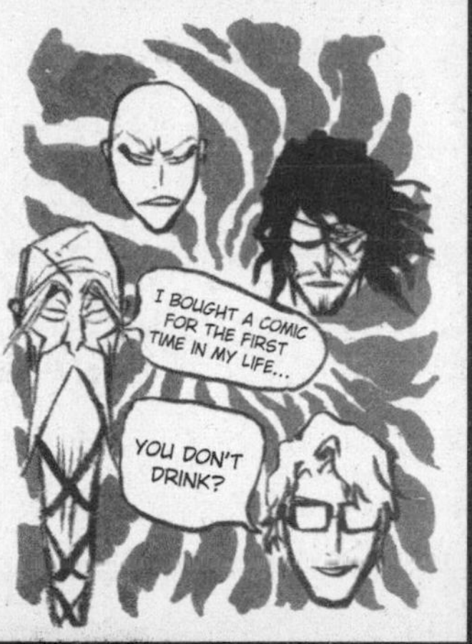
I BOUGHT A COMIC FOR THE FIRST TIME IN MY LIFE...
YOU DON'T DRINK?

I went to a mid-season production party.

I drank surrounded by men like them. It was pretty intense, but it was fun.

-Tite Kubo

BLEACH is author Tite Kubo's second title. Kubo made his debut with *ZOMBIEPOWDER.*, a four-volume series for *WEEKLY SHONEN JUMP*. To date, *BLEACH* has been translated into numerous languages and has also inspired an animated TV series that began airing in the U.S. in 2006. Beginning its serialization in 2001, *BLEACH* is still a mainstay in the pages of *WEEKLY SHONEN JUMP*. In 2005, *BLEACH* was awarded the prestigious Shogakukan Manga Award in the *shonen* (boys) category.

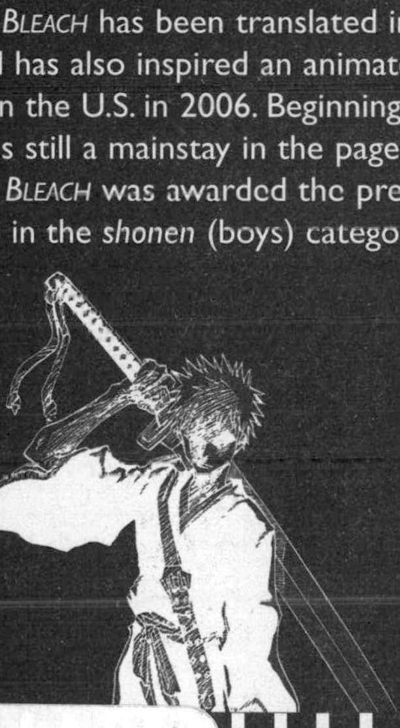

BLEACH
Vol. 21: Be My Family or Not
SHONEN JUMP Manga Edition

This volume contains material that was originally published in SHONEN
JUMP #59. Artwork in the magazine may have been altered slightly from
what is presented in this volume.

STORY AND ART BY
TITE KUBO

English Adaptation/Lance Caselman
Translation/Joe Yamazaki
Touch-Up Art & Lettering/Evan Waldinger
Design/Sean Lee
Editor/Pancha Diaz

Printed in the U.S.A.

Published by VIZ Media, LLC
P.O. Box 77010
San Francisco, CA 94107

10 9 8 7 6 5
First printing, October 2007
Fifth printing, August 2014

Everything in this world
Exists to wear you down

BLEACH21

BE MY FAMILY OR NOT

Shonen Jump Manga

STARS AND

Rukia Kuchiki

Orihime Inoue

Ichigo Kurosaki

plot

After a fateful encounter with Soul Reaper Rukia Kuchiki, Ichigo becomes a Soul Reaper himself. Now he and his friends have traveled to the Soul Society to save Rukia from execution.

In the aftermath of Ichigo's daring rescue of Rukia and the defeat of her brother, Captain Aizen's scheme to Hollowfy Soul Reapers is revealed! The Thirteen Court Guard Companies confront Aizen, but they are powerless to prevent his escape. Leaving both Ichigo and Byakuya Kuchiki near death, Aizen and his henchmen flee to the world of the Menos Grandes.

BLEACH ALL

茶渡泰虎

Chad Yasutora

平子真子

Shinji Hirako

Uryû Ishida

石田雨竜

STORIES

BLEACH 21

BE MY FAMILY OR NOT

Contents

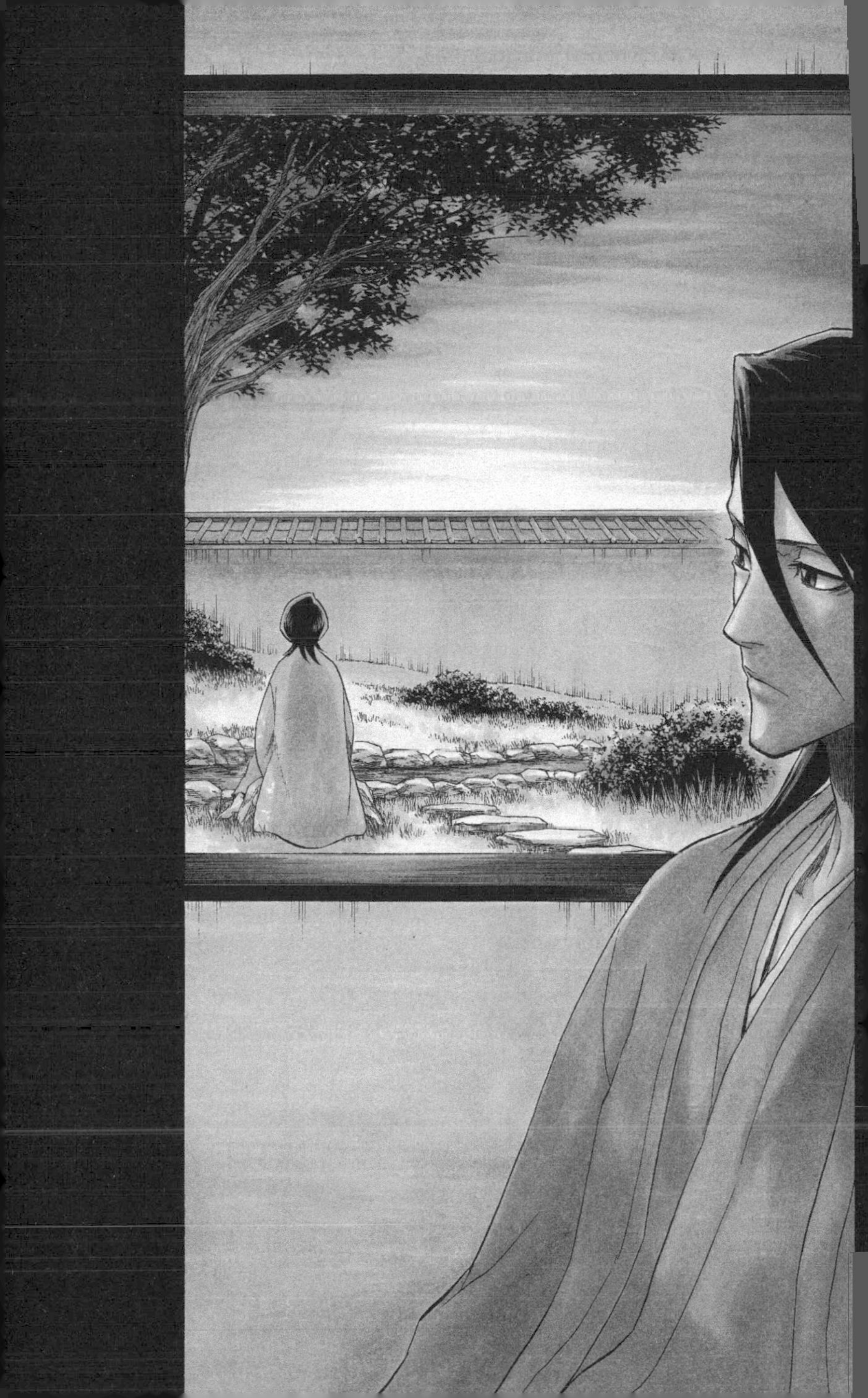

BLEACH
ブリーチ

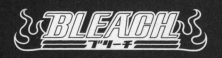

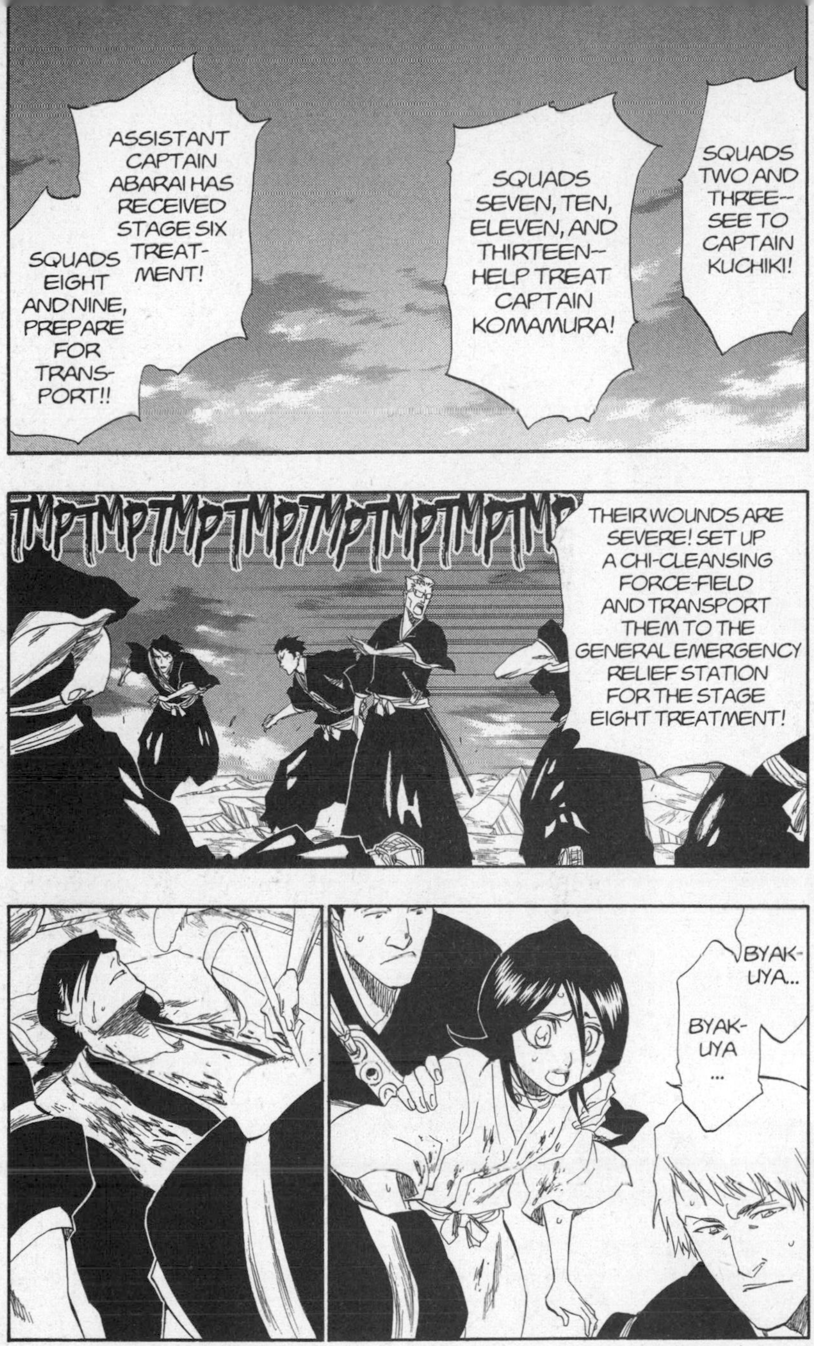
SQUADS TWO AND THREE-- SEE TO CAPTAIN KUCHIKI!
SQUADS SEVEN, TEN, ELEVEN, AND THIRTEEN-- HELP TREAT CAPTAIN KOMAMURA!
ASSISTANT CAPTAIN ABARAI HAS RECEIVED STAGE SIX TREATMENT!
SQUADS EIGHT AND NINE, PREPARE FOR TRANSPORT!!
THEIR WOUNDS ARE SEVERE! SET UP A CHI-CLEANSING FORCE-FIELD AND TRANSPORT THEM TO THE GENERAL EMERGENCY RELIEF STATION FOR THE STAGE EIGHT TREATMENT!
TMP TMP TMP TMP TMP TMP TMP TMP TMP
BYAKUYA...
BYAKUYA...

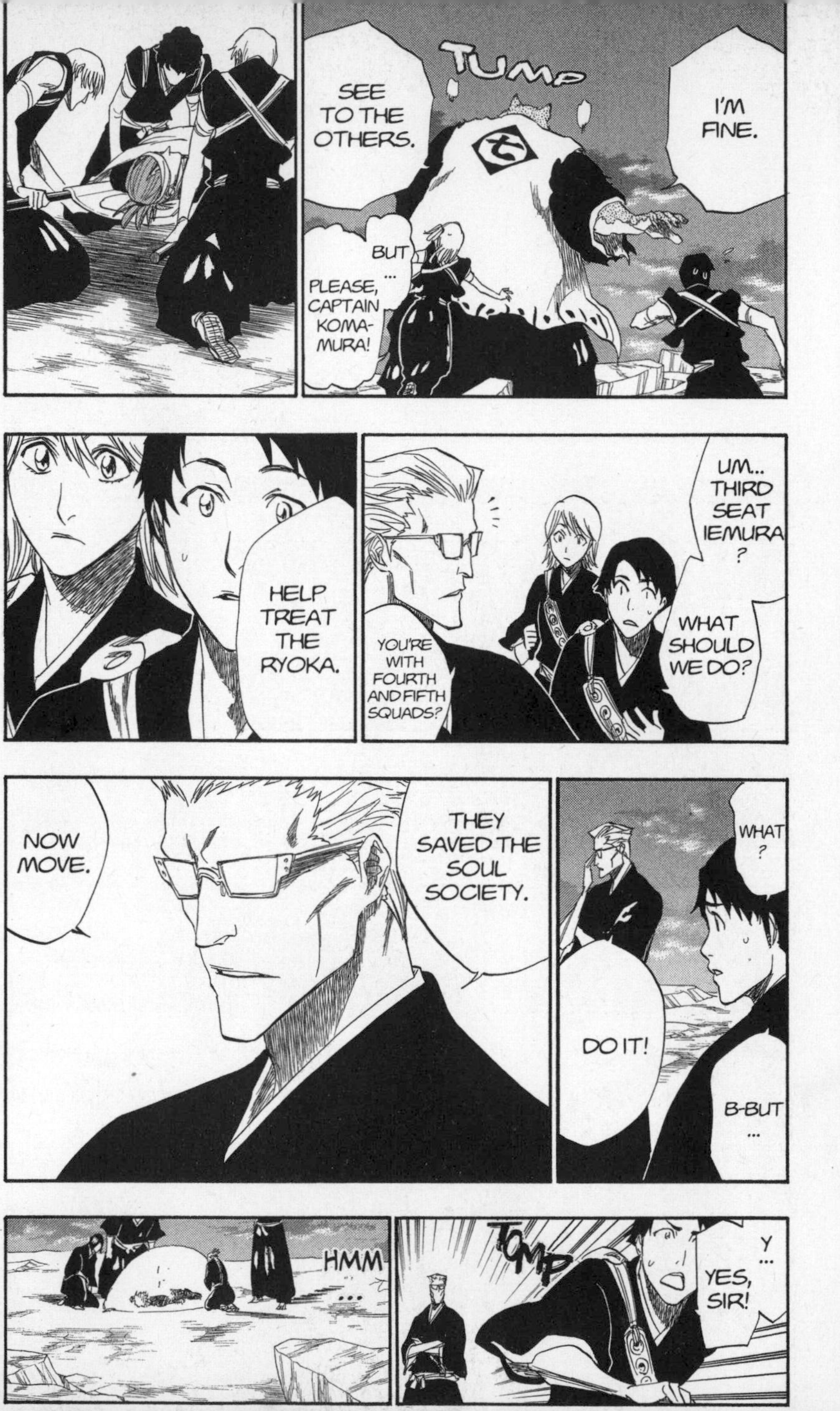
TUMP
I'M FINE.
SEE TO THE OTHERS.
BUT ... PLEASE, CAPTAIN KOMAMURA!
UM... THIRD SEAT IEMURA?
WHAT SHOULD WE DO?
YOU'RE WITH FOURTH AND FIFTH SQUADS?
HELP TREAT THE RYOKA.
WHAT?
DO IT!
B-BUT ...
THEY SAVED THE SOUL SOCIETY.
NOW MOVE.
Y ... YES, SIR!
TOMP
HMM ...

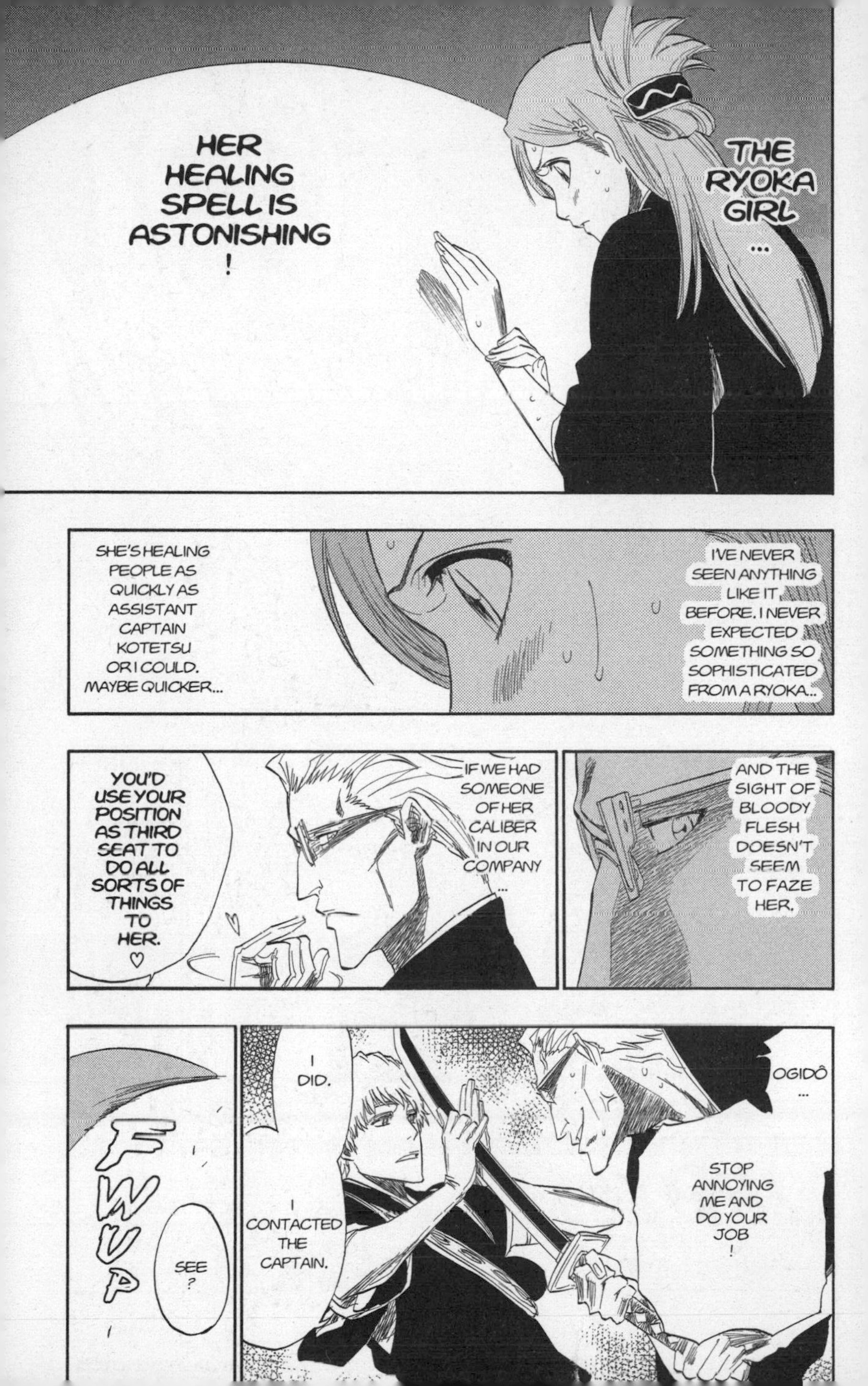

THE RYOKA GIRL...
HER HEALING SPELL IS ASTONISHING!
I'VE NEVER SEEN ANYTHING LIKE IT BEFORE. I NEVER EXPECTED SOMETHING SO SOPHISTICATED FROM A RYOKA...
SHE'S HEALING PEOPLE AS QUICKLY AS ASSISTANT CAPTAIN KOTETSU OR I COULD. MAYBE QUICKER...
AND THE SIGHT OF BLOODY FLESH DOESN'T SEEM TO FAZE HER.
IF WE HAD SOMEONE OF HER CALIBER IN OUR COMPANY...
YOU'D USE YOUR POSITION AS THIRD SEAT TO DO ALL SORTS OF THINGS TO HER. ♡
OGIDÔ...
I DID.
STOP ANNOYING ME AND DO YOUR JOB!
I CONTACTED THE CAPTAIN.
FWUP
SEE?

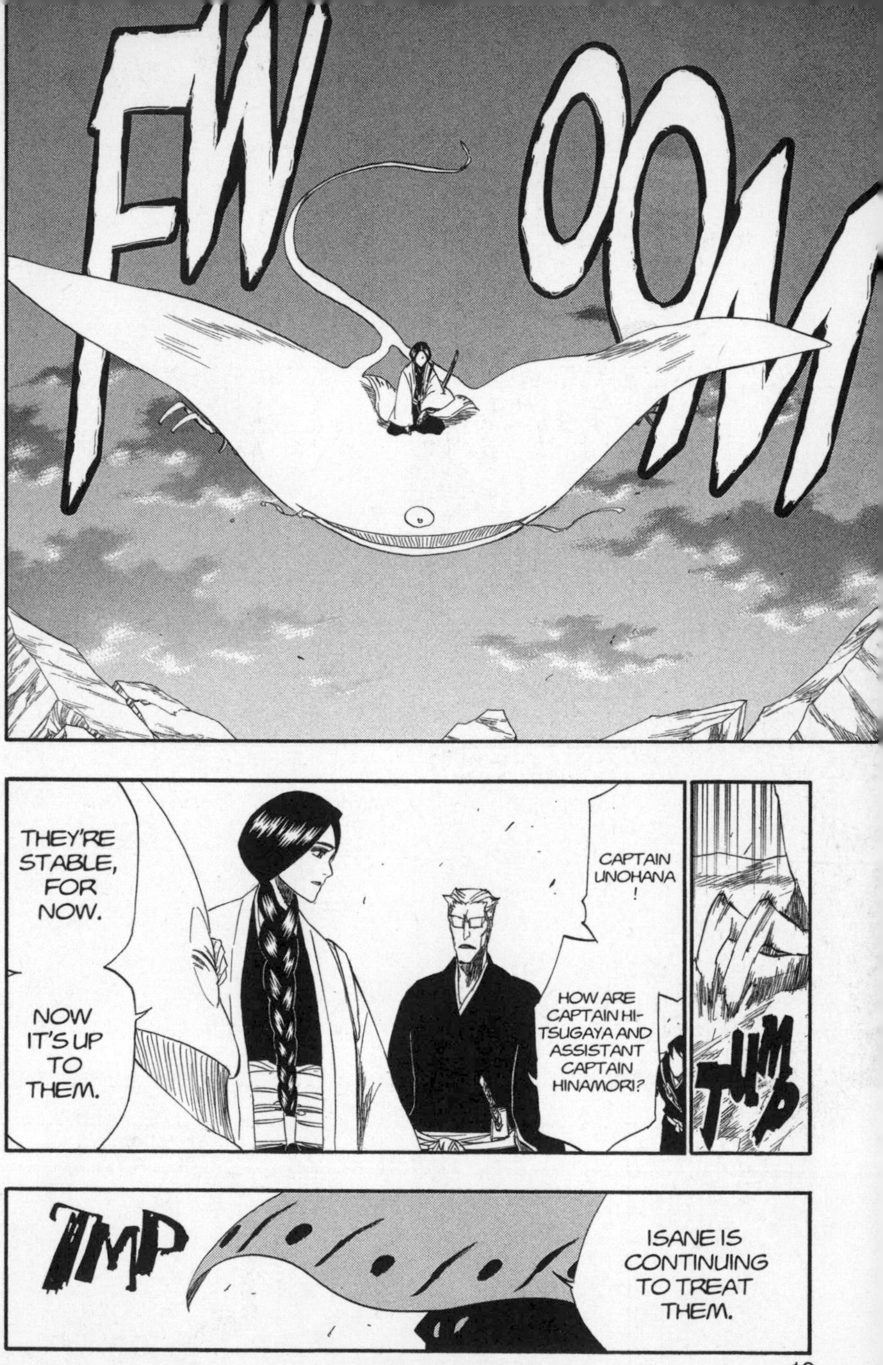
FWOOM
TUMP
CAPTAIN UNOHANA!
HOW ARE CAPTAIN HITSUGAYA AND ASSISTANT CAPTAIN HINAMORI?
THEY'RE STABLE, FOR NOW.
NOW IT'S UP TO THEM.
ISANE IS CONTINUING TO TREAT THEM.
TMP

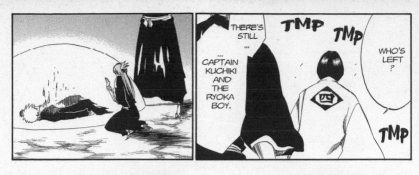

THERE'S STILL ...

CAPTAIN KUCHIKI AND THE RYOKA BOY.

TMP

TMP

WHO'S LEFT?

TMP

EH ?!

Y-YES ...

LOOKS LIKE THE RYOKA GIRL DOESN'T NEED OUR HELP.

SWUFF

YOU WERE RECKLESS ...

... CAP-TAIN KUCHIKI ...

!

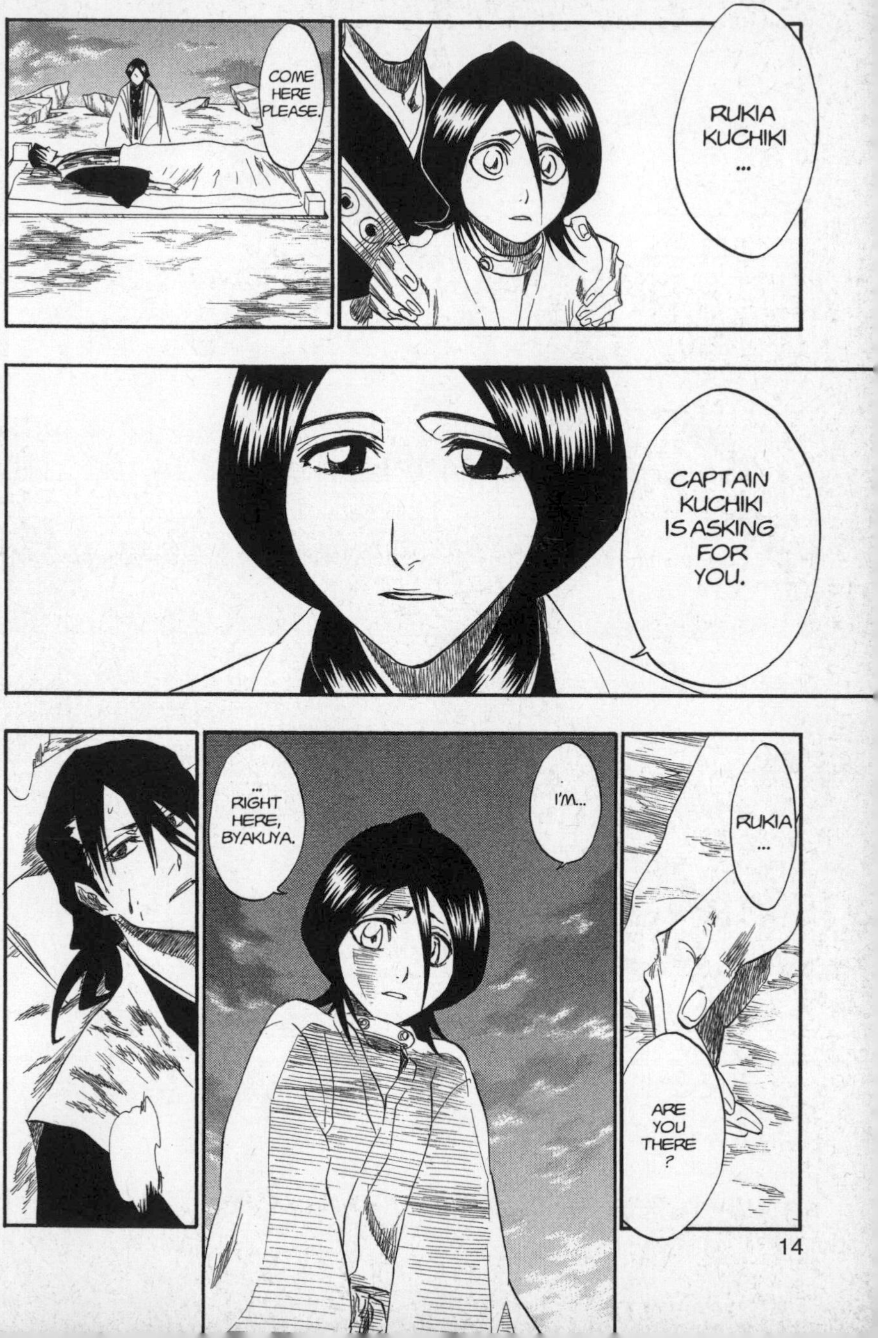
RUKIA KUCHIKI ...
COME HERE PLEASE.
CAPTAIN KUCHIKI IS ASKING FOR YOU.
RUKIA ...
ARE YOU THERE ?
I'M...
... RIGHT HERE, BYAKUYA.

READ THIS WAY

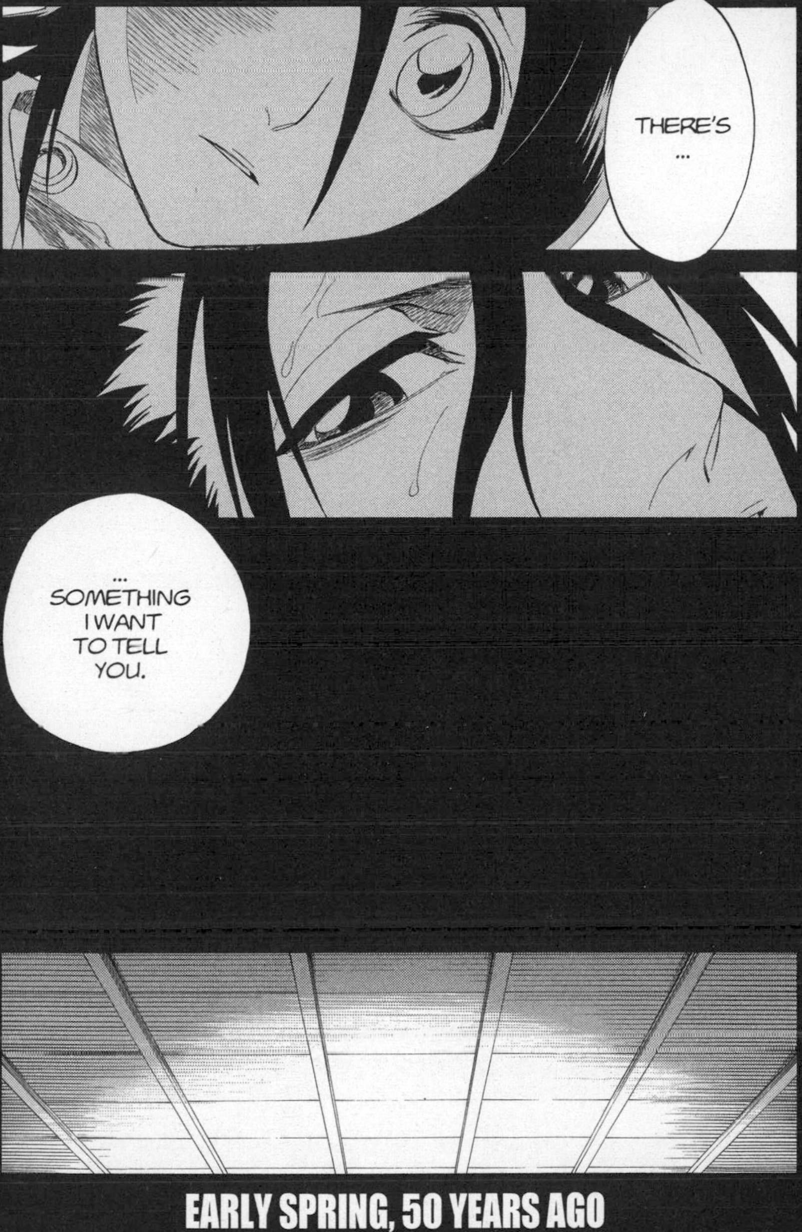
THERE'S ...
... SOMETHING I WANT TO TELL YOU.
EARLY SPRING, 50 YEARS AGO

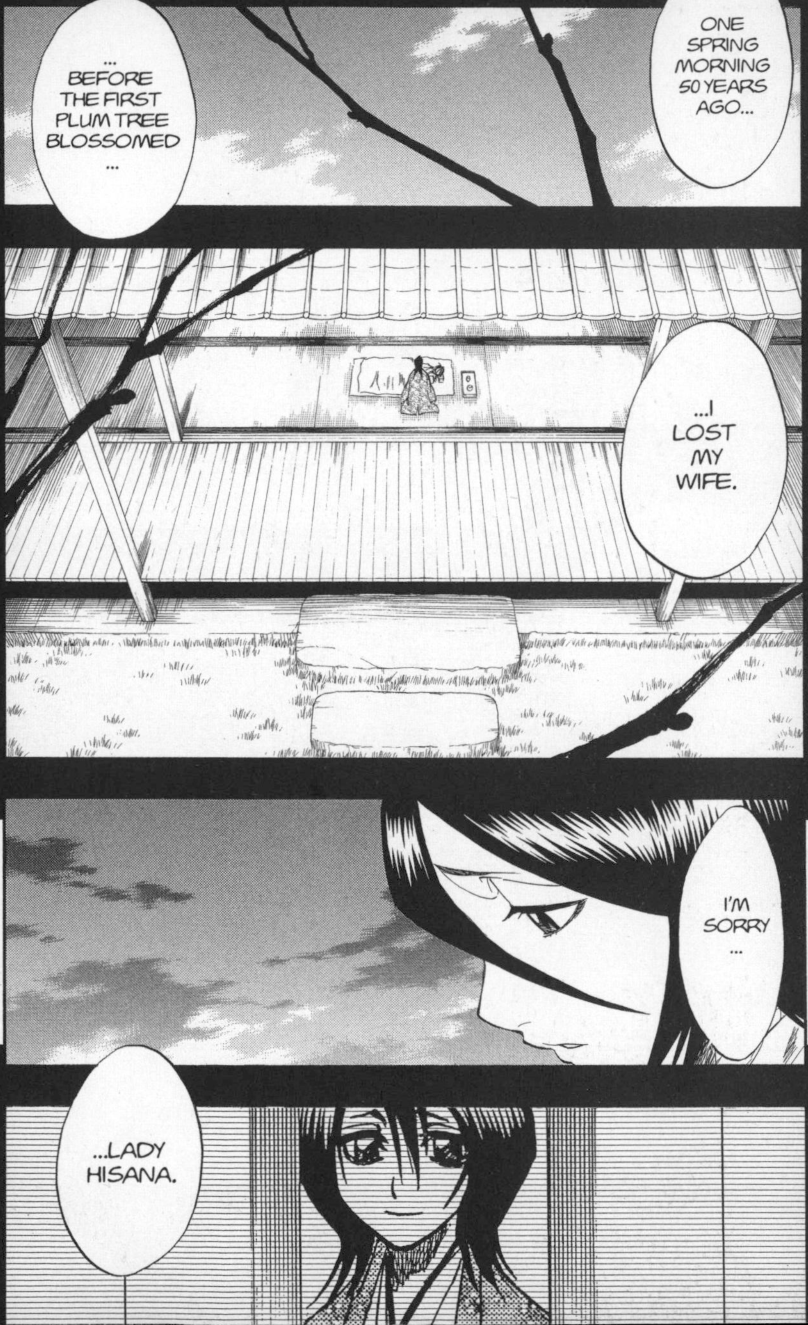
ONE SPRING MORNING 50 YEARS AGO...
... BEFORE THE FIRST PLUM TREE BLOSSOMED ...
...I LOST MY WIFE.
I'M SORRY ...
...LADY HISANA.

READ THIS WAY

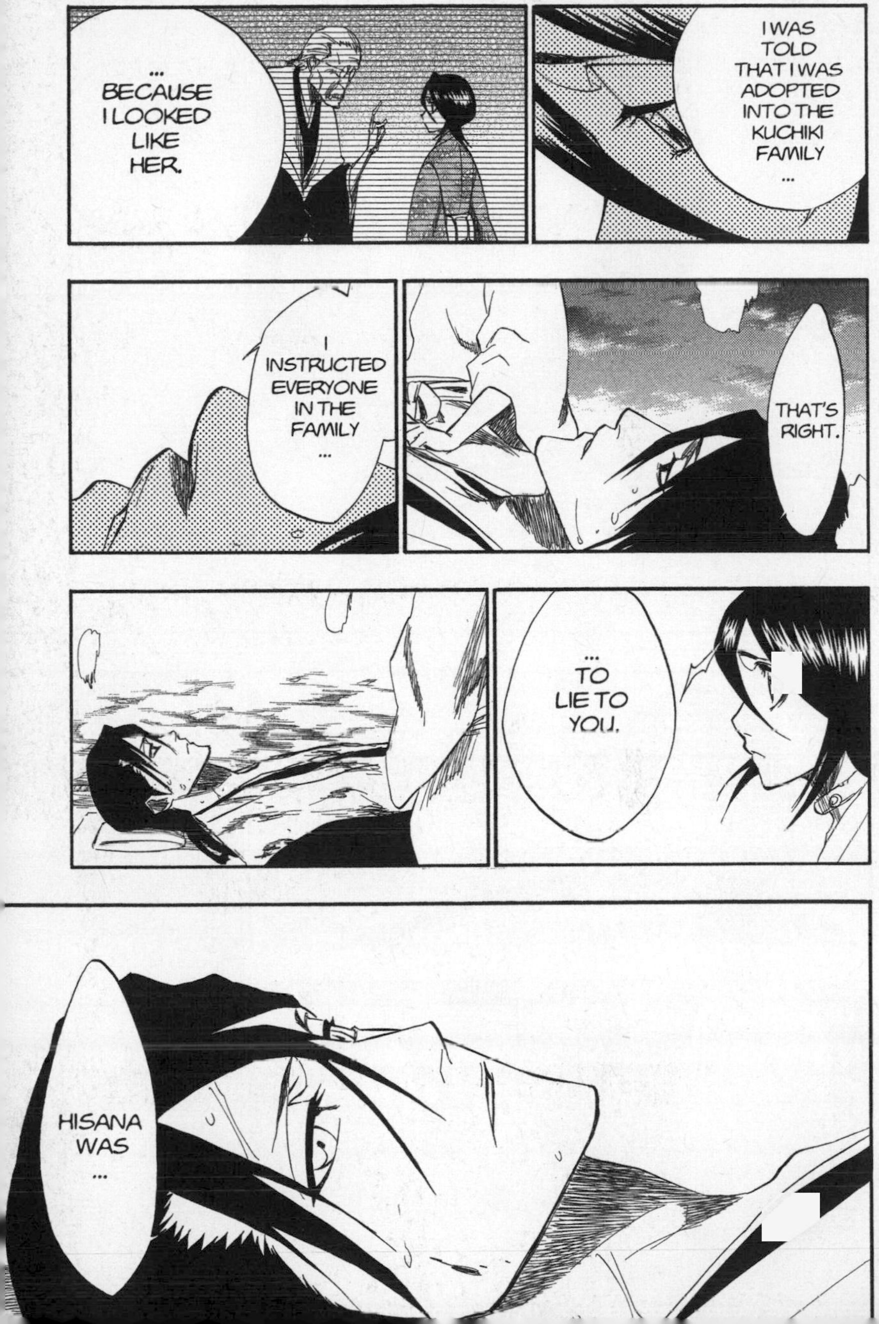

I WAS TOLD THAT I WAS ADOPTED INTO THE KUCHIKI FAMILY ...
... BECAUSE I LOOKED LIKE HER.
THAT'S RIGHT.
I INSTRUCTED EVERYONE IN THE FAMILY ...
... TO LIE TO YOU.
HISANA WAS ...

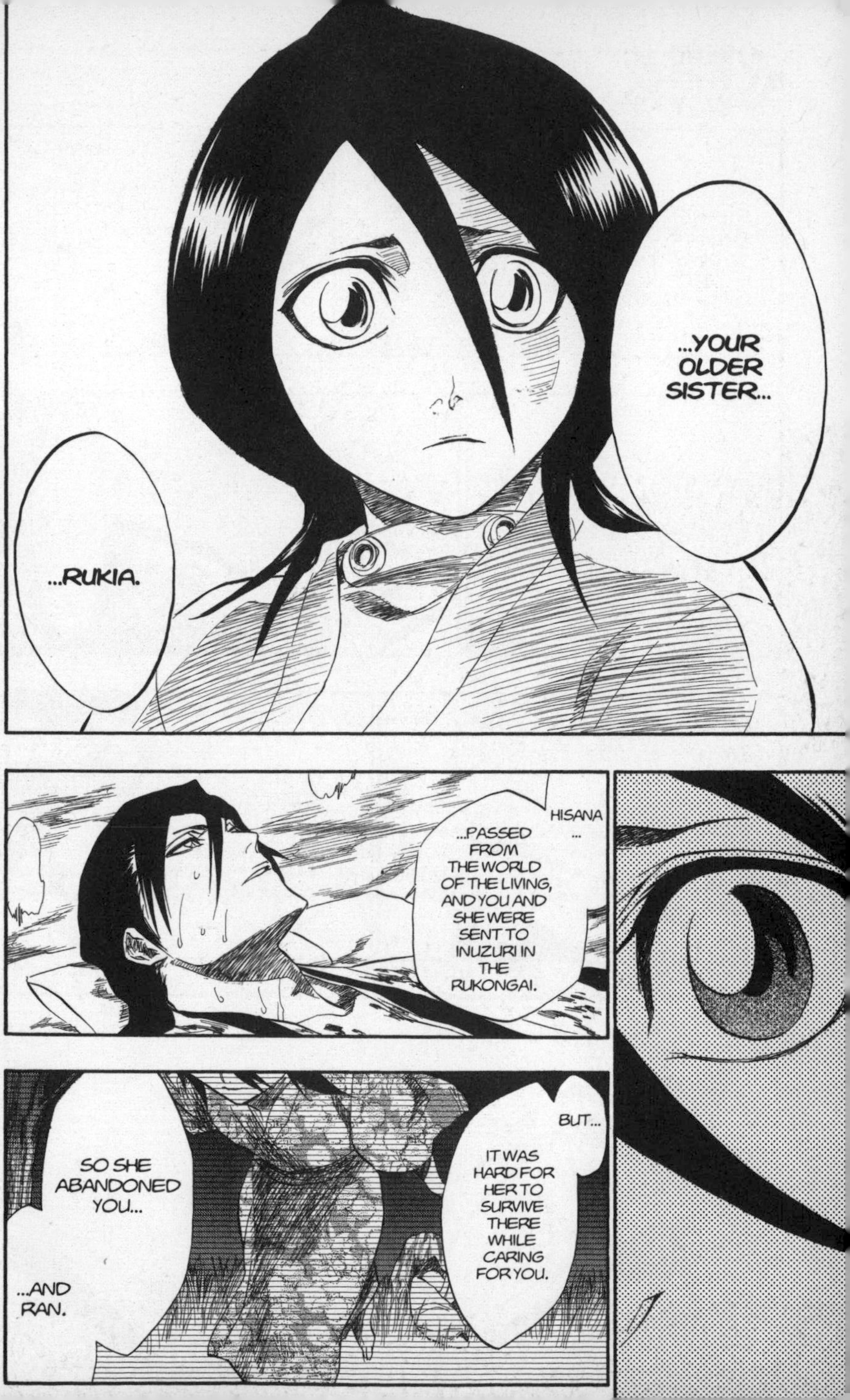
...YOUR OLDER SISTER...
...RUKIA.
HISANA ...
...PASSED FROM THE WORLD OF THE LIVING, AND YOU AND SHE WERE SENT TO INUZURI IN THE RUKONGAI.
BUT...
IT WAS HARD FOR HER TO SURVIVE THERE WHILE CARING FOR YOU.
SO SHE ABANDONED YOU...
...AND RAN.

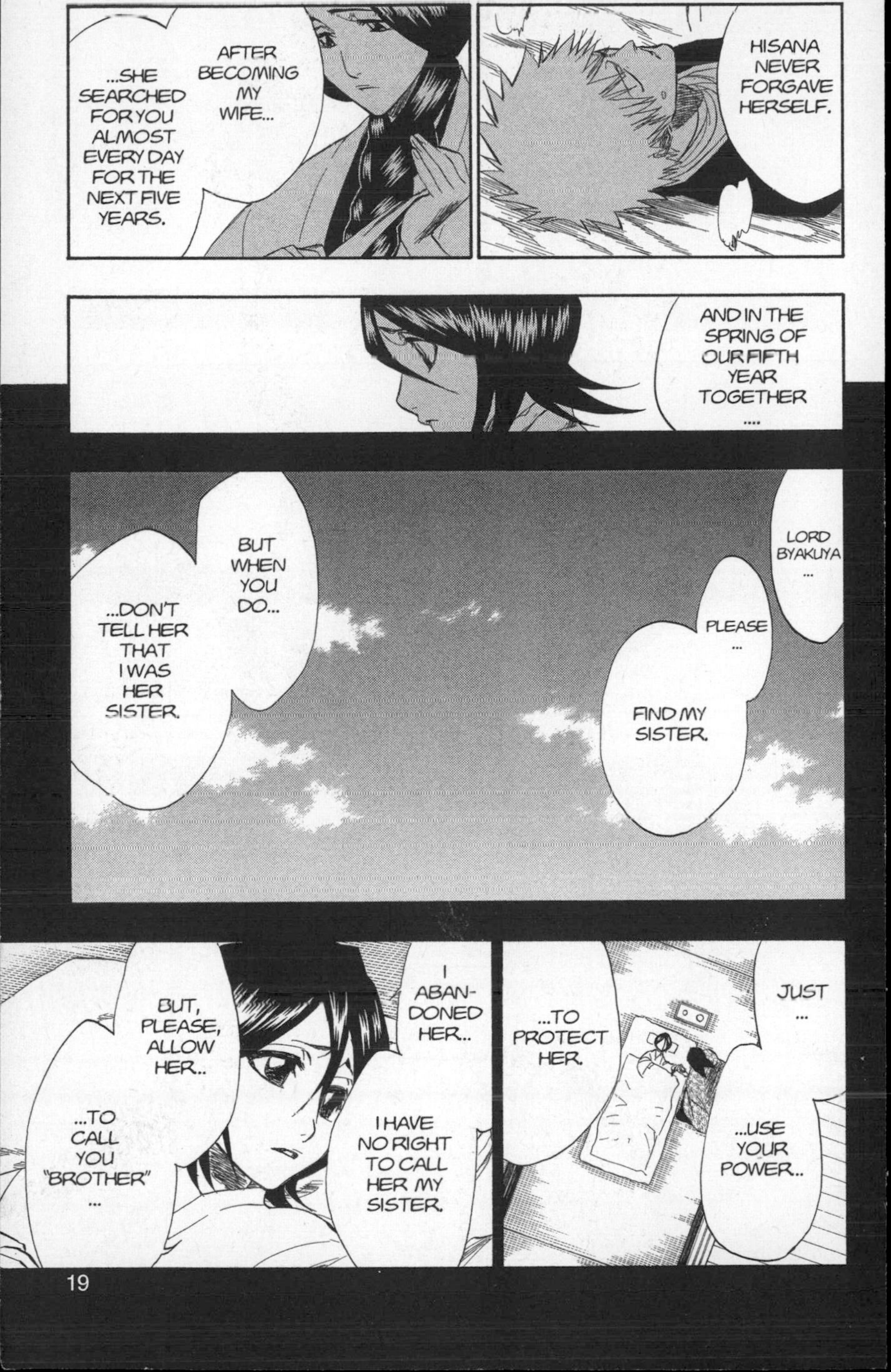
HISANA NEVER FORGAVE HERSELF.
AFTER BECOMING MY WIFE...
...SHE SEARCHED FOR YOU ALMOST EVERY DAY FOR THE NEXT FIVE YEARS.
AND IN THE SPRING OF OUR FIFTH YEAR TOGETHER ....
LORD BYAKUYA ...
PLEASE ...
FIND MY SISTER.
BUT WHEN YOU DO...
...DON'T TELL HER THAT I WAS HER SISTER.
JUST ...
...USE YOUR POWER..
...TO PROTECT HER.
I ABAN-DONED HER..
I HAVE NO RIGHT TO CALL HER MY SISTER.
BUT, PLEASE, ALLOW HER..
...TO CALL YOU "BROTHER" ...

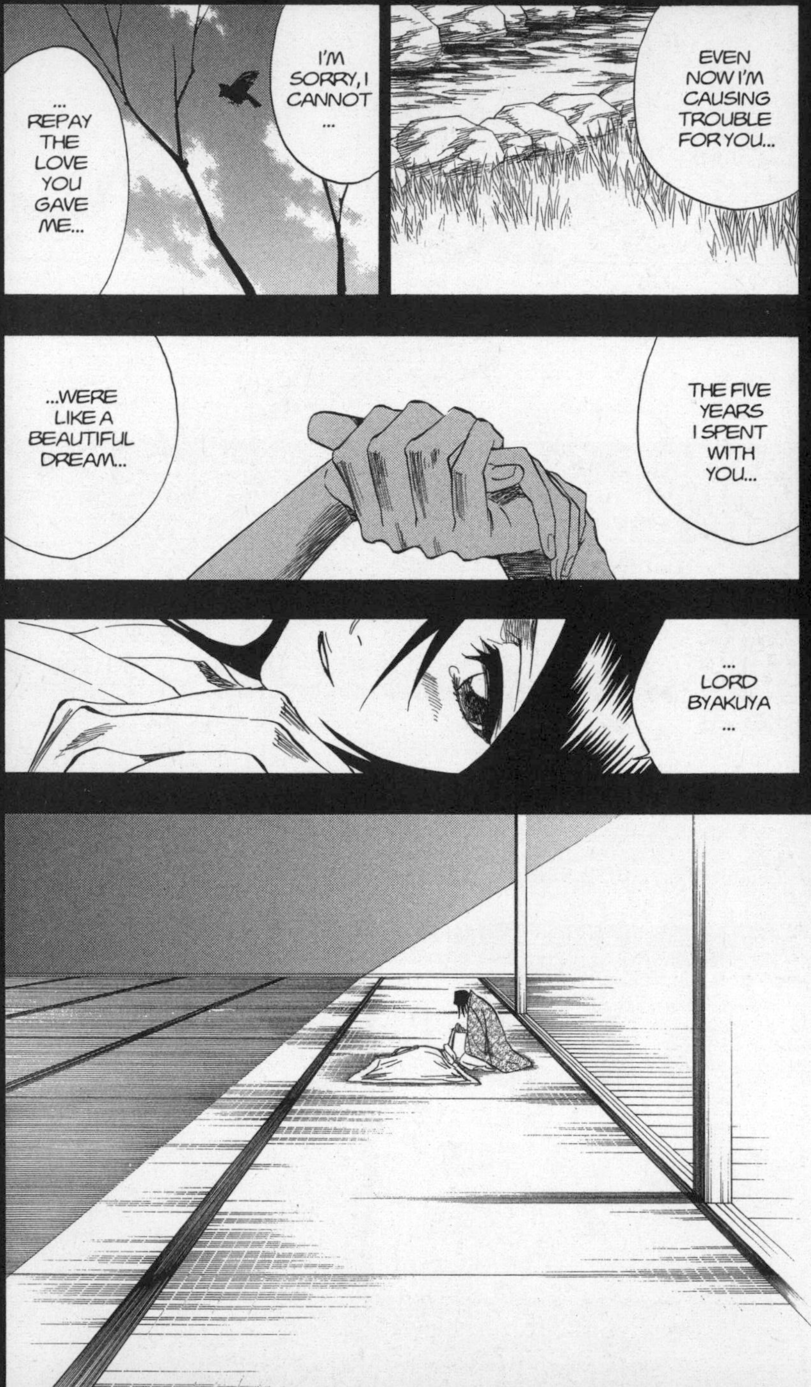
EVEN NOW I'M CAUSING TROUBLE FOR YOU...
I'M SORRY, I CANNOT ...
... REPAY THE LOVE YOU GAVE ME...
THE FIVE YEARS I SPENT WITH YOU...
...WERE LIKE A BEAUTIFUL DREAM...
... LORD BYAKUYA ...

READ THIS WAY

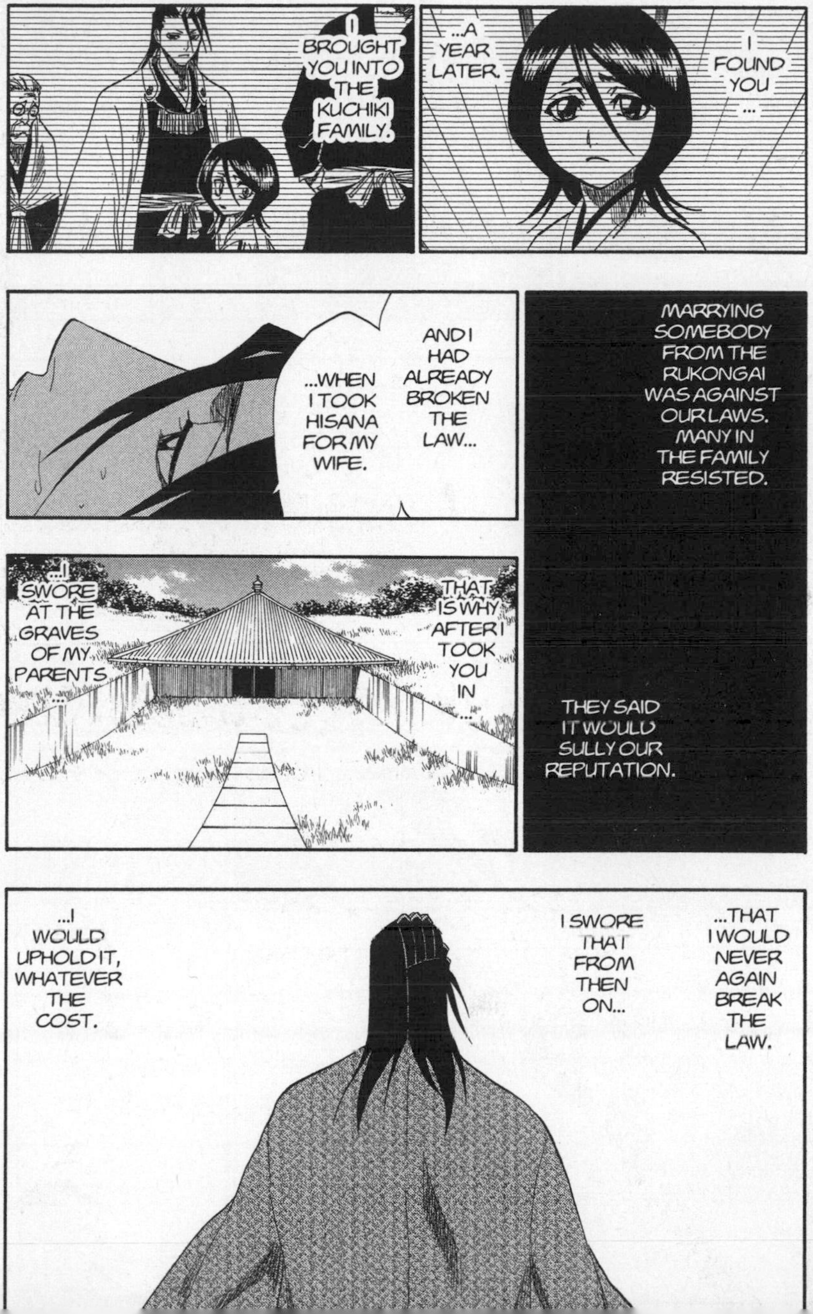
I FOUND YOU ...
...A YEAR LATER.
I BROUGHT YOU INTO THE KUCHIKI FAMILY.
MARRYING SOMEBODY FROM THE RUKONGAI WAS AGAINST OUR LAWS. MANY IN THE FAMILY RESISTED.
THEY SAID IT WOULD SULLY OUR REPUTATION.
AND I HAD ALREADY BROKEN THE LAW...
...WHEN I TOOK HISANA FOR MY WIFE.
THAT IS WHY AFTER I TOOK YOU IN ...
...I SWORE AT THE GRAVES OF MY PARENTS ...
...THAT I WOULD NEVER AGAIN BREAK THE LAW.
I SWORE THAT FROM THEN ON...
...I WOULD UPHOLD IT, WHATEVER THE COST.

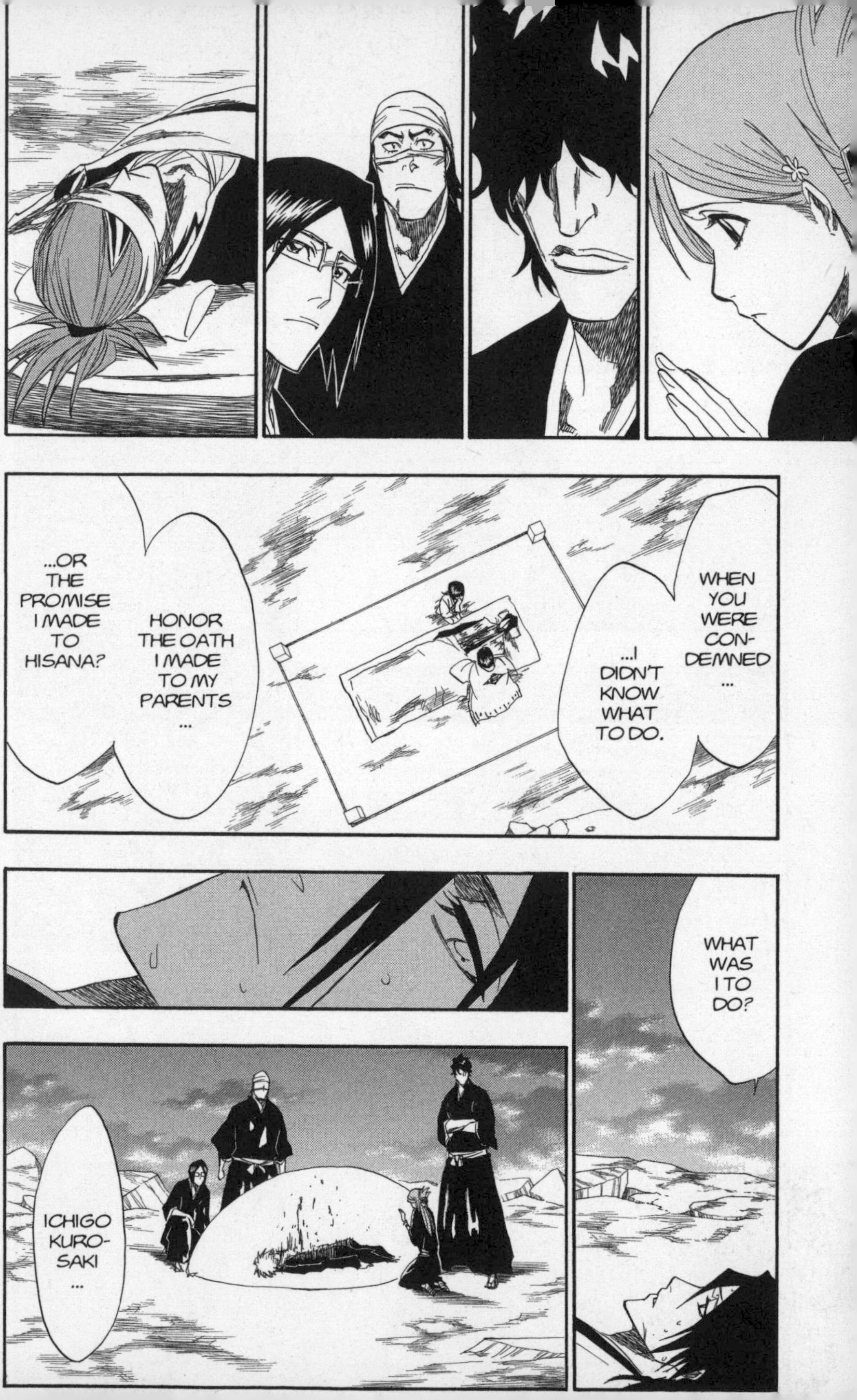
WHEN YOU WERE CON-DEMNED ...
...I DIDN'T KNOW WHAT TO DO.
HONOR THE OATH I MADE TO MY PARENTS ...
...OR THE PROMISE I MADE TO HISANA?
WHAT WAS I TO DO?
ICHIGO KURO-SAKI ...

I THANK YOU.

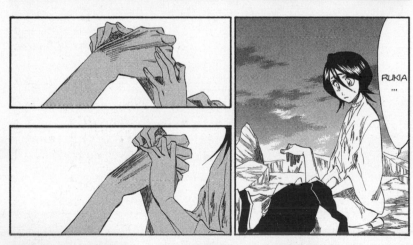

RUKIA
...

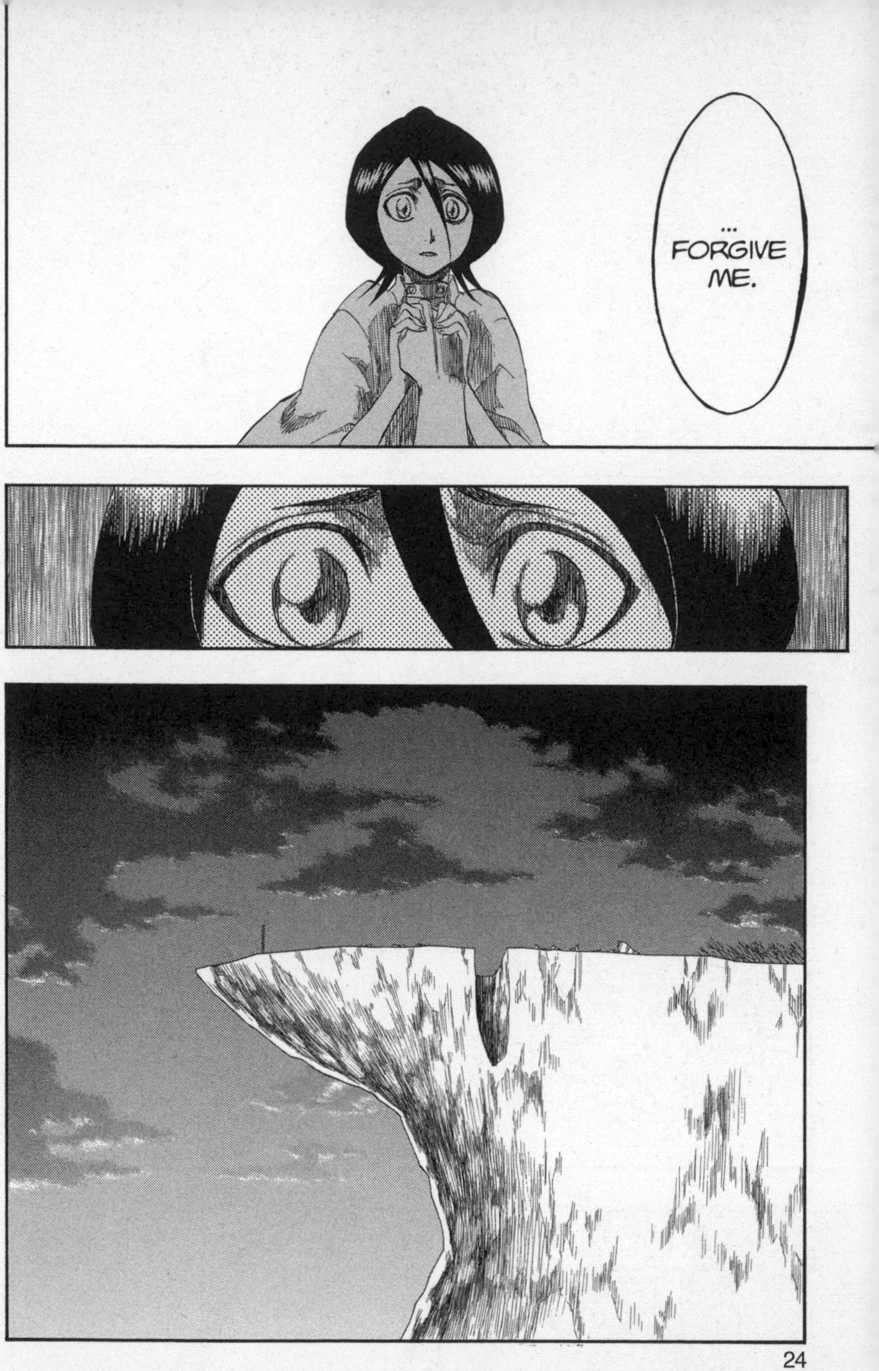
... FORGIVE ME.

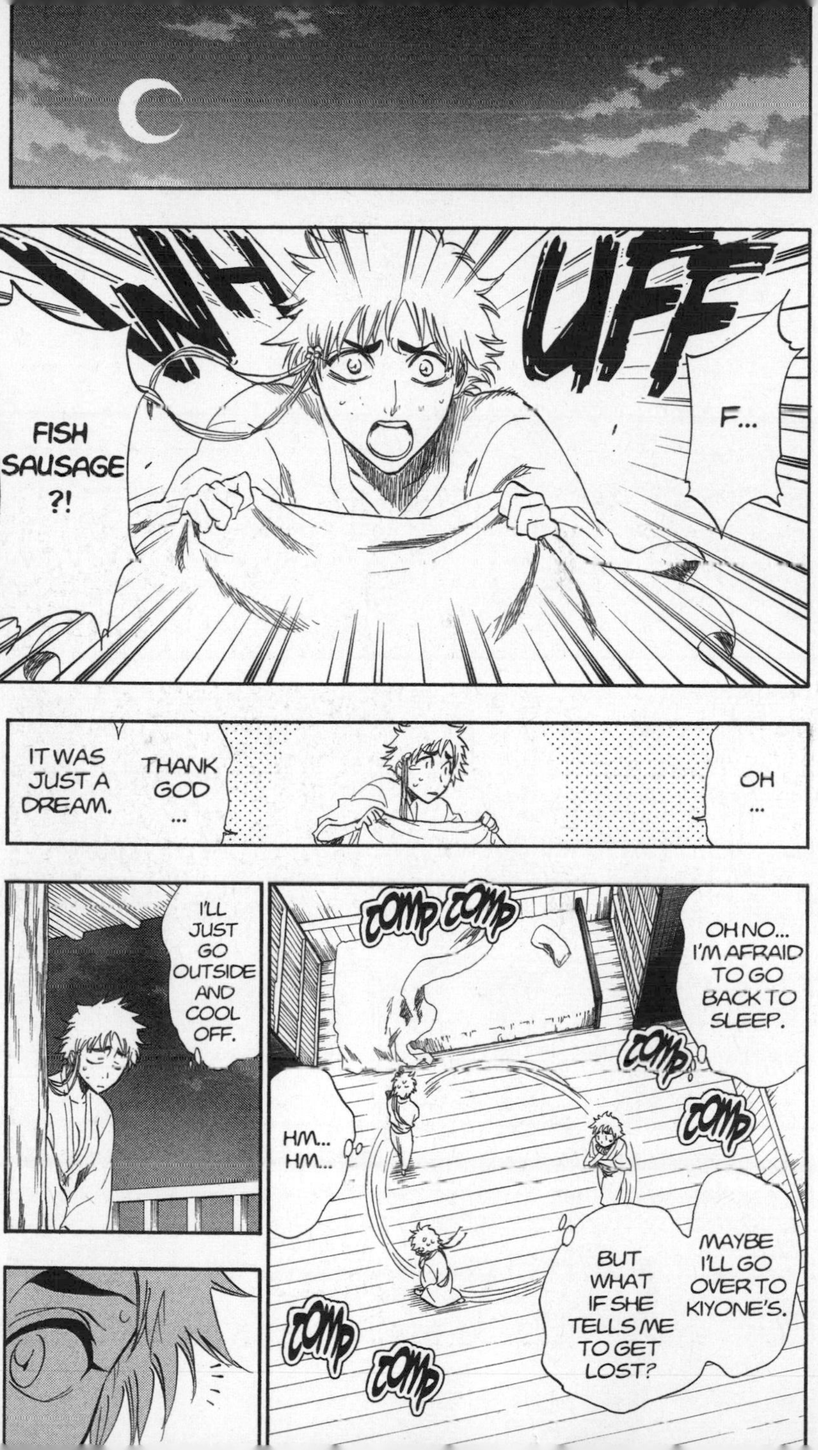
UNH UFF
F...
FISH SAUSAGE ?!
OH ...
THANK GOD ...
IT WAS JUST A DREAM.
COMP COMP
OH NO... I'M AFRAID TO GO BACK TO SLEEP.
COMP
COMP
HM... HM...
MAYBE I'LL GO OVER TO KIYONE'S.
BUT WHAT IF SHE TELLS ME TO GET LOST?
COMP
COMP
I'LL JUST GO OUTSIDE AND COOL OFF.

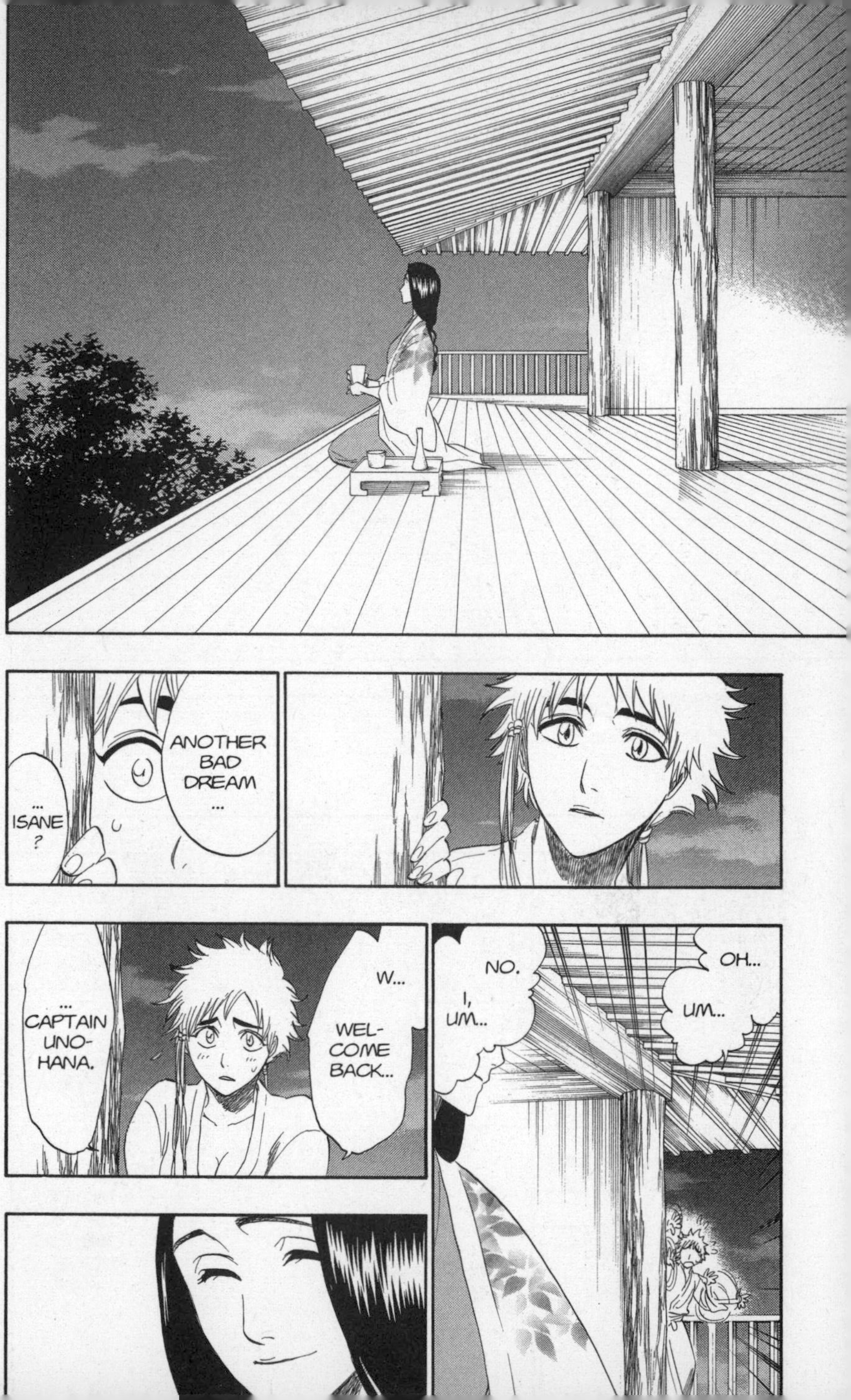
ANOTHER BAD DREAM ...
... ISANE ?
OH...
UM...
NO.
I, UM...
W... WELCOME BACK...
... CAPTAIN UNO-HANA.

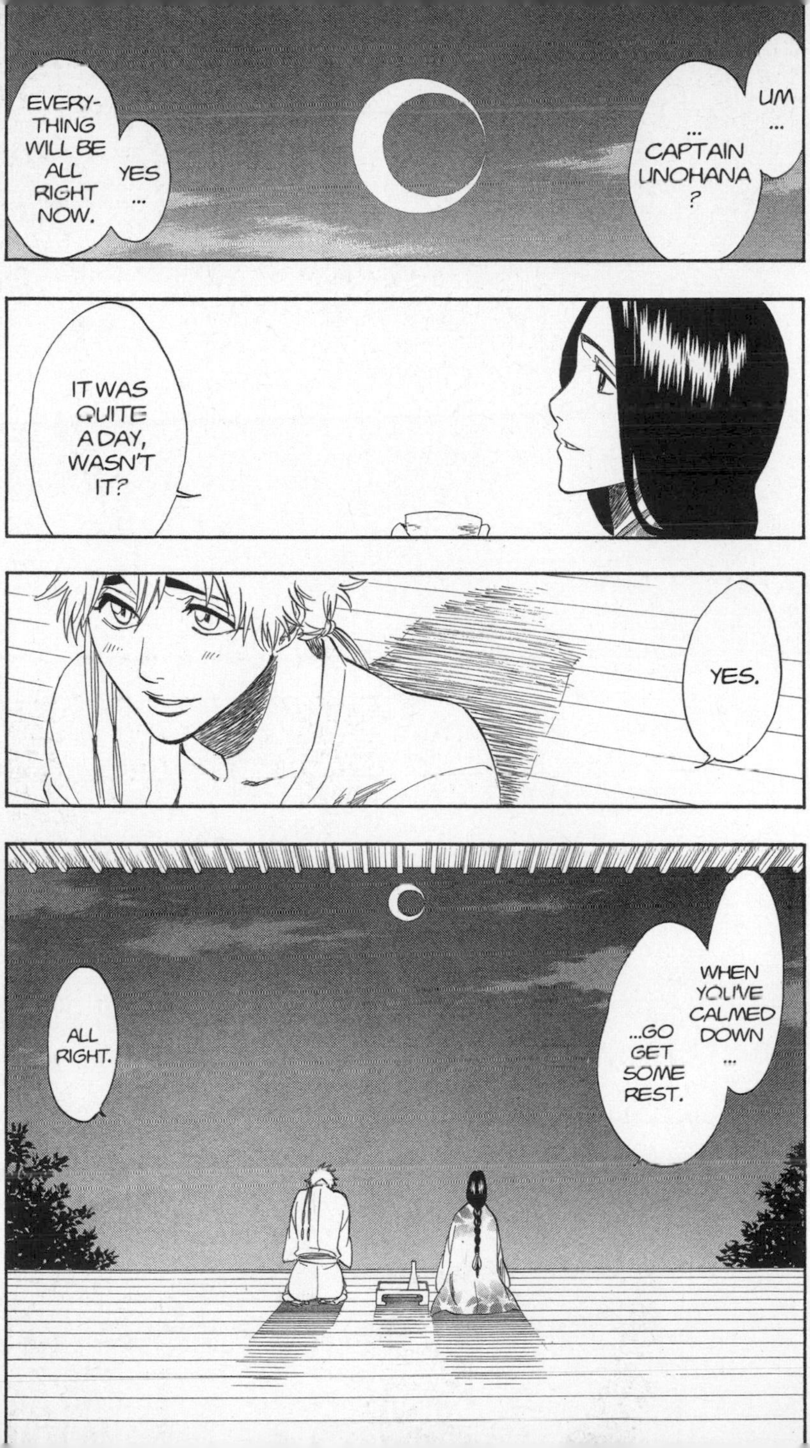
UM ... ... CAPTAIN UNOHANA ?
YES ...
EVERY-THING WILL BE ALL RIGHT NOW.
IT WAS QUITE A DAY, WASN'T IT?
YES.
WHEN YOU'VE CALMED DOWN ...
...GO GET SOME REST.
ALL RIGHT.

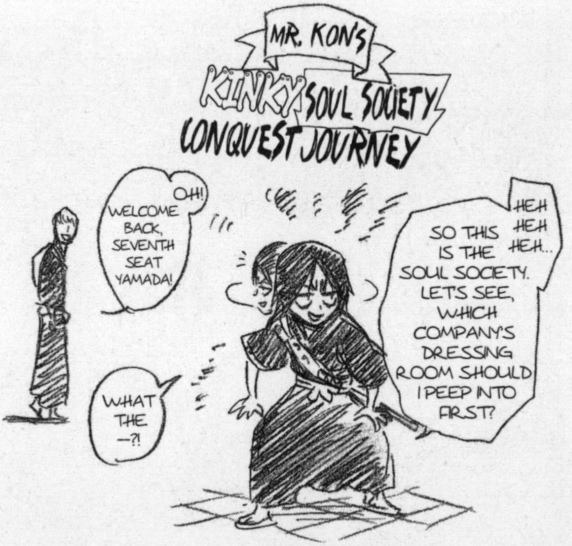
MR. KON'S
KINKY SOUL SOCIETY
CONQUEST JOURNEY
HEH HEH HEH...
SO THIS IS THE SOUL SOCIETY. LET'S SEE, WHICH COMPANY'S DRESSING ROOM SHOULD I PEEP INTO FIRST?
OH!
WELCOME BACK, SEVENTH SEAT YAMADA!
WHAT THE—?!

180. SOMETHING IN THE AFTERMATH

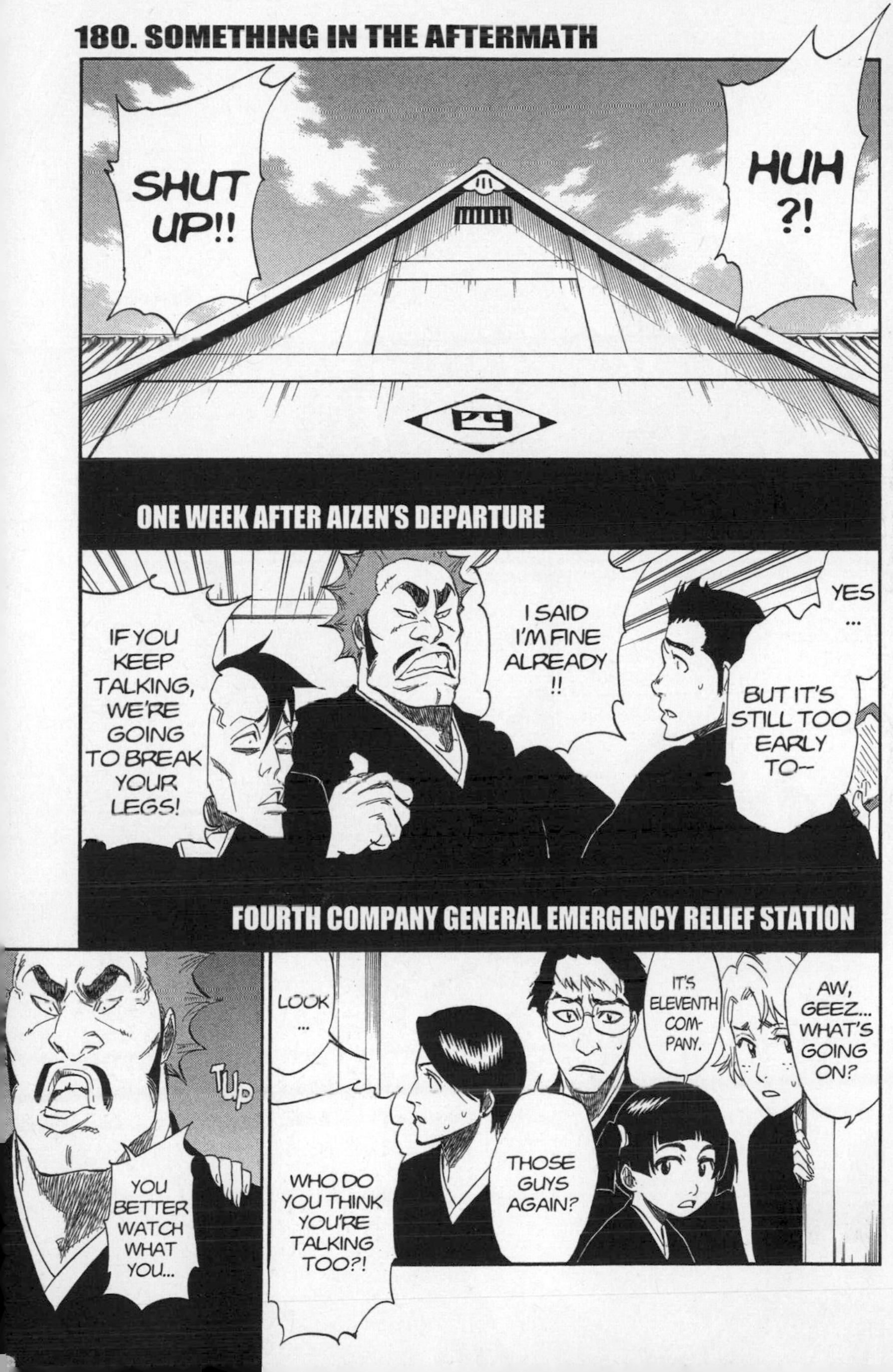

HUH ?!
SHUT UP!!
ONE WEEK AFTER AIZEN'S DEPARTURE
YES ...
BUT IT'S STILL TOO EARLY TO--
I SAID I'M FINE ALREADY !!
IF YOU KEEP TALKING, WE'RE GOING TO BREAK YOUR LEGS!
FOURTH COMPANY GENERAL EMERGENCY RELIEF STATION
AW, GEEZ... WHAT'S GOING ON?
IT'S ELEVENTH COM-PANY.
LOOK ...
THOSE GUYS AGAIN?
WHO DO YOU THINK YOU'RE TALKING TOO?!
TUP
YOU BETTER WATCH WHAT YOU...

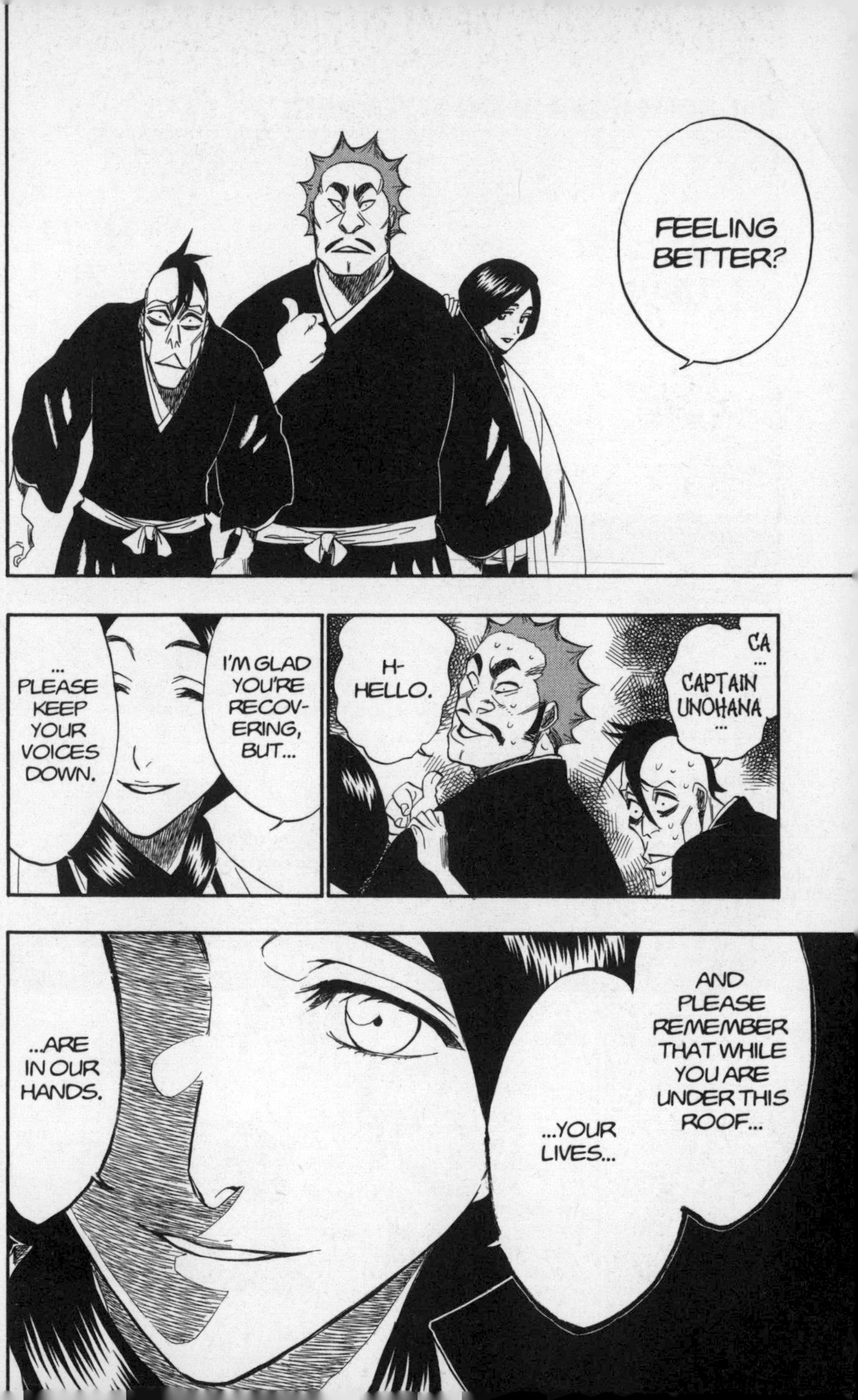
FEELING BETTER?
CA... CAPTAIN UNOHANA...
H-HELLO.
I'M GLAD YOU'RE RECOVERING, BUT...
...PLEASE KEEP YOUR VOICES DOWN.
AND PLEASE REMEMBER THAT WHILE YOU ARE UNDER THIS ROOF...
...YOUR LIVES...
...ARE IN OUR HANDS.

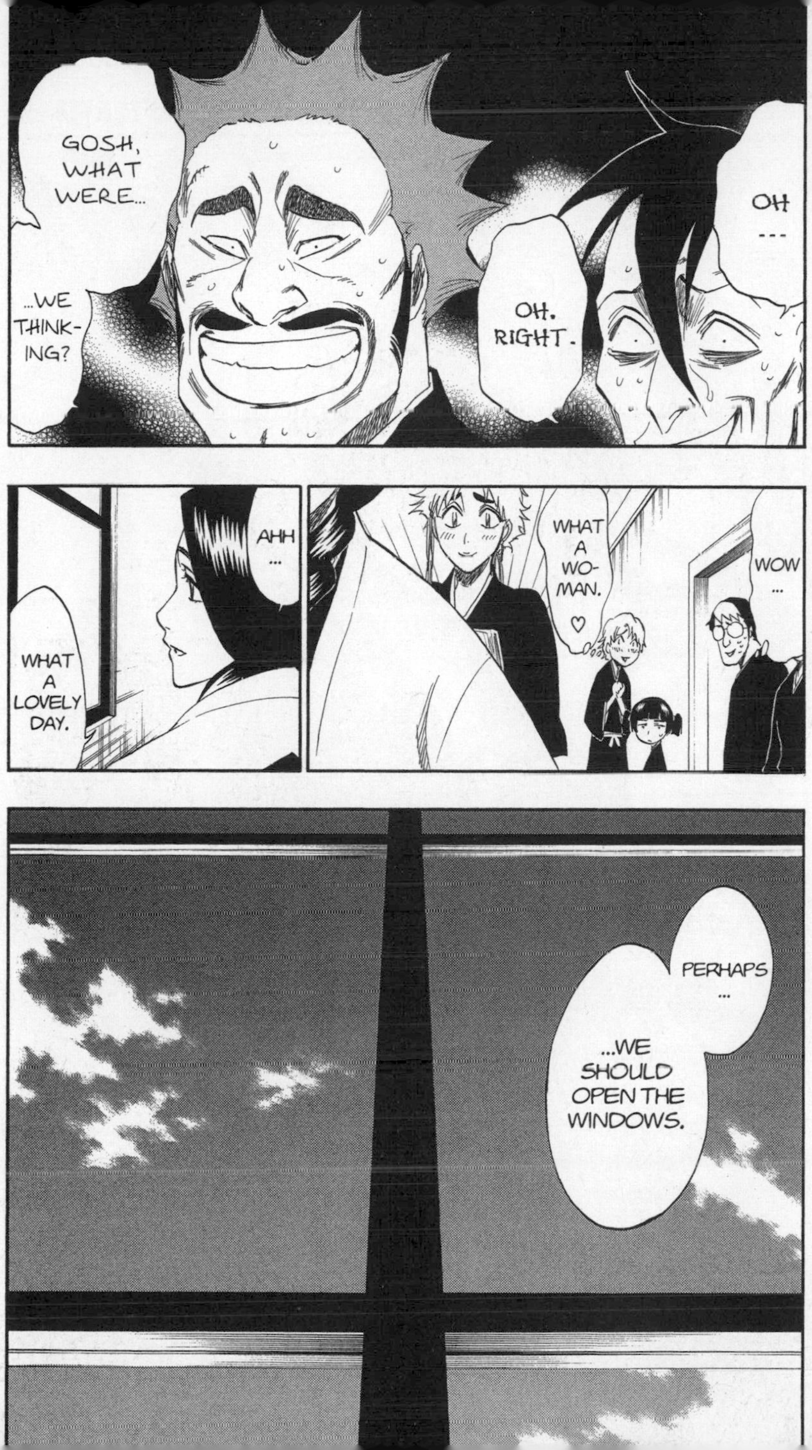
OH ---
GOSH, WHAT WERE...
...WE THINKING?
OH. RIGHT.
WOW ...
WHAT A WOMAN. ♡
AHH ...
WHAT A LOVELY DAY.
PERHAPS ...
...WE SHOULD OPEN THE WINDOWS.

180. SOMETHING IN THE AFTERMATH

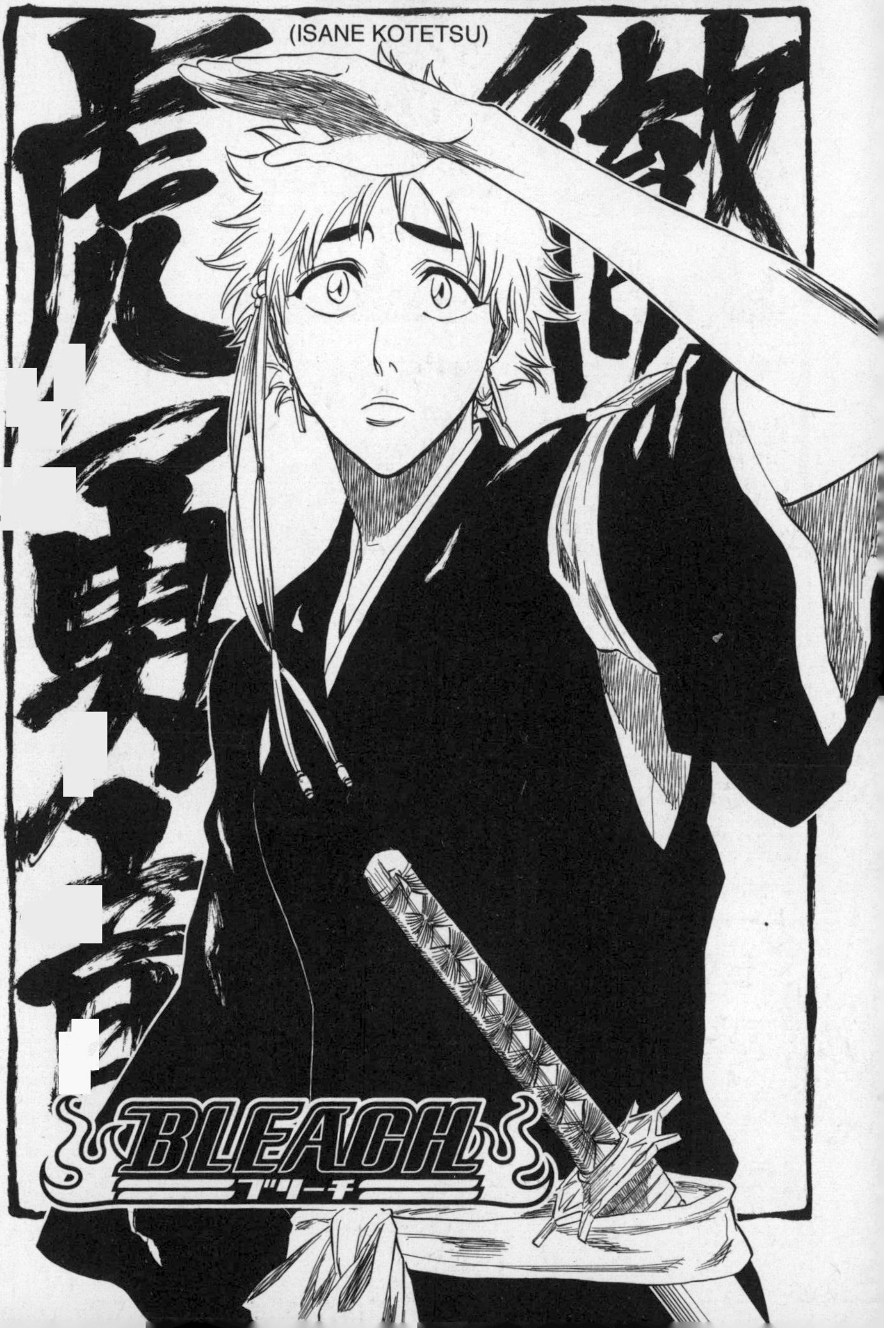
(ISANE KOTETSU)
BLEACH
ブリーチ

READ THIS WAY

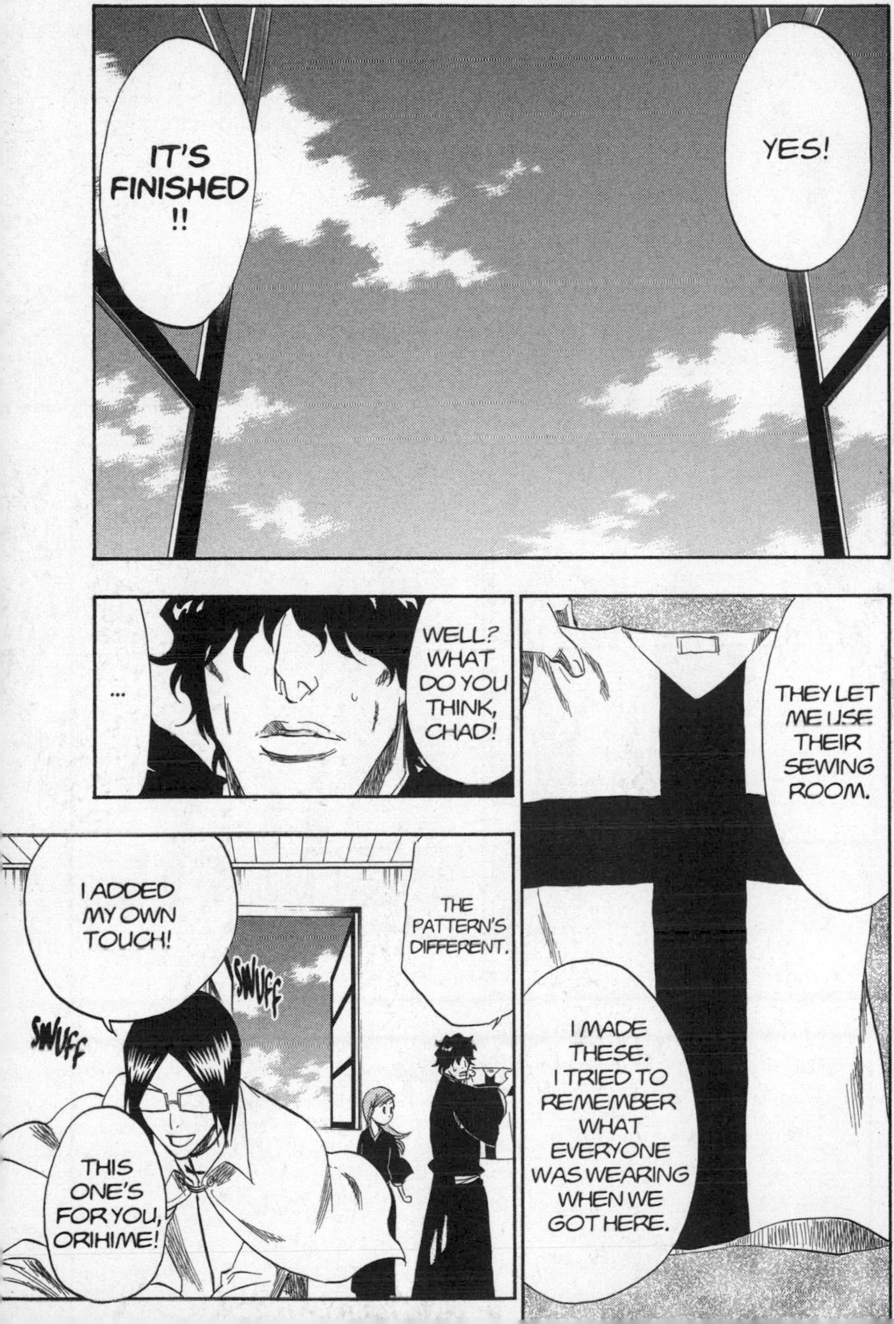
YES!
IT'S FINISHED!!
THEY LET ME USE THEIR SEWING ROOM.
I MADE THESE. I TRIED TO REMEMBER WHAT EVERYONE WAS WEARING WHEN WE GOT HERE.
WELL? WHAT DO YOU THINK, CHAD!
...
THE PATTERN'S DIFFERENT.
I ADDED MY OWN TOUCH!
SNUFF
SNUFF
THIS ONE'S FOR YOU, ORIHIME!

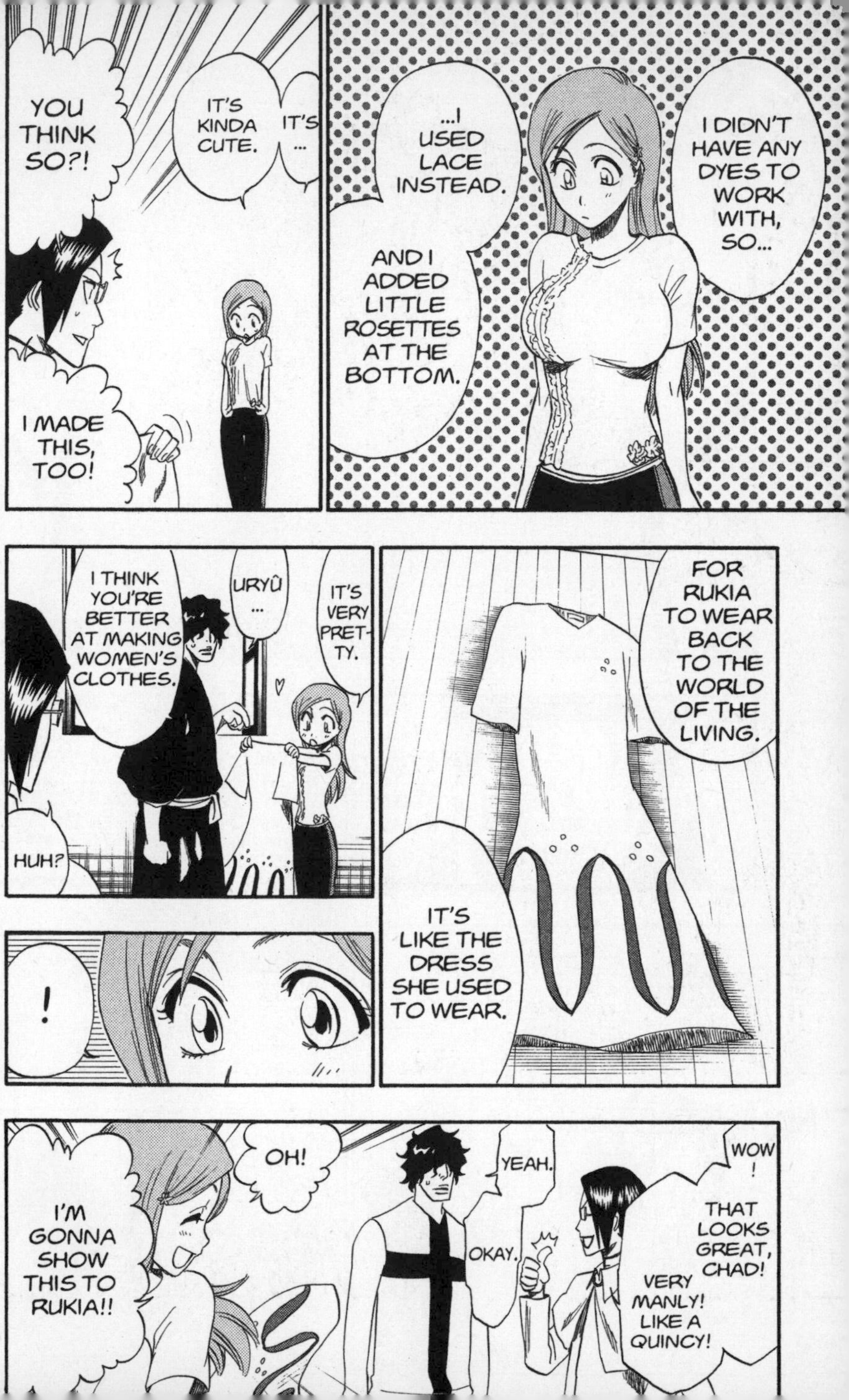
I DIDN'T HAVE ANY DYES TO WORK WITH, SO...
...I USED LACE INSTEAD.
AND I ADDED LITTLE ROSETTES AT THE BOTTOM.
IT'S ...
IT'S KINDA CUTE.
YOU THINK SO?!
I MADE THIS, TOO!
FOR RUKIA TO WEAR BACK TO THE WORLD OF THE LIVING.
IT'S LIKE THE DRESS SHE USED TO WEAR.
IT'S VERY PRET-TY.
URYÛ ...
I THINK YOU'RE BETTER AT MAKING WOMEN'S CLOTHES.
HUH?
!
WOW!
THAT LOOKS GREAT, CHAD!
VERY MANLY! LIKE A QUINCY!
YEAH.
OKAY.
OH!
I'M GONNA SHOW THIS TO RUKIA!!

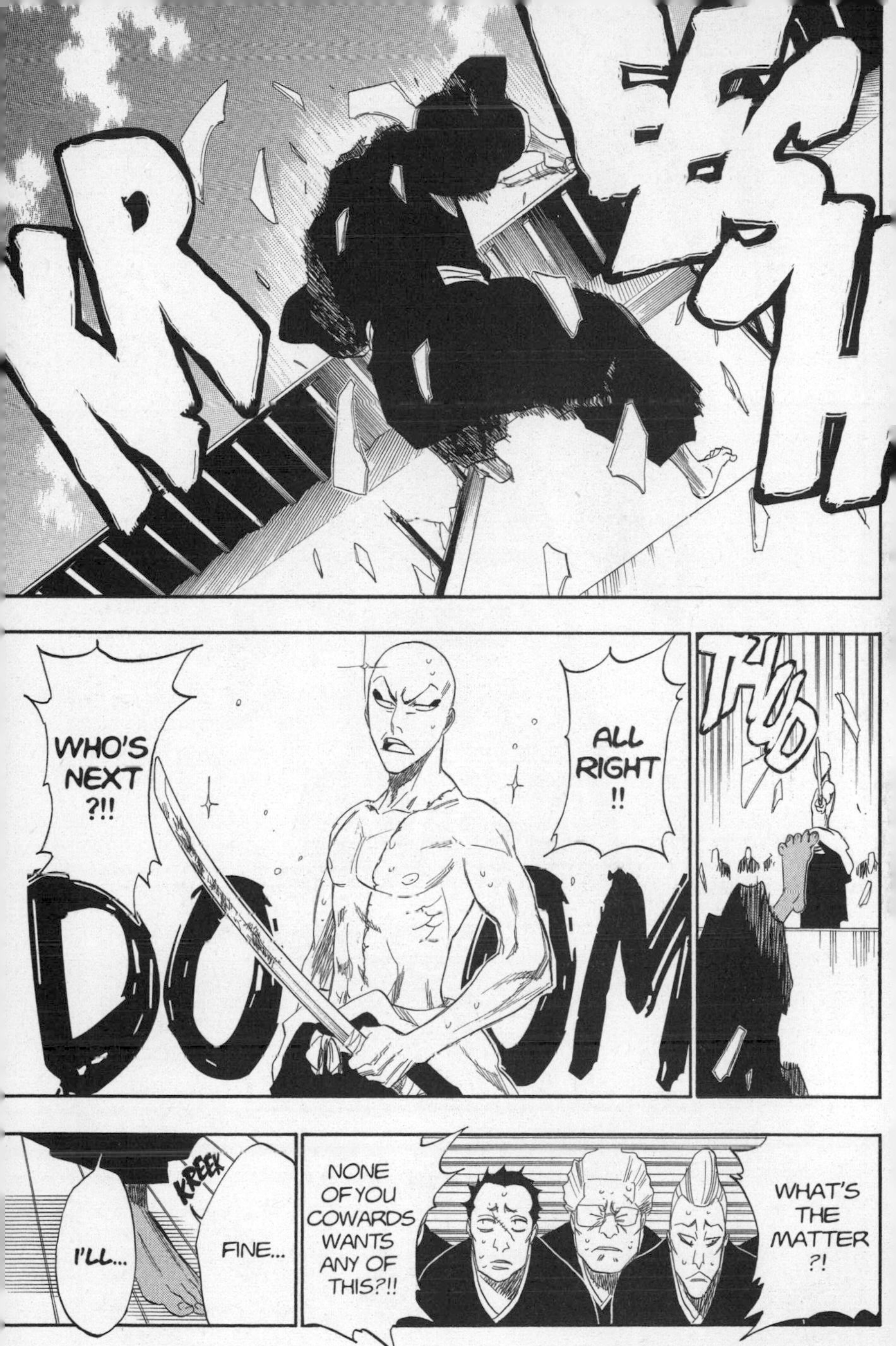
KRASH
THUD
ALL RIGHT !!
WHO'S NEXT ?!!
DOOM
WHAT'S THE MATTER ?!
NONE OF YOU COWARDS WANTS ANY OF THIS?!!
KREEK
FINE...
I'LL...

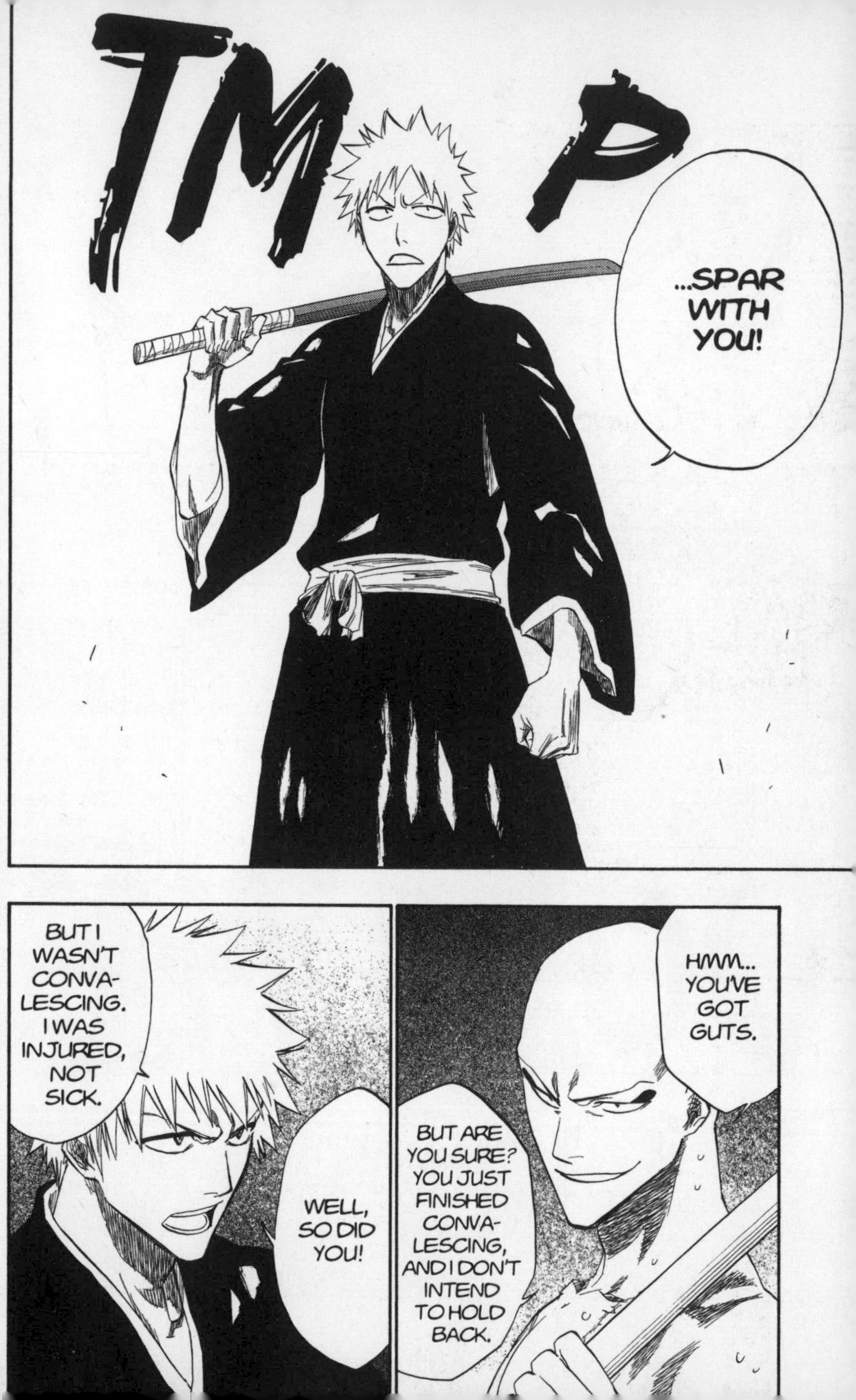
TMP
...SPAR WITH YOU!
HMM... YOU'VE GOT GUTS.
BUT ARE YOU SURE? YOU JUST FINISHED CONVA-LESCING, AND I DON'T INTEND TO HOLD BACK.
WELL, SO DID YOU!
BUT I WASN'T CONVA-LESCING. I WAS INJURED, NOT SICK.

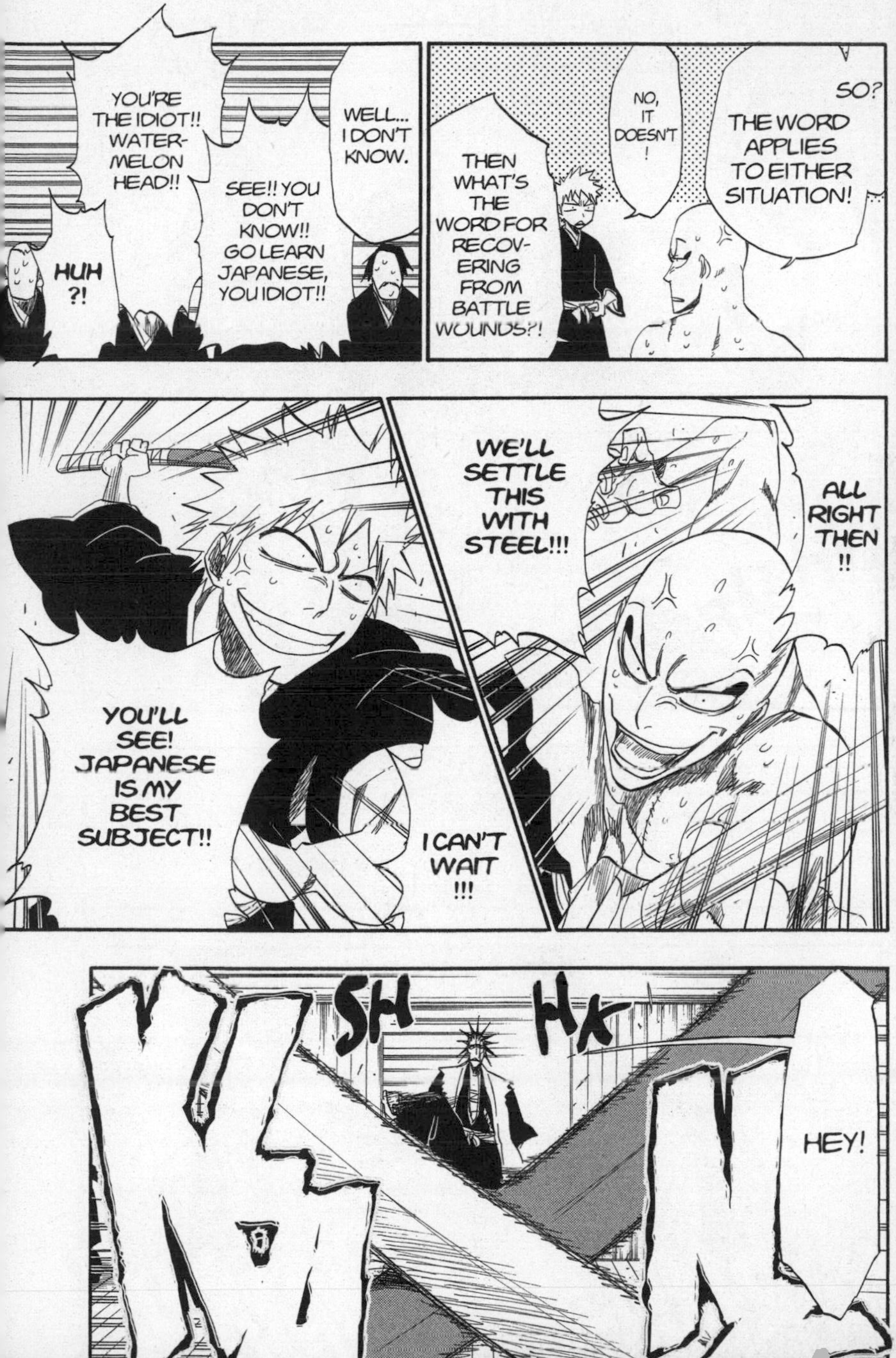
SO?
THE WORD APPLIES TO EITHER SITUATION!
NO, IT DOESN'T!
THEN WHAT'S THE WORD FOR RECOVERING FROM BATTLE WOUNDS?!
WELL... I DON'T KNOW.
SEE!! YOU DON'T KNOW!! GO LEARN JAPANESE, YOU IDIOT!!
YOU'RE THE IDIOT!! WATER-MELON HEAD!!
HUH?!
ALL RIGHT THEN!!
WE'LL SETTLE THIS WITH STEEL!!!
I CAN'T WAIT!!!
YOU'LL SEE! JAPANESE IS MY BEST SUBJECT!!
HEY!
SH
HK

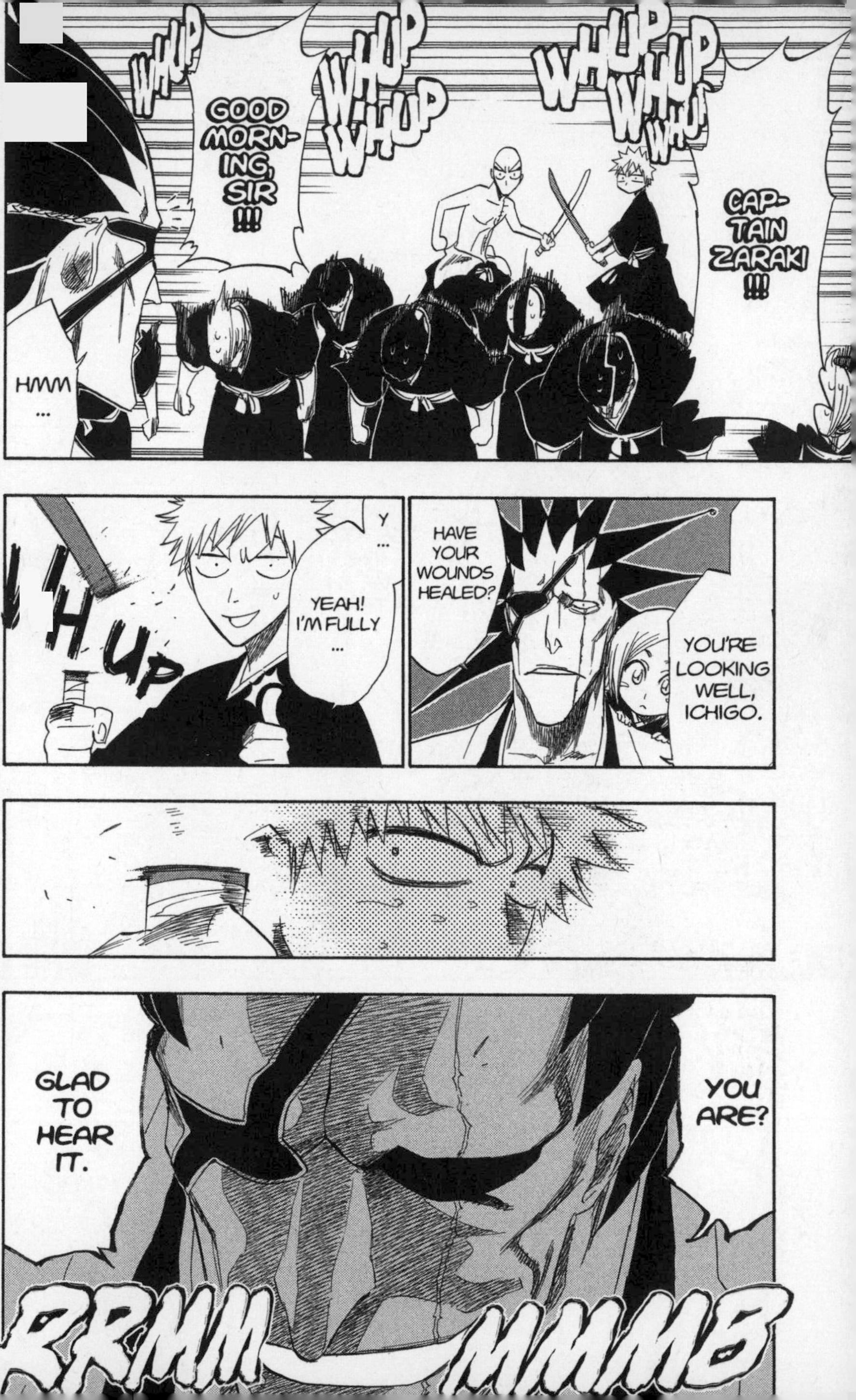
CAP-TAIN ZARAKI !!!
WHUP WHUP WHUP
WHUP WHUP WHUP
GOOD MORN-ING, SIR !!!
WHUP
HMM ...
YOU'RE LOOKING WELL, ICHIGO.
HAVE YOUR WOUNDS HEALED?
Y ...
YEAH! I'M FULLY ...
WHUP
YOU ARE?
GLAD TO HEAR IT.
RRMMMMMB

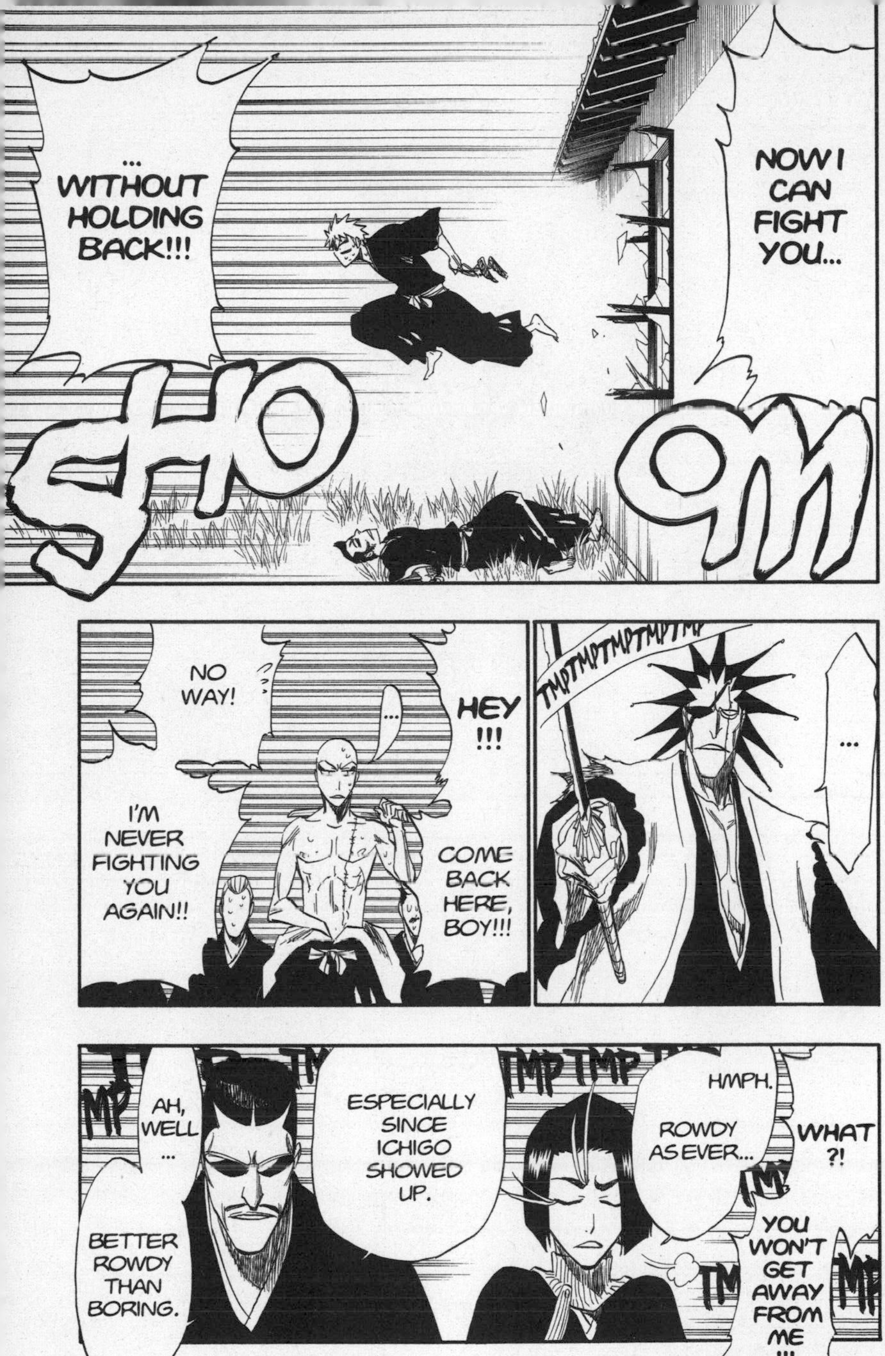
NOW I CAN FIGHT YOU...
...WITHOUT HOLDING BACK!!!
SHOOM
TMPTMPTMPTMPTMP
...
HEY!!!
COME BACK HERE, BOY!!!
...
NO WAY!
I'M NEVER FIGHTING YOU AGAIN!!
TMPTMP
HMPH.
ROWDY AS EVER...
WHAT?!
YOU WON'T GET AWAY FROM ME!!!
ESPECIALLY SINCE ICHIGO SHOWED UP.
AH, WELL...
BETTER ROWDY THAN BORING.

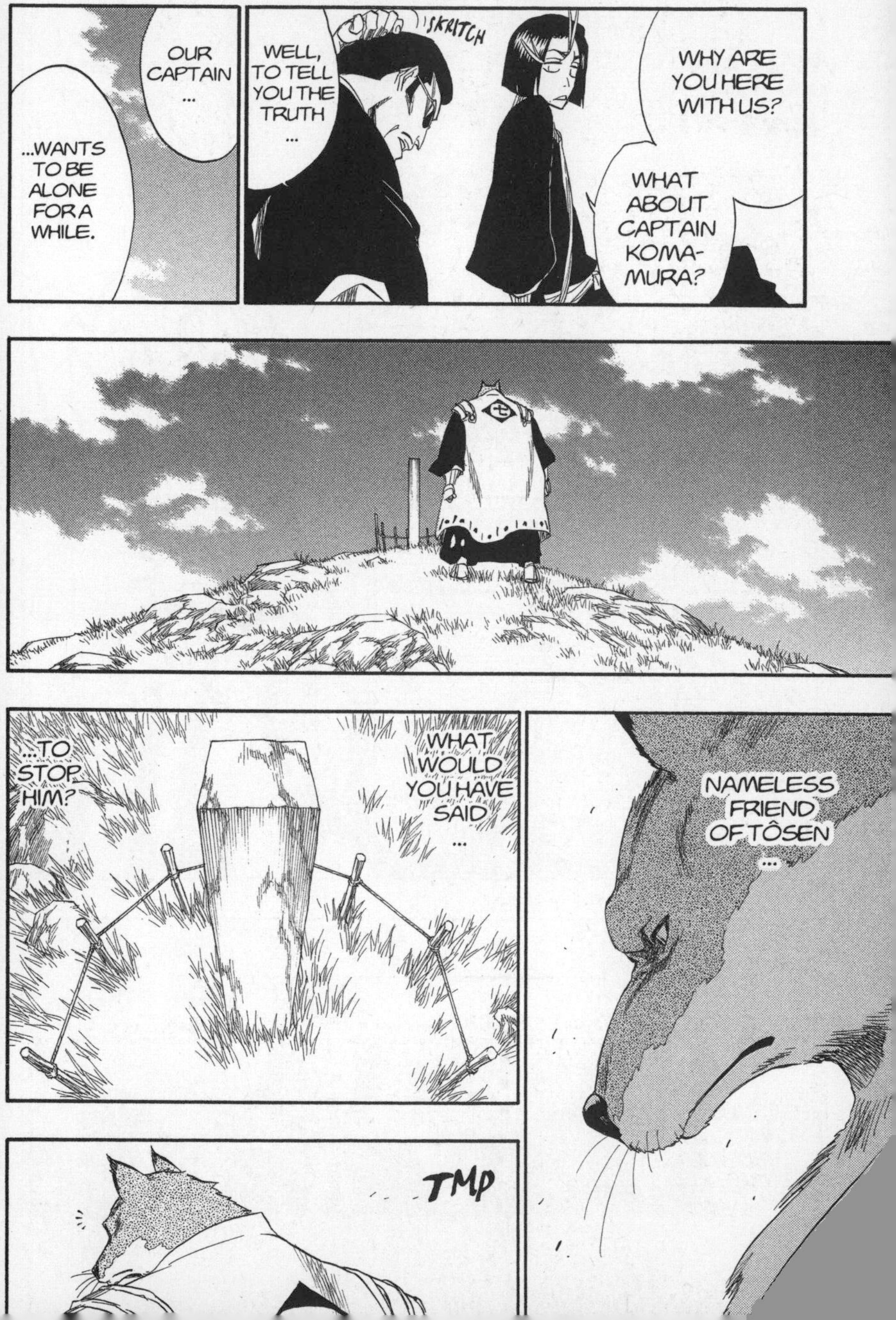
WHY ARE YOU HERE WITH US?
WHAT ABOUT CAPTAIN KOMAMURA?
SKRITCH
WELL, TO TELL YOU THE TRUTH ...
OUR CAPTAIN ...
...WANTS TO BE ALONE FOR A WHILE.
NAMELESS FRIEND OF TÔSEN ...
WHAT WOULD YOU HAVE SAID ...
...TO STOP HIM?
TMP

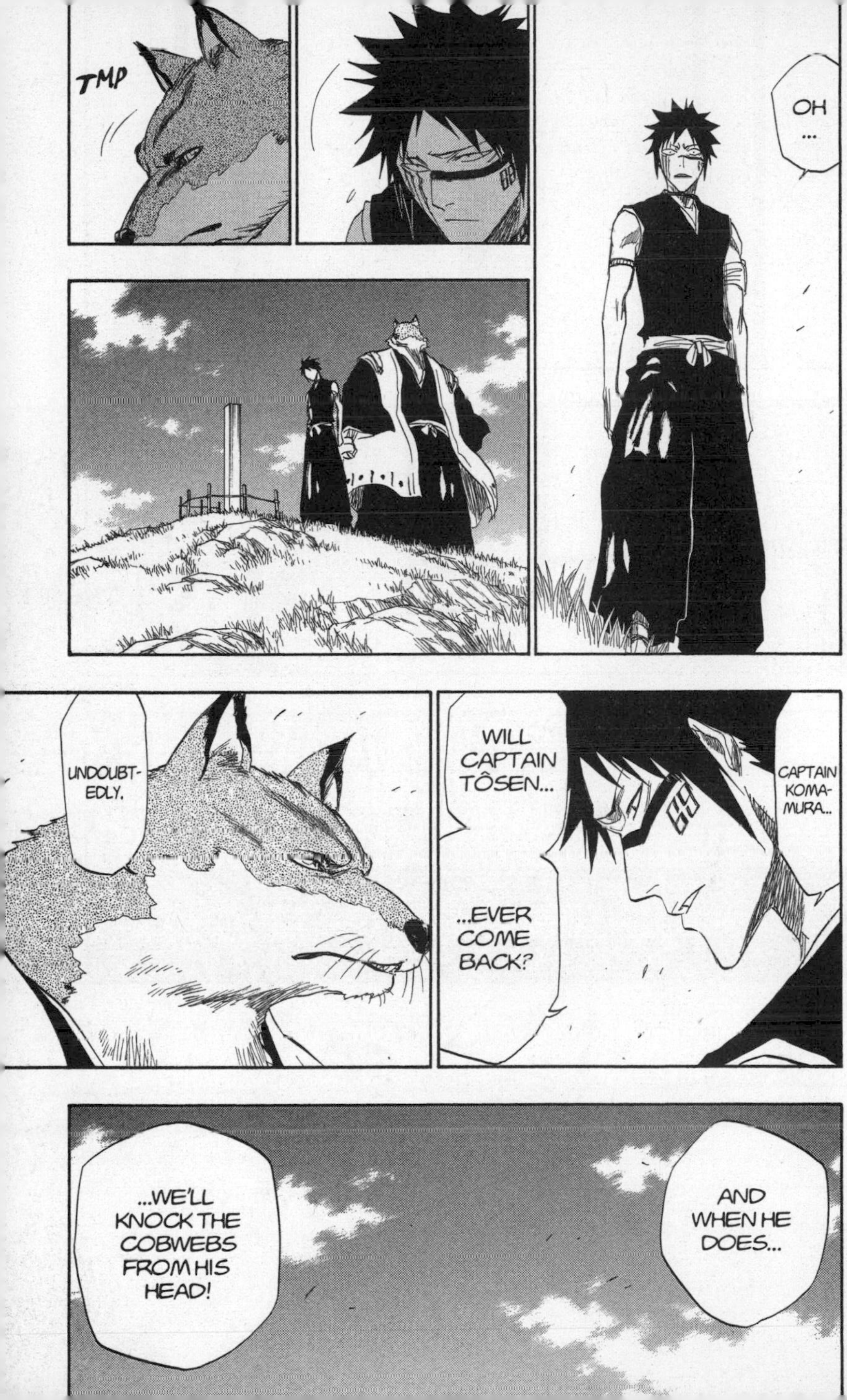
OH ...
TMP
CAPTAIN KOMAMURA...
WILL CAPTAIN TÔSEN...
...EVER COME BACK?
UNDOUBTEDLY.
AND WHEN HE DOES...
...WE'LL KNOCK THE COBWEBS FROM HIS HEAD!

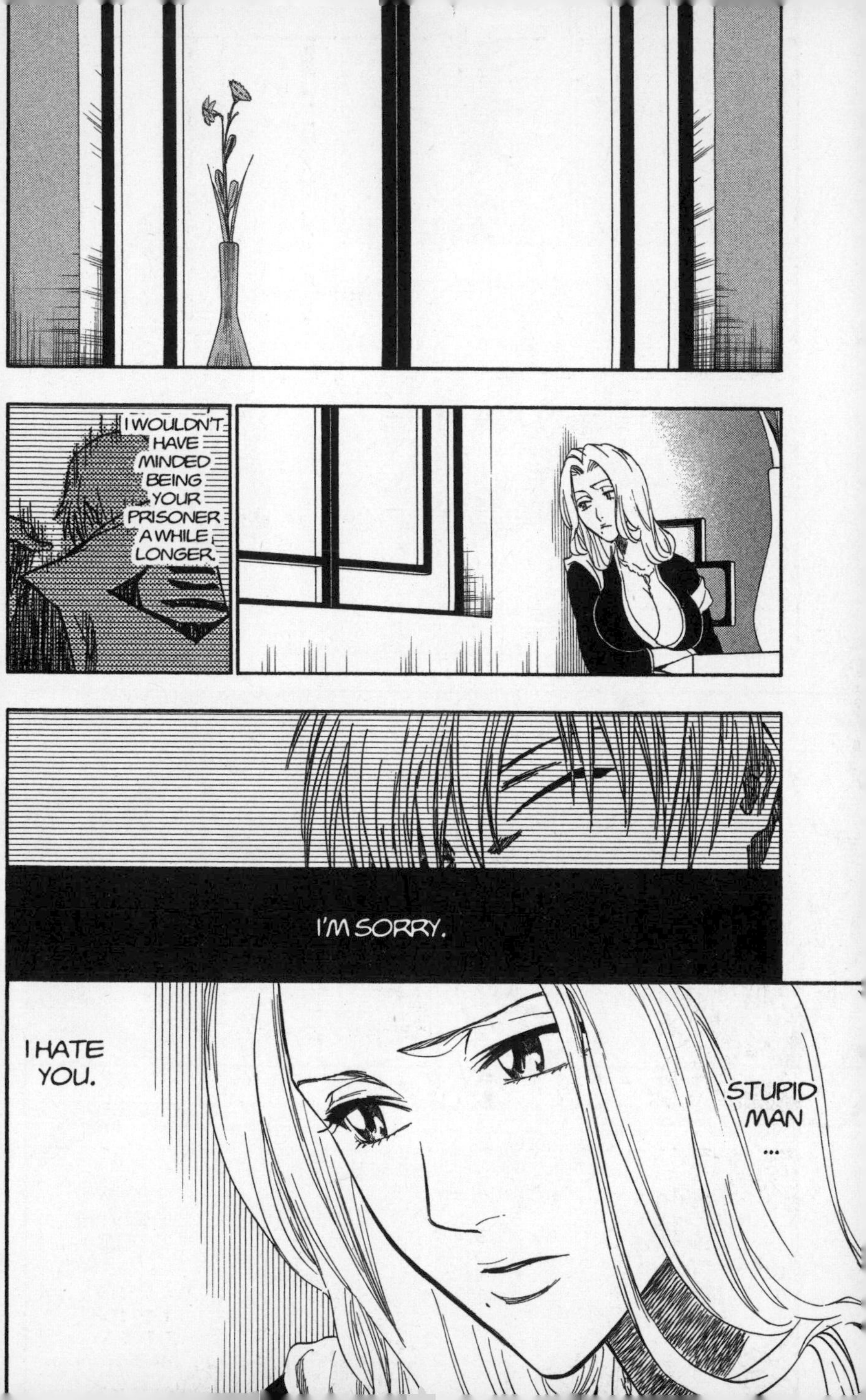
I WOULDN'T HAVE MINDED BEING YOUR PRISONER A WHILE LONGER.
I'M SORRY.
STUPID MAN ...
I HATE YOU.

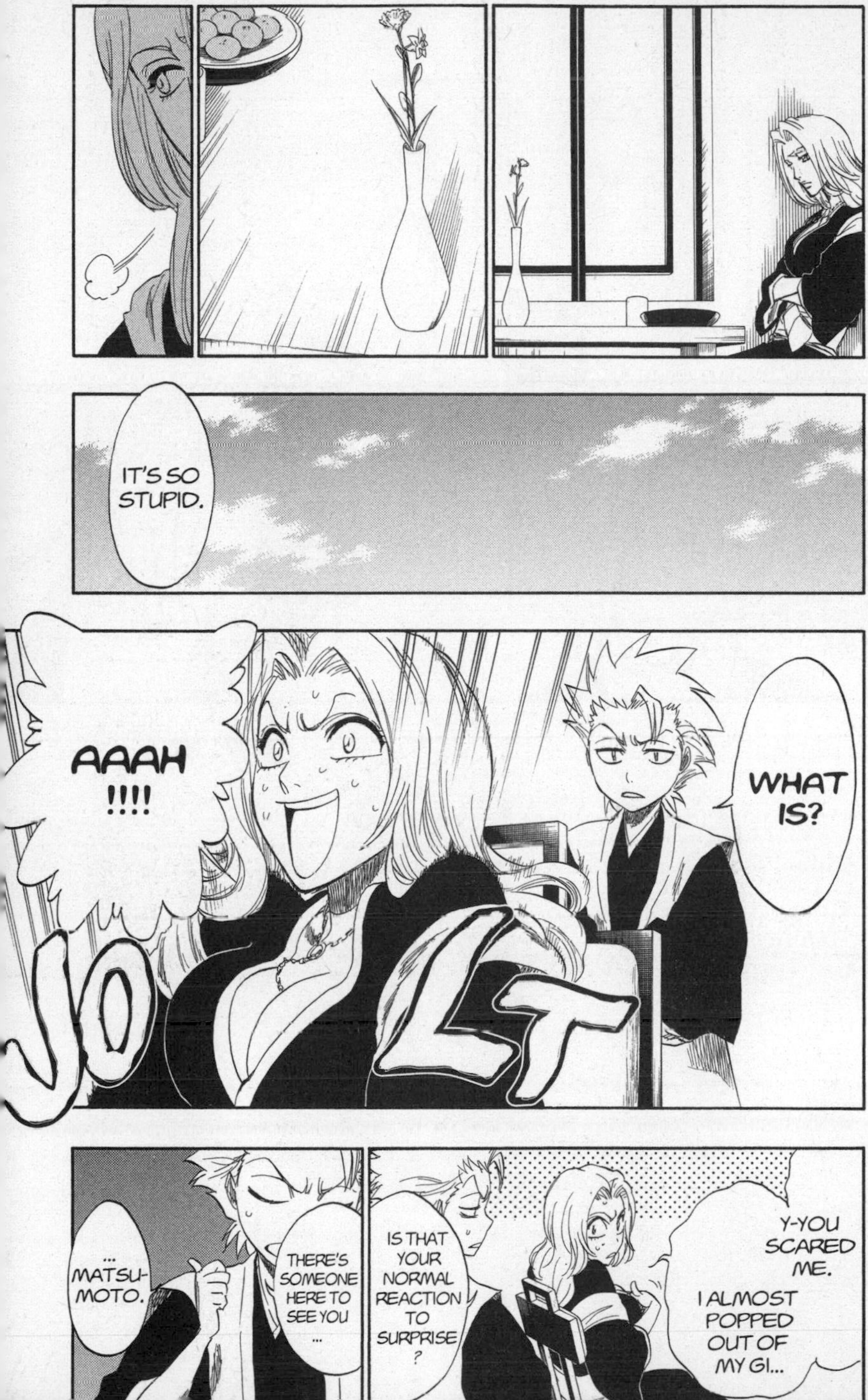
IT'S SO STUPID.
WHAT IS?
AAAH !!!!
JOLT
Y-YOU SCARED ME.
I ALMOST POPPED OUT OF MY GI...
IS THAT YOUR NORMAL REACTION TO SURPRISE?
THERE'S SOMEONE HERE TO SEE YOU ...
... MATSU-MOTO.

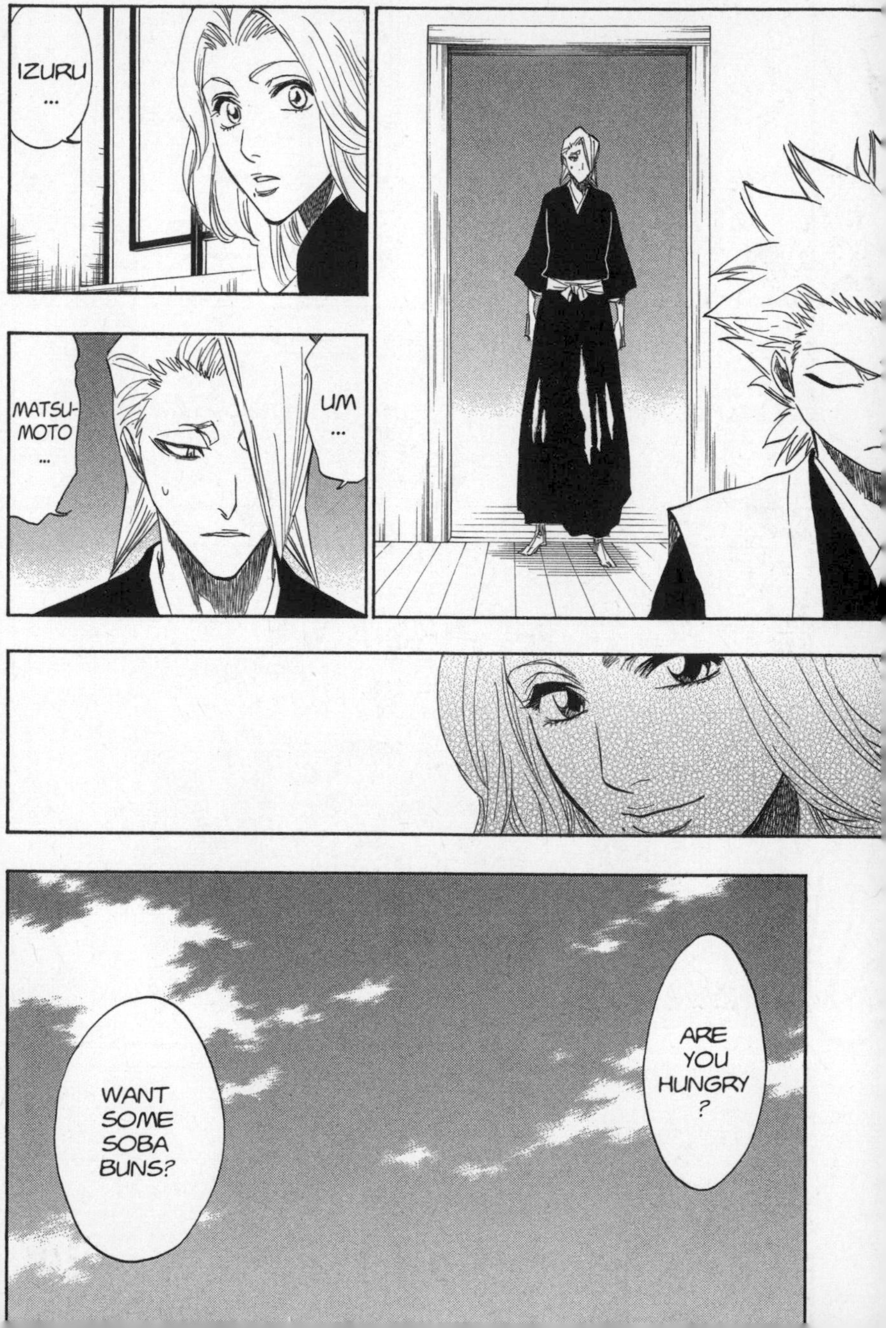
IZURU ...
UM ...
MATSU-MOTO ...
ARE YOU HUNGRY?
WANT SOME SOBA BUNS?

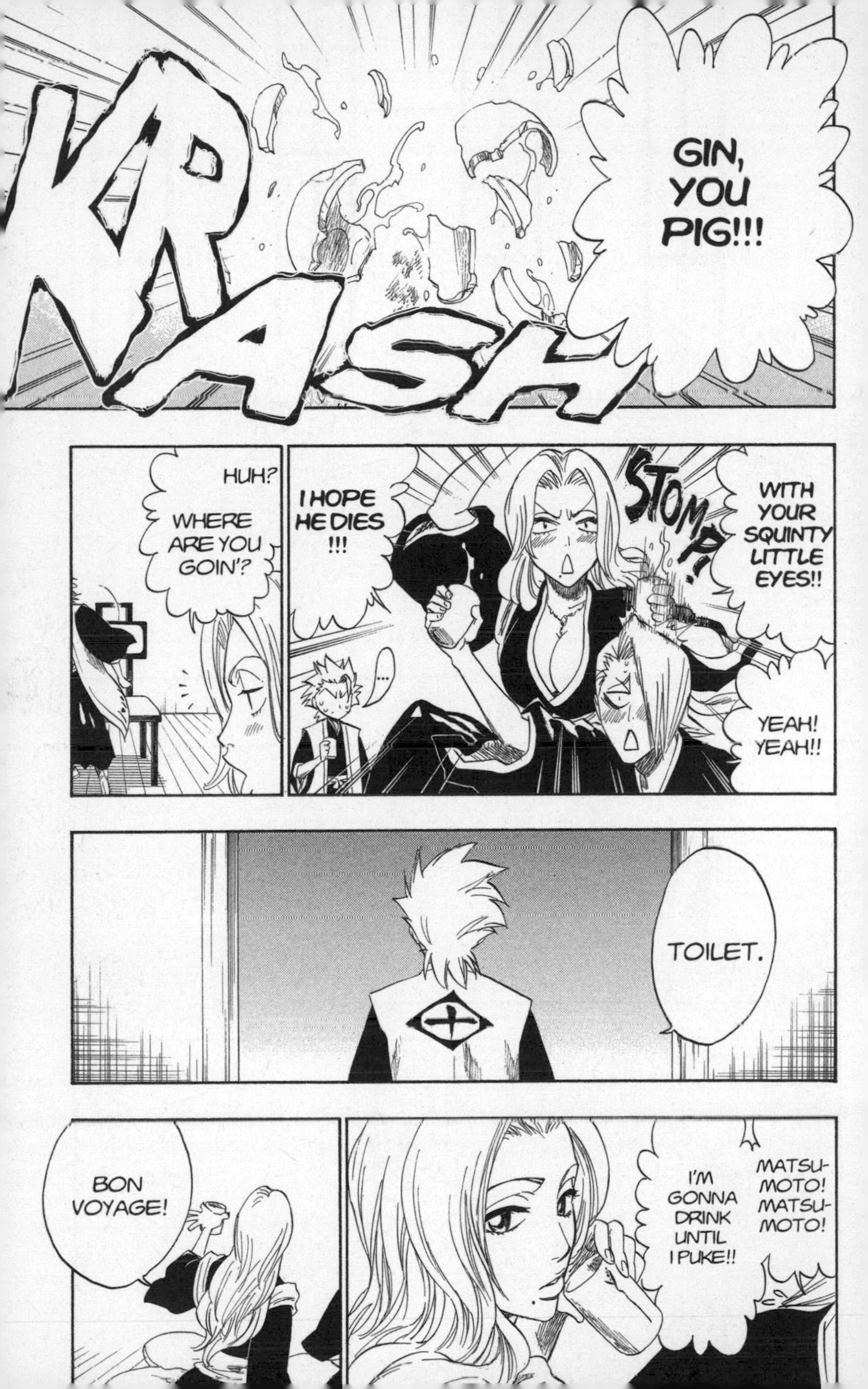
GIN, YOU PIG!!!
KRASH
WITH YOUR SQUINTY LITTLE EYES!!
STOMP
I HOPE HE DIES !!!
YEAH! YEAH!!
...
HUH?
WHERE ARE YOU GOIN'?
TOILET.
MATSU-MOTO! MATSU-MOTO!
I'M GONNA DRINK UNTIL I PUKE!!
BON VOYAGE!

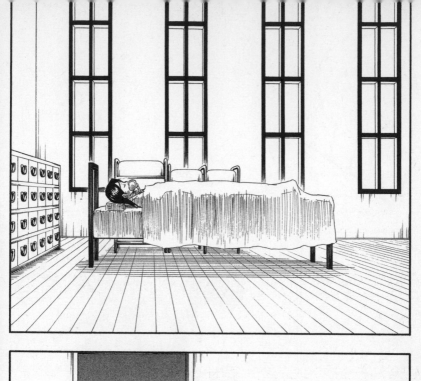

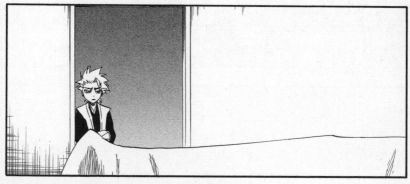

HINA-
MORI
...

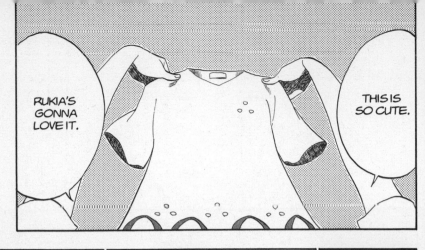

THIS IS SO CUTE.
RUKIA'S GONNA LOVE IT.
SHE'S BEEN PRETTY DOWN LATELY...
...BUT THIS SHOULD LIFT HER SPIRITS.
I WON-DER WHY...
...URYÛ WOULD GO TO SO MUCH TROUBLE.
!!!!
O-OH!
MAYBE URYÛ...
I'M SO SMART!!
WOW!!
ORIHIME INOUE HAS HAD HER FIRST WOMAN'S INTUITION AT THE AGE OF 15!!!
WAY OFF MARK
OH, HERE IT IS!
RU-KI-AAA...
YOO-HOO! ♪

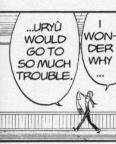

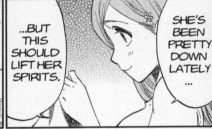

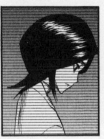

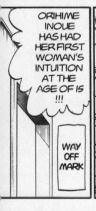

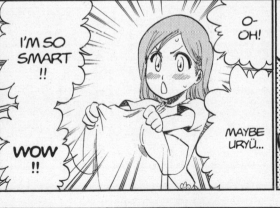

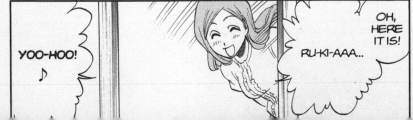

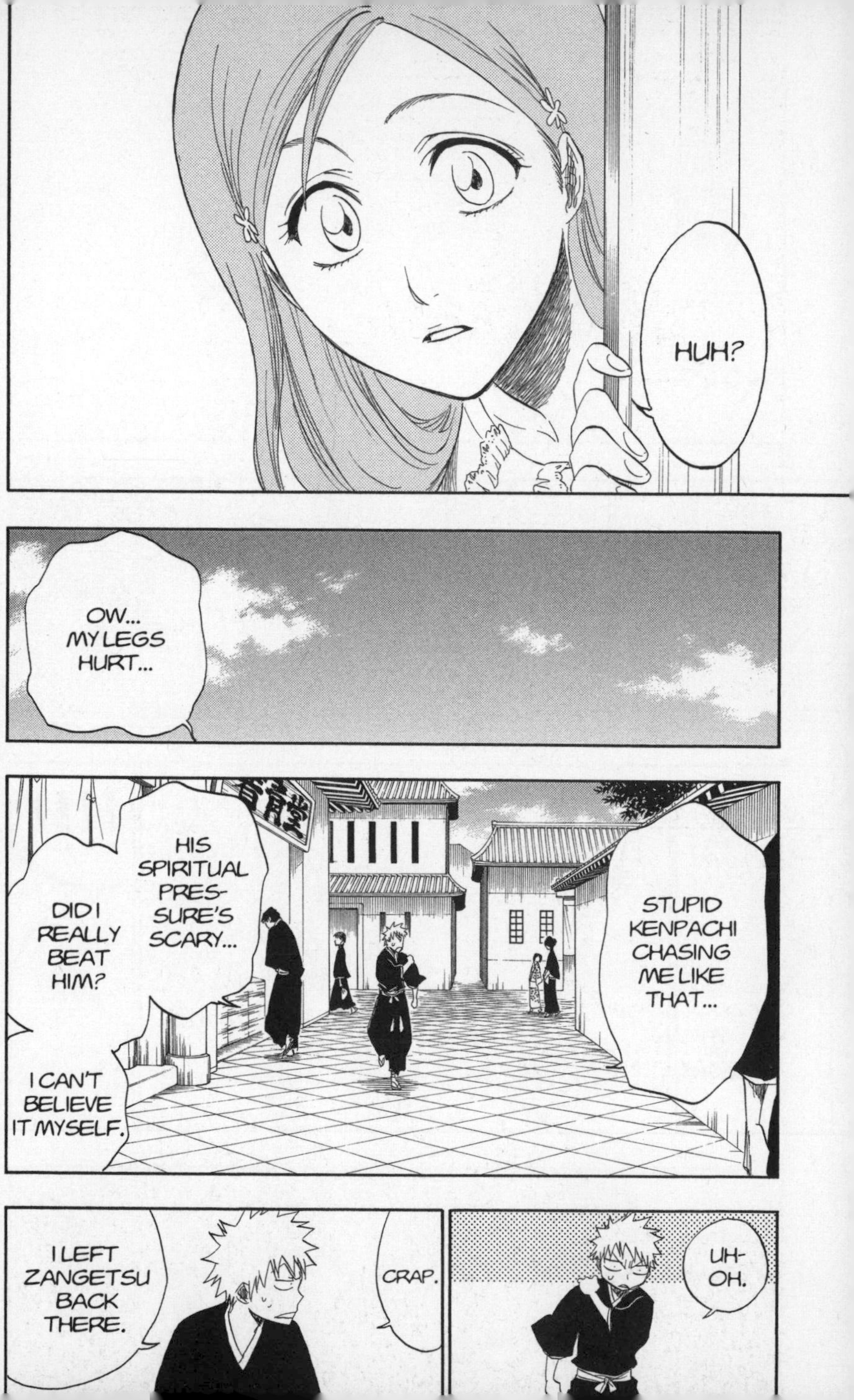
HUH?
OW... MY LEGS HURT...
STUPID KENPACHI CHASING ME LIKE THAT...
HIS SPIRITUAL PRES-SURE'S SCARY...
DID I REALLY BEAT HIM?
I CAN'T BELIEVE IT MYSELF.
UH-OH.
CRAP.
I LEFT ZANGETSU BACK THERE.

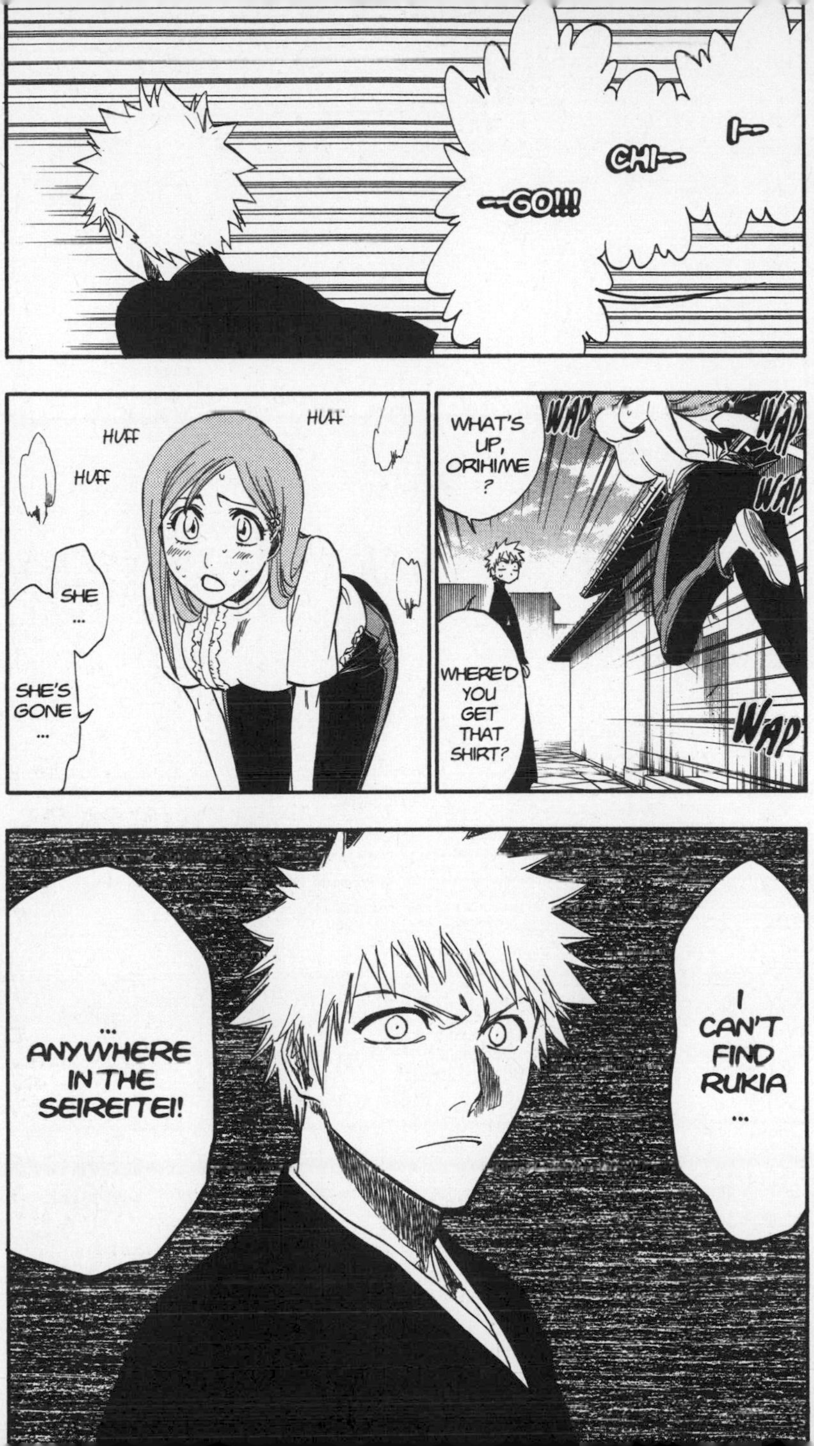
I—
CHI—
—GO!!!
WAP
WAP
WAP
WHAT'S UP, ORIHIME?
WHERE'D YOU GET THAT SHIRT?
WAP
HUFF
HUFF
HUFF
SHE...
SHE'S GONE...
I CAN'T FIND RUKIA...
...ANYWHERE IN THE SEIREITEI!

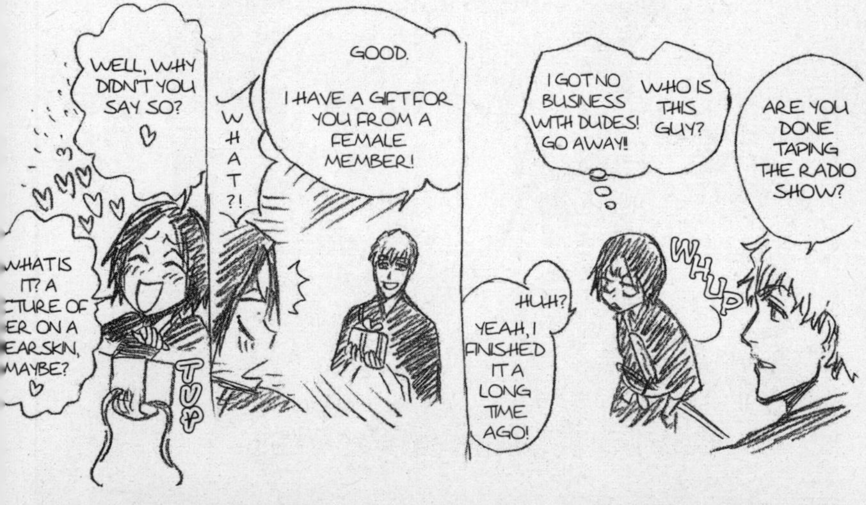
ARE YOU DONE TAPING THE RADIO SHOW?
WHUP
WHO IS THIS GUY?
I GOT NO BUSINESS WITH DUDES! GO AWAY!!
HUH? YEAH, I FINISHED IT A LONG TIME AGO!
GOOD. I HAVE A GIFT FOR YOU FROM A FEMALE MEMBER!
WHAT?!
WELL, WHY DIDN'T YOU SAY SO?
WHAT IS IT? A CTURE OF ER ON A EARSKIN, MAYBE?
TUP

181. AND THE RAIN LEFT OFF

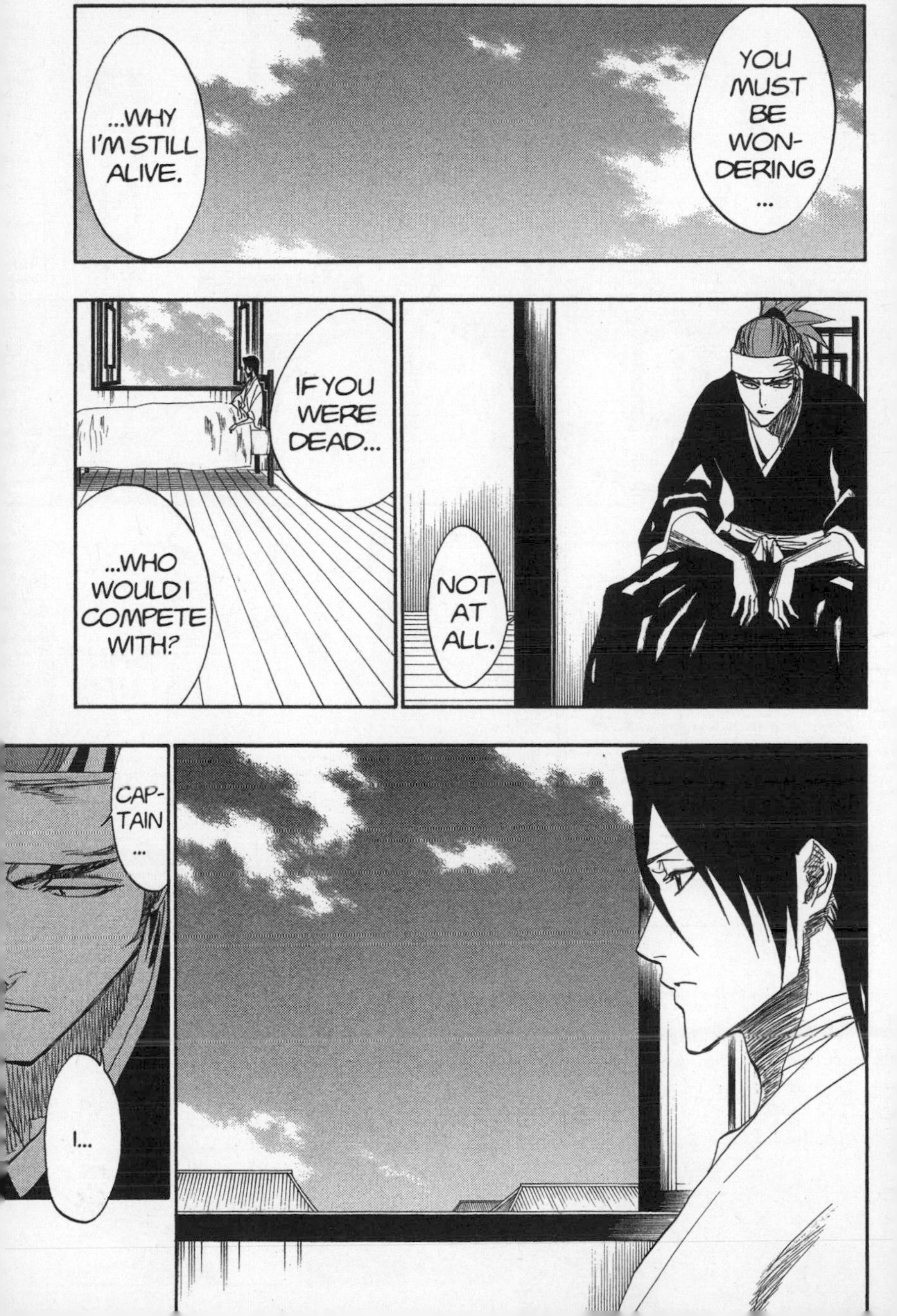
YOU MUST BE WON-DERING...
...WHY I'M STILL ALIVE.
NOT AT ALL.
IF YOU WERE DEAD...
...WHO WOULD I COMPETE WITH?
CAP-TAIN...
I...

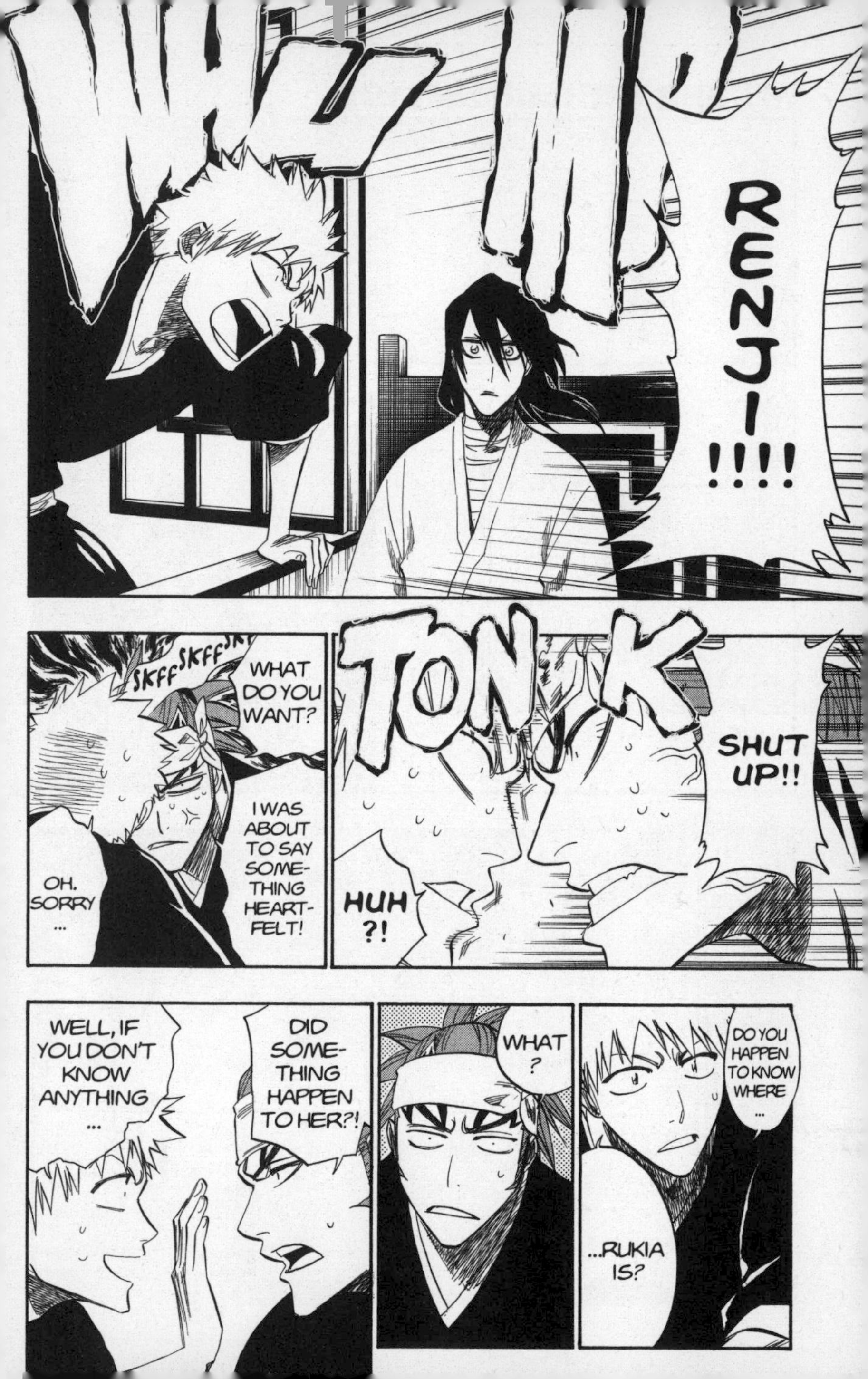
RENJI!!!!
SHUT UP!!
TONK
HUH ?!
WHAT DO YOU WANT?
SKFF SKFF SKFF
I WAS ABOUT TO SAY SOME-THING HEART-FELT!
OH. SORRY ...
DO YOU HAPPEN TO KNOW WHERE ...
...RUKIA IS?
WHAT ?
DID SOME-THING HAPPEN TO HER?!
WELL, IF YOU DON'T KNOW ANYTHING ...

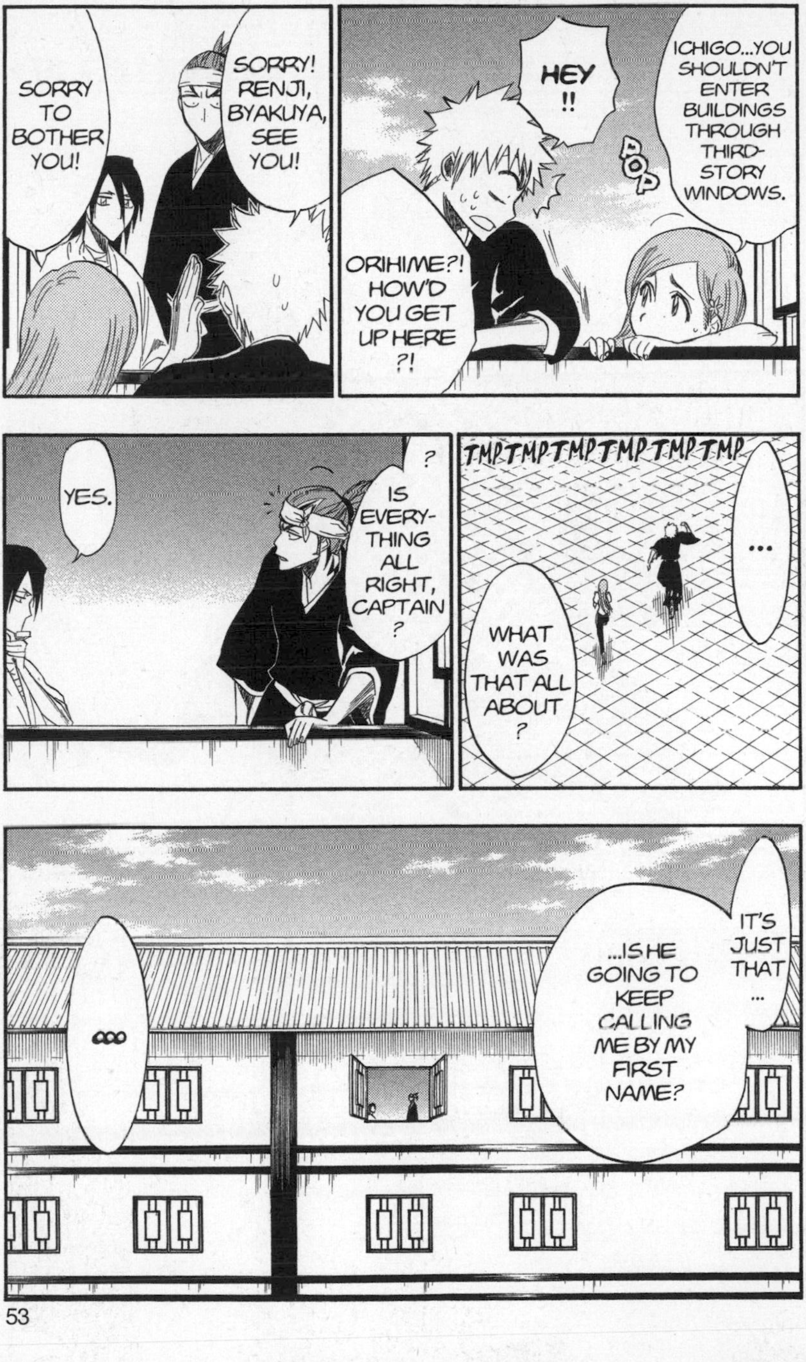
HEY !!
ICHIGO...YOU SHOULDN'T ENTER BUILDINGS THROUGH THIRD-STORY WINDOWS.
POP
ORIHIME?! HOW'D YOU GET UP HERE ?!
SORRY! RENJI, BYAKUYA, SEE YOU!
SORRY TO BOTHER YOU!
TMP TMP TMP TMP TMP TMP TMP
...
WHAT WAS THAT ALL ABOUT ?
? IS EVERY-THING ALL RIGHT, CAPTAIN ?
YES.
IT'S JUST THAT ...
...IS HE GOING TO KEEP CALLING ME BY MY FIRST NAME?
...

BLEACH 181. AND THE RAIN LEFT OFF

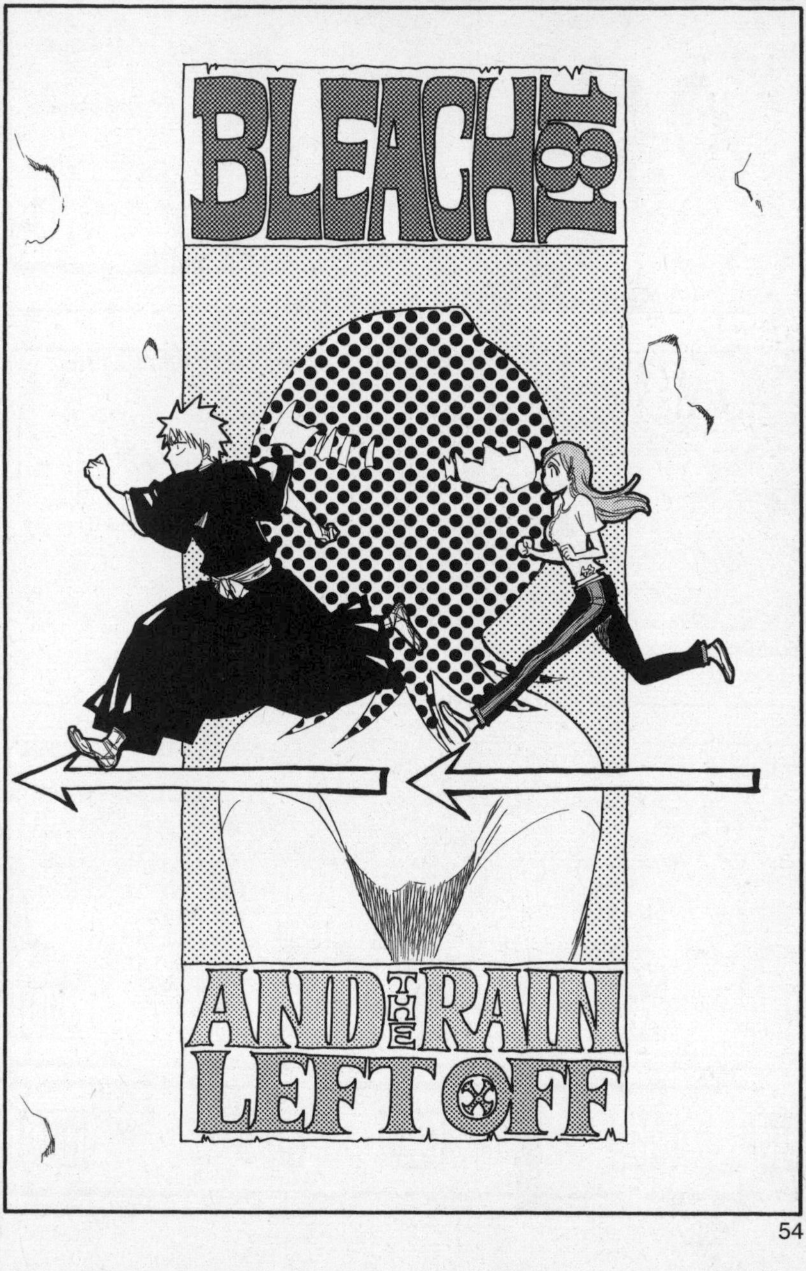
BLEACH 181
AND THE RAIN LEFT OFF

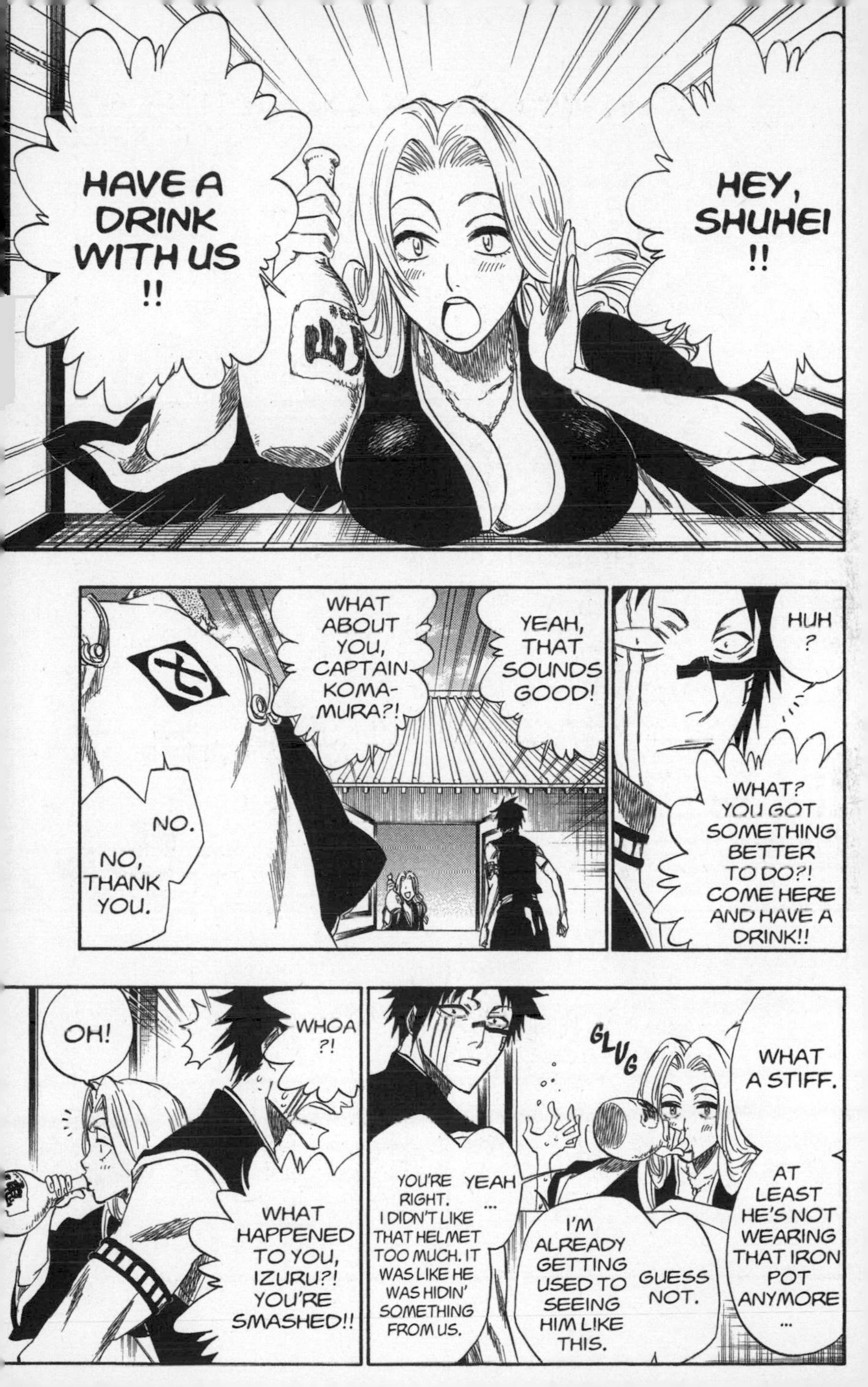
HEY, SHUHEI!!
HAVE A DRINK WITH US!!
HUH?
WHAT? YOU GOT SOMETHING BETTER TO DO?! COME HERE AND HAVE A DRINK!!
YEAH, THAT SOUNDS GOOD!
WHAT ABOUT YOU, CAPTAIN KOMAMURA?!
NO.
NO, THANK YOU.
WHAT A STIFF.
GLUG
AT LEAST HE'S NOT WEARING THAT IRON POT ANYMORE...
GUESS NOT.
I'M ALREADY GETTING USED TO SEEING HIM LIKE THIS.
YEAH...
YOU'RE RIGHT. I DIDN'T LIKE THAT HELMET TOO MUCH. IT WAS LIKE HE WAS HIDIN' SOMETHING FROM US.
WHOA?!
OH!
WHAT HAPPENED TO YOU, IZURU?! YOU'RE SMASHED!!

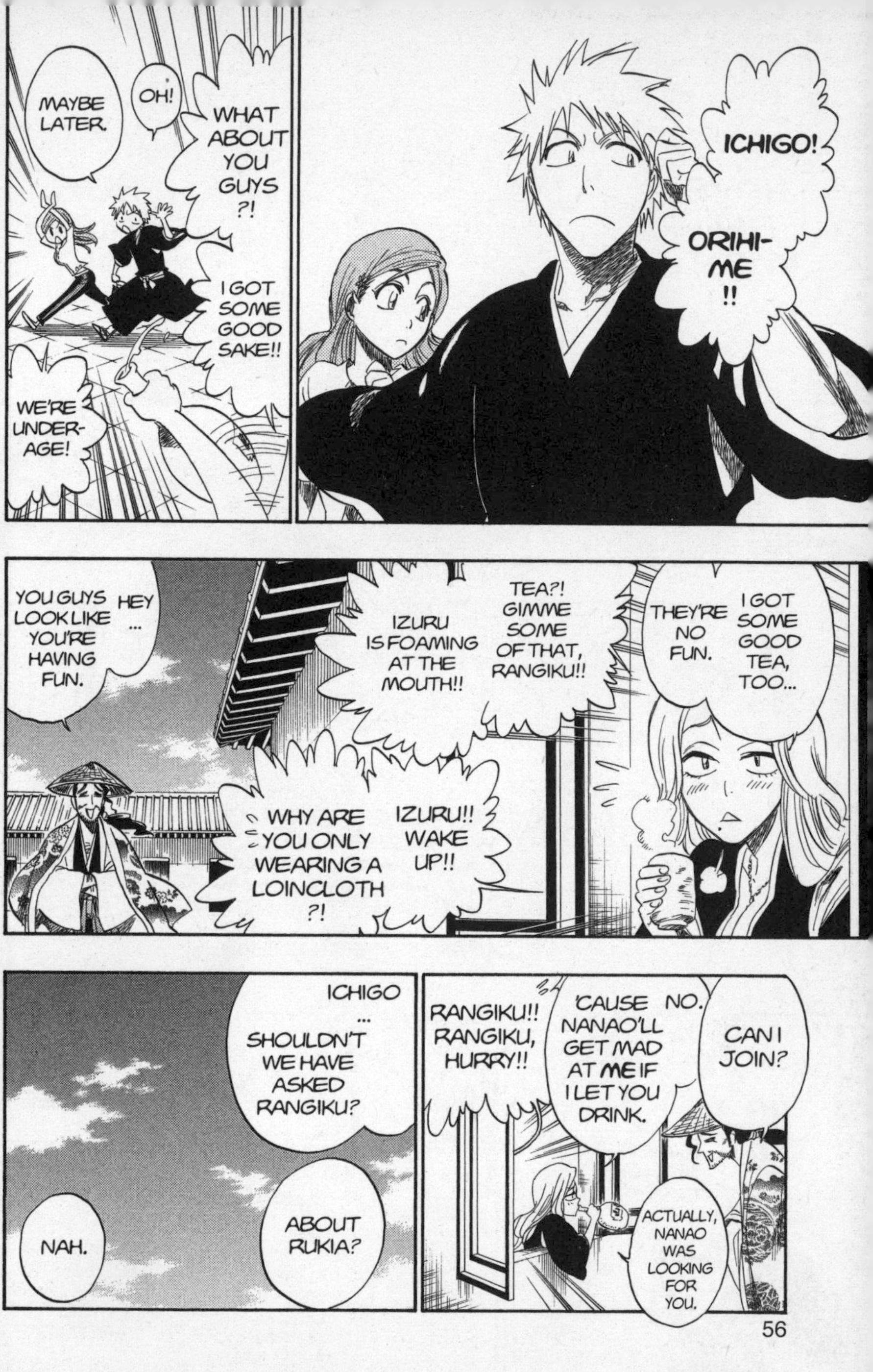
ICHIGO!
ORIHI-ME!!
WHAT ABOUT YOU GUYS?!
OH!
MAYBE LATER.
I GOT SOME GOOD SAKE!!
WE'RE UNDER-AGE!
I GOT SOME GOOD TEA, TOO...
THEY'RE NO FUN.
TEA?! GIMME SOME OF THAT, RANGIKU!!
IZURU IS FOAMING AT THE MOUTH!!
HEY ...
YOU GUYS LOOK LIKE YOU'RE HAVING FUN.
IZURU!! WAKE UP!!
WHY ARE YOU ONLY WEARING A LOINCLOTH?!
CAN I JOIN?
NO.
'CAUSE NANAO'LL GET MAD AT ME IF I LET YOU DRINK.
RANGIKU!! RANGIKU, HURRY!!
ACTUALLY, NANAO WAS LOOKING FOR YOU.
ICHIGO ... SHOULDN'T WE HAVE ASKED RANGIKU?
ABOUT RUKIA?
NAH.

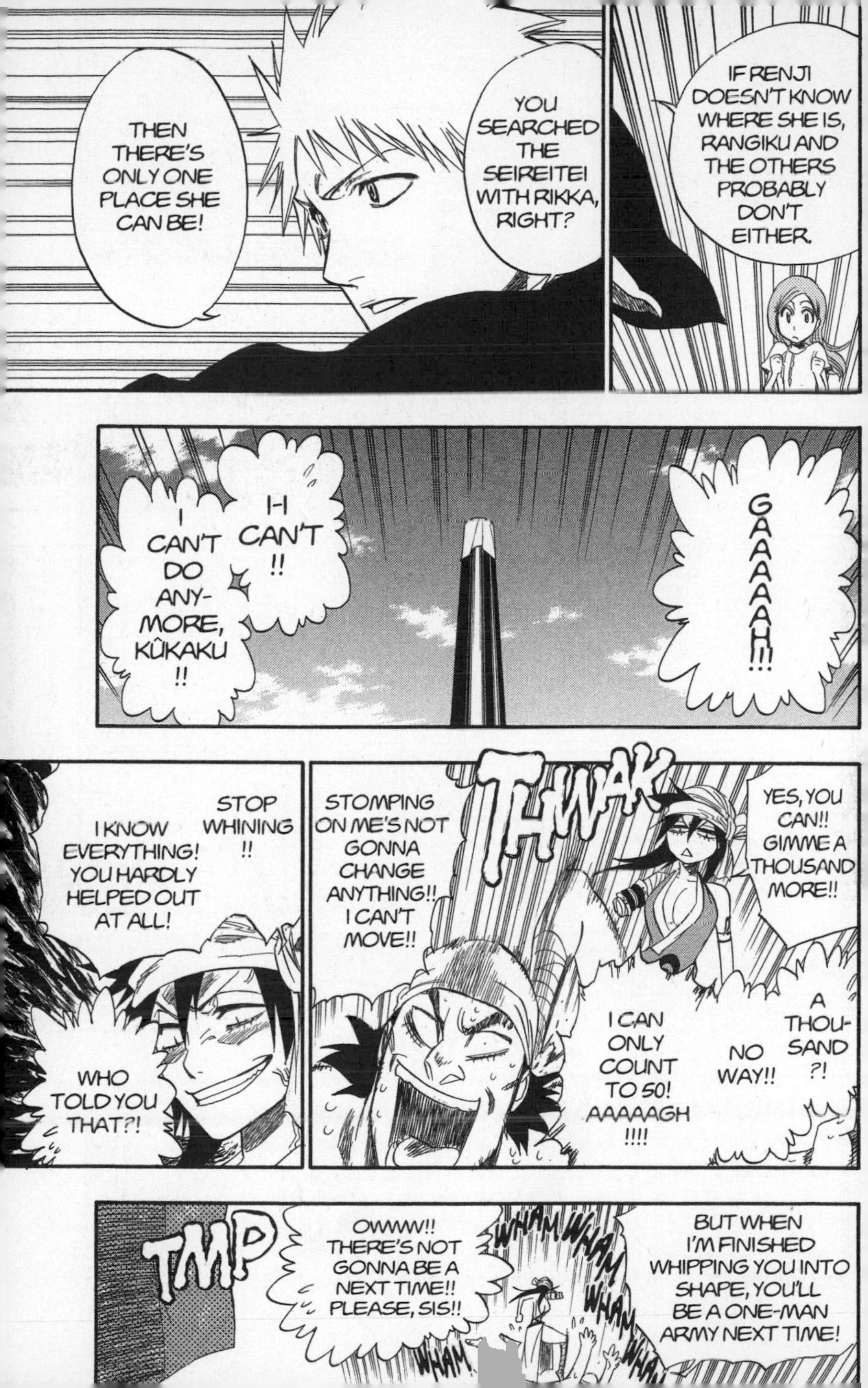
IF RENJI DOESN'T KNOW WHERE SHE IS, RANGIKU AND THE OTHERS PROBABLY DON'T EITHER.
YOU SEARCHED THE SEIREITEI WITH RIKKA, RIGHT?
THEN THERE'S ONLY ONE PLACE SHE CAN BE!
GAAAAAAH!!!
H-I CAN'T!!
I CAN'T DO ANYMORE, KÛKAKU!!
THWAK
YES, YOU CAN!! GIMME A THOUSAND MORE!!
STOMPING ON ME'S NOT GONNA CHANGE ANYTHING!! I CAN'T MOVE!!
A THOUSAND?!
NO WAY!!
I CAN ONLY COUNT TO 50! AAAAAGH!!!!
STOP WHINING!!
I KNOW EVERYTHING! YOU HARDLY HELPED OUT AT ALL!
WHO TOLD YOU THAT?!
BUT WHEN I'M FINISHED WHIPPING YOU INTO SHAPE, YOU'LL BE A ONE-MAN ARMY NEXT TIME!
WHAM WHAM WHAM WHAM WHAM WHAM
OWWW!! THERE'S NOT GONNA BE A NEXT TIME!! PLEASE, SIS!!
TMP

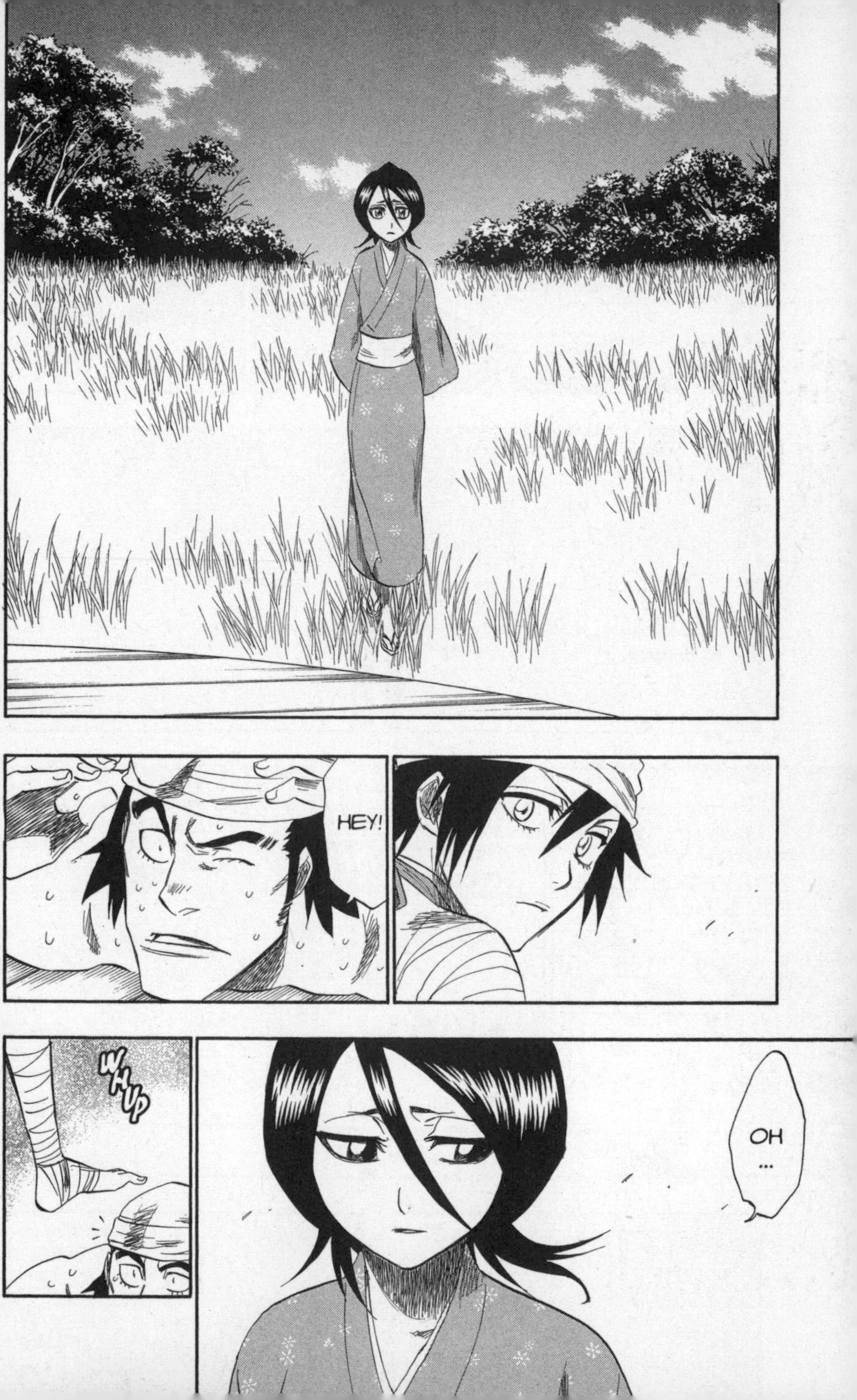
HEY!
WHUP
OH ...

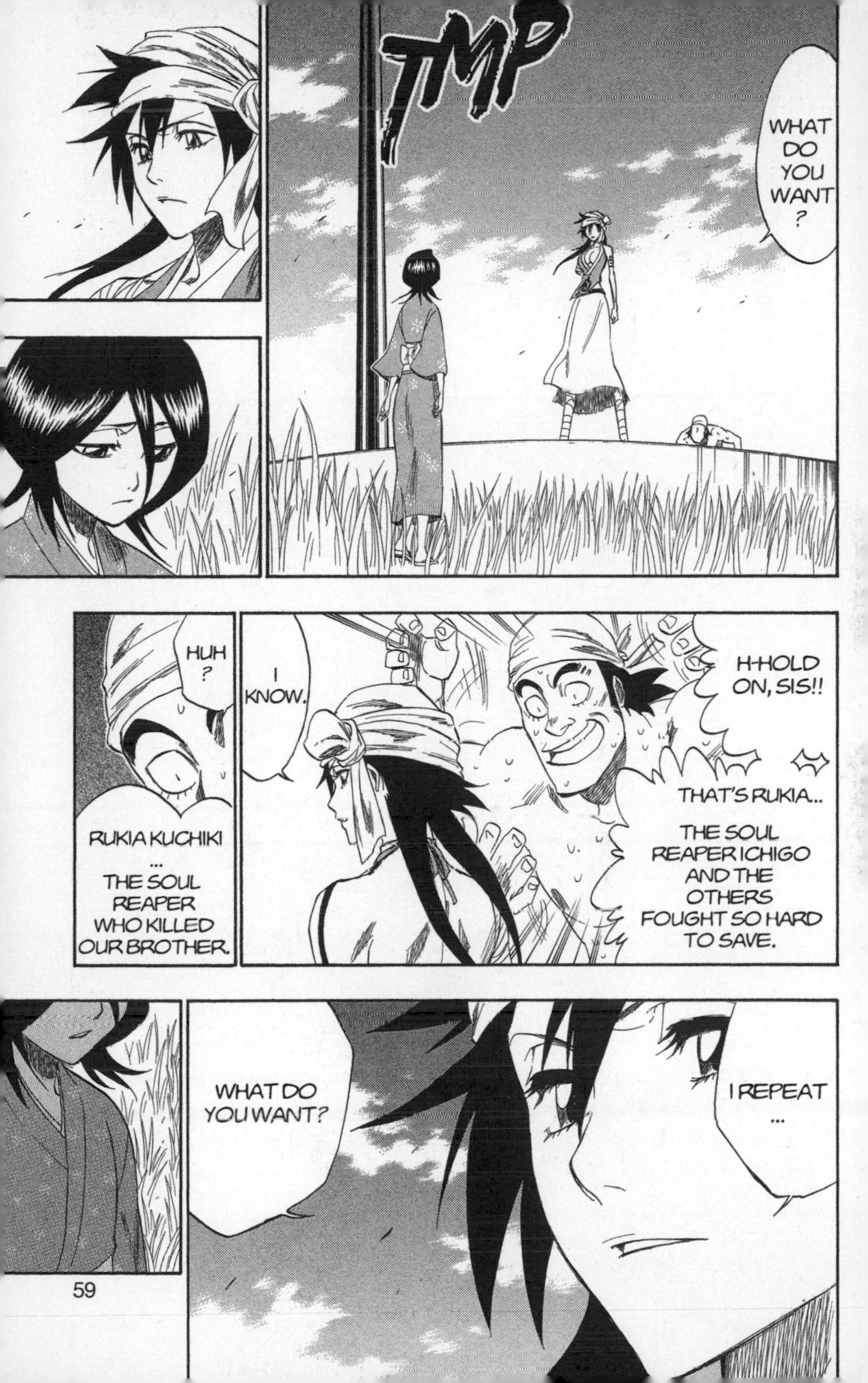
TMP
WHAT DO YOU WANT?
H-HOLD ON, SIS!!
THAT'S RUKIA...
THE SOUL REAPER ICHIGO AND THE OTHERS FOUGHT SO HARD TO SAVE.
I KNOW.
HUH?
RUKIA KUCHIKI ... THE SOUL REAPER WHO KILLED OUR BROTHER.
I REPEAT ...
WHAT DO YOU WANT?

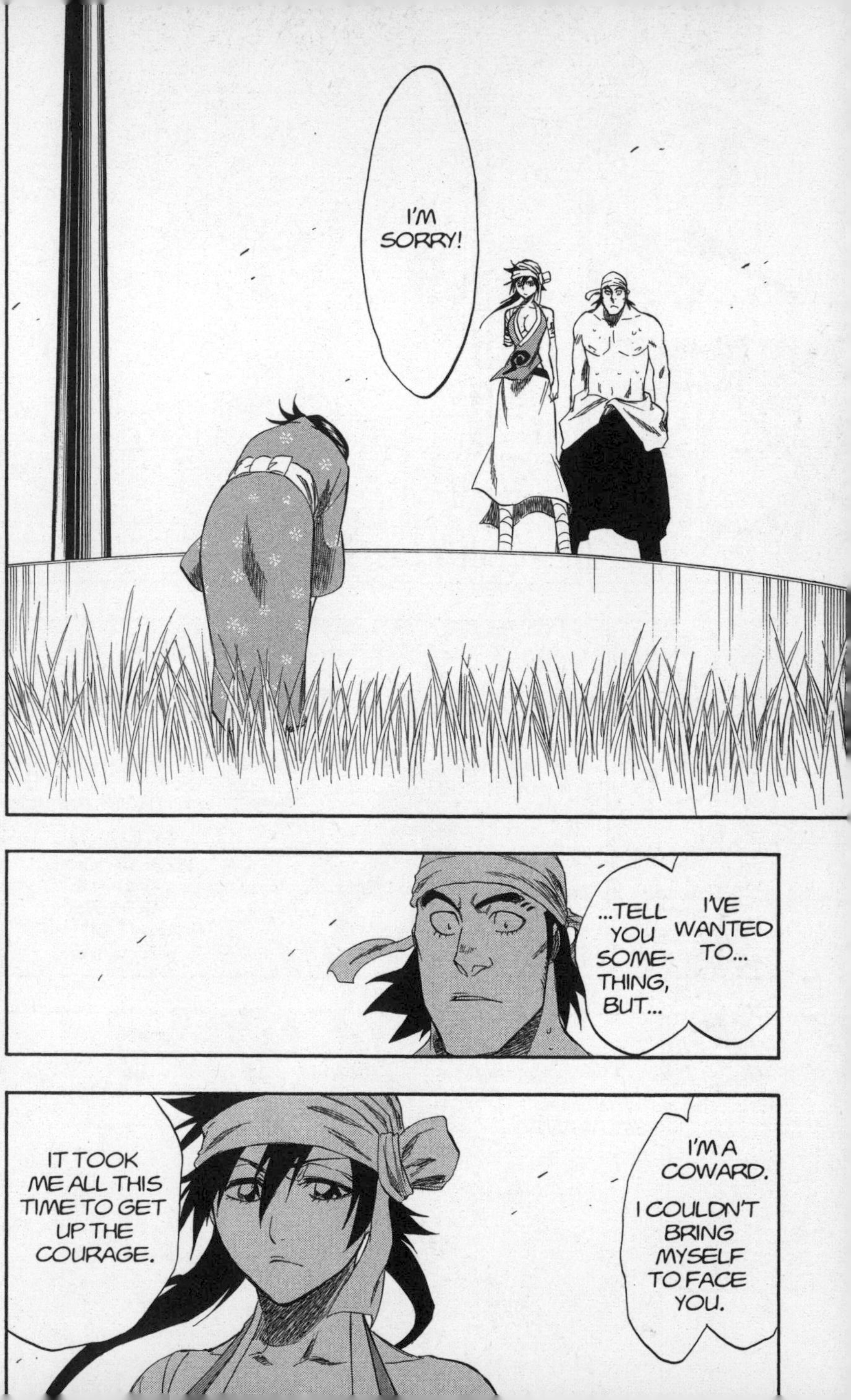
I'M SORRY!
I'VE WANTED TO... ...TELL YOU SOMETHING, BUT...
I'M A COWARD.
I COULDN'T BRING MYSELF TO FACE YOU.
IT TOOK ME ALL THIS TIME TO GET UP THE COURAGE.

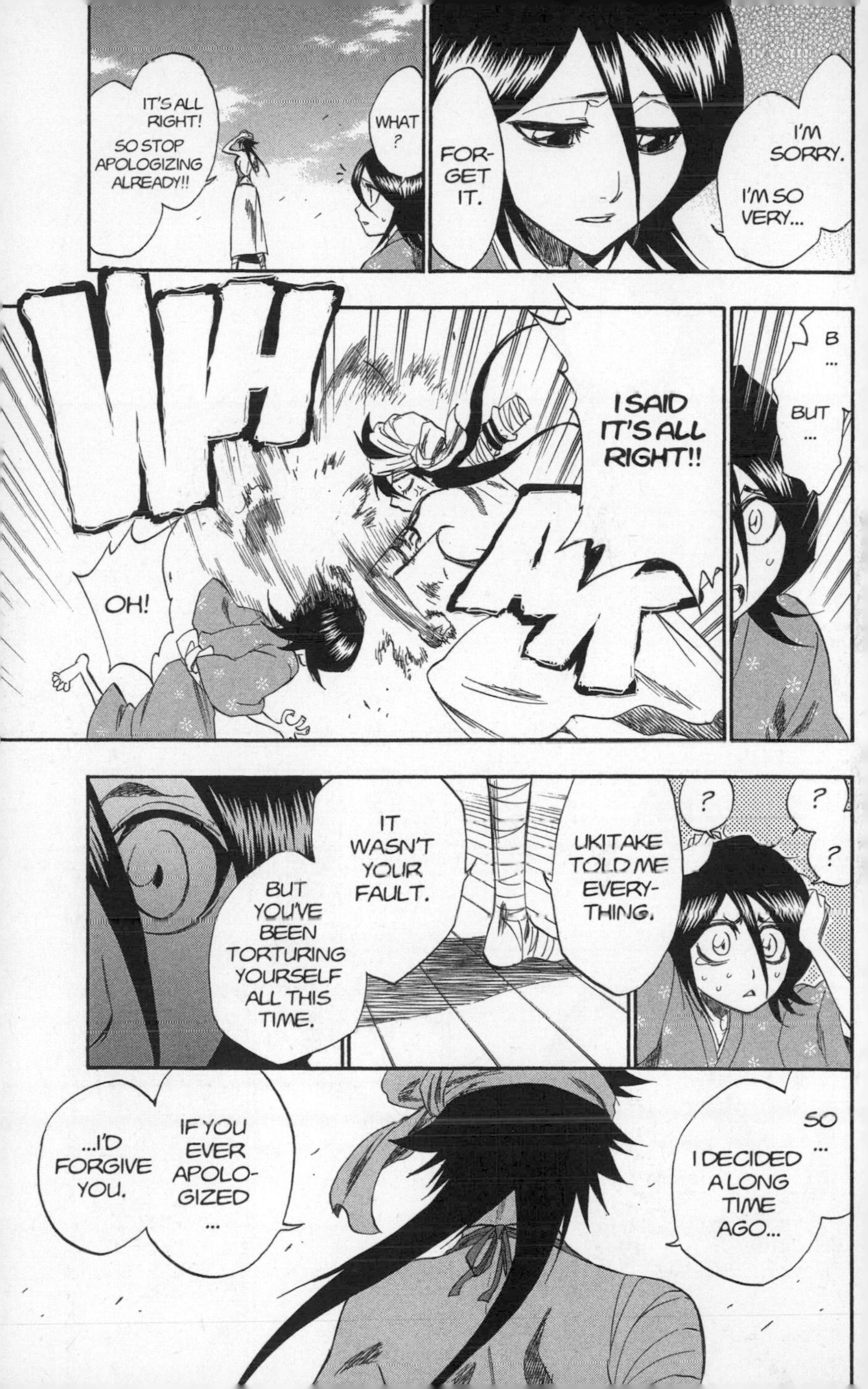
I'M SORRY.
I'M SO VERY...
FOR-GET IT.
WHAT?
IT'S ALL RIGHT! SO STOP APOLOGIZING ALREADY!!
B...
BUT...
I SAID IT'S ALL RIGHT!!
WHAM
OH!
?
?
?
UKITAKE TOLD ME EVERY-THING.
IT WASN'T YOUR FAULT.
BUT YOU'VE BEEN TORTURING YOURSELF ALL THIS TIME.
SO...
I DECIDED A LONG TIME AGO...
IF YOU EVER APOLO-GIZED...
...I'D FORGIVE YOU.

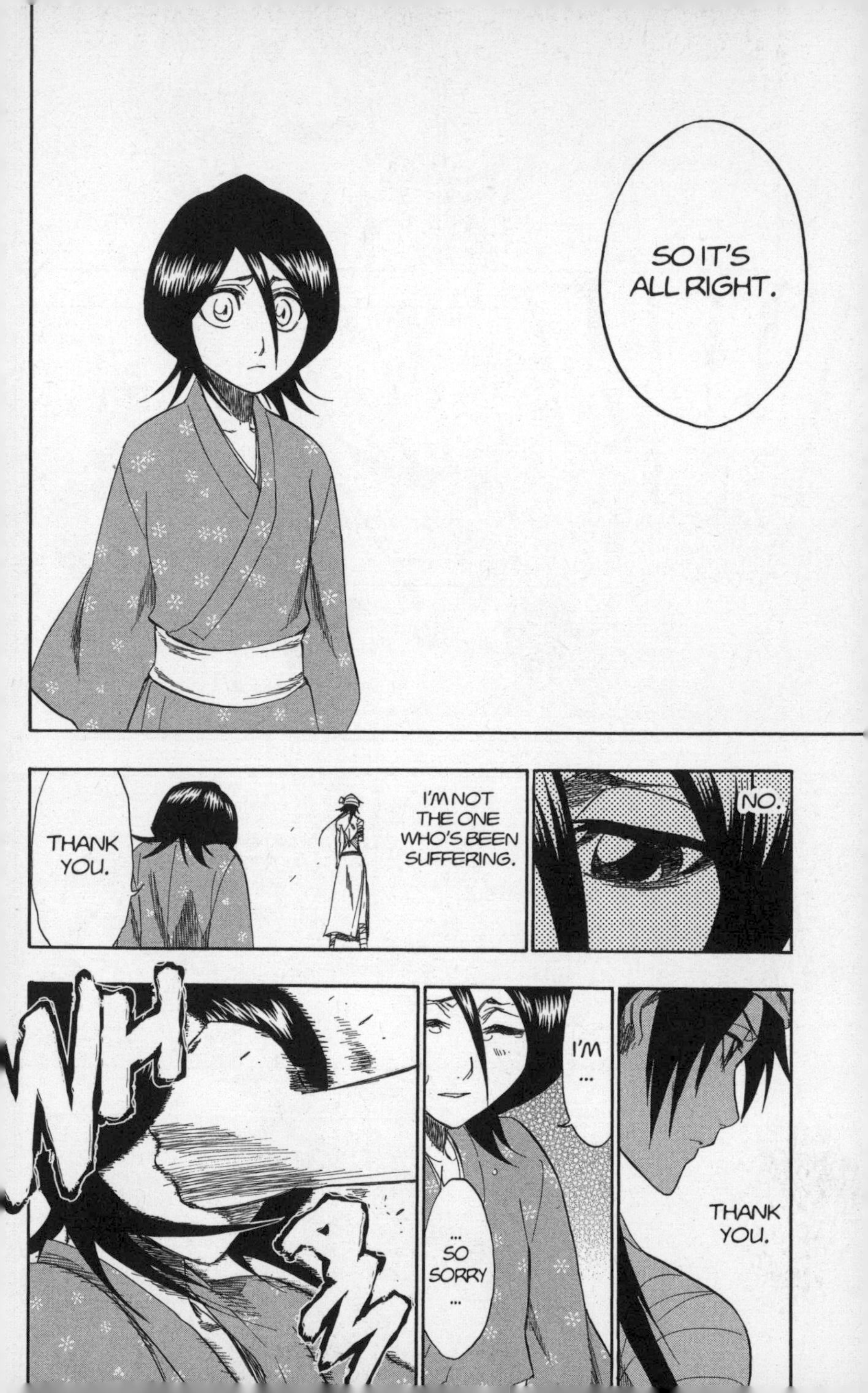
SO IT'S ALL RIGHT.
NO.
I'M NOT THE ONE WHO'S BEEN SUFFERING.
THANK YOU.
THANK YOU.
I'M ...
... SO SORRY ...
WHAM

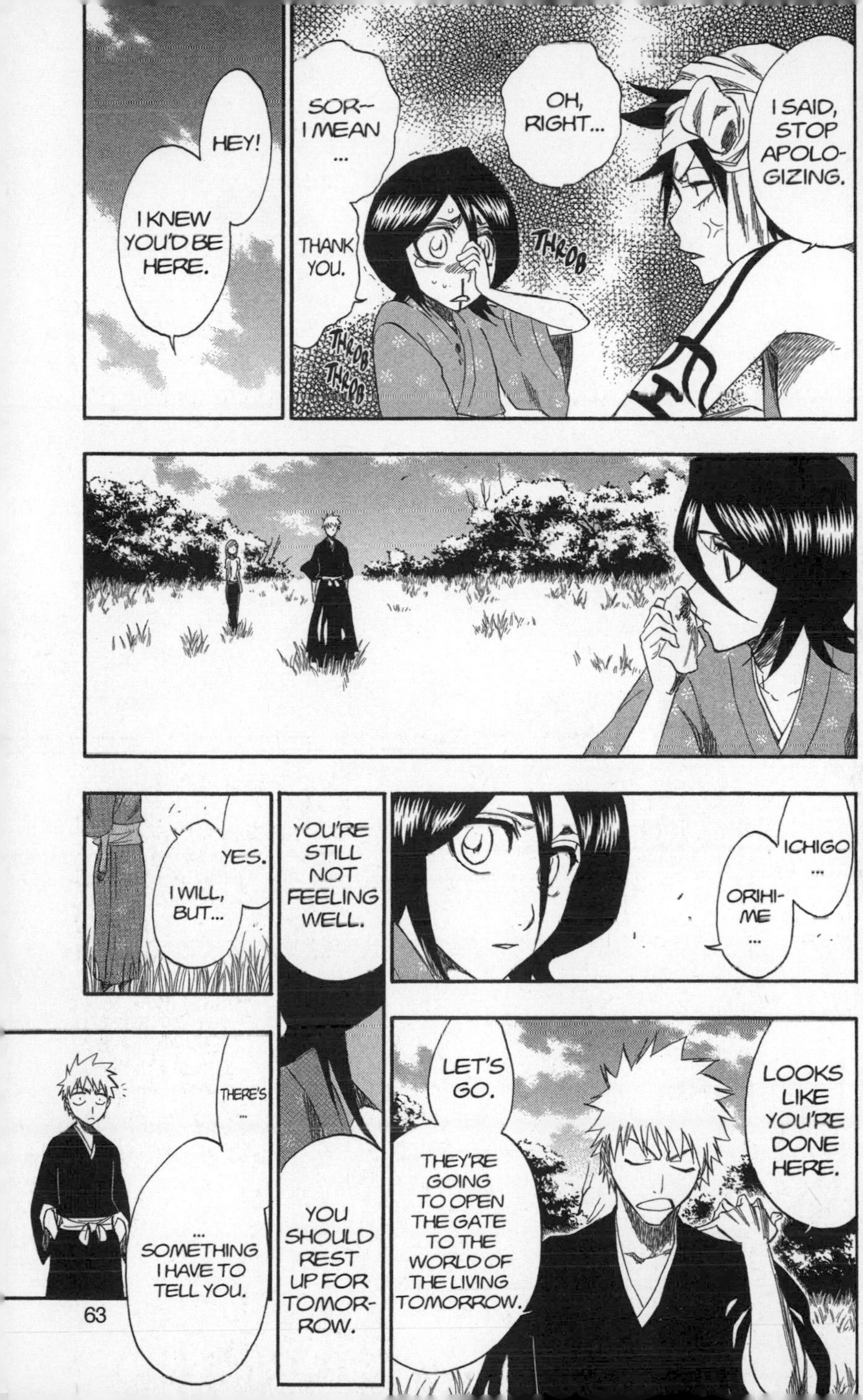
I SAID, STOP APOLO-GIZING.
OH, RIGHT...
SOR-- I MEAN ...
THANK YOU.
THROB
THROB THROB
HEY!
I KNEW YOU'D BE HERE.
ICHIGO ...
ORIHI-ME ...
LOOKS LIKE YOU'RE DONE HERE.
LET'S GO.
THEY'RE GOING TO OPEN THE GATE TO THE WORLD OF THE LIVING TOMORROW.
YOU'RE STILL NOT FEELING WELL.
YOU SHOULD REST UP FOR TOMOR-ROW.
YES.
I WILL, BUT...
THERE'S ...
... SOMETHING I HAVE TO TELL YOU.

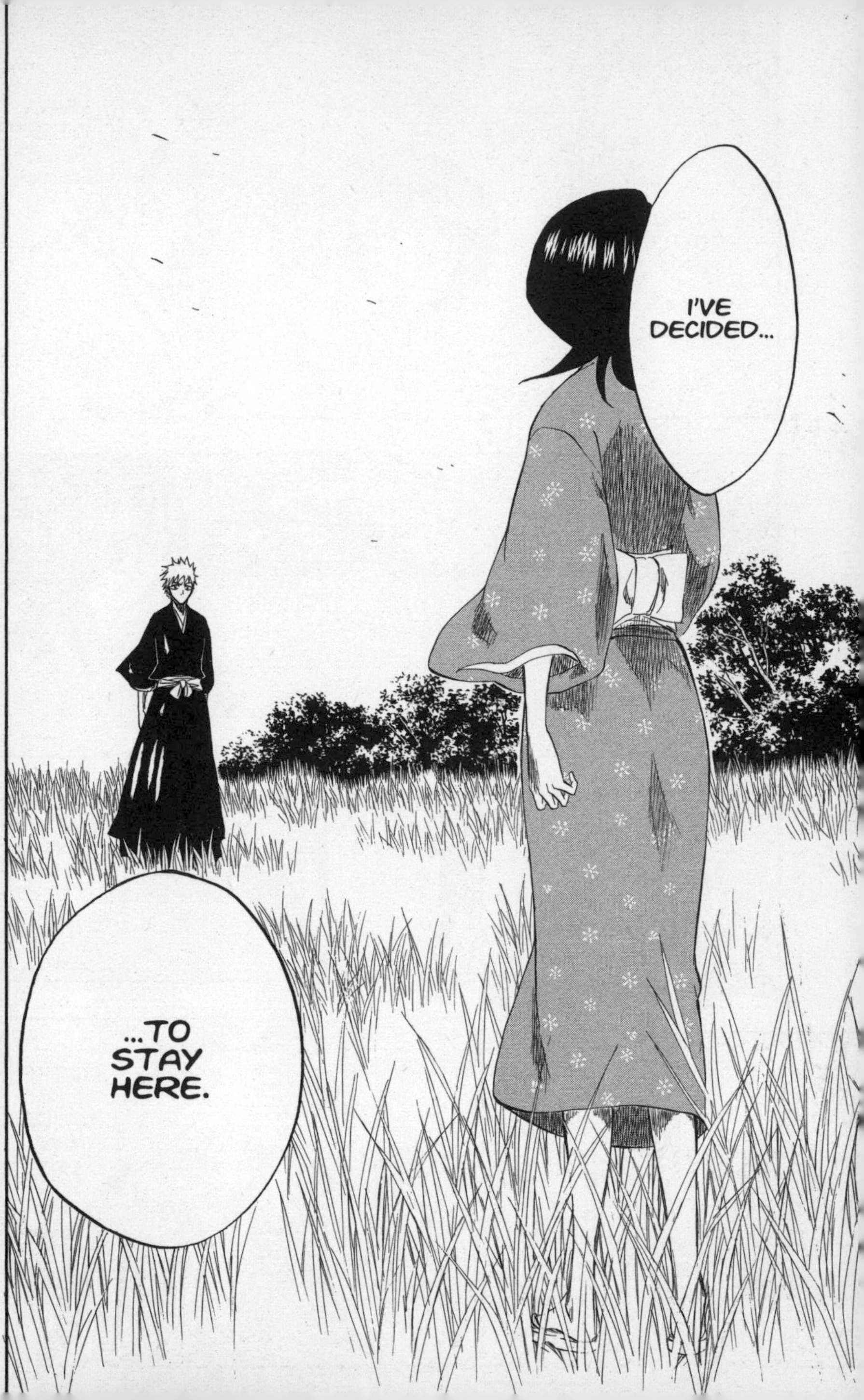
I'VE DECIDED...
...TO STAY HERE.

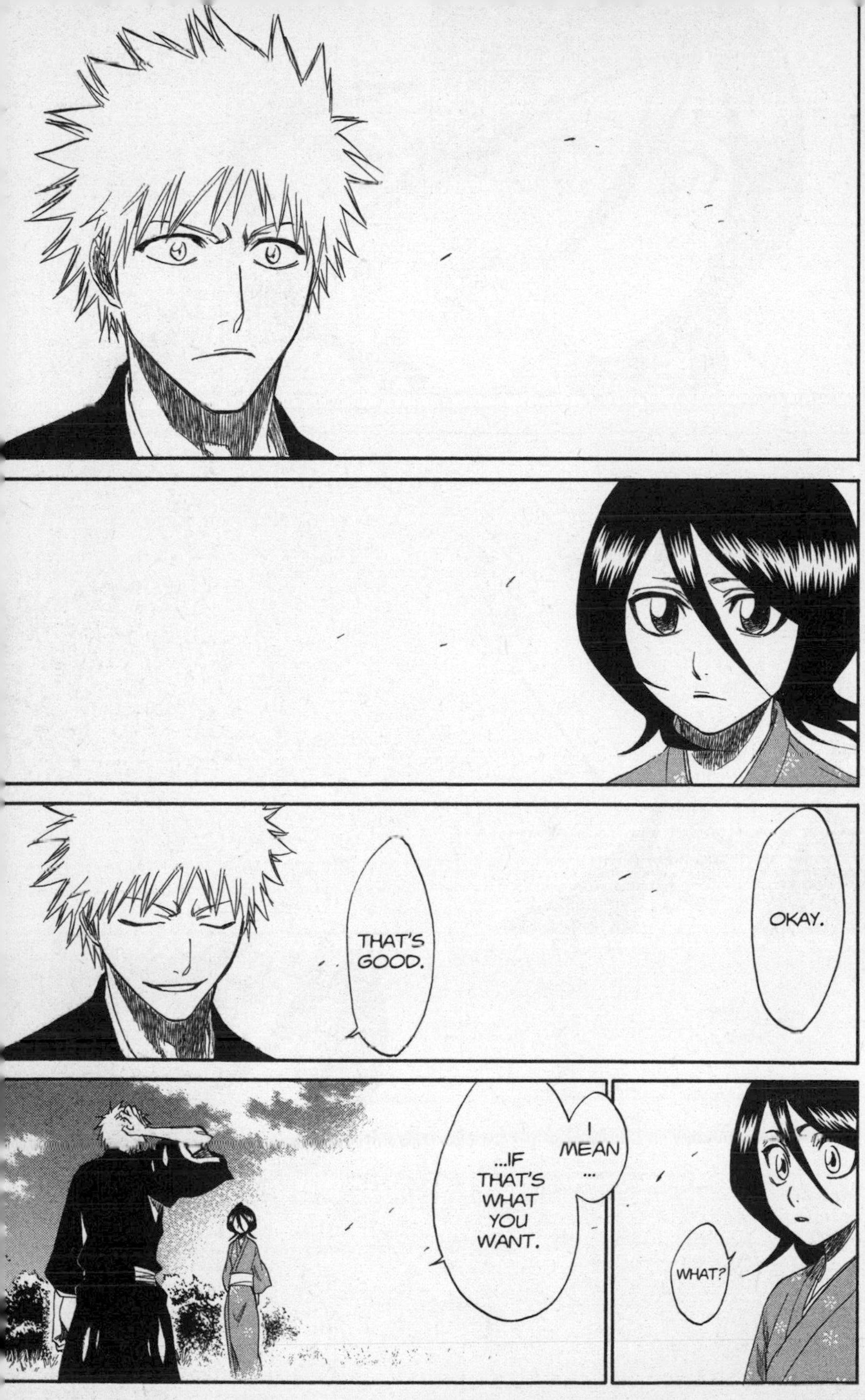
OKAY.
THAT'S GOOD.
WHAT?
I MEAN ...
...IF THAT'S WHAT YOU WANT.

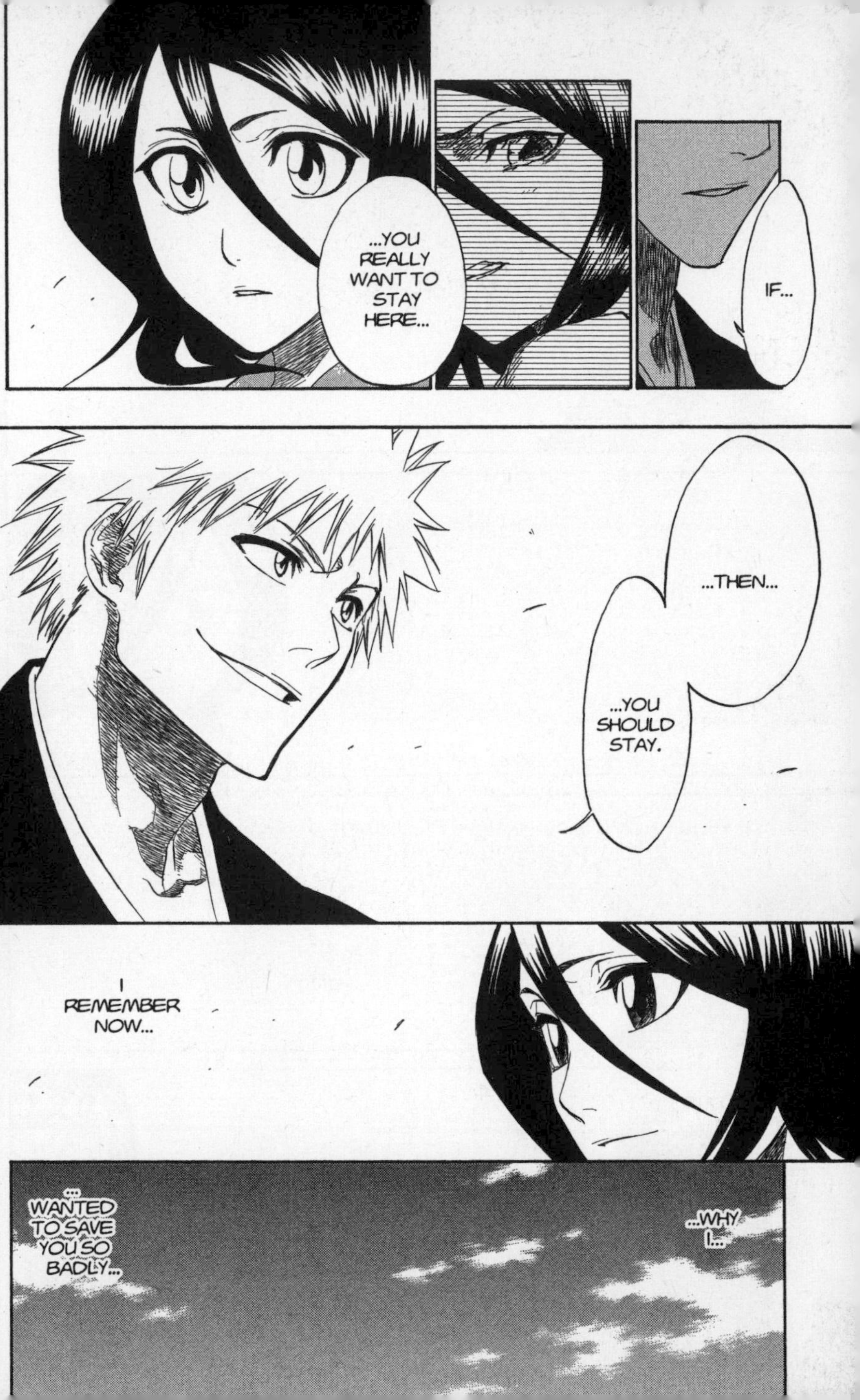
IF...
...YOU REALLY WANT TO STAY HERE...
...THEN...
...YOU SHOULD STAY.
I REMEMBER NOW...
...WHY I...
...WANTED TO SAVE YOU SO BADLY...

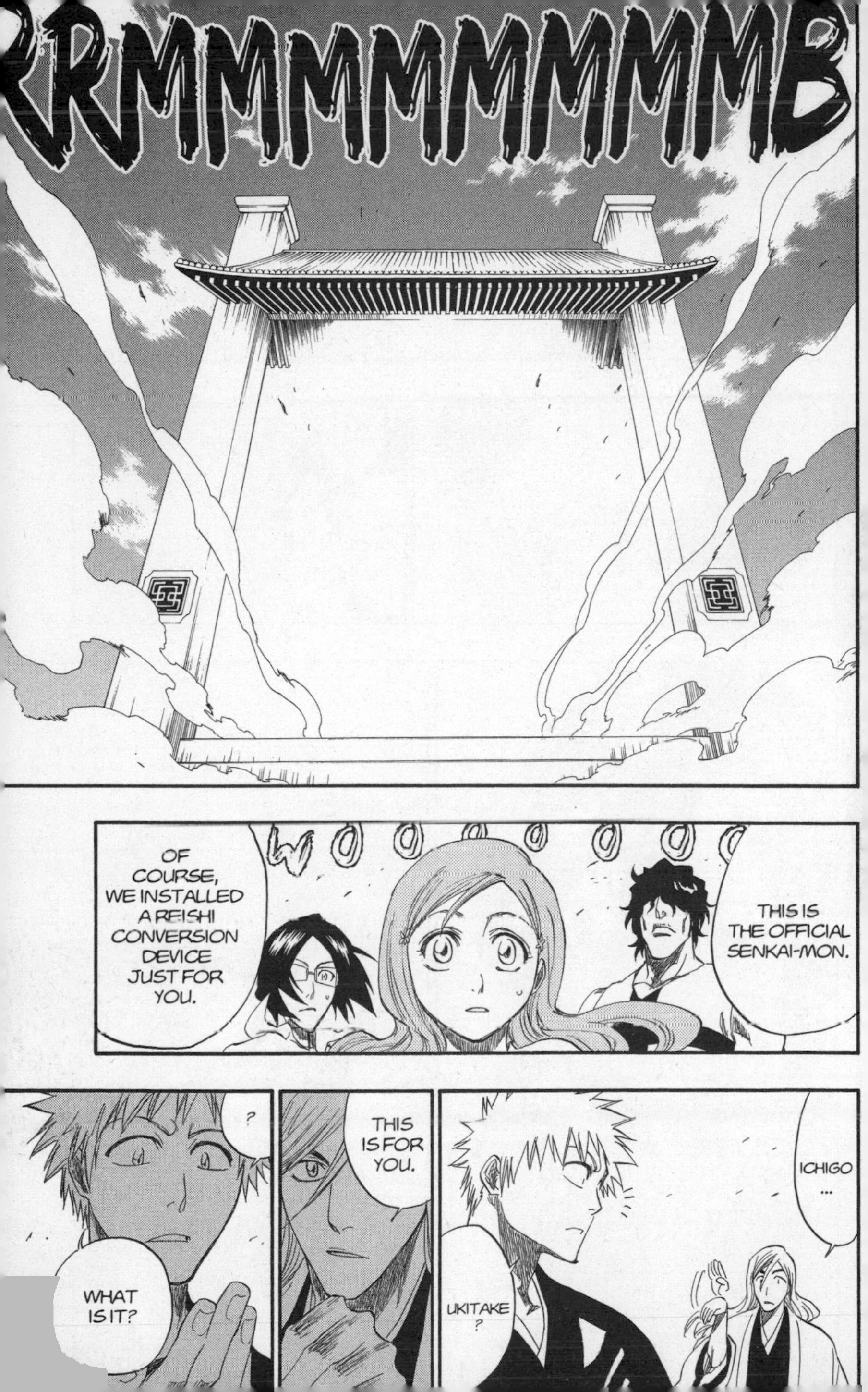

RMMMMMMMMMB
THIS IS THE OFFICIAL SENKAI-MON.
WOOOOOOOO
OF COURSE, WE INSTALLED A REISHI CONVERSION DEVICE JUST FOR YOU.
ICHIGO ...
UKITAKE ?
THIS IS FOR YOU.
?
WHAT IS IT?

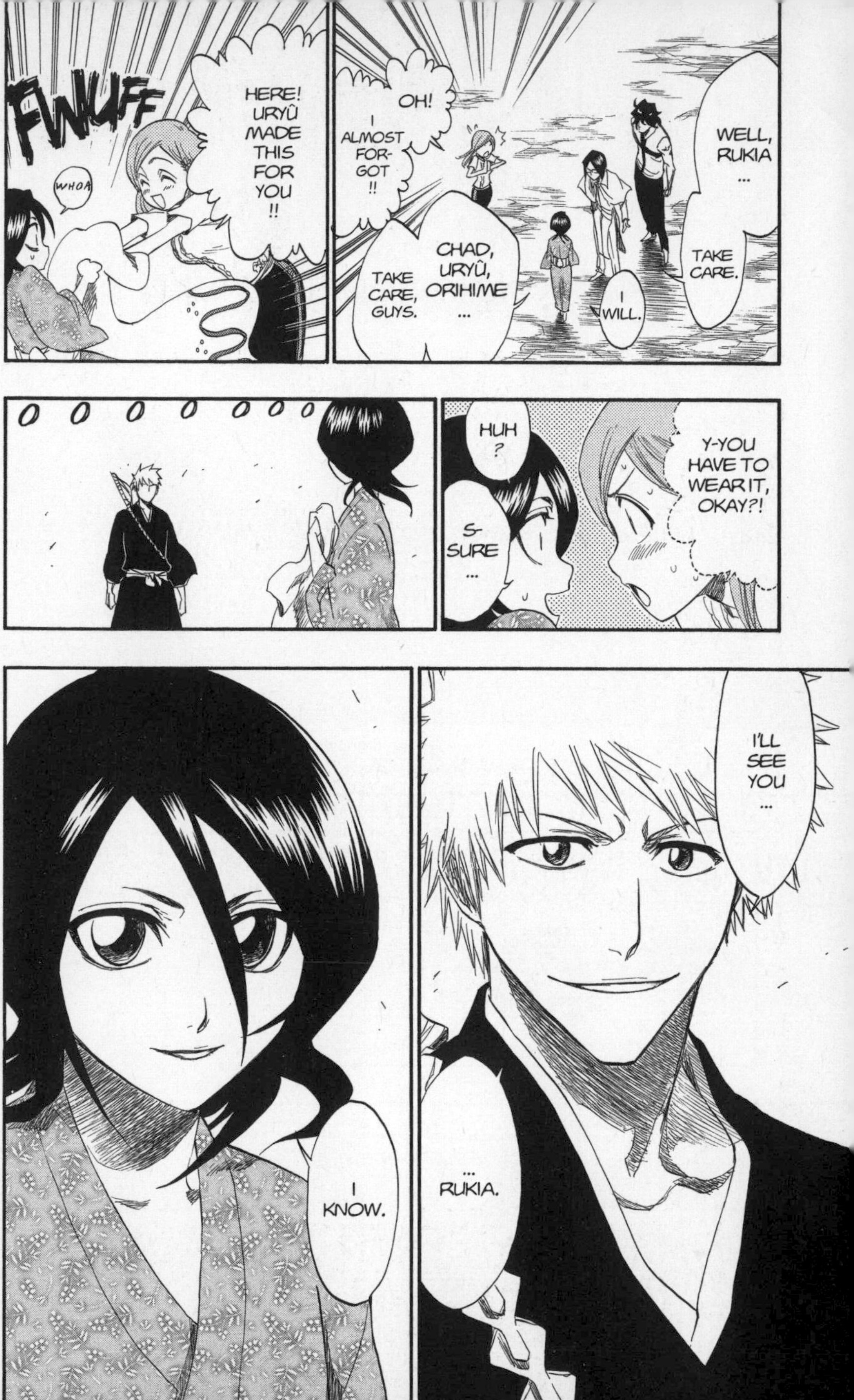
WELL, RUKIA ...
TAKE CARE.
I WILL.
CHAD, URYÛ, ORIHIME ...
TAKE CARE, GUYS.
OH! I ALMOST FOR-GOT !!
FWUFF
HERE! URYÛ MADE THIS FOR YOU !!
WHOA
Y-YOU HAVE TO WEAR IT, OKAY?!
HUH ?
S-SURE ...
O O O O O O O
I'LL SEE YOU ...
... RUKIA.
I KNOW.

THAT'S MY LINE.

... ICHIGO.

THANK YOU ...

BECAUSE OF YOU ...

THANKS, RUKIA.

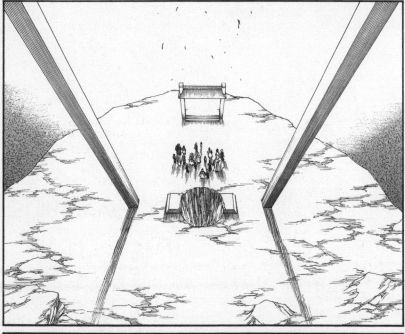

THE RAIN HAS FINALLY STOPPED...

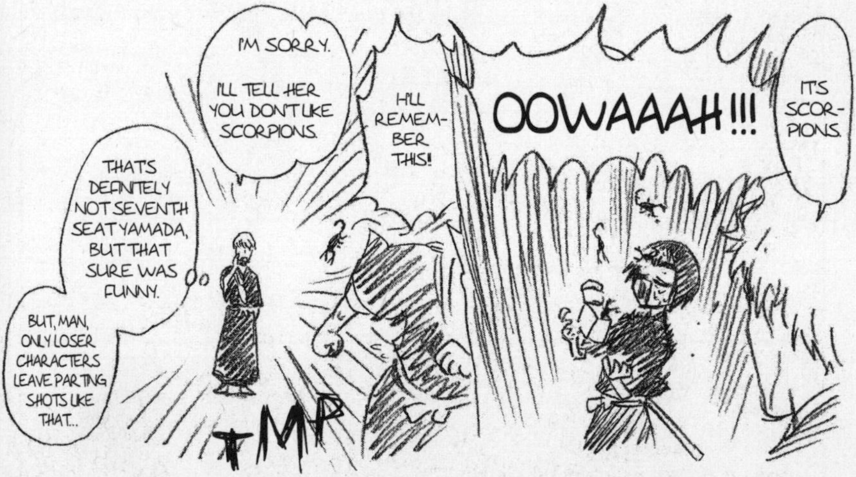
IT'S SCORPIONS.
OOWAAAH!!!
I'LL REMEMBER THIS!
I'M SORRY.
I'LL TELL HER YOU DON'T LIKE SCORPIONS.
THATS DEFINITELY NOT SEVENTH SEAT YAMADA, BUT THAT SURE WAS FUNNY.
BUT, MAN, ONLY LOSER CHARACTERS LEAVE PARTING SHOTS LIKE THAT...
TMP

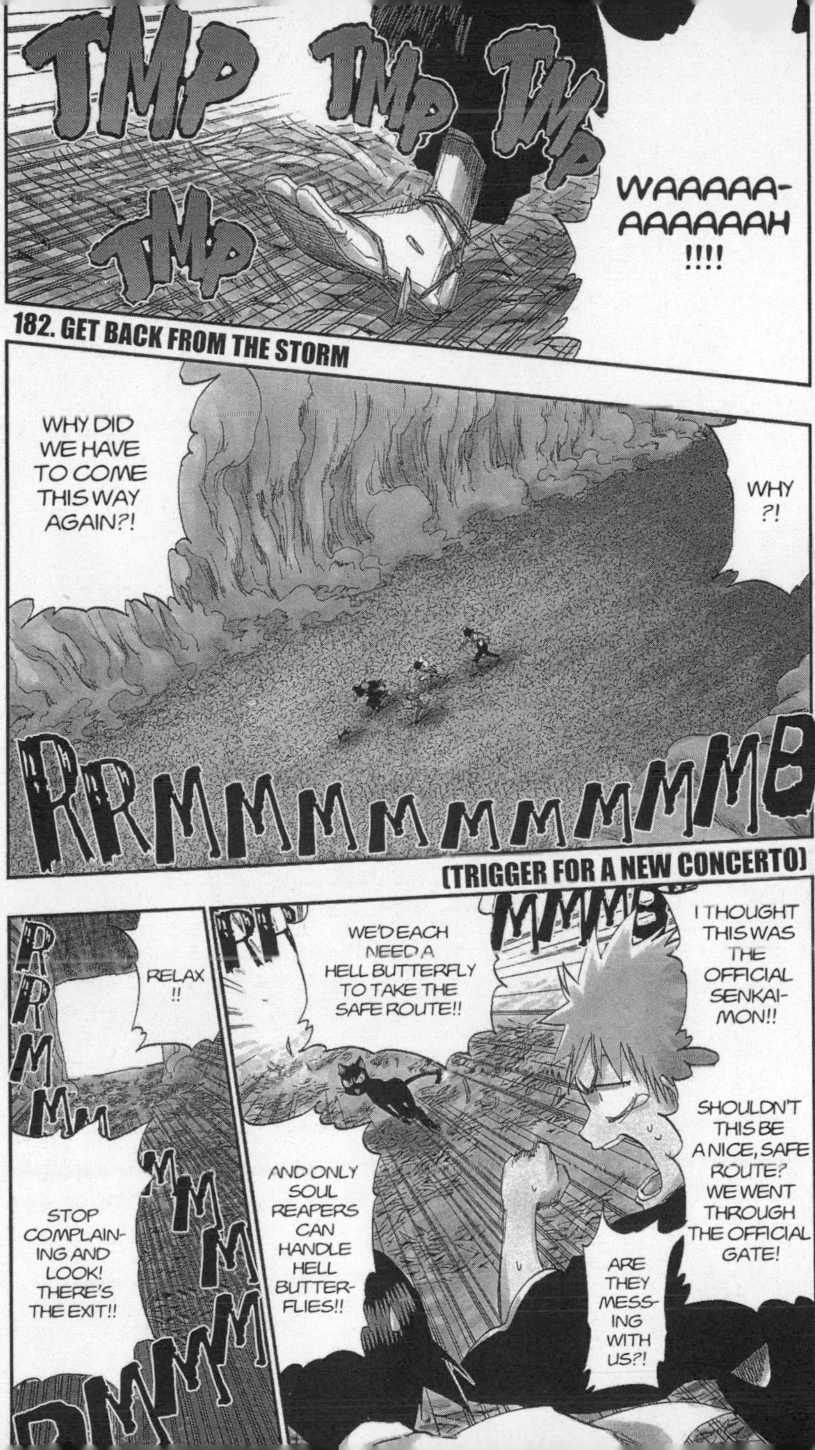
WAAAAA-AAAAAAH!!!!
TMP TMP TMP TMP
182. GET BACK FROM THE STORM
WHY ?!
WHY DID WE HAVE TO COME THIS WAY AGAIN?!
RRMMMMMMMMMMMB
(TRIGGER FOR A NEW CONCERTO)
I THOUGHT THIS WAS THE OFFICIAL SENKAI-MON!!
SHOULDN'T THIS BE A NICE, SAFE ROUTE? WE WENT THROUGH THE OFFICIAL GATE!
ARE THEY MESS-ING WITH US?!
WE'D EACH NEED A HELL BUTTERFLY TO TAKE THE SAFE ROUTE!!
AND ONLY SOUL REAPERS CAN HANDLE HELL BUTTER-FLIES!!
RELAX !!
STOP COMPLAIN-ING AND LOOK! THERE'S THE EXIT!!

ACH

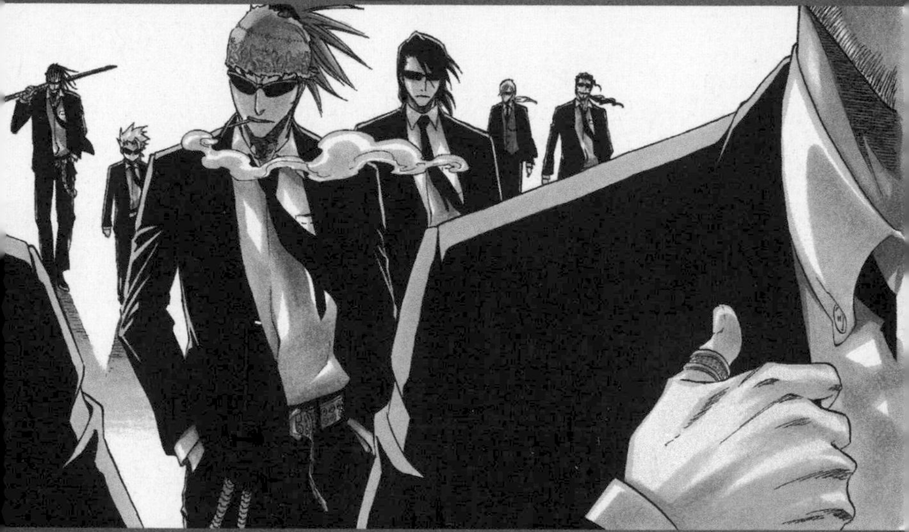

BACK FROM STORM

[TRIGGER FOR A NEW CONCERTO]

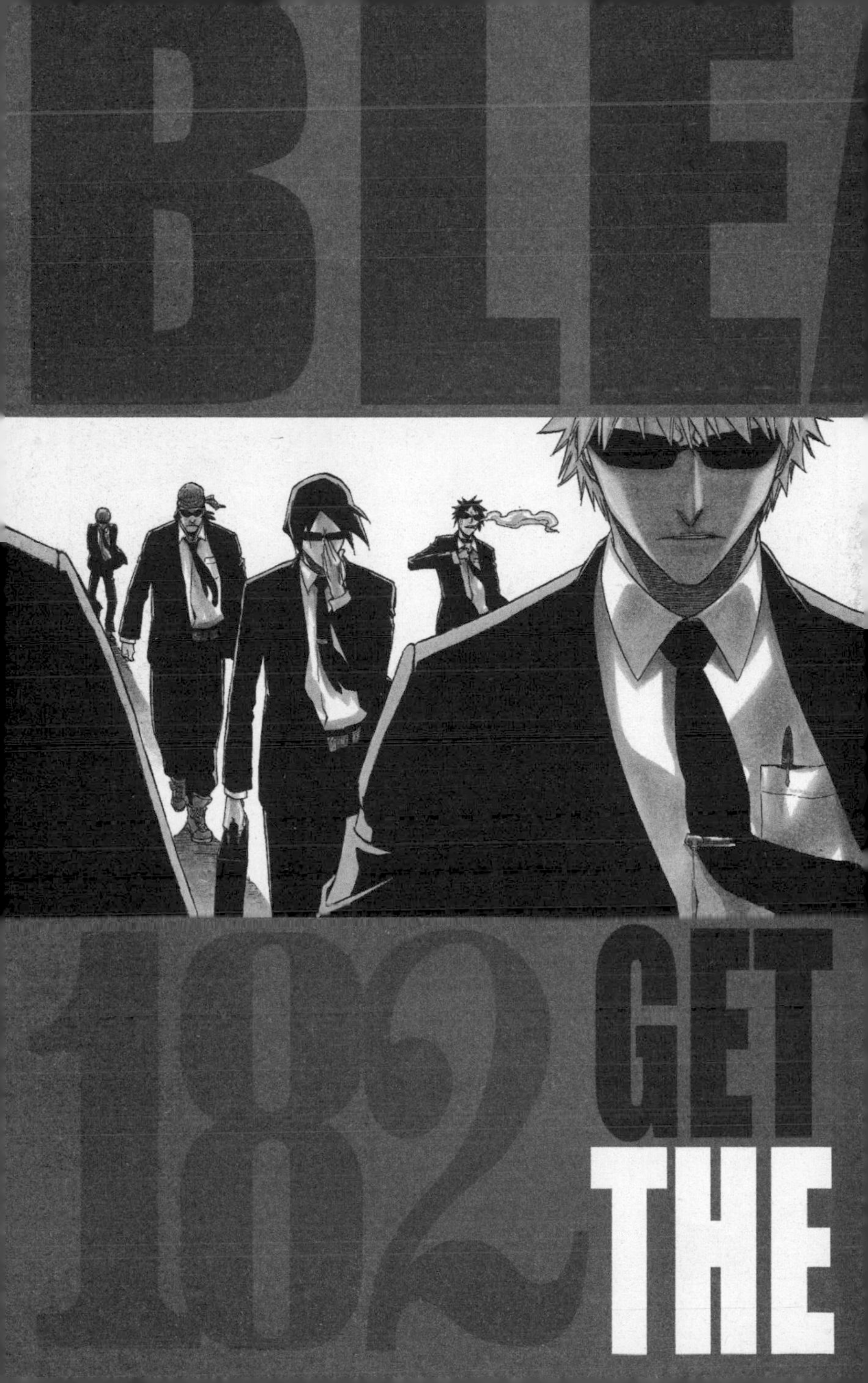
BLE
182
GET
THE

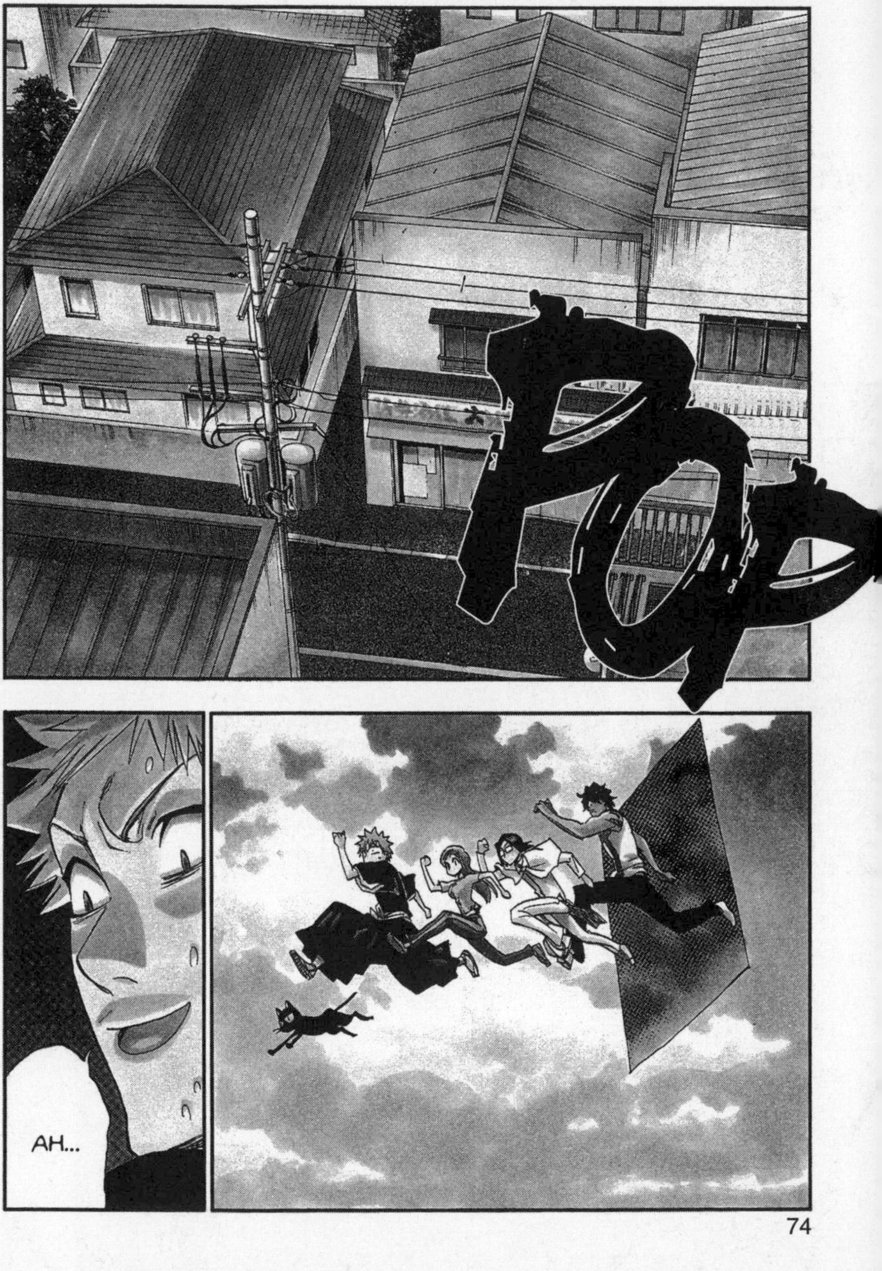
POP
AH...

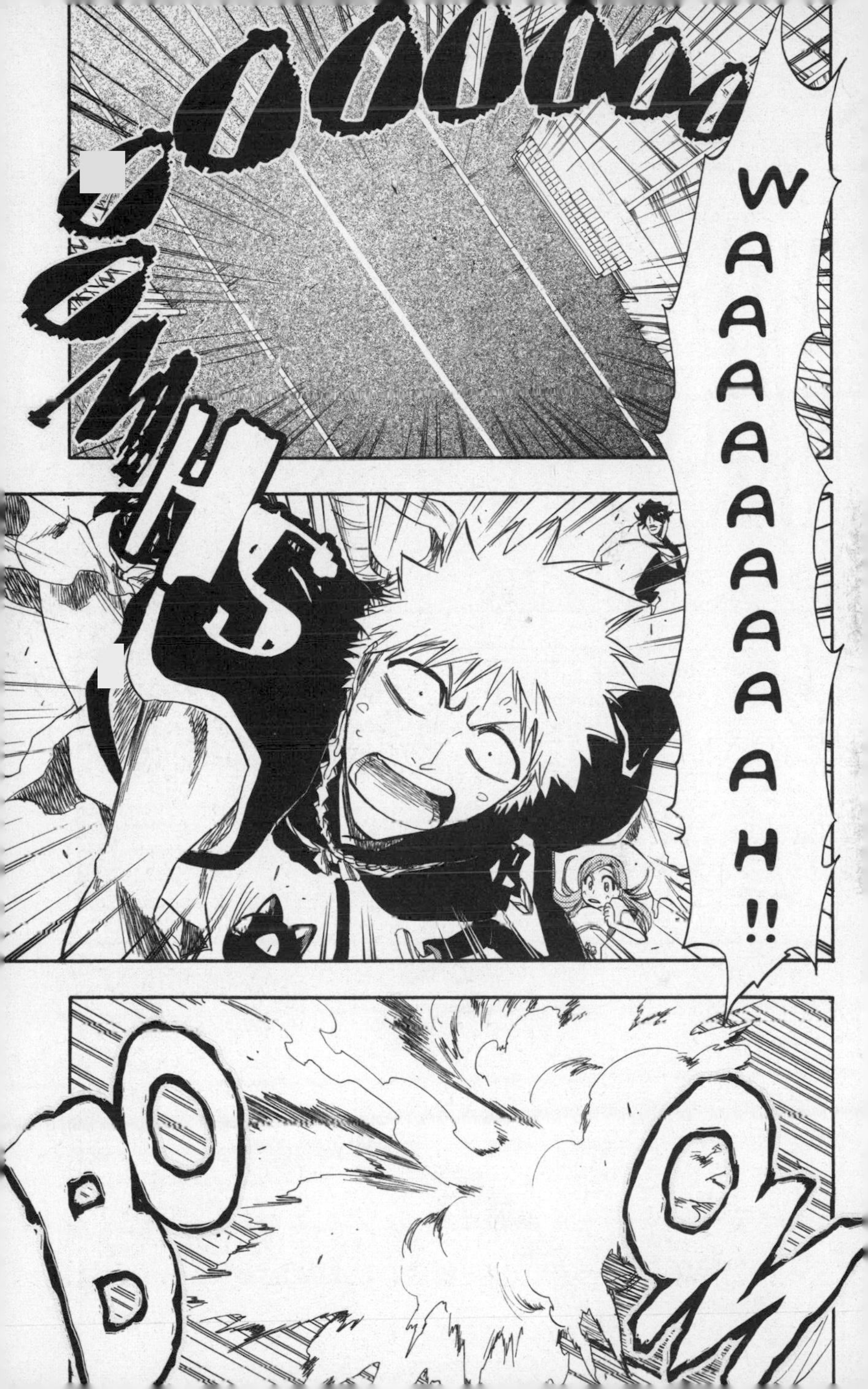
WAAAAAAAAH!!
BOOM

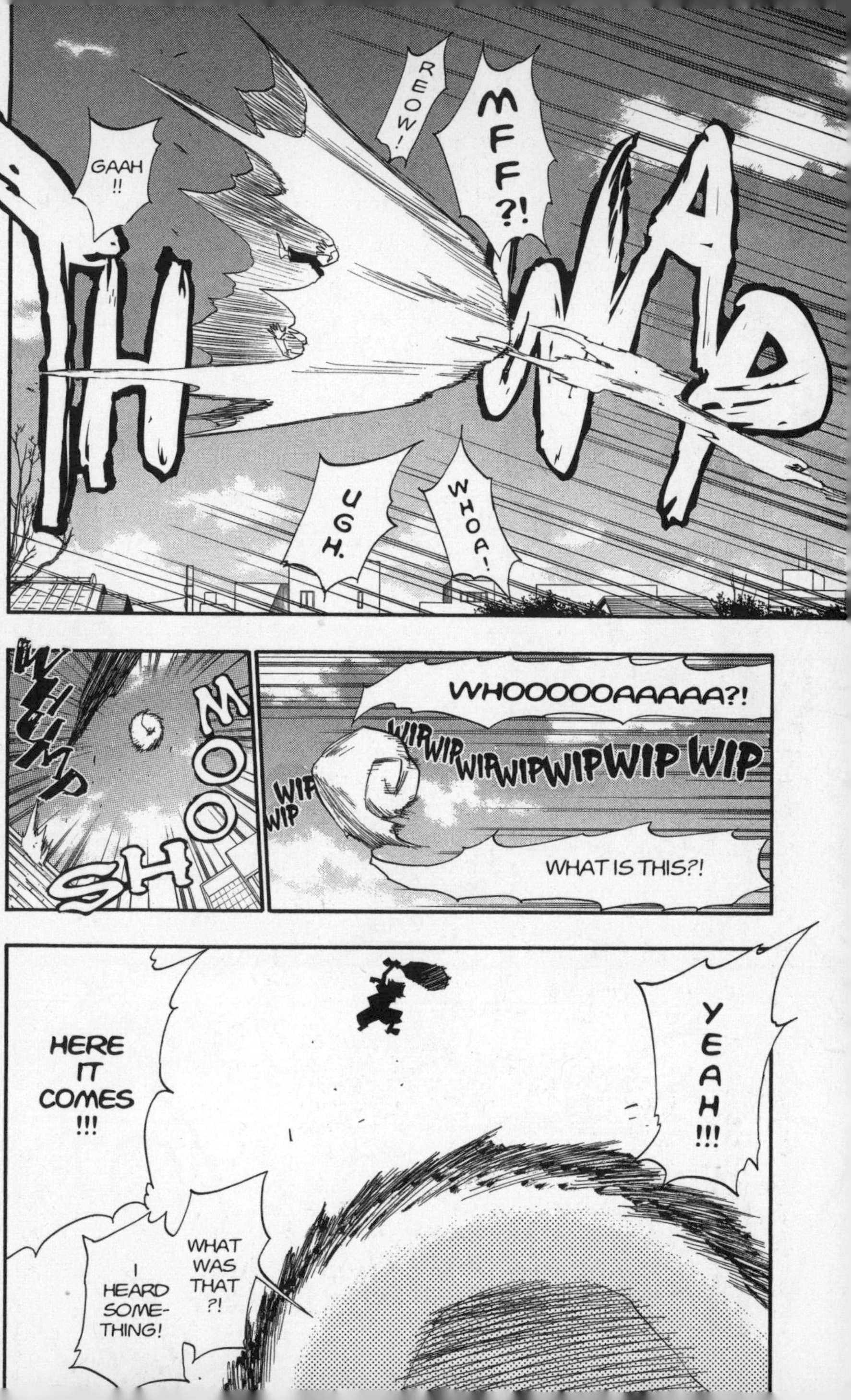
MFF?!
REOW!
GAAH!!
THWAP
WHOA!
UGH.
WHOOOOOAAAAA?!
WIP WIP WIP WIP WIP WIP WIP WIP WIP
WHAT IS THIS?!
WHUMP
SHOOOM
YEAH!!!
HERE IT COMES!!!
WHAT WAS THAT?!
I HEARD SOME-THING!

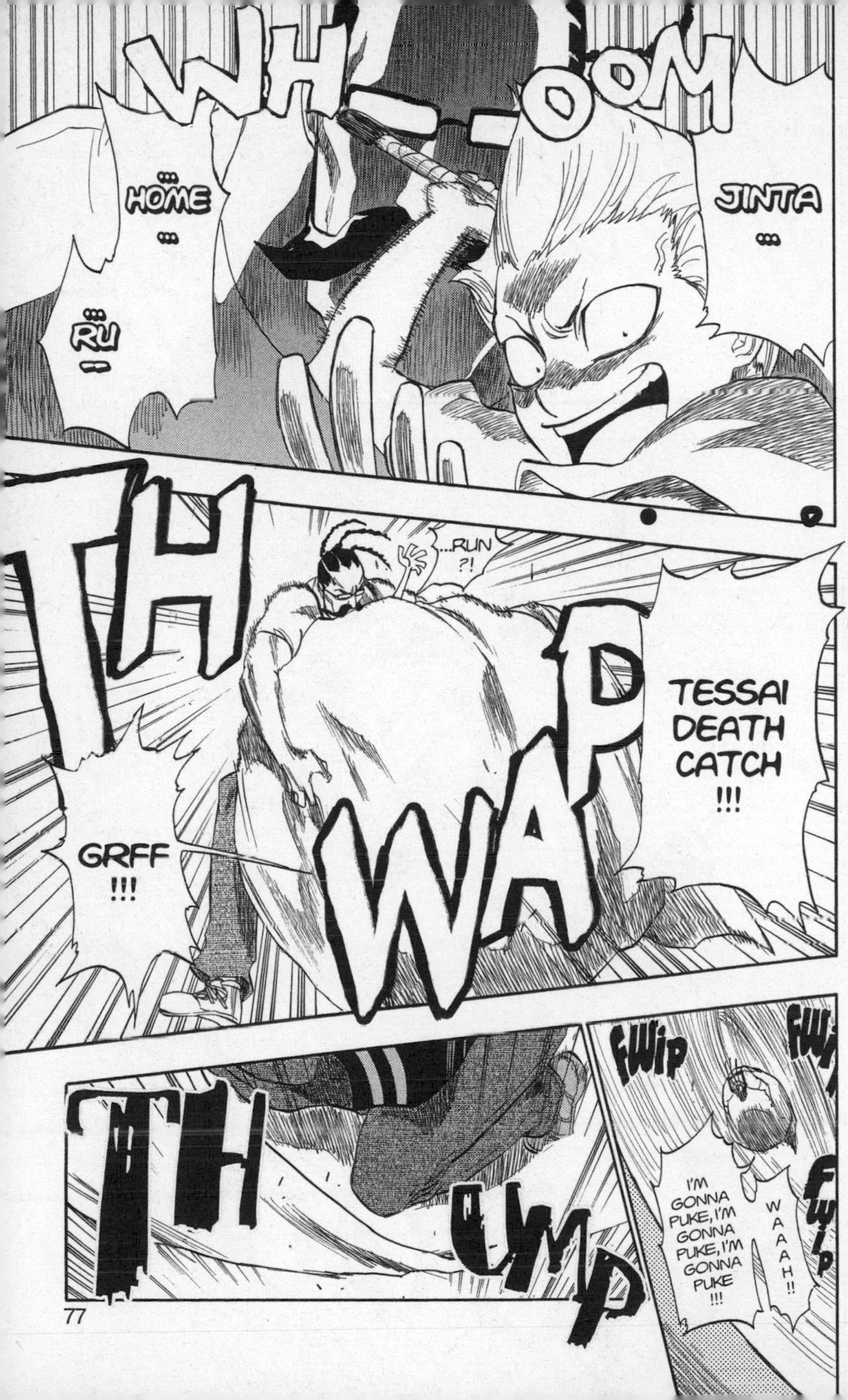
WH-OOM
JINTA ...
... HOME ...
... RU -
...RUN ?!
TESSAI DEATH CATCH !!!
THWAP
GRFF !!!
FWIP
FWIP
WAAAH!!
I'M GONNA PUKE, I'M GONNA PUKE, I'M GONNA PUKE !!!
FWIP
THUMP

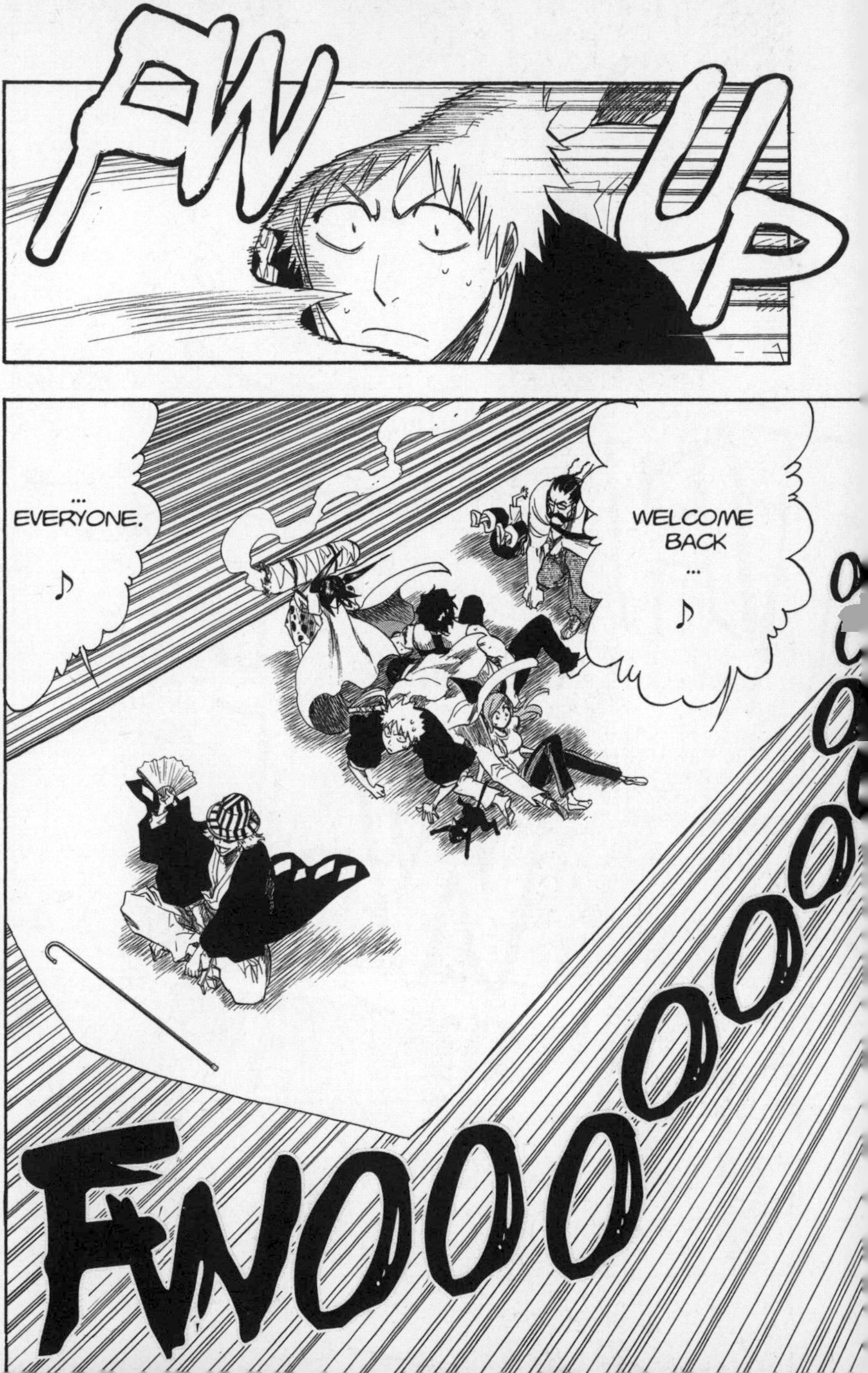
FWUP
WELCOME BACK ... ♪
... EVERYONE. ♪
FWOOOOOOOOOOOO

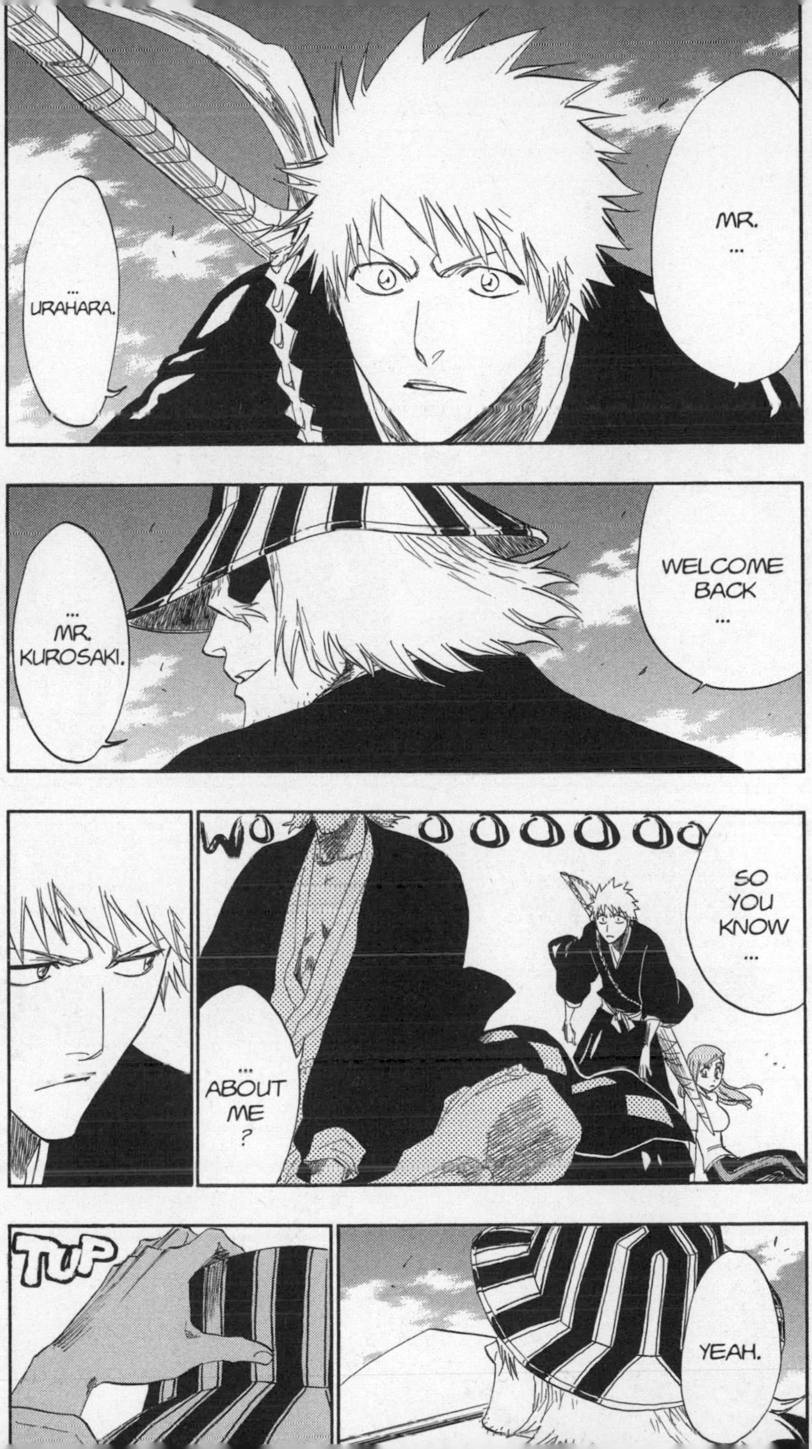
MR. ...
... URAHARA.
WELCOME BACK ...
... MR. KUROSAKI.
WOOOOOOOO
SO YOU KNOW ...
... ABOUT ME ?
YEAH.
TUP

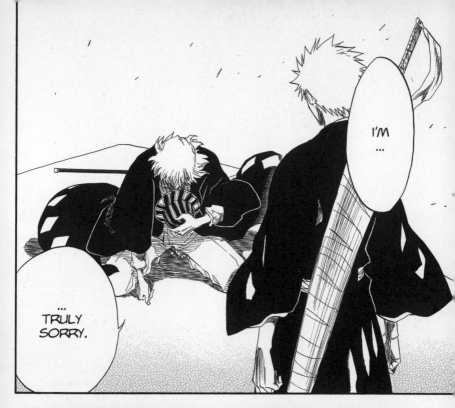

I'M ...

... TRULY SORRY.

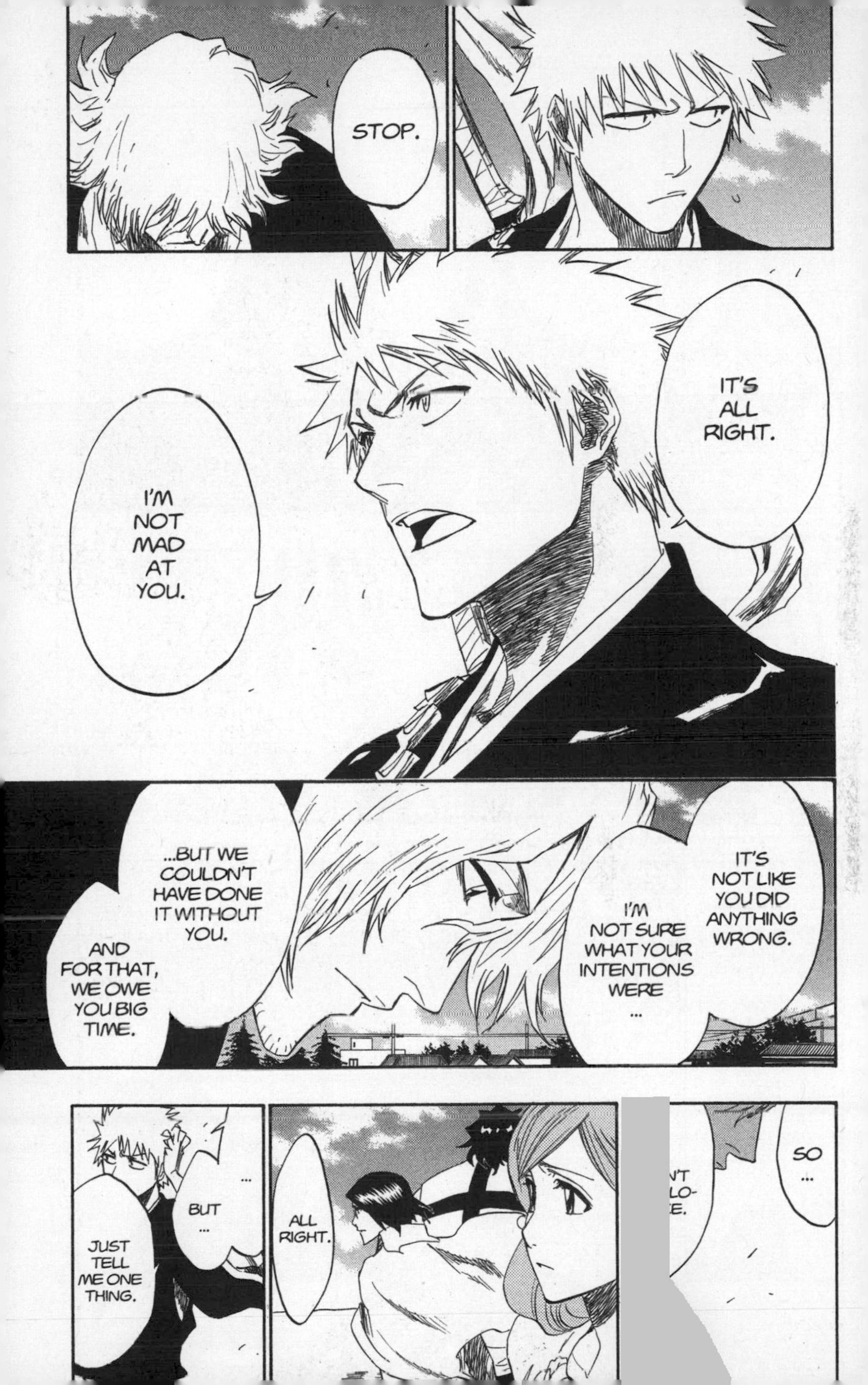
STOP.
IT'S ALL RIGHT.
I'M NOT MAD AT YOU.
IT'S NOT LIKE YOU DID ANYTHING WRONG.
I'M NOT SURE WHAT YOUR INTENTIONS WERE ...
...BUT WE COULDN'T HAVE DONE IT WITHOUT YOU.
AND FOR THAT, WE OWE YOU BIG TIME.
SO ...
ALL RIGHT.
...
BUT ...
JUST TELL ME ONE THING.

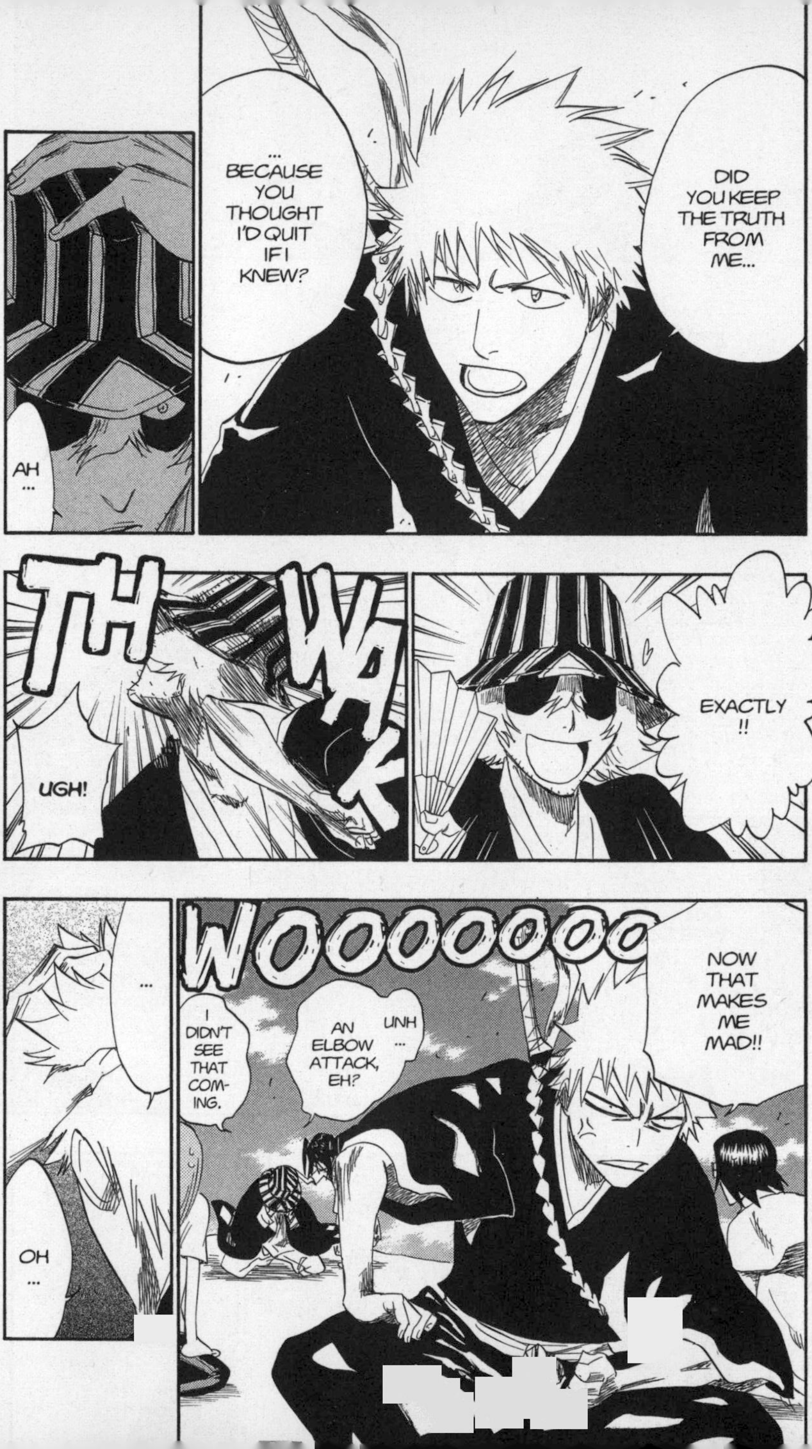
DID YOU KEEP THE TRUTH FROM ME...
... BECAUSE YOU THOUGHT I'D QUIT IF I KNEW?
AH ...
EXACTLY !!
THWAK
UGH!
WOOOOOOO
NOW THAT MAKES ME MAD!!
UNH ...
AN ELBOW ATTACK, EH?
I DIDN'T SEE THAT COM-ING.
...
OH ...

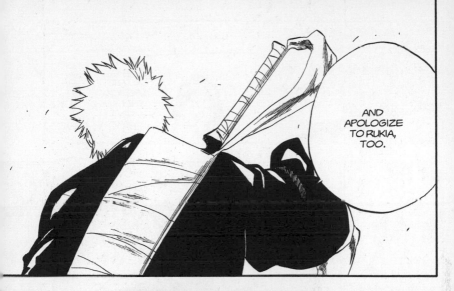

AND APOLOGIZE TO RUKIA, TOO.

...SHE'LL PROBABLY TELL YOU THE SAME THING I DID.

EVEN THOUGH...

I WILL.

FWOOOOOOOO

BY THE WAY, ICHIGO...

...!

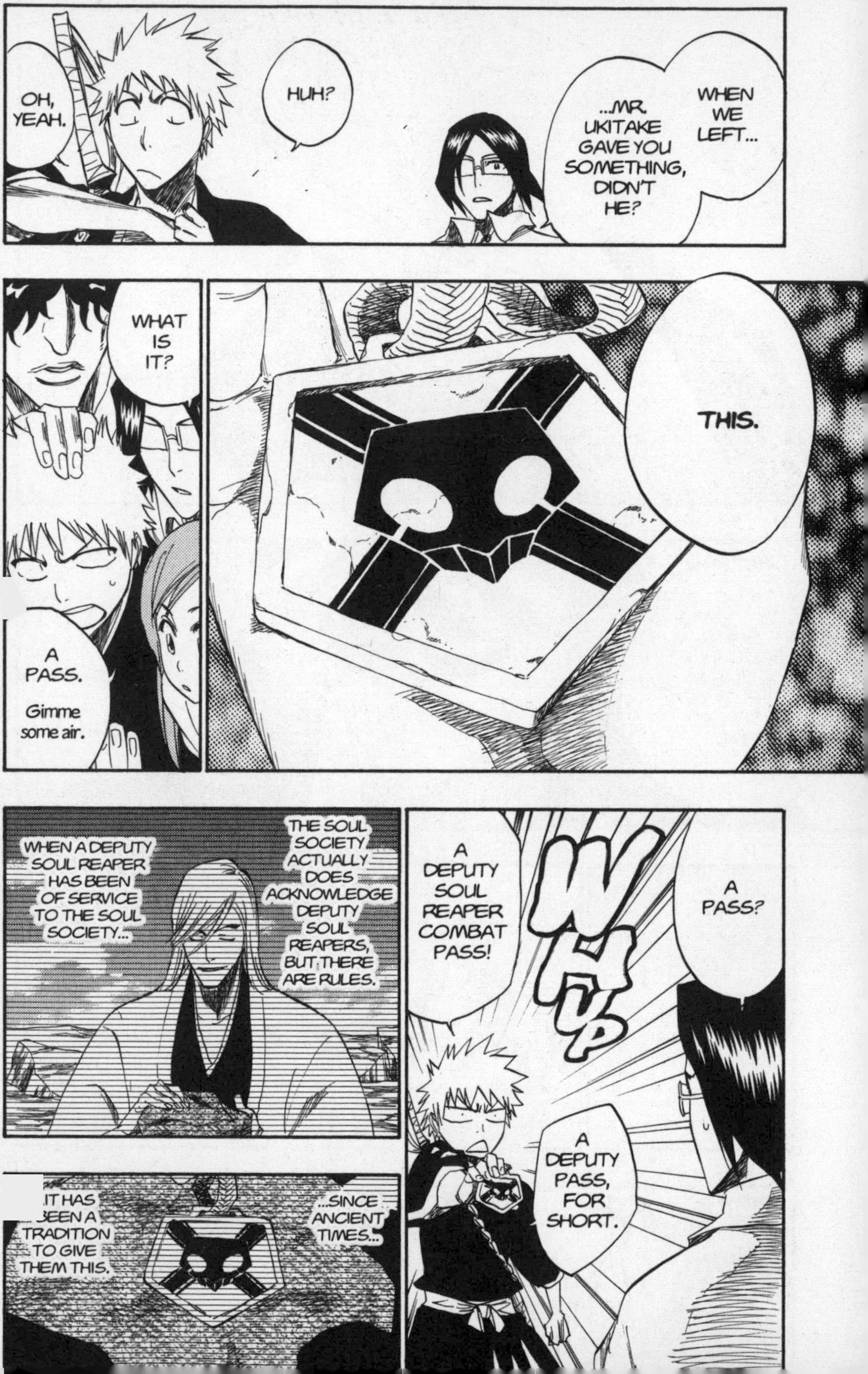
WHEN WE LEFT...
...MR. UKITAKE GAVE YOU SOMETHING, DIDN'T HE?
HUH?
OH, YEAH.
THIS.
WHAT IS IT?
A PASS.
Gimme some air.
A PASS?
WHUP
A DEPUTY SOUL REAPER COMBAT PASS!
A DEPUTY PASS, FOR SHORT.
THE SOUL SOCIETY ACTUALLY DOES ACKNOWLEDGE DEPUTY SOUL REAPERS, BUT THERE ARE RULES.
WHEN A DEPUTY SOUL REAPER HAS BEEN OF SERVICE TO THE SOUL SOCIETY...
...SINCE ANCIENT TIMES...
IT HAS BEEN A TRADITION TO GIVE THEM THIS.

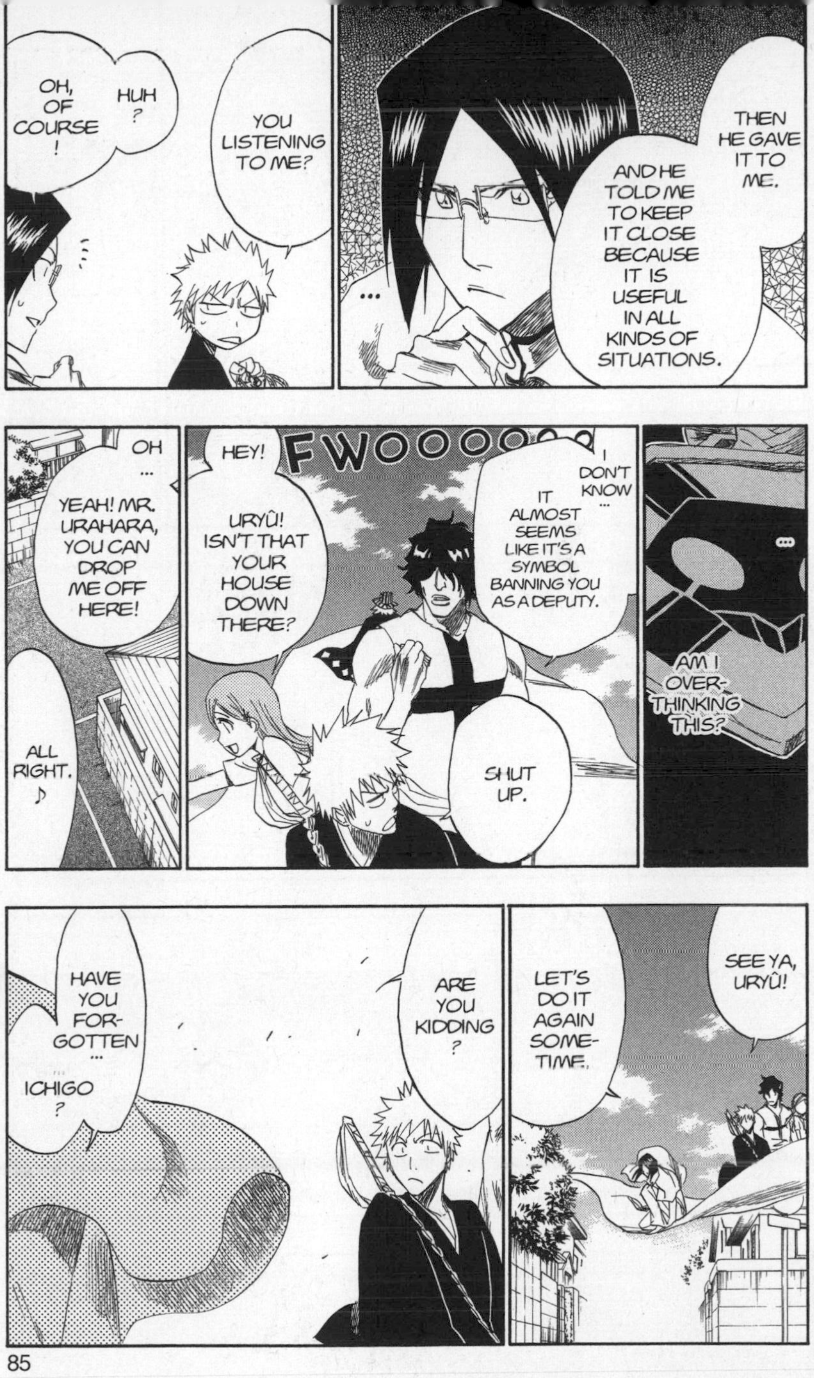

THEN HE GAVE IT TO ME.
AND HE TOLD ME TO KEEP IT CLOSE BECAUSE IT IS USEFUL IN ALL KINDS OF SITUATIONS.
...
YOU LISTENING TO ME?
HUH?
OH, OF COURSE!
...
...
AM I OVER-THINKING THIS?
FWOOOOOOO
I DON'T KNOW...
IT ALMOST SEEMS LIKE IT'S A SYMBOL BANNING YOU AS A DEPUTY.
HEY!
URYÛ! ISN'T THAT YOUR HOUSE DOWN THERE?
SHUT UP.
OH... YEAH! MR. URAHARA, YOU CAN DROP ME OFF HERE!
ALL RIGHT. ♪
SEE YA, URYÛ!
LET'S DO IT AGAIN SOMETIME.
ARE YOU KIDDING?
HAVE YOU FORGOTTEN... ...ICHIGO?

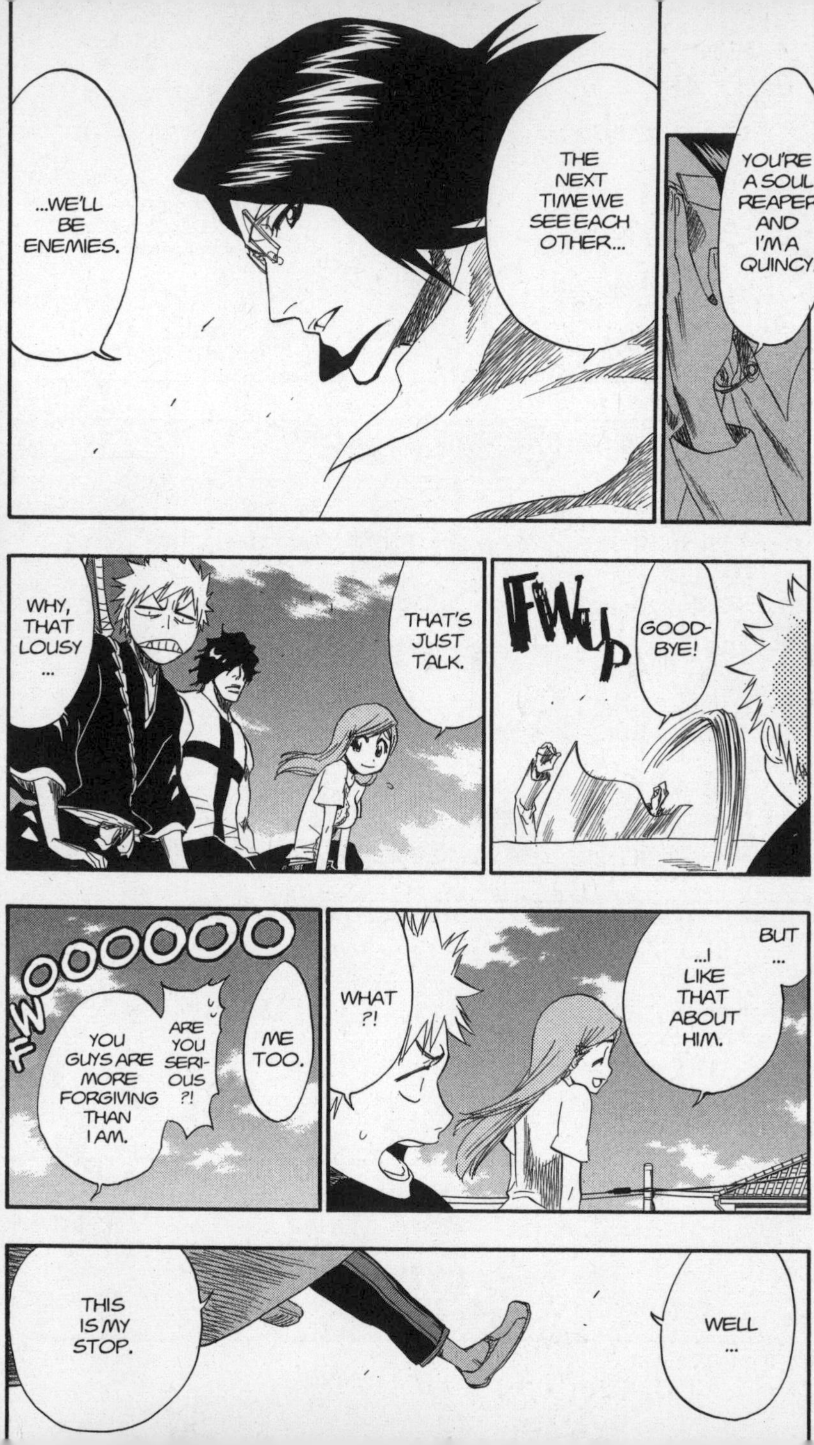
YOU'RE A SOUL REAPER AND I'M A QUINCY.
THE NEXT TIME WE SEE EACH OTHER...
...WE'LL BE ENEMIES.
GOOD-BYE!
FWUP
THAT'S JUST TALK.
WHY, THAT LOUSY ...
BUT ...
...I LIKE THAT ABOUT HIM.
WHAT ?!
ME TOO.
ARE YOU SERI-OUS ?!
YOU GUYS ARE MORE FORGIVING THAN I AM.
FWOOOOOOO
WELL ...
THIS IS MY STOP.

READ THIS WAY

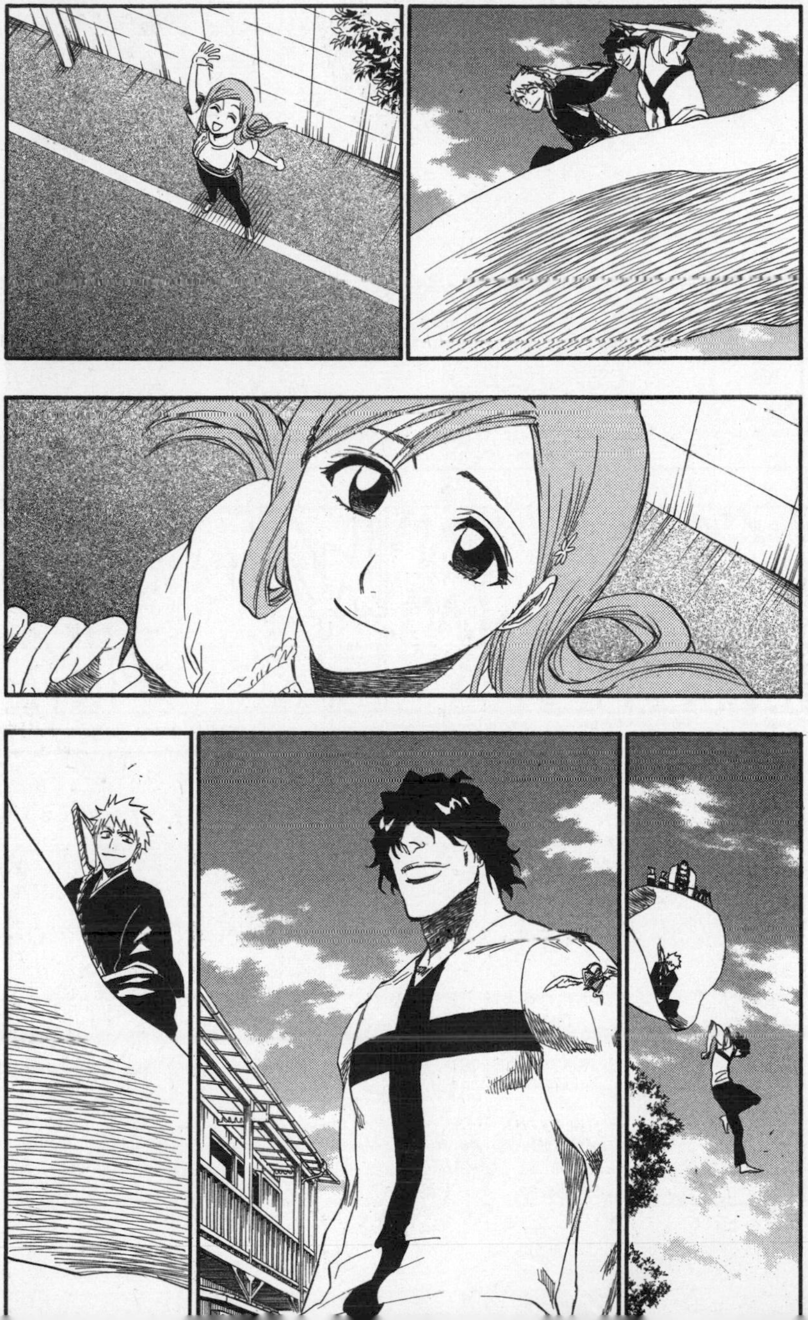

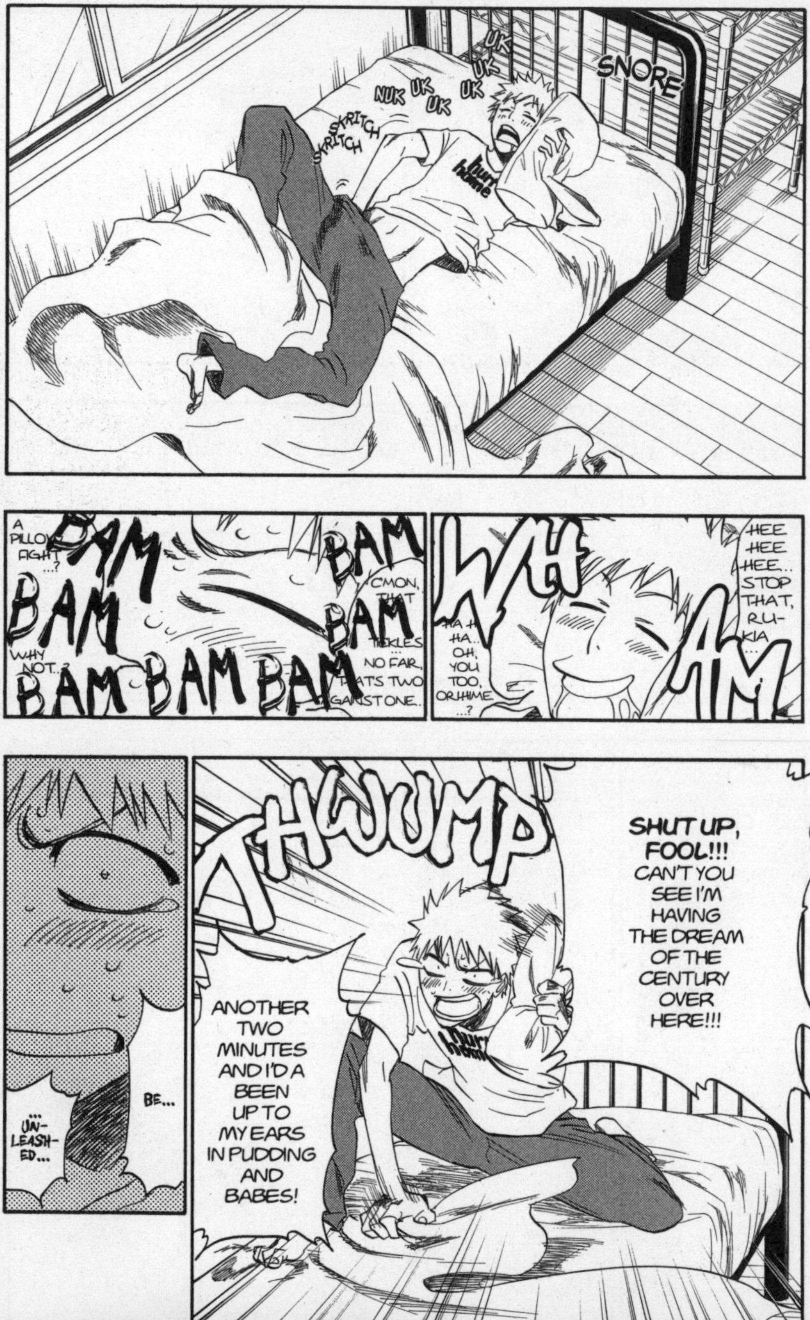
SNORE
UK UK UK
NUK UK UK
SKRITCH SKRITCH
HEE HEE HEE... STOP THAT, RU-KIA...
WHAM
HA HA... OH, YOU TOO, ORIHIME...?
C'MON, THAT TICKLES... NO FAIR, THAT'S TWO GAINST ONE.
BAM BAM
A PILLOW FIGHT...?
BAM BAM
WHY NOT...?
BAM BAM BAM
SHUT UP, FOOL!!! CAN'T YOU SEE I'M HAVING THE DREAM OF THE CENTURY OVER HERE!!!
THWUMP
ANOTHER TWO MINUTES AND I'DA BEEN UP TO MY EARS IN PUDDING AND BABES!
BE...
...UN-LEASHED...

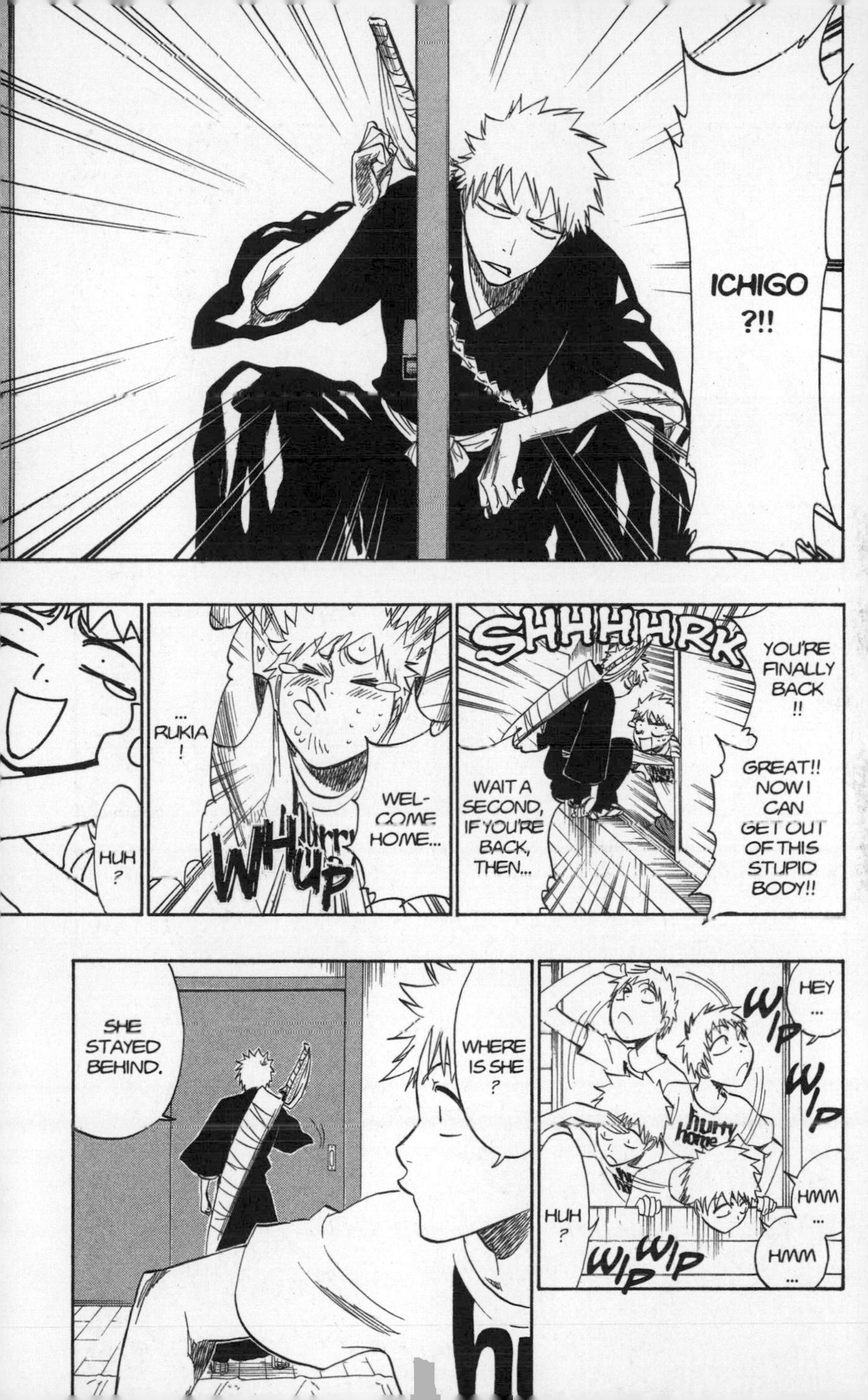
ICHIGO ?!!
YOU'RE FINALLY BACK !!
GREAT!! NOW I CAN GET OUT OF THIS STUPID BODY!!
SHHHHRK
WAIT A SECOND, IF YOU'RE BACK, THEN...
WEL-COME HOME...
... RUKIA !
WHUP
HUH ?
HEY ...
WIP WIP
HMM ...
HMM ...
HUH ?
WIP WIP
WHERE IS SHE ?
SHE STAYED BEHIND.

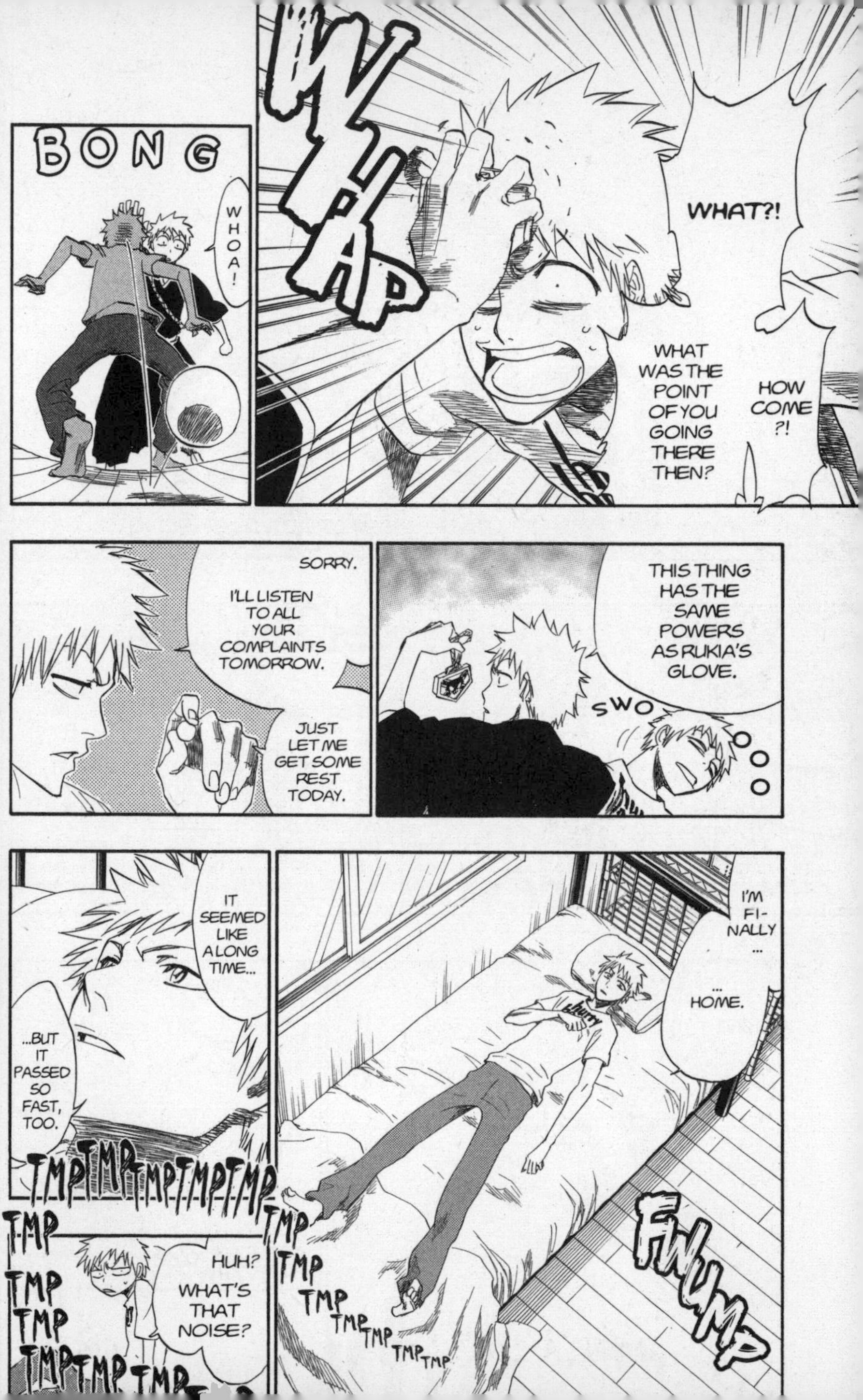
WHAT?!
HOW COME?!
WHAT WAS THE POINT OF YOU GOING THERE THEN?
WHAP
BONG
WHOA!
THIS THING HAS THE SAME POWERS AS RUKIA'S GLOVE.
SWOOOO
SORRY.
I'LL LISTEN TO ALL YOUR COMPLAINTS TOMORROW.
JUST LET ME GET SOME REST TODAY.
I'M FI-NALLY...
...HOME.
FWUMP
IT SEEMED LIKE A LONG TIME...
...BUT IT PASSED SO FAST, TOO.
TMP TMP TMP TMP TMP TMP TMP TMP TMP TMP TMP TMP TMP TMP TMP
HUH? WHAT'S THAT NOISE?
TMP TMP TMP TMP TMP TMP TMP TMP TMP TMP

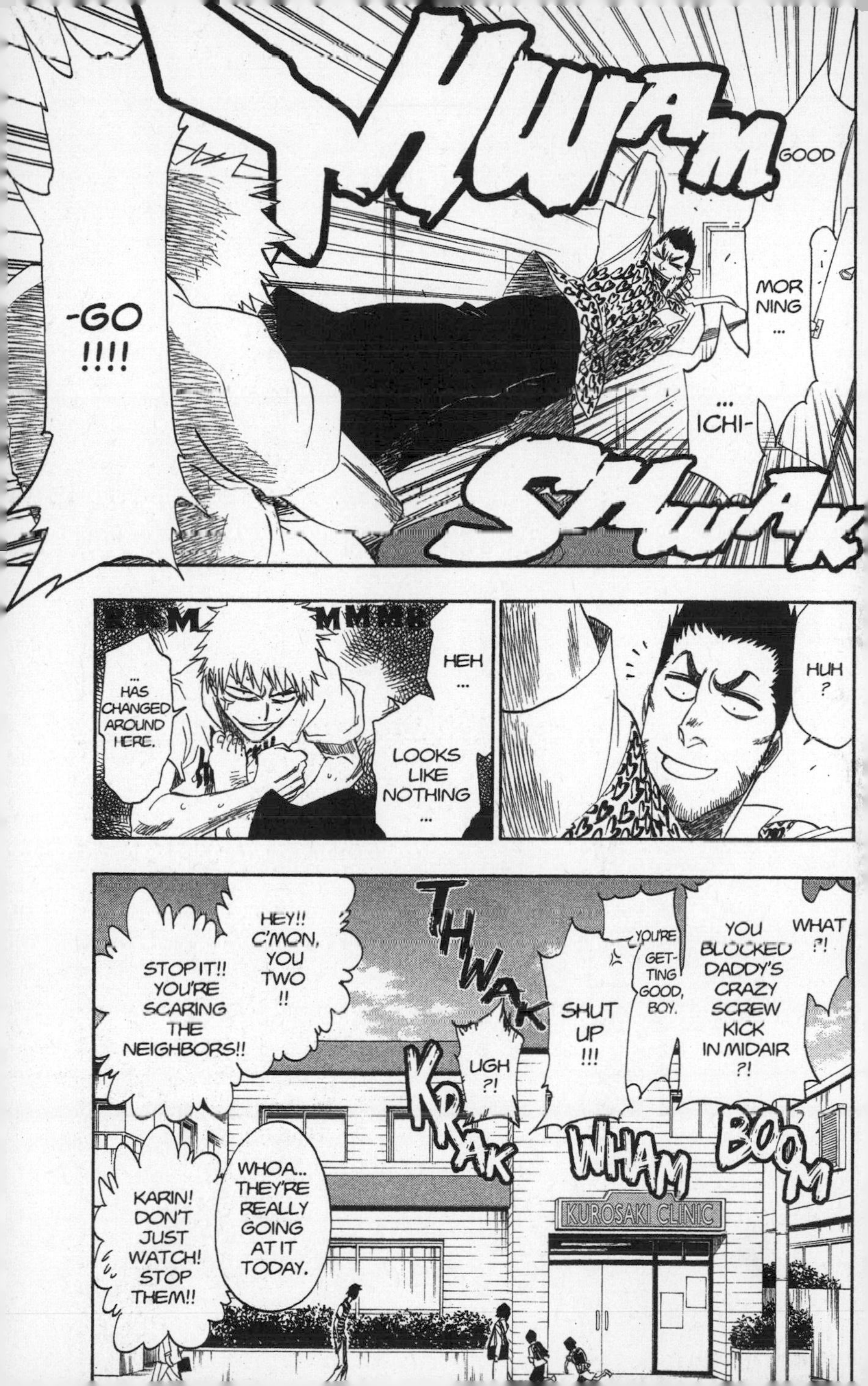
GOOD MORNING ...
... ICHI-
-GO !!!!
HUH ?
HEH ...
LOOKS LIKE NOTHING ...
... HAS CHANGED AROUND HERE.
WHAT ?!
YOU BLOCKED DADDY'S CRAZY SCREW KICK IN MIDAIR ?!
YOU'RE GETTING GOOD, BOY.
SHUT UP !!!
THWAK
UGH ?!
HEY!! C'MON, YOU TWO !!
STOP IT!! YOU'RE SCARING THE NEIGHBORS!!
BOOM
WHAM
KUROSAKI CLINIC
WHOA.. THEY'RE REALLY GOING AT IT TODAY.
KARIN! DON'T JUST WATCH! STOP THEM!!

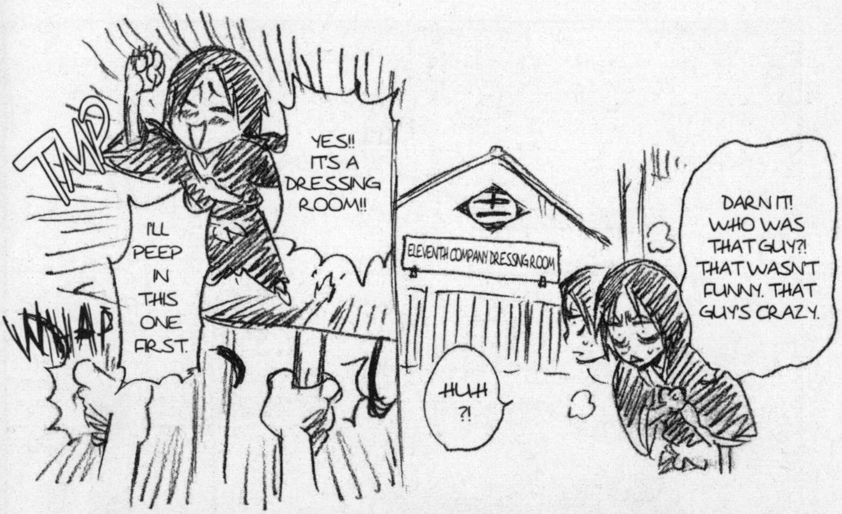
DARN IT! WHO WAS THAT GUY?! THAT WASN'T FUNNY. THAT GUY'S CRAZY.
HUH ?!
ELEVENTH COMPANY DRESSNG ROOM
YES!! IT'S A DRESSING ROOM!!
I'LL PEEP IN THIS ONE FIRST.
TMP
WHAP

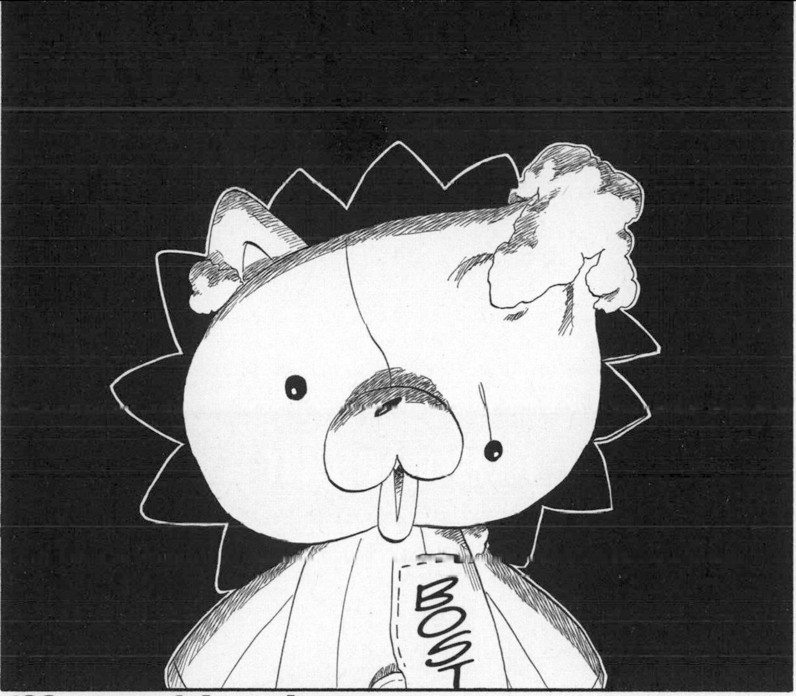
BOST

183. eyes of the unknown

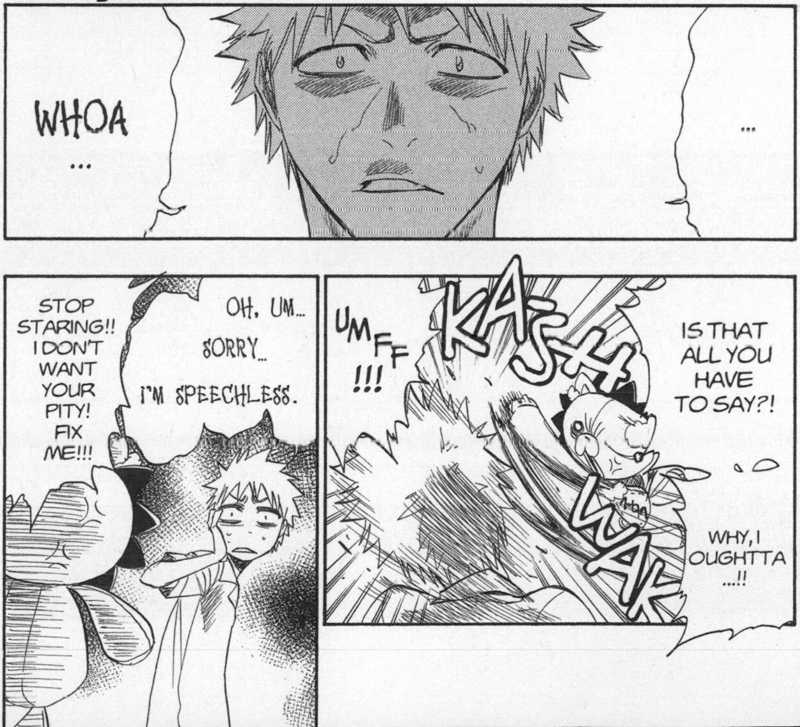
...
WHOA
...
IS THAT ALL YOU HAVE TO SAY?!
KA-SHH
UMFF!!!
WHAK
WHY, I OUGHTTA ...!!
OH, UM... SORRY... I'M SPEECHLESS.
STOP STARING!! I DON'T WANT YOUR PITY! FIX ME!!!

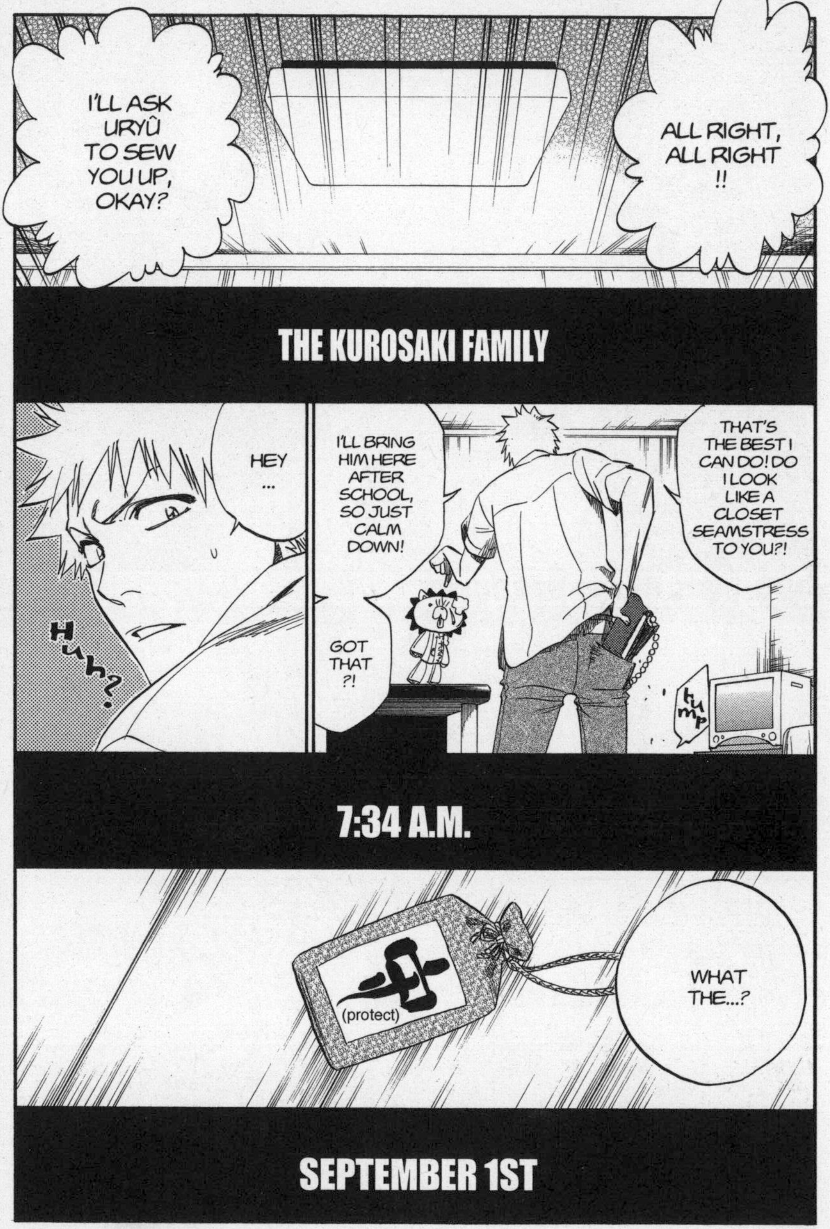
ALL RIGHT, ALL RIGHT !!
I'LL ASK URYÛ TO SEW YOU UP, OKAY?
THE KUROSAKI FAMILY
THAT'S THE BEST I CAN DO! DO I LOOK LIKE A CLOSET SEAMSTRESS TO YOU?!
I'LL BRING HIM HERE AFTER SCHOOL, SO JUST CALM DOWN!
thump
GOT THAT ?!
HEY ...
Huh?
7:34 A.M.
WHAT THE...?
(protect)
SEPTEMBER 1ST

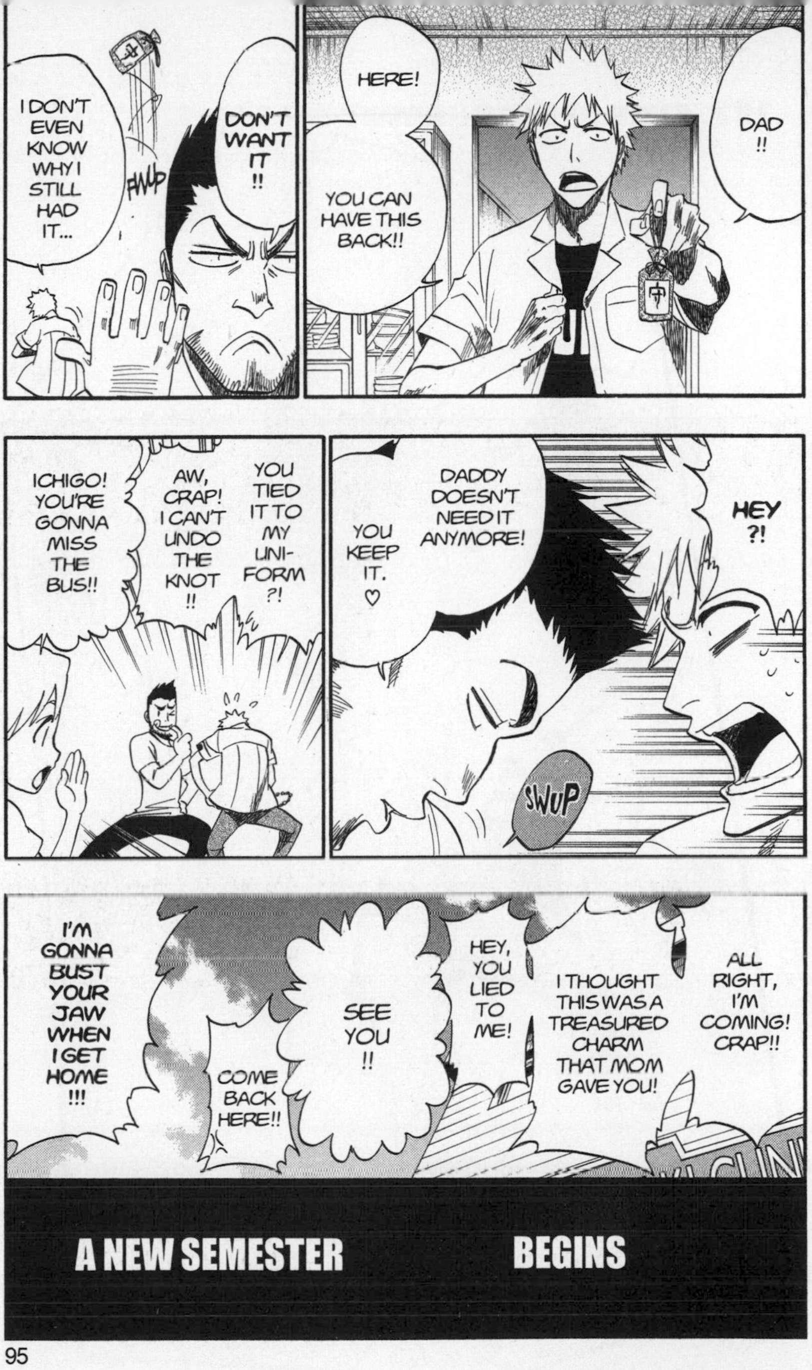
DAD!!
HERE!
YOU CAN HAVE THIS BACK!!
DON'T WANT IT!!
FWUP
I DON'T EVEN KNOW WHY I STILL HAD IT...
HEY?!
DADDY DOESN'T NEED IT ANYMORE!
YOU KEEP IT. ♡
SWUP
YOU TIED IT TO MY UNI-FORM?!
AW, CRAP! I CAN'T UNDO THE KNOT!!
ICHIGO! YOU'RE GONNA MISS THE BUS!!
ALL RIGHT, I'M COMING! CRAP!!
I THOUGHT THIS WAS A TREASURED CHARM THAT MOM GAVE YOU!
HEY, YOU LIED TO ME!
SEE YOU!!
COME BACK HERE!!
I'M GONNA BUST YOUR JAW WHEN I GET HOME!!!
A NEW SEMESTER BEGINS

183. eyes of the unkown

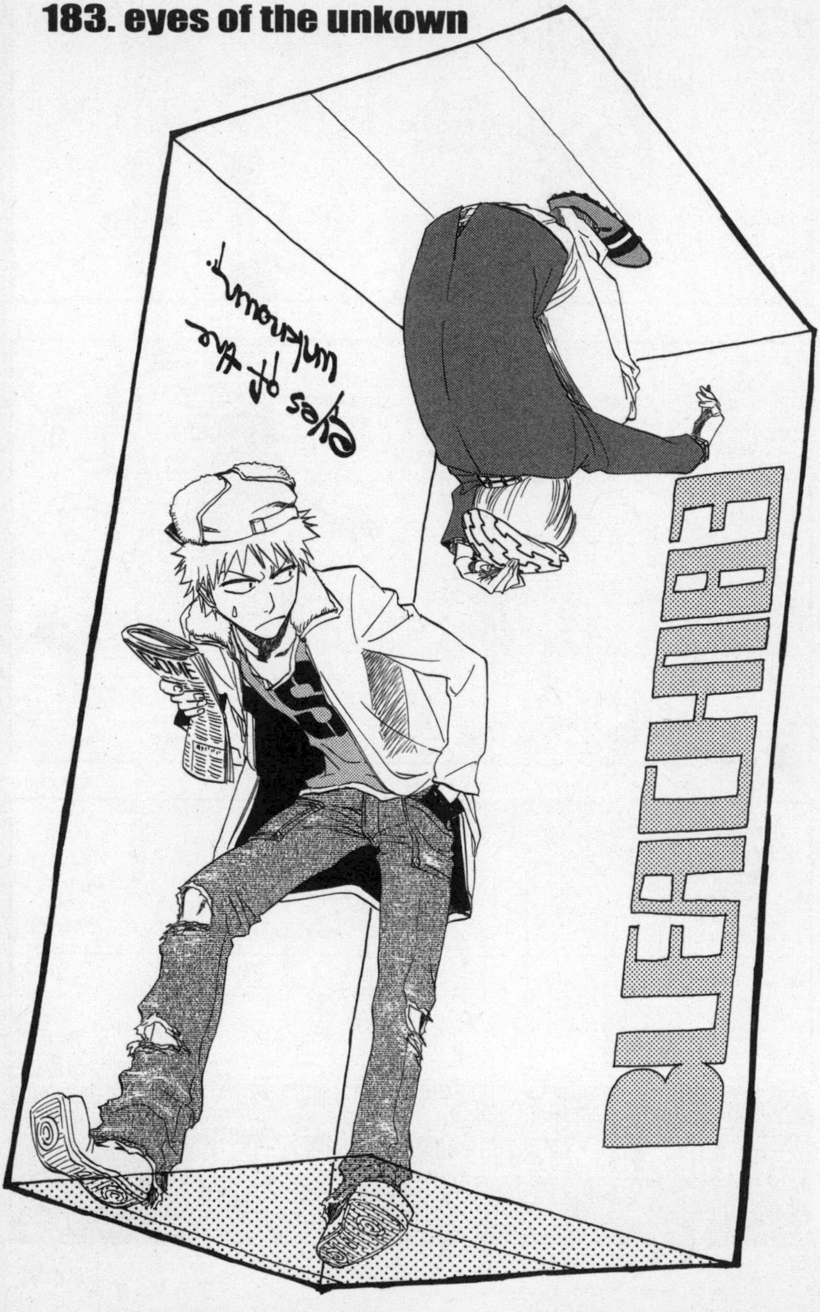
eyes of the unknown
BLEACH

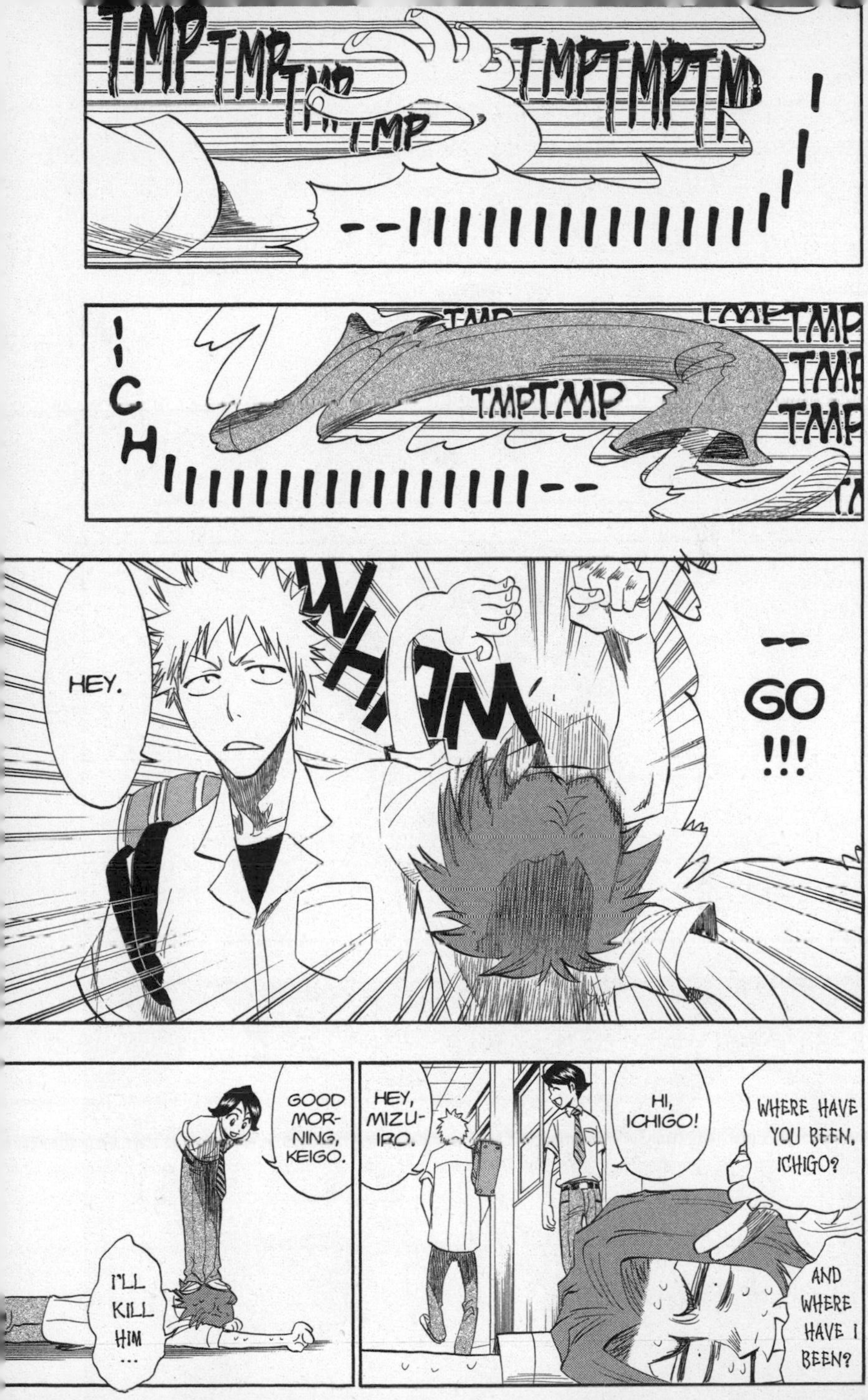

TMP TMP TMP TMP
TMPTMPTMP
--IIIIIIIIIIIIIIII
TMPTMP TMP TMP TMP
TMPTMP
ICH IIIIIIIIIIIIIIII--
-- GO !!!
WHAM
HEY.
WHERE HAVE YOU BEEN, ICHIGO?
AND WHERE HAVE I BEEN?
HI, ICHIGO!
HEY, MIZU-IRO.
GOOD MOR-NING, KEIGO.
I'LL KILL HIM ...

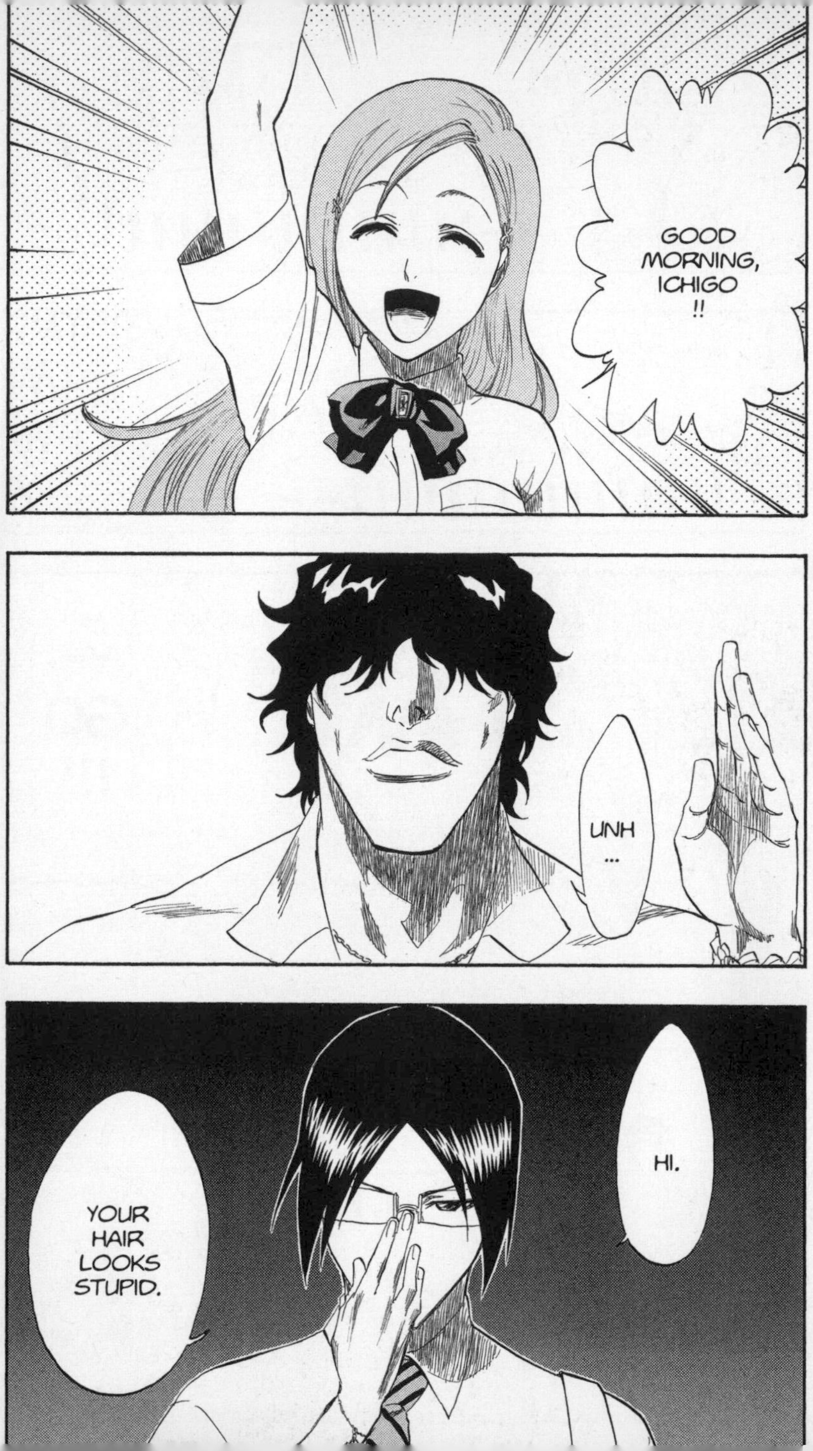
GOOD MORNING, ICHIGO!!
UNH...
HI.
YOUR HAIR LOOKS STUPID.

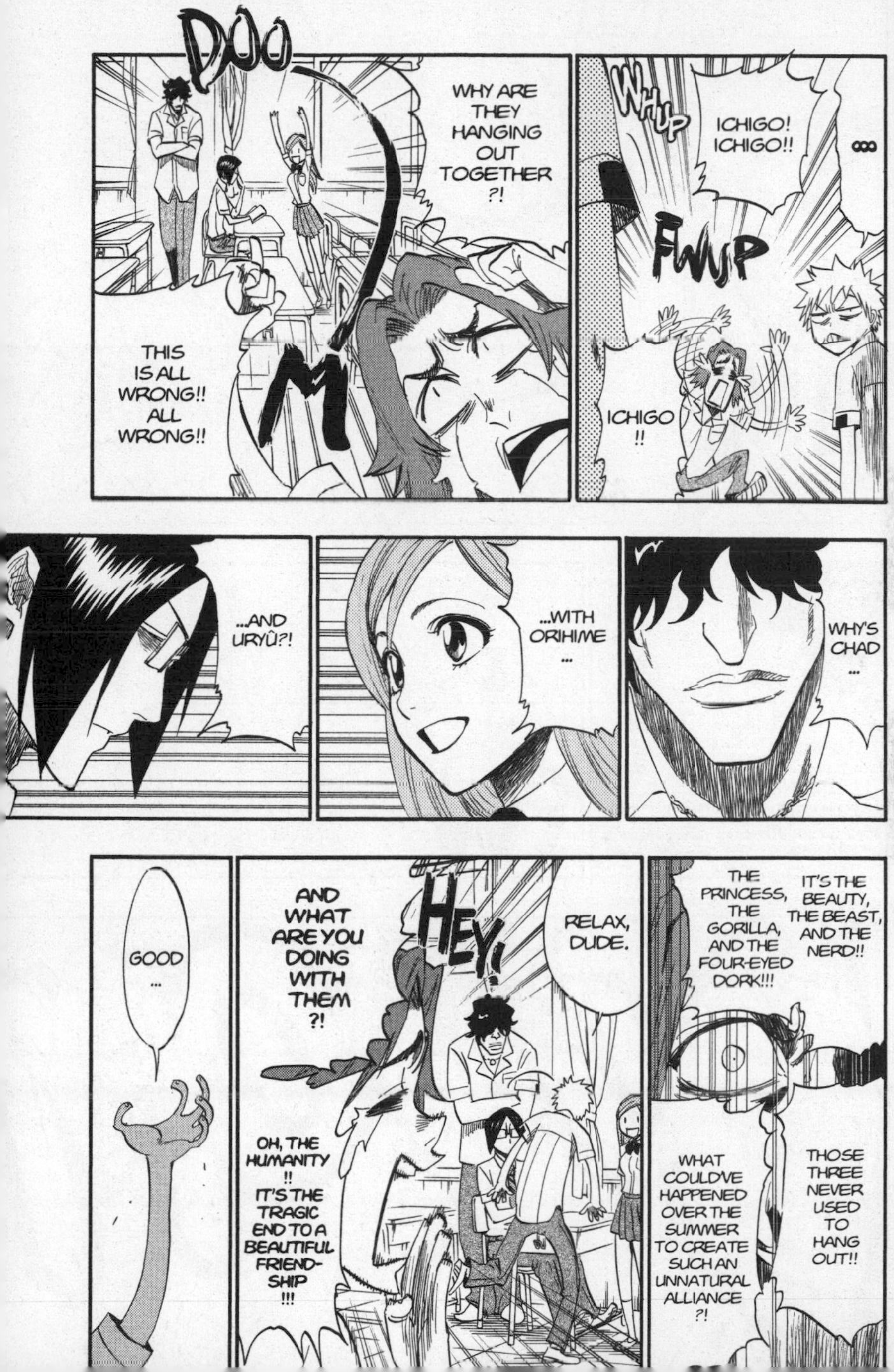
WHUP
ICHIGO! ICHIGO!!
...
FWUP
ICHIGO !!
DOO
M
WHY ARE THEY HANGING OUT TOGETHER ?!
THIS IS ALL WRONG!! ALL WRONG!!
WHY'S CHAD ...
...WITH ORIHIME ...
...AND URYÛ?!
IT'S THE BEAUTY, THE BEAST, AND THE NERD!!
THE PRINCESS, THE GORILLA, AND THE FOUR-EYED DORK!!!
THOSE THREE NEVER USED TO HANG OUT!!
WHAT COULD'VE HAPPENED OVER THE SUMMER TO CREATE SUCH AN UNNATURAL ALLIANCE ?!
RELAX, DUDE.
HEY,
AND WHAT ARE YOU DOING WITH THEM ?!
OH, THE HUMANITY !! IT'S THE TRAGIC END TO A BEAUTIFUL FRIEND-SHIP !!!
GOOD ...

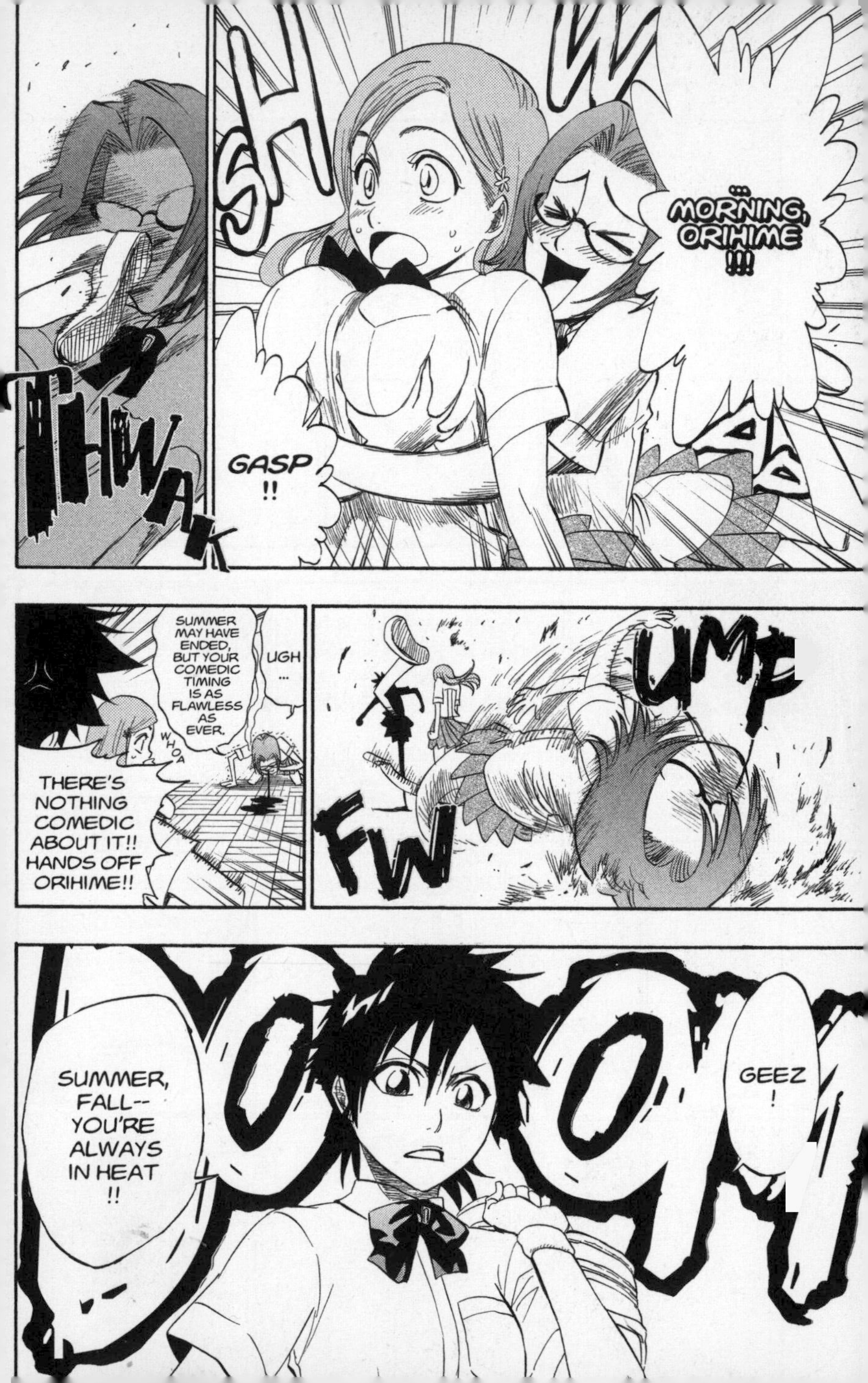
... MORNING, ORIHIME !!!
GASP !!
THWAK
UMP
FW
UGH ...
SUMMER MAY HAVE ENDED, BUT YOUR COMEDIC TIMING IS AS FLAWLESS AS EVER.
WHOA
THERE'S NOTHING COMEDIC ABOUT IT!! HANDS OFF ORIHIME!!
GEEZ !
SUMMER, FALL-- YOU'RE ALWAYS IN HEAT !!

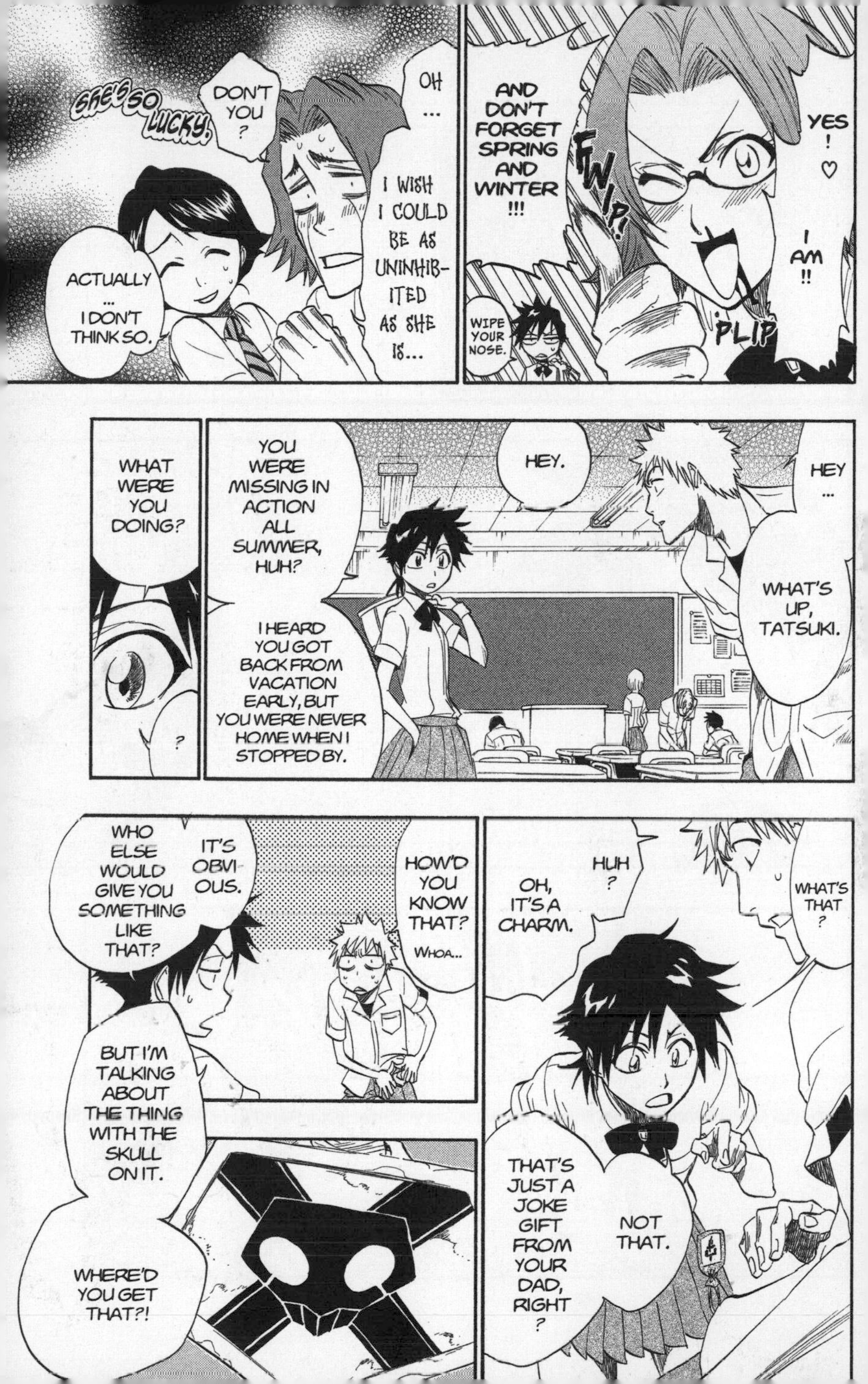
YES! ♡ I AM!!
FWIP!
AND DON'T FORGET SPRING AND WINTER!!!
PLIP
WIPE YOUR NOSE.
OH ...
I WISH I COULD BE AS UNINHIBITED AS SHE IS...
DON'T YOU?
SHE'S SO LUCKY!
ACTUALLY ... I DON'T THINK SO.
HEY ...
HEY.
WHAT'S UP, TATSUKI.
YOU WERE MISSING IN ACTION ALL SUMMER, HUH?
I HEARD YOU GOT BACK FROM VACATION EARLY, BUT YOU WERE NEVER HOME WHEN I STOPPED BY.
WHAT WERE YOU DOING?
?
WHAT'S THAT?
HUH?
OH, IT'S A CHARM.
NOT THAT.
THAT'S JUST A JOKE GIFT FROM YOUR DAD, RIGHT?
HOW'D YOU KNOW THAT?
WHOA...
IT'S OBVIOUS.
WHO ELSE WOULD GIVE YOU SOMETHING LIKE THAT?
BUT I'M TALKING ABOUT THE THING WITH THE SKULL ON IT.
WHERE'D YOU GET THAT?!

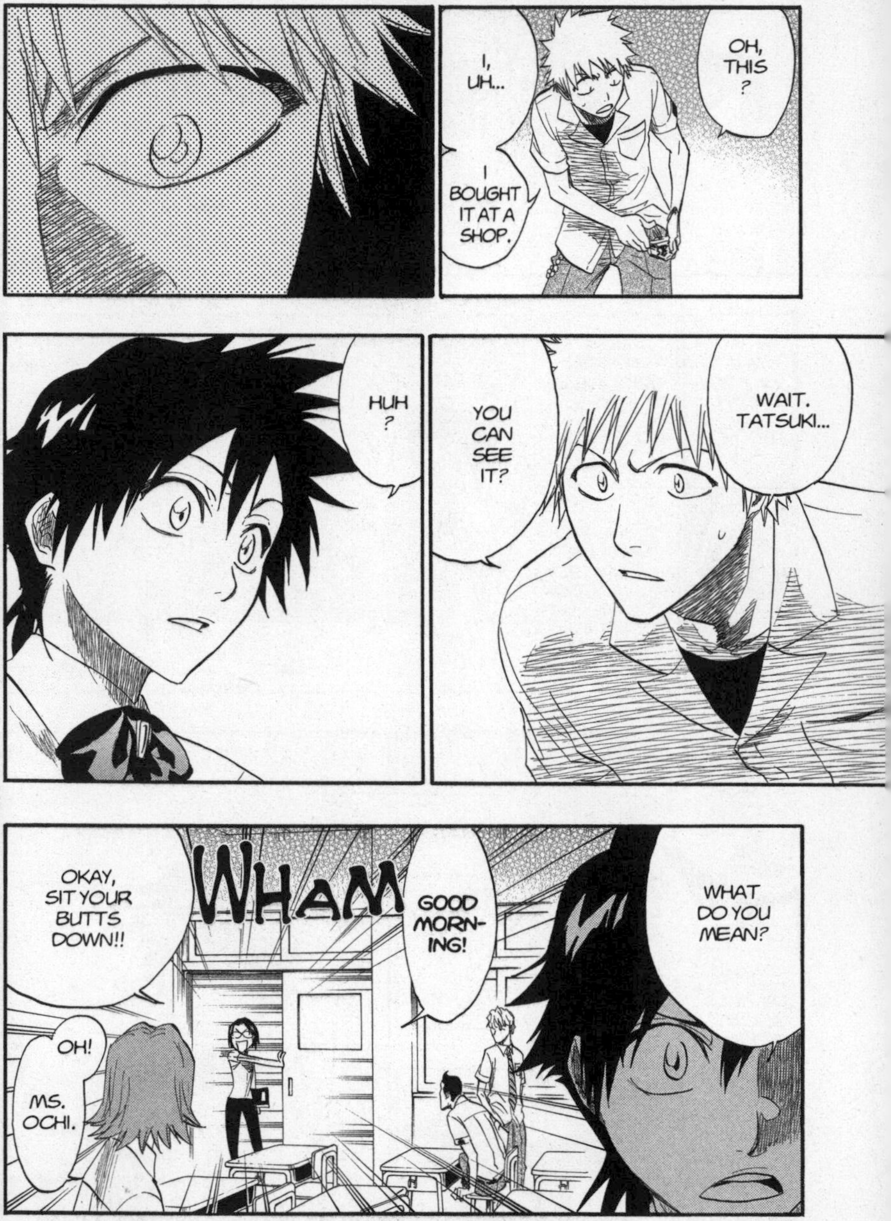
OH, THIS ?
I, UH...
I BOUGHT IT AT A SHOP.
WAIT. TATSUKI...
YOU CAN SEE IT?
HUH ?
WHAT DO YOU MEAN?
GOOD MORN-ING!
WHAM
OKAY, SIT YOUR BUTTS DOWN!!
OH!
MS. OCHI.

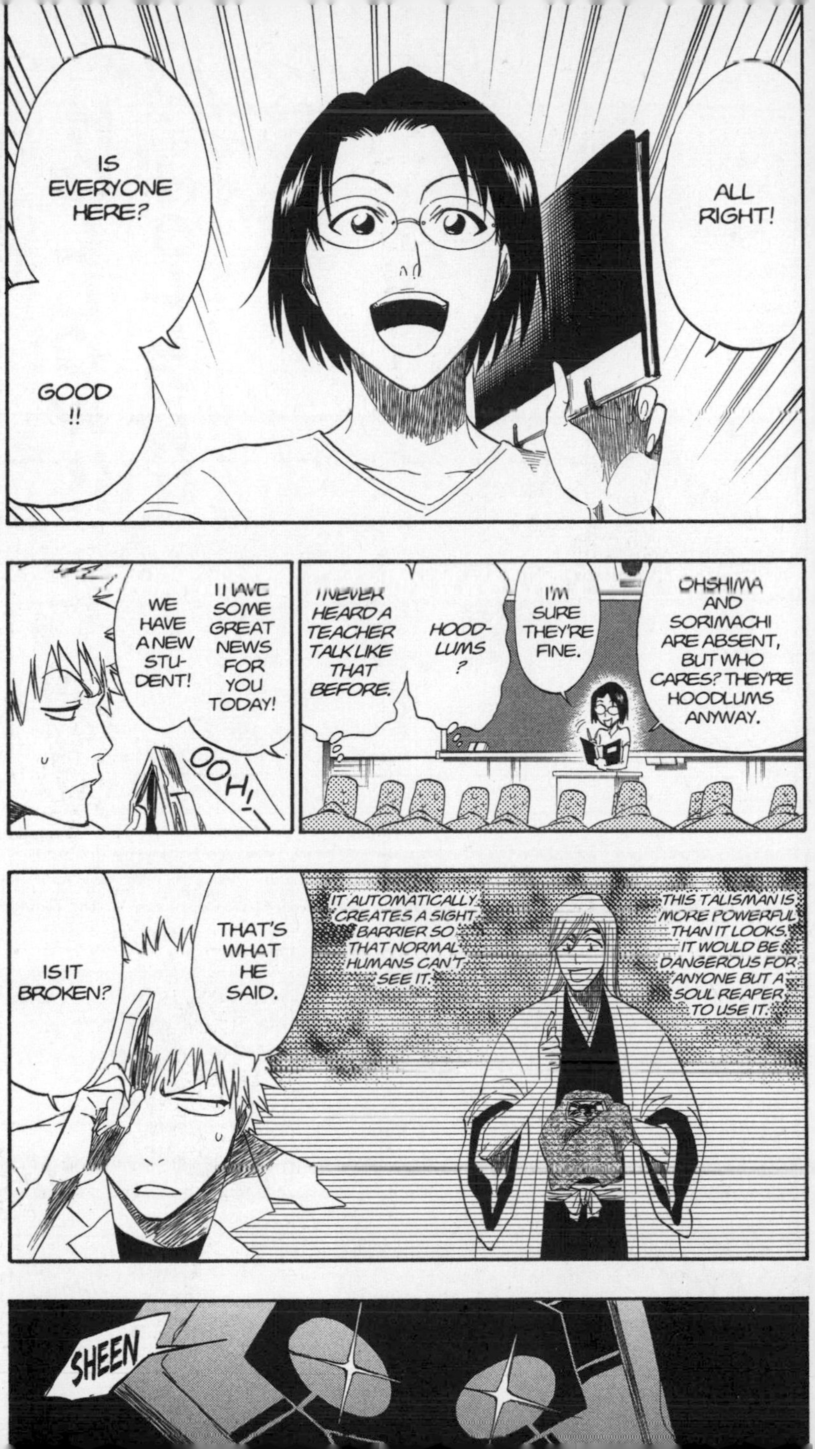
ALL RIGHT!
IS EVERYONE HERE?
GOOD!!
OHSHIMA AND SORIMACHI ARE ABSENT, BUT WHO CARES? THEY'RE HOODLUMS ANYWAY.
I'M SURE THEY'RE FINE.
HOOD-LUMS?
I NEVER HEARD A TEACHER TALK LIKE THAT BEFORE.
I HAVE SOME GREAT NEWS FOR YOU TODAY!
WE HAVE A NEW STU-DENT!
OOH!
THIS TALISMAN IS MORE POWERFUL THAN IT LOOKS. IT WOULD BE DANGEROUS FOR ANYONE BUT A SOUL REAPER TO USE IT.
IT AUTOMATICALLY CREATES A SIGHT BARRIER SO THAT NORMAL HUMANS CAN'T SEE IT.
THAT'S WHAT HE SAID.
IS IT BROKEN?
SHEEN

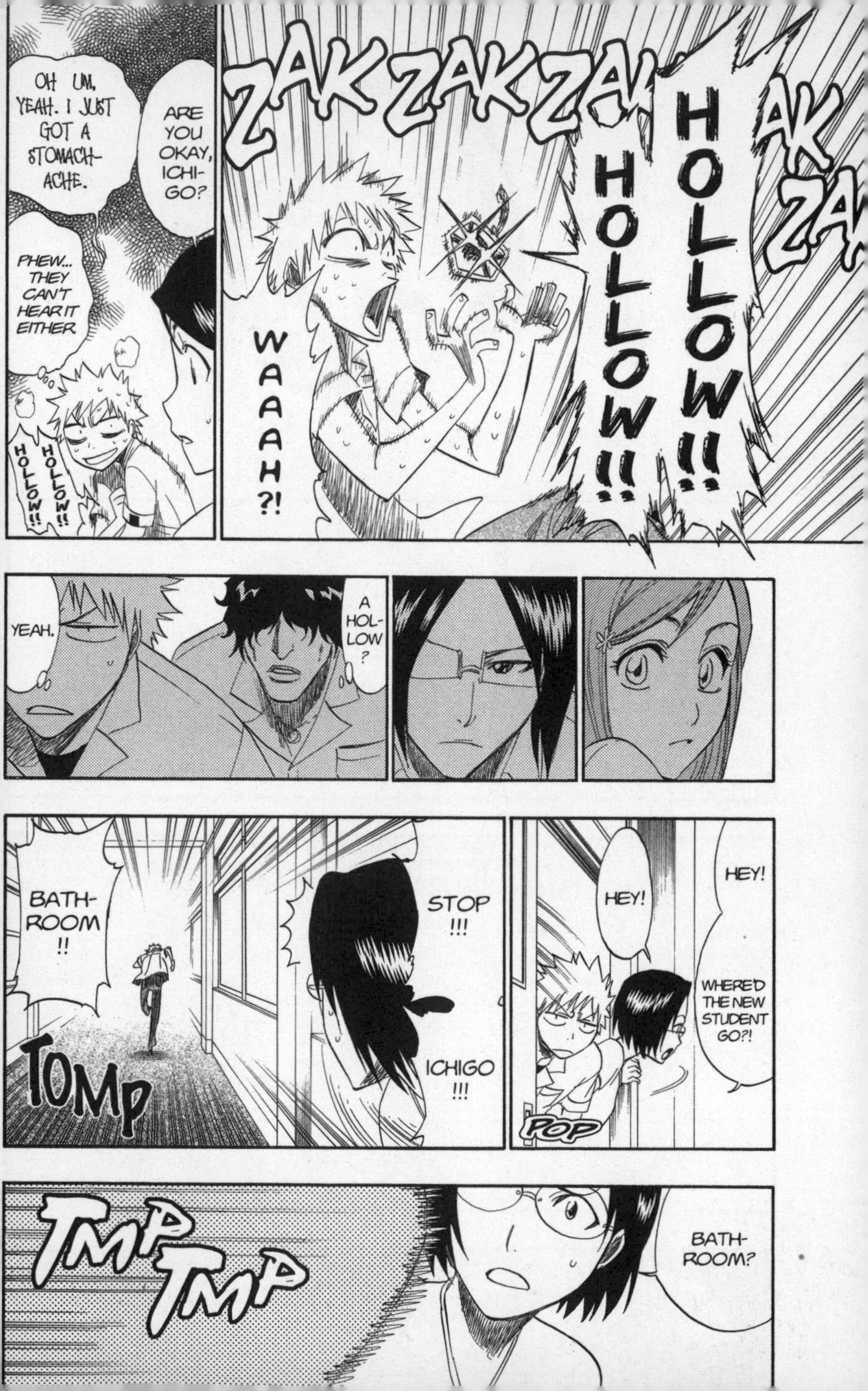
AK ZA
HOLLOW!!
HOLLOW!!
ZAK ZAK ZA
WAAAAH?!
ARE YOU OKAY, ICHIGO?
OH UM, YEAH. I JUST GOT A STOMACHACHE.
PHEW... THEY CAN'T HEAR IT EITHER
HOLLOW!!
HOLLOW!!
A HOLLOW?
YEAH.
HEY!
WHERE'D THE NEW STUDENT GO?!
HEY!
POP
STOP!!!
ICHIGO!!!
BATHROOM!!
TOMP
BATHROOM?
TMP TMP

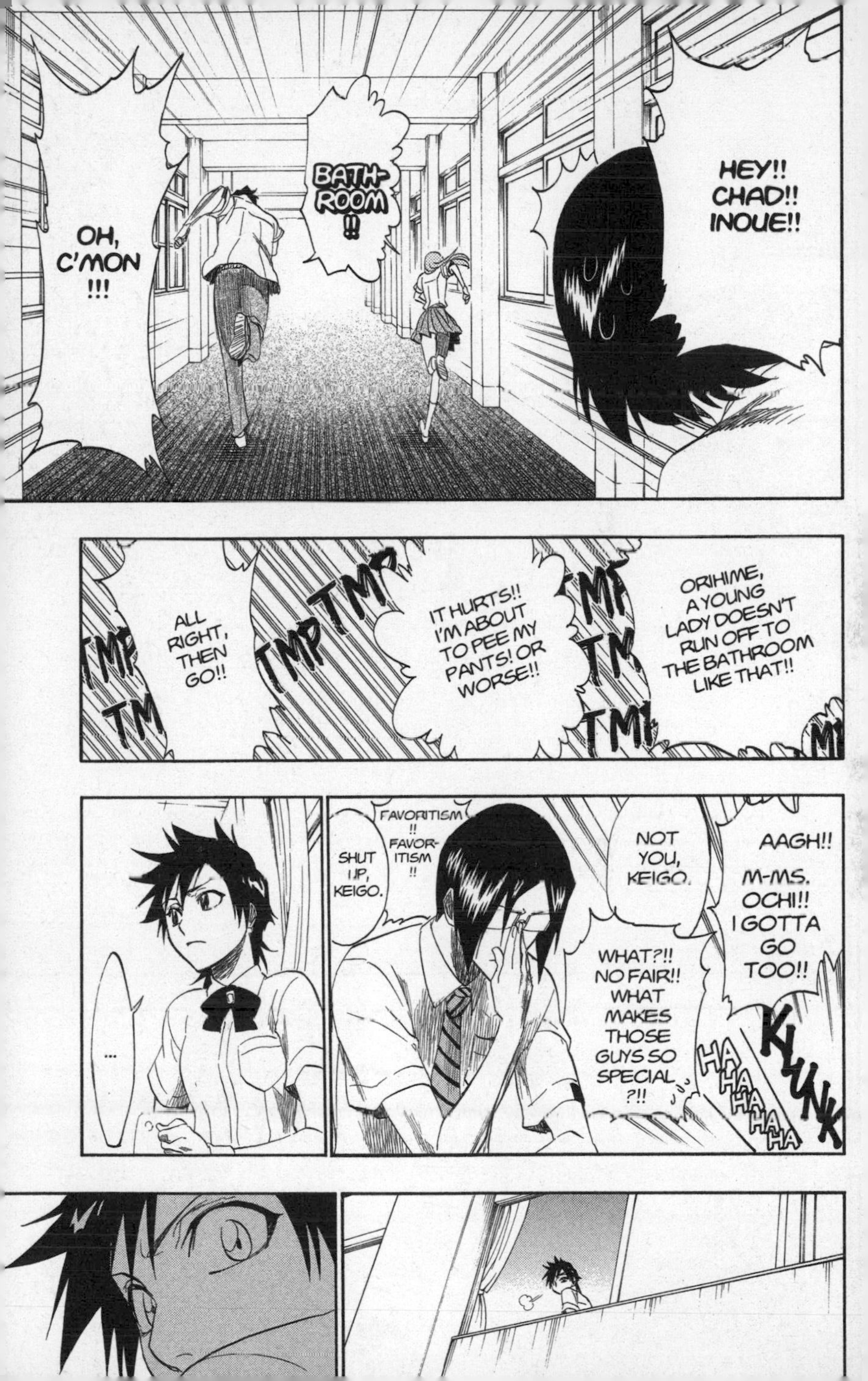
HEY!! CHAD!! INOUE!!
BATH-ROOM!!
OH, C'MON!!!
ORIHIME, A YOUNG LADY DOESN'T RUN OFF TO THE BATHROOM LIKE THAT!!
TMP TMP TM
IT HURTS!! I'M ABOUT TO PEE MY PANTS! OR WORSE!!
TMP TMP
ALL RIGHT, THEN GO!!
TMP TM
AAGH!!
M-MS. OCHI!! I GOTTA GO TOO!!
NOT YOU, KEIGO.
WHAT?!! NO FAIR!! WHAT MAKES THOSE GUYS SO SPECIAL?!!
KLUNK
HA HA HA HA HA HA
FAVORITISM!! FAVORITISM!!
SHUT UP, KEIGO.
...

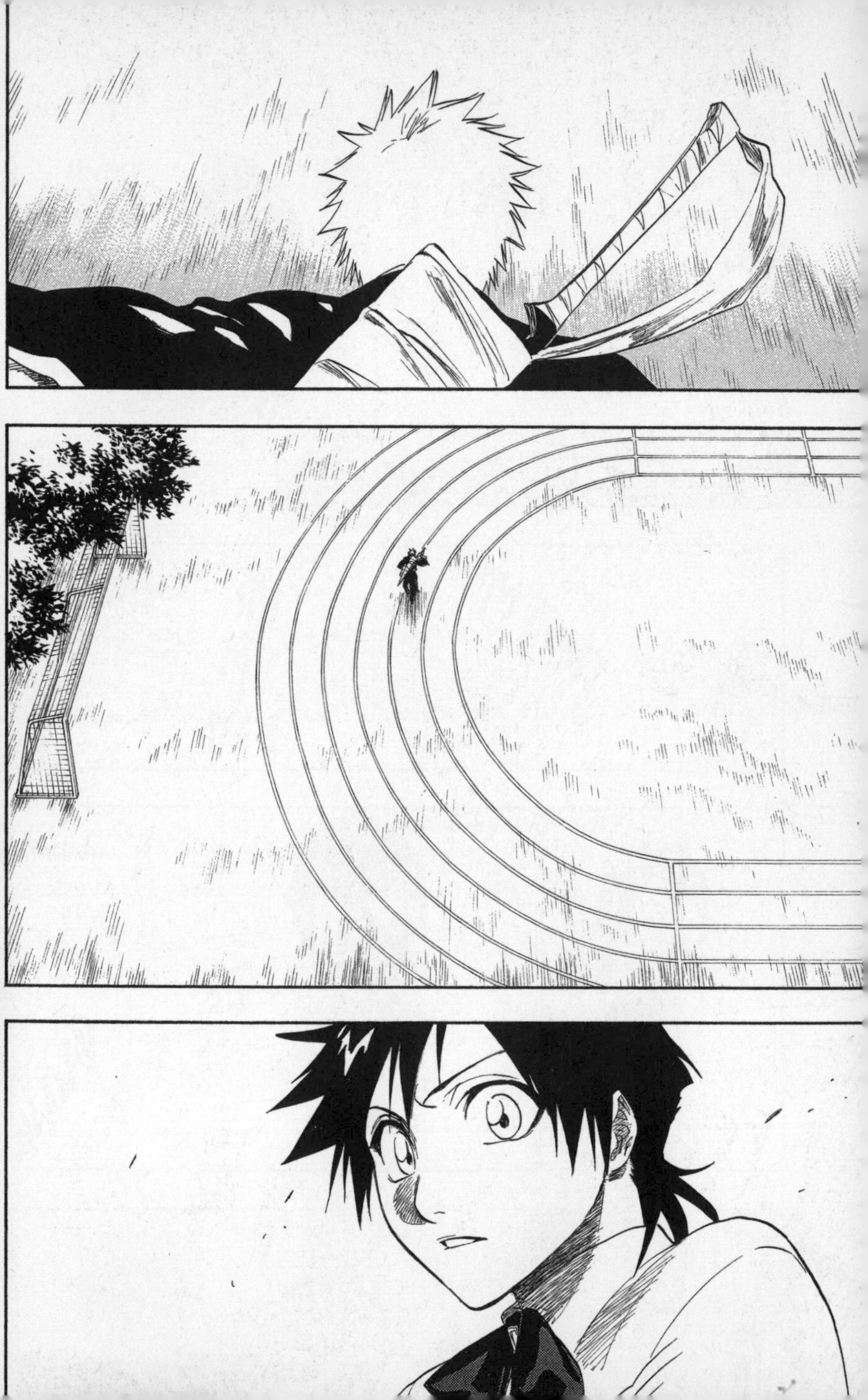

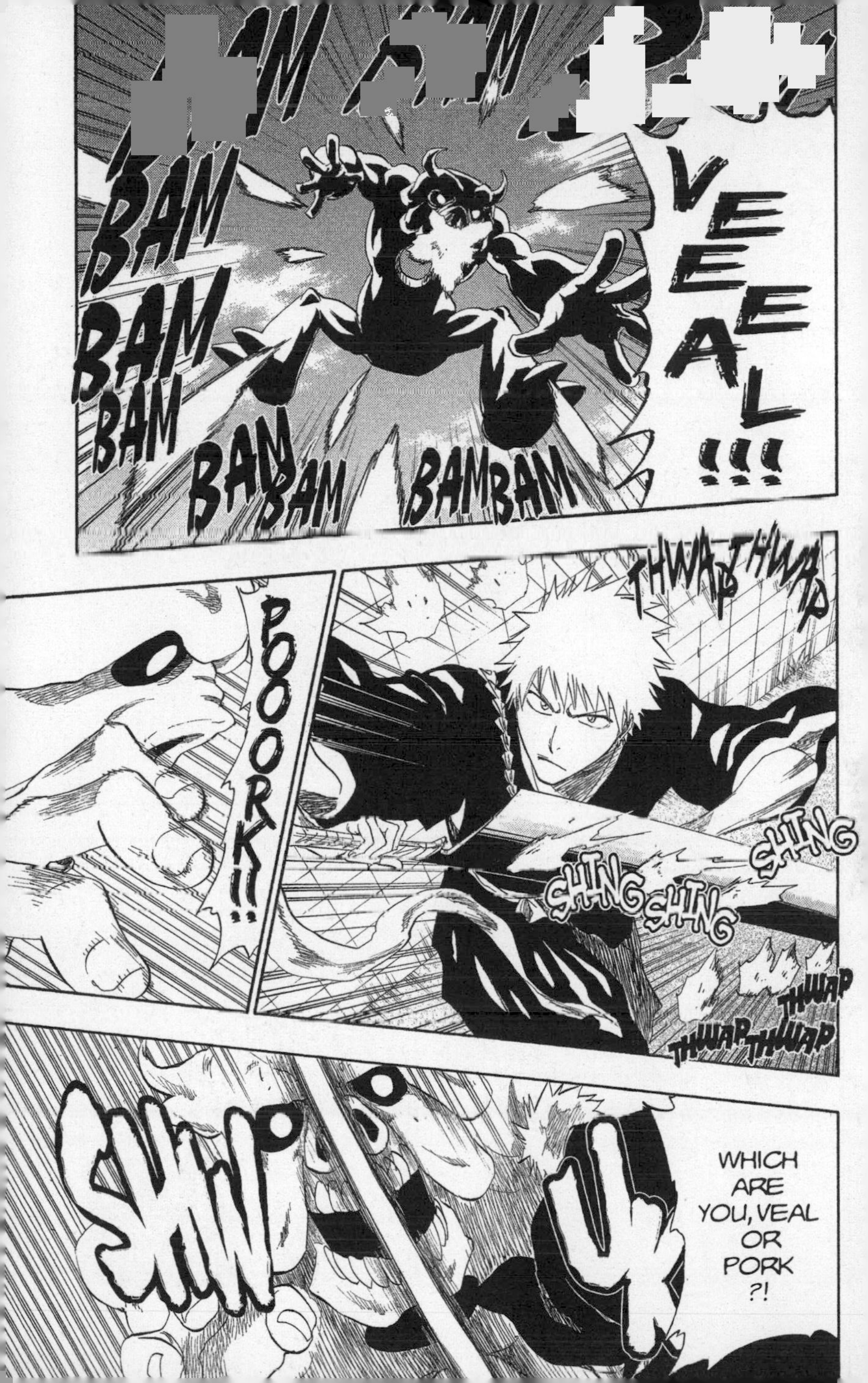
VEEEAL!!!
BAM
BAM
BAM
BAM BAM
BAMBAM
THWAP THWAP
SHING SHING SHING
THWAP THWAP THWAP
POOOORK!!
WHICH ARE YOU, VEAL OR PORK?!

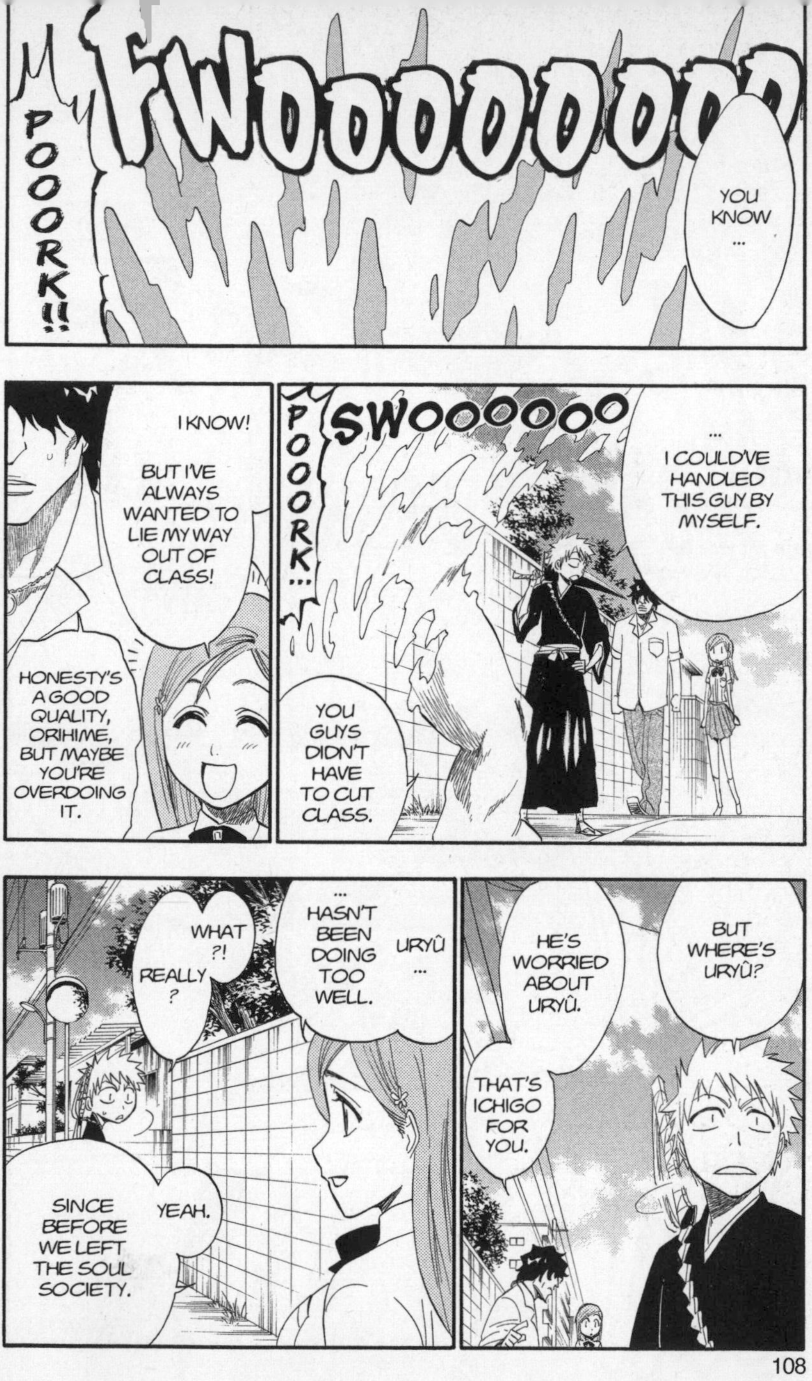
FWOOOOOOOO
POOOORK!!
YOU KNOW ...
... I COULD'VE HANDLED THIS GUY BY MYSELF.
SWOOOOOO
POOOORK...
YOU GUYS DIDN'T HAVE TO CUT CLASS.
I KNOW!
BUT I'VE ALWAYS WANTED TO LIE MY WAY OUT OF CLASS!
HONESTY'S A GOOD QUALITY, ORIHIME, BUT MAYBE YOU'RE OVERDOING IT.
BUT WHERE'S URYÛ?
HE'S WORRIED ABOUT URYÛ.
THAT'S ICHIGO FOR YOU.
URYÛ ...
... HASN'T BEEN DOING TOO WELL.
WHAT?!
REALLY?
YEAH.
SINCE BEFORE WE LEFT THE SOUL SOCIETY.

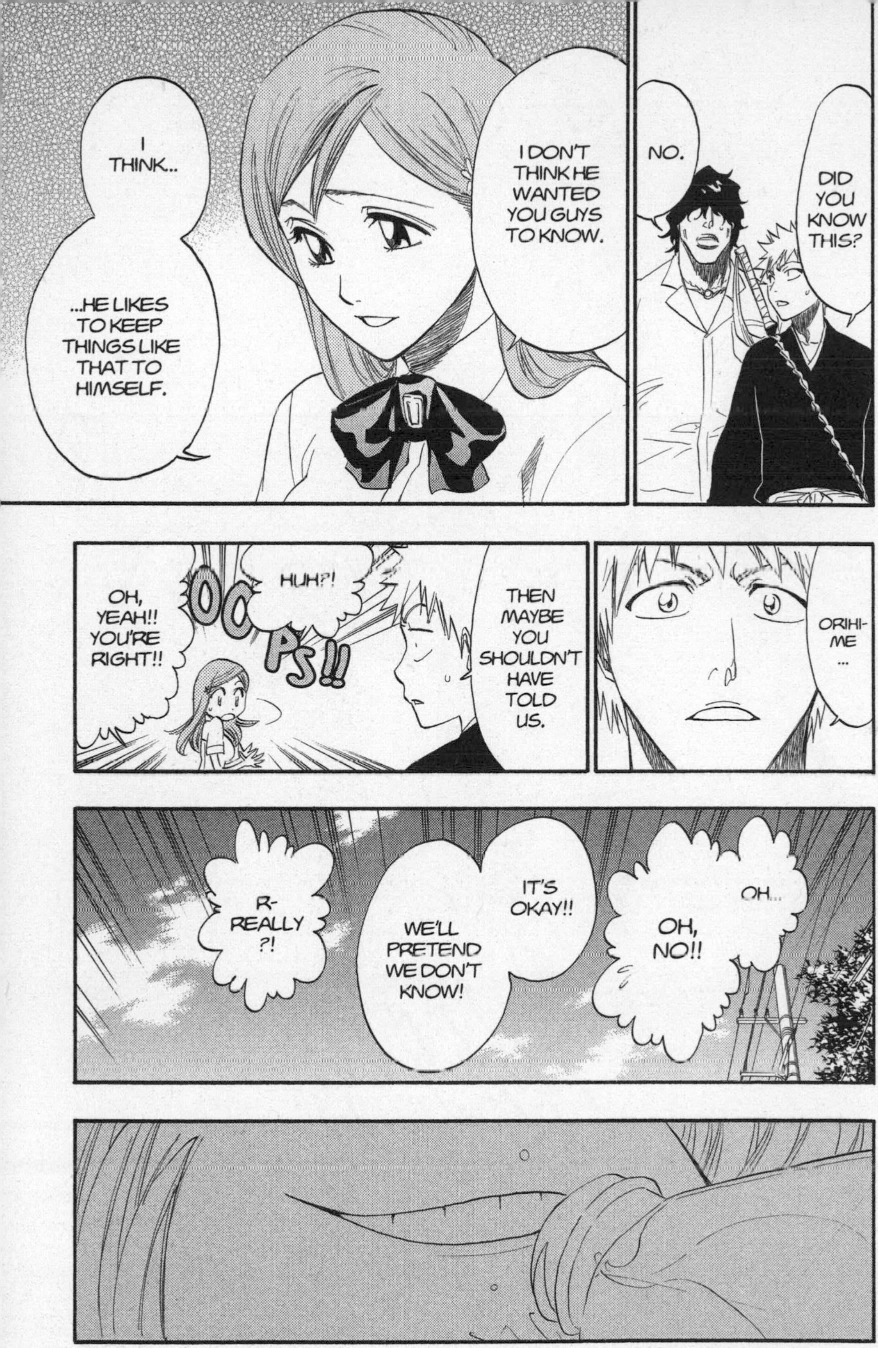
DID YOU KNOW THIS?
NO.
I DON'T THINK HE WANTED YOU GUYS TO KNOW.
I THINK...
...HE LIKES TO KEEP THINGS LIKE THAT TO HIMSELF.
ORIHIME...
THEN MAYBE YOU SHOULDN'T HAVE TOLD US.
HUH?!
OOPS!!
OH, YEAH!! YOU'RE RIGHT!!
OH...
OH, NO!!
IT'S OKAY!!
WE'LL PRETEND WE DON'T KNOW!
R-REALLY?!

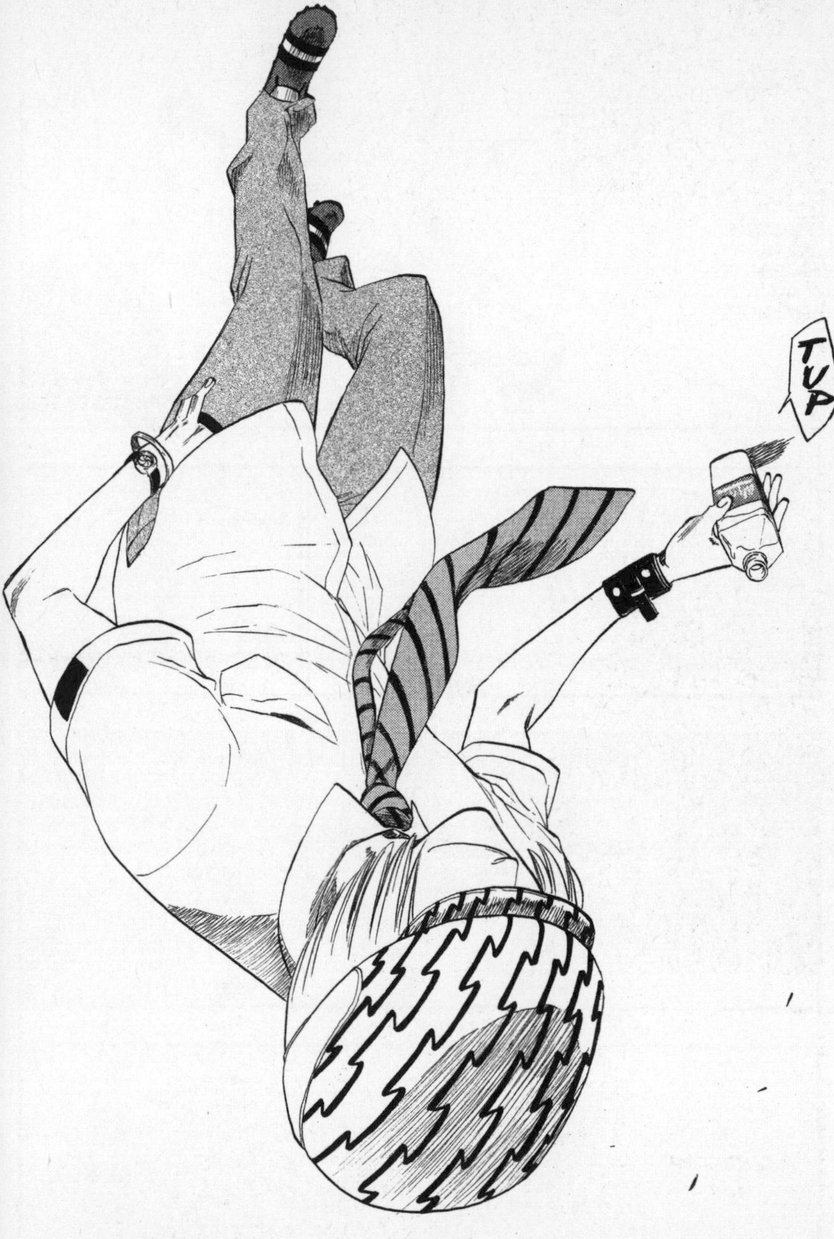
TUP

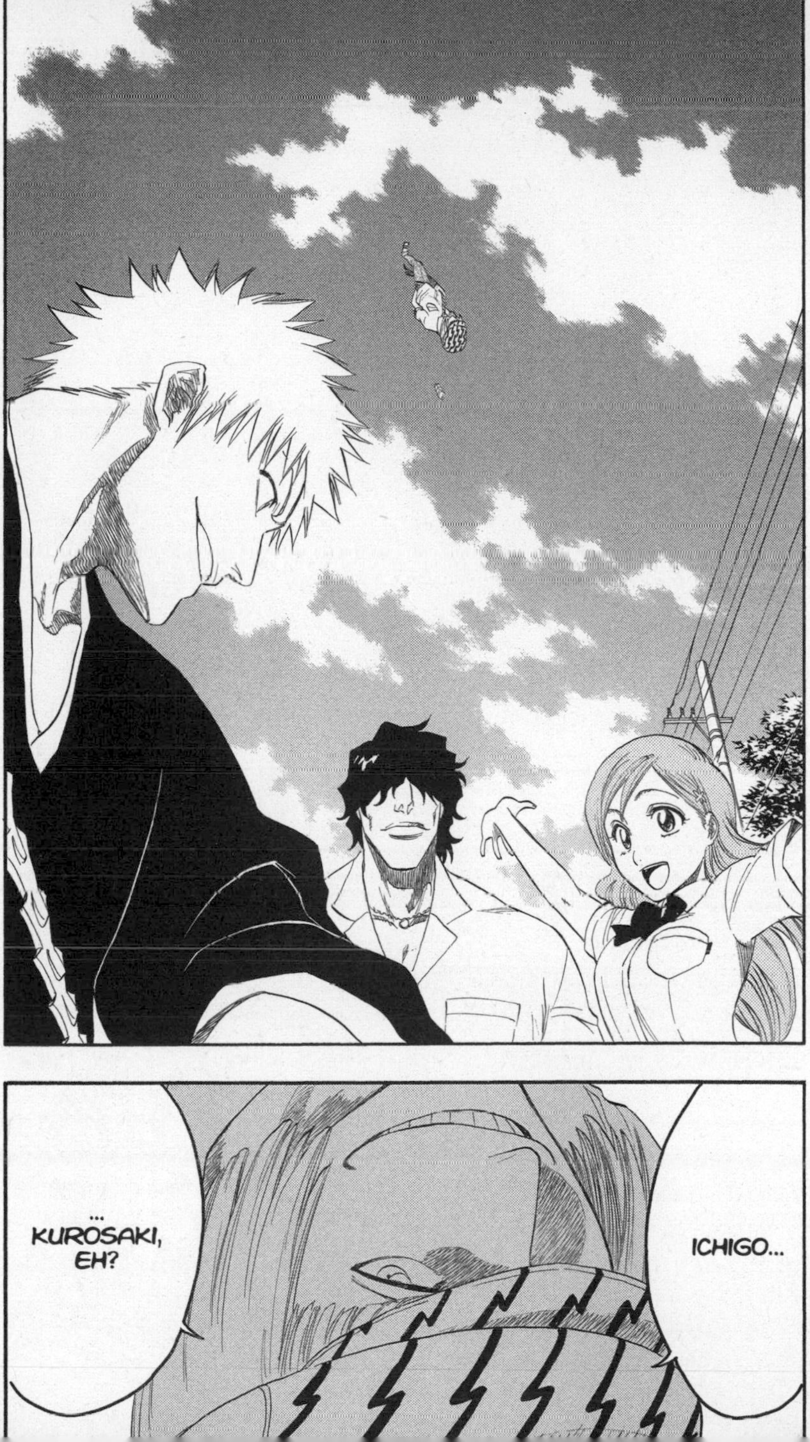
ICHIGO...
... KUROSAKI, EH?

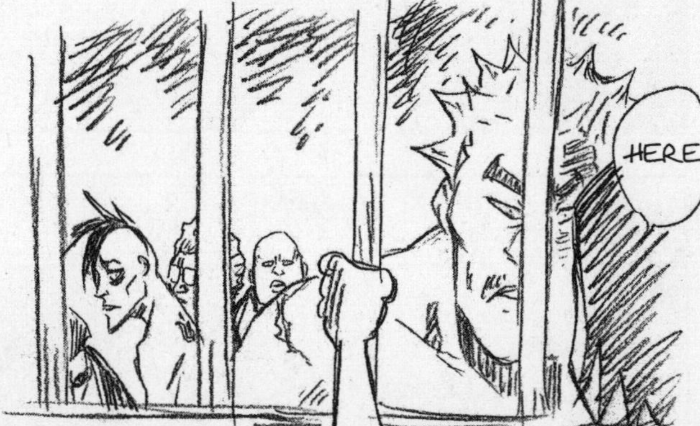
HERE

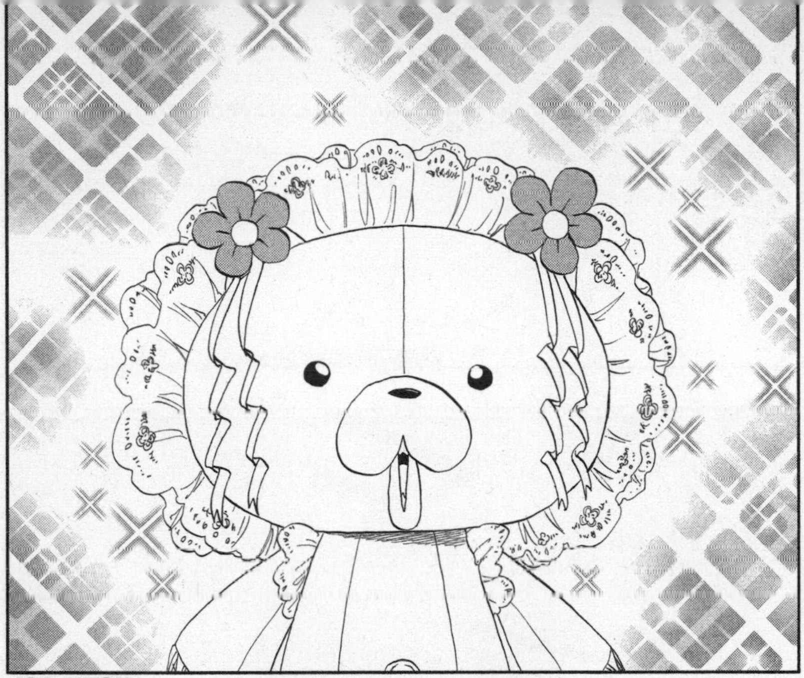

184. HUSH

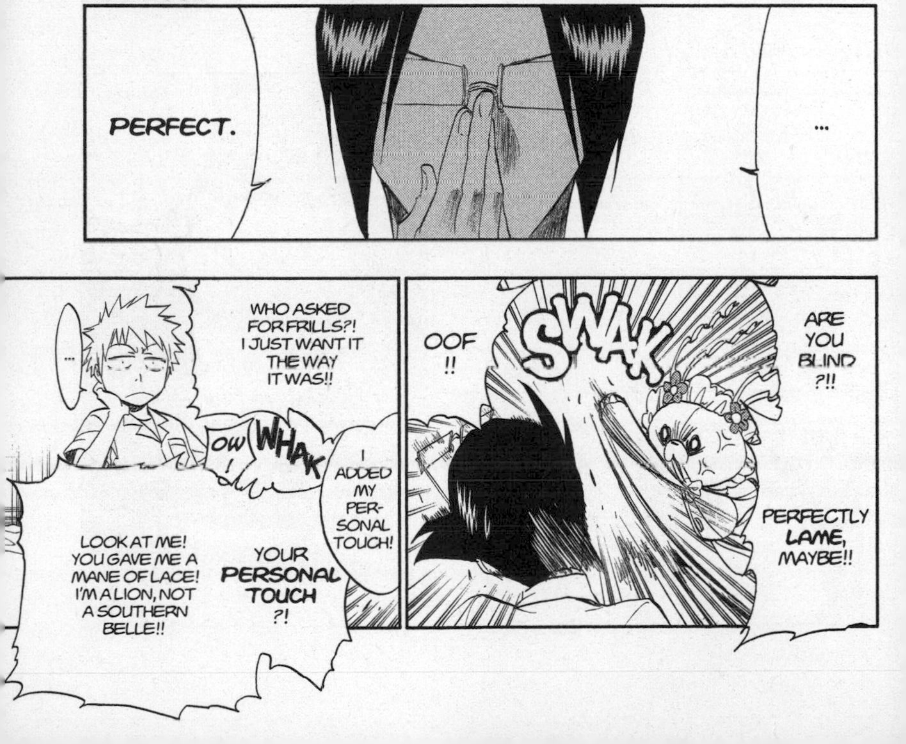
...
PERFECT.
ARE YOU BLIND ?!!
SWAK
OOF !!
PERFECTLY LAME, MAYBE!!
WHO ASKED FOR FRILLS?! I JUST WANT IT THE WAY IT WAS!!
...
I ADDED MY PER-SONAL TOUCH!
WHAK
OW !
YOUR PERSONAL TOUCH ?!
LOOK AT ME! YOU GAVE ME A MANE OF LACE! I'M A LION, NOT A SOUTHERN BELLE!!

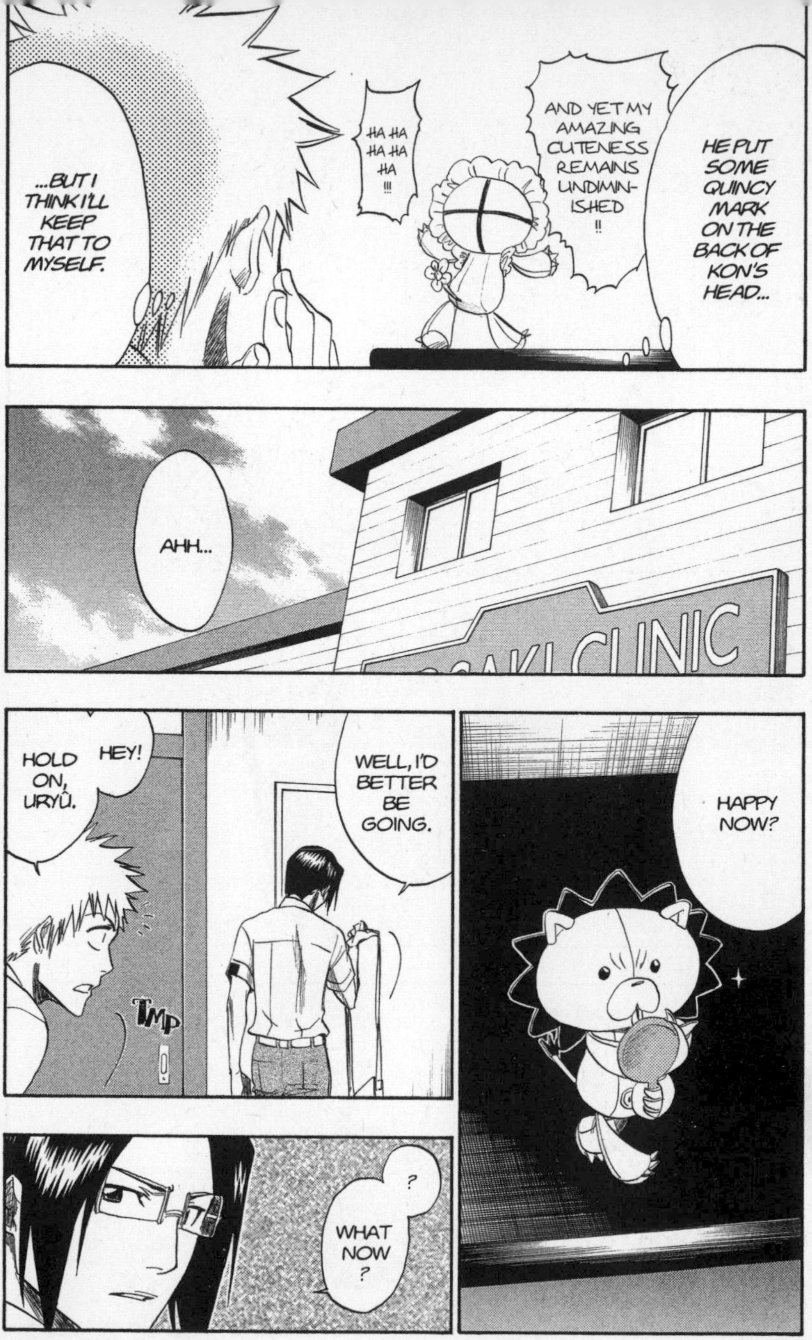
HE PUT SOME QUINCY MARK ON THE BACK OF KON'S HEAD...
AND YET MY AMAZING CUTENESS REMAINS UNDIMIN-ISHED !!
HA HA HA HA HA !!!
...BUT I THINK I'LL KEEP THAT TO MYSELF.
AHH...
HAPPY NOW?
WELL, I'D BETTER BE GOING.
HEY!
HOLD ON, URYŪ.
TMP
?
WHAT NOW ?

READ THIS WAY

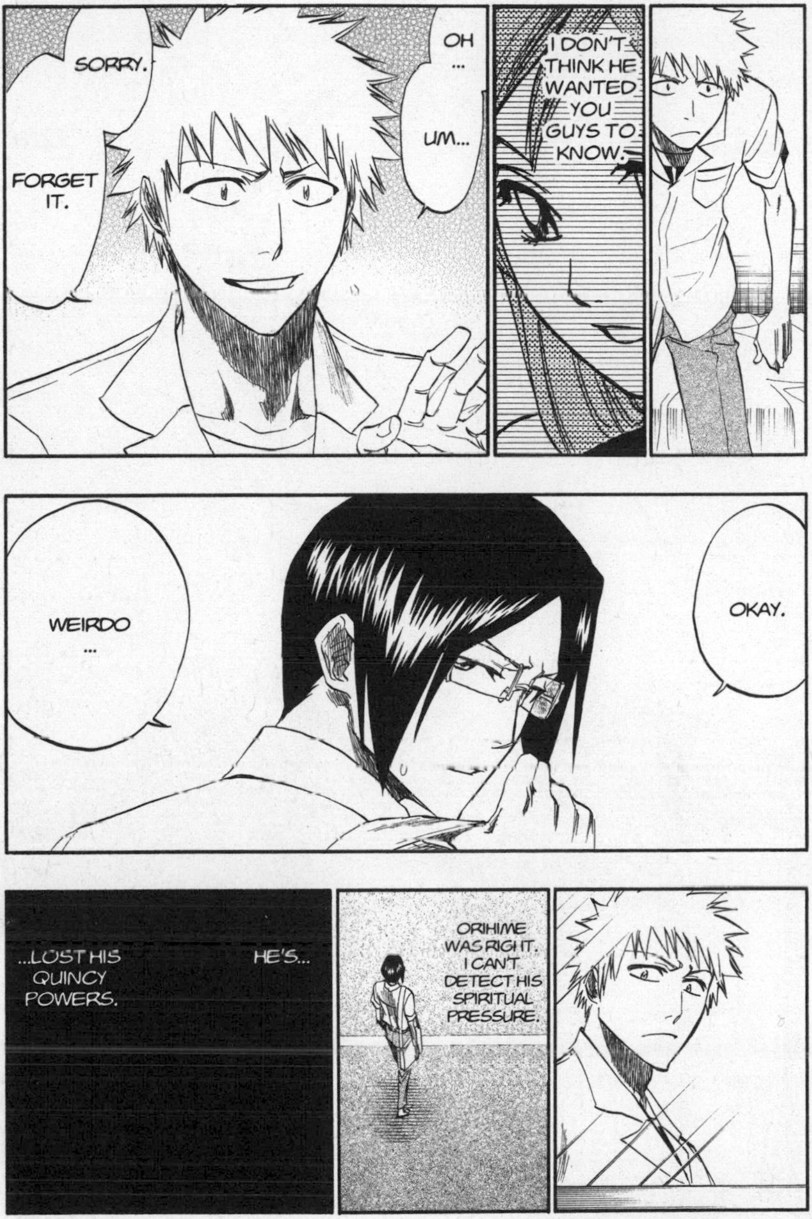
I DON'T THINK HE WANTED YOU GUYS TO KNOW.
OH ...
UM...
SORRY.
FORGET IT.
OKAY.
WEIRDO ...
ORIHIME WAS RIGHT. I CAN'T DETECT HIS SPIRITUAL PRESSURE.
HE'S...
...LOST HIS QUINCY POWERS.

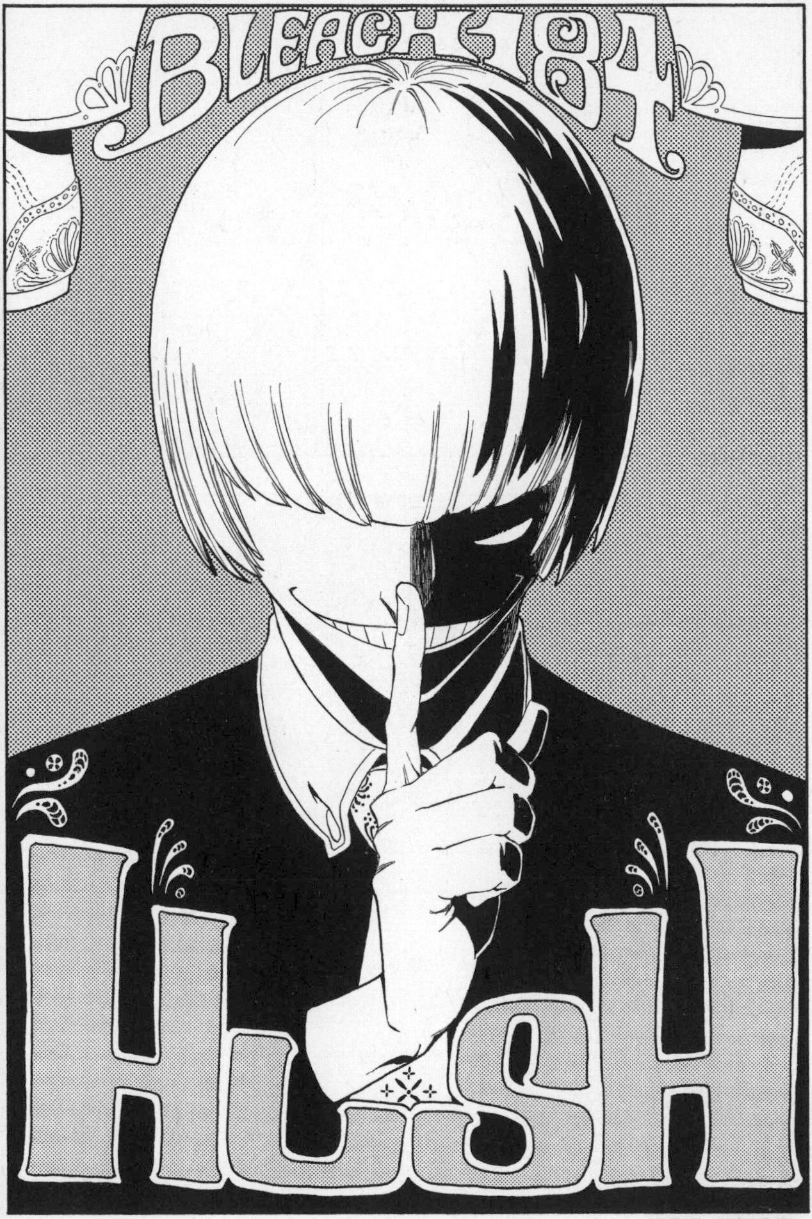
BLEACH 184
HUSH

184. HUSH

READ THIS WAY

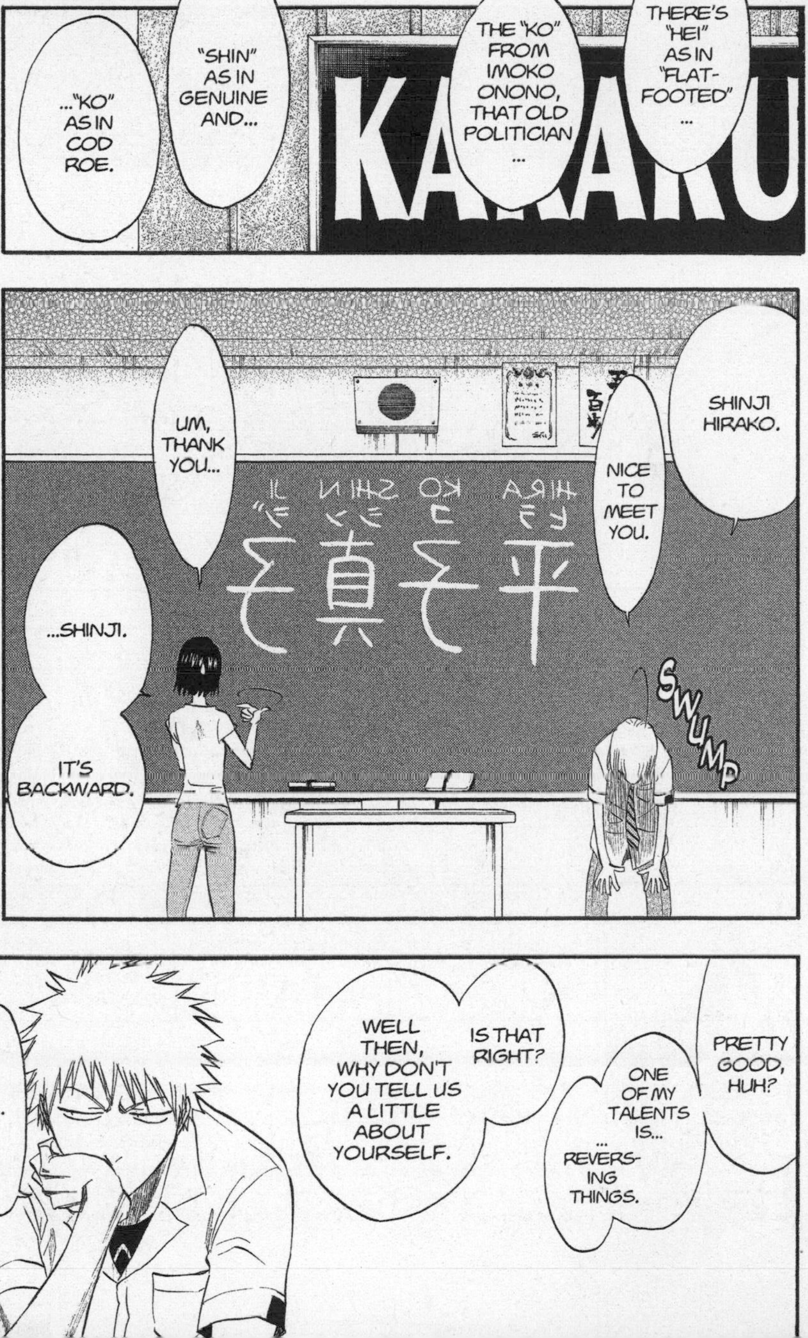
THERE'S "HEI" AS IN "FLAT-FOOTED" ...
THE "KO" FROM IMOKO ONONO, THAT OLD POLITICIAN ...
"SHIN" AS IN GENUINE AND...
..."KO" AS IN COD ROE.
SHINJI HIRAKO.
NICE TO MEET YOU.
SWUMP
UM, THANK YOU...
...SHINJI.
IT'S BACKWARD.
PRETTY GOOD, HUH?
ONE OF MY TALENTS IS... ...REVERSING THINGS.
IS THAT RIGHT?
WELL THEN, WHY DON'T YOU TELL US A LITTLE ABOUT YOURSELF.
...

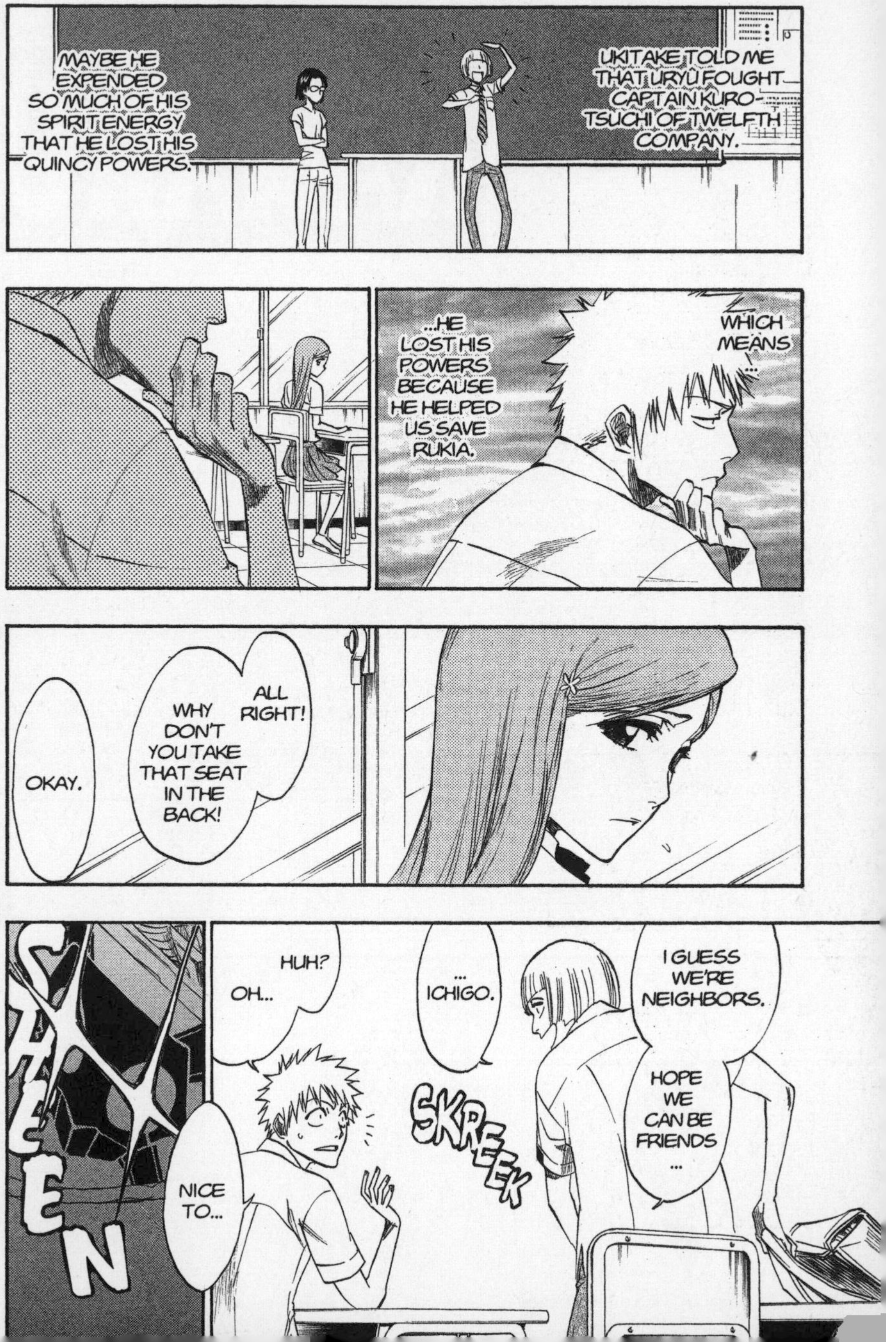
UKITAKE TOLD ME THAT URYŪ FOUGHT CAPTAIN KURO-TSUCHI OF TWELFTH COMPANY.
MAYBE HE EXPENDED SO MUCH OF HIS SPIRIT ENERGY THAT HE LOST HIS QUINCY POWERS.
WHICH MEANS...
...HE LOST HIS POWERS BECAUSE HE HELPED US SAVE RUKIA.
ALL RIGHT!
WHY DON'T YOU TAKE THAT SEAT IN THE BACK!
OKAY.
I GUESS WE'RE NEIGHBORS.
HOPE WE CAN BE FRIENDS...
SKREEEK
...ICHIGO.
HUH? OH...
NICE TO...
SHEEEN

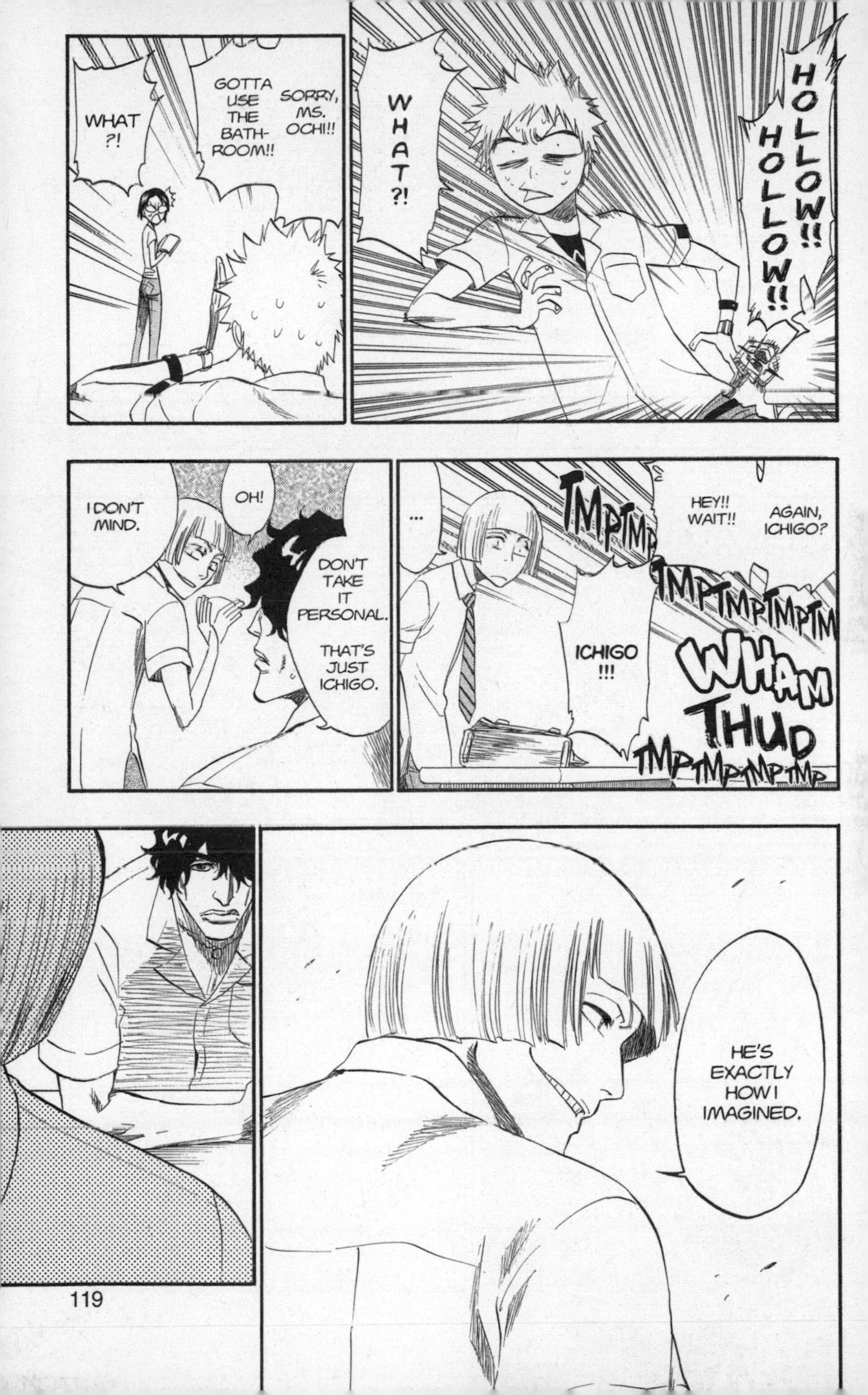
HOLLOW!! HOLLOW!!
WHAT?!
SORRY, MS. OCHI!!
GOTTA USE THE BATH-ROOM!!
WHAT?!
AGAIN, ICHIGO?
HEY!! WAIT!!
TMPTMP
TMPTMPTMPTMPTM
ICHIGO!!!
WHAM
THUD
TMPTMPTMPTMP
...
DON'T TAKE IT PERSONAL.
THAT'S JUST ICHIGO.
OH!
I DON'T MIND.
HE'S EXACTLY HOW I IMAGINED.

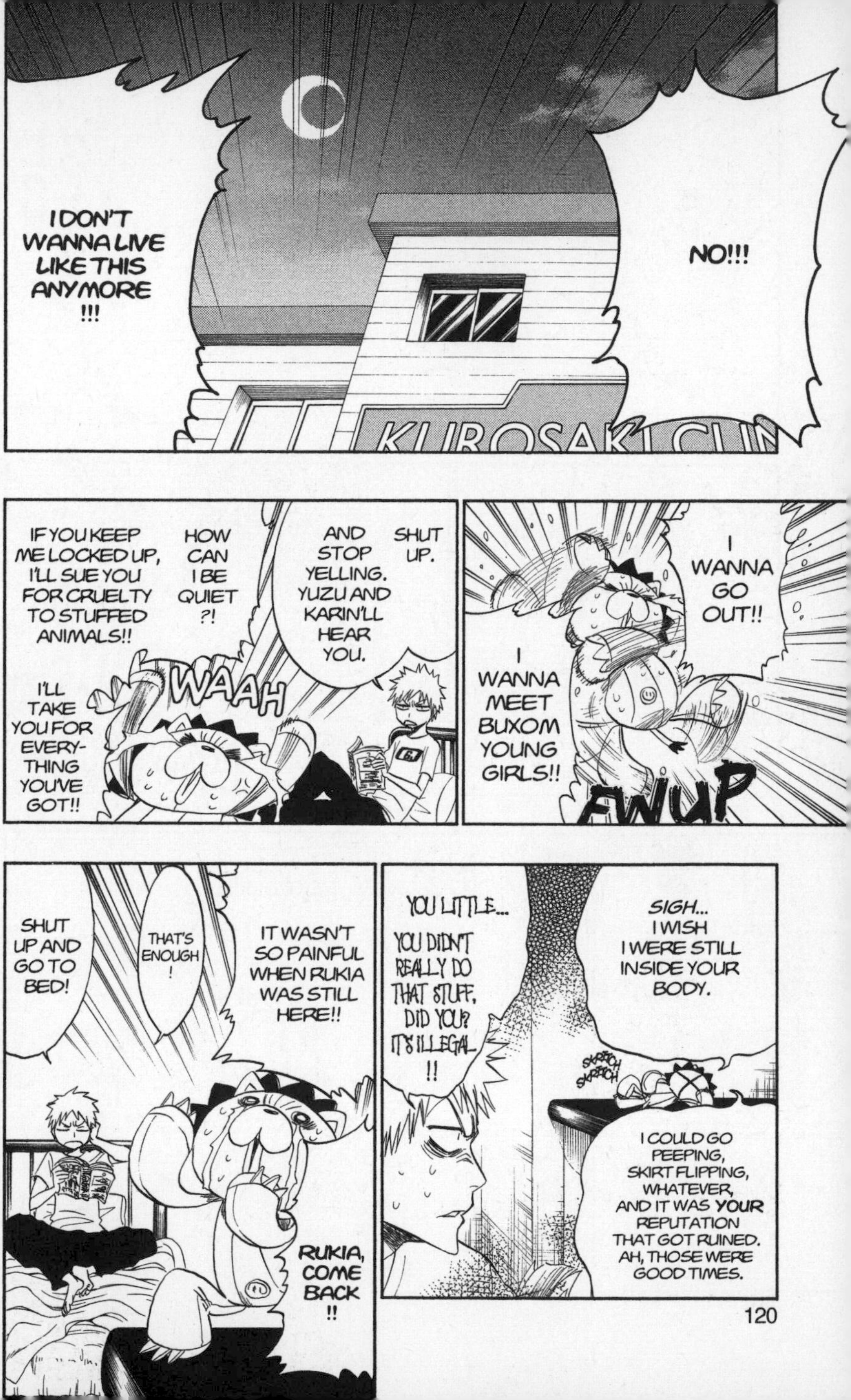
NO!!!
I DON'T WANNA LIVE LIKE THIS ANYMORE!!!
KUROSAKI CLIN
I WANNA GO OUT!!
I WANNA MEET BUXOM YOUNG GIRLS!!
FWUP
SHUT UP.
AND STOP YELLING. YUZU AND KARIN'LL HEAR YOU.
HOW CAN I BE QUIET?!
IF YOU KEEP ME LOCKED UP, I'LL SUE YOU FOR CRUELTY TO STUFFED ANIMALS!!
WAAAH
I'LL TAKE YOU FOR EVERYTHING YOU'VE GOT!!
SIGH... I WISH I WERE STILL INSIDE YOUR BODY.
YOU LITTLE...
YOU DIDN'T REALLY DO THAT STUFF, DID YOU? IT'S ILLEGAL!!
SKRITCH SKRITCH
I COULD GO PEEPING, SKIRT FLIPPING, WHATEVER, AND IT WAS **YOUR** REPUTATION THAT GOT RUINED. AH, THOSE WERE GOOD TIMES.
IT WASN'T SO PAINFUL WHEN RUKIA WAS STILL HERE!!
THAT'S ENOUGH!
SHUT UP AND GO TO BED!
RUKIA, COME BACK!!

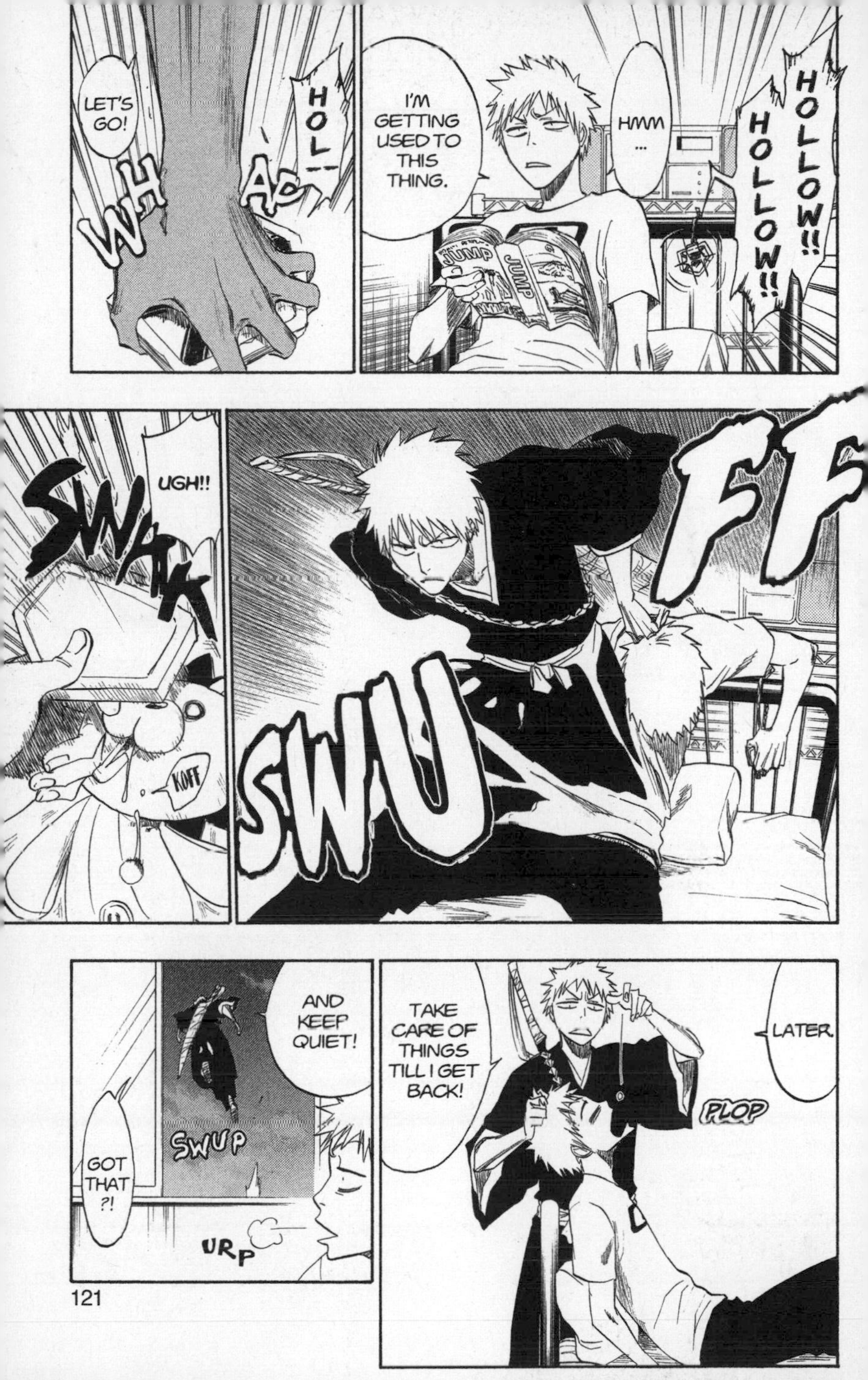

HOLLOW!!
HOLLOW!!
HMM...
I'M GETTING USED TO THIS THING.
HOL--
WHAD
LET'S GO!
FF
SWU
UGH!!
SWAK
KOFF
LATER.
PLOP
TAKE CARE OF THINGS TILL I GET BACK!
AND KEEP QUIET!
SWUP
GOT THAT?!
URP

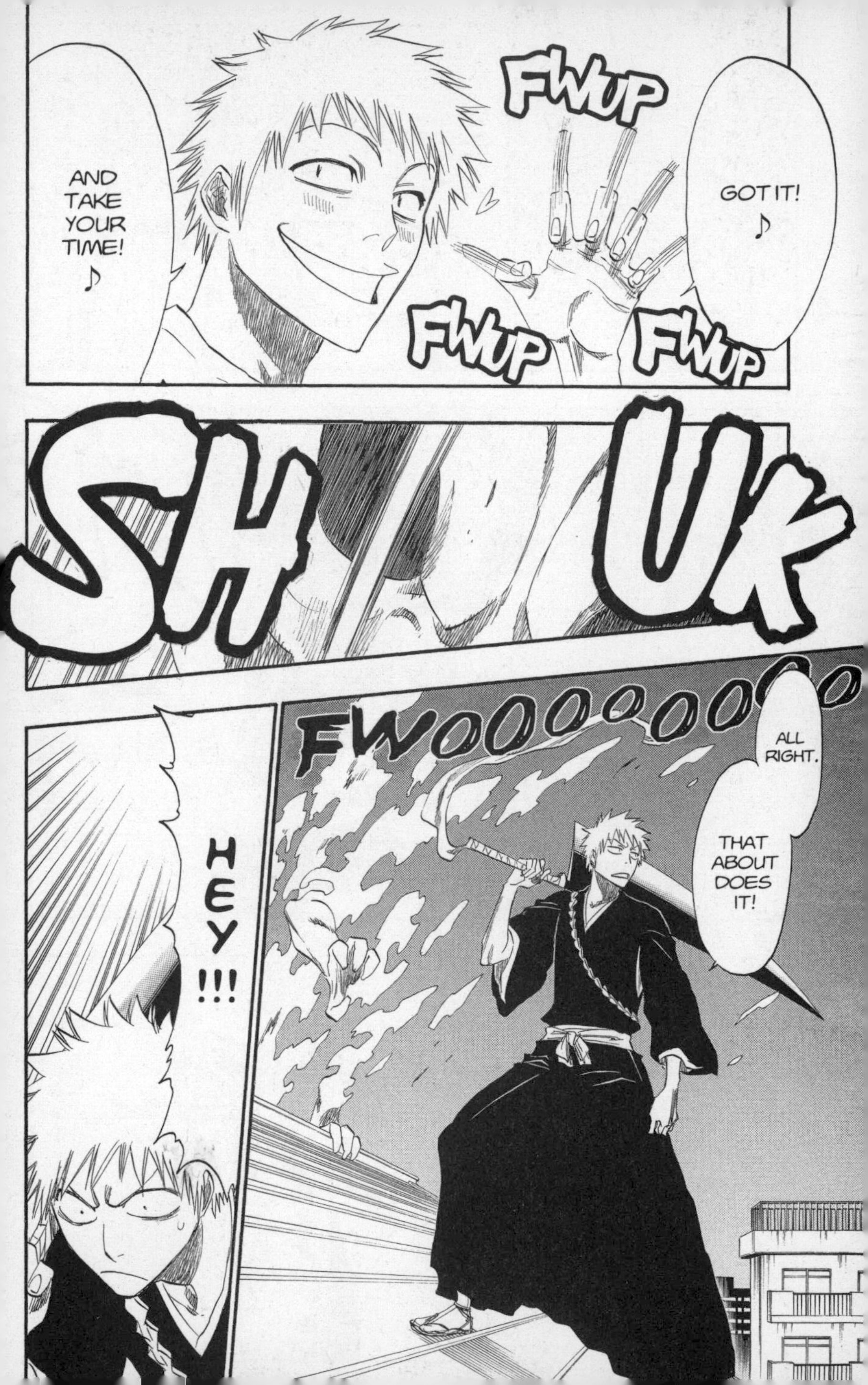
FWUP
GOT IT! ♪
FWUP FWUP
AND TAKE YOUR TIME! ♪
SHUNK
FWOOOOOOOOO
ALL RIGHT.
THAT ABOUT DOES IT!
HEY!!!

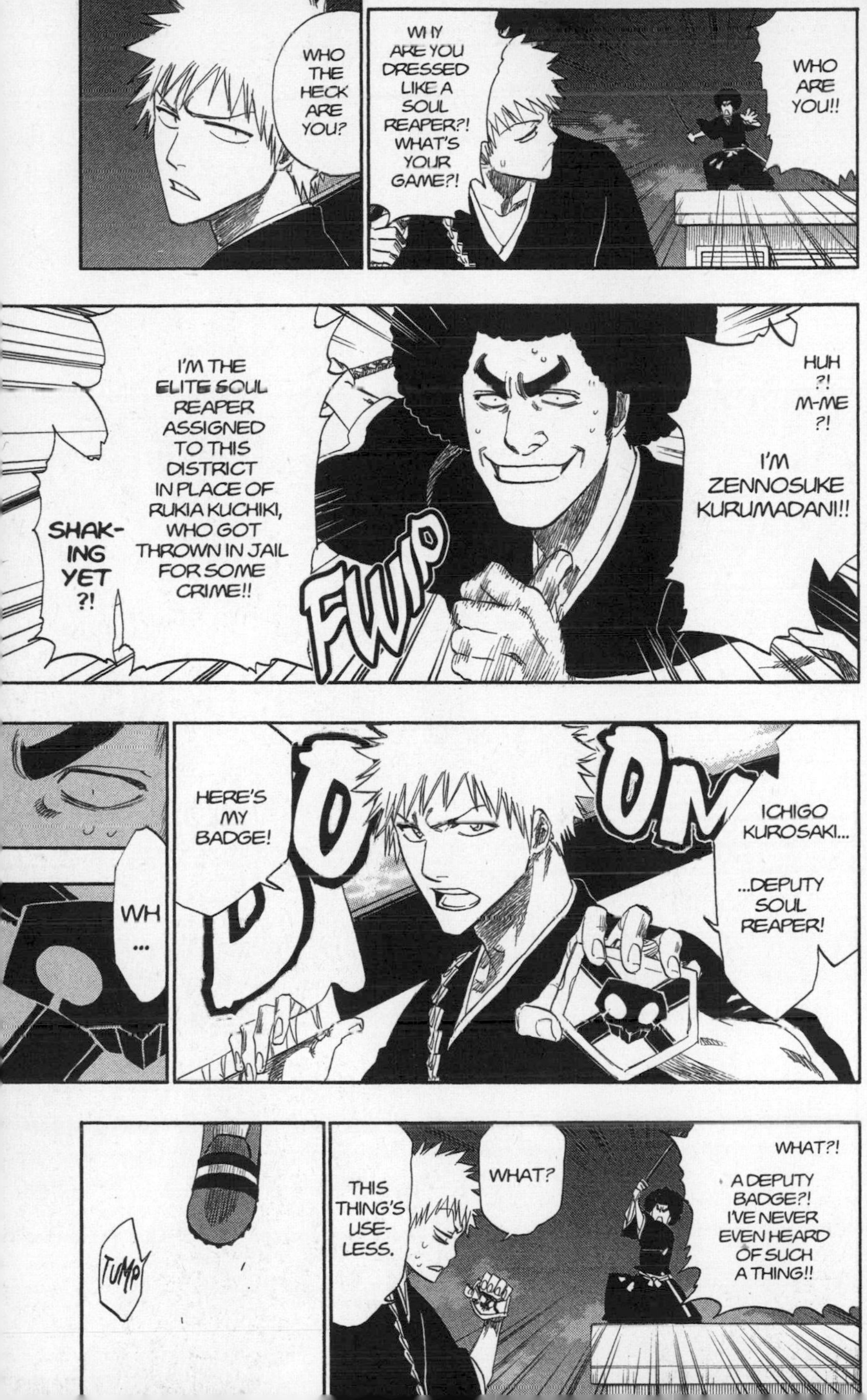

WHO ARE YOU!!
WHY ARE YOU DRESSED LIKE A SOUL REAPER?! WHAT'S YOUR GAME?!
WHO THE HECK ARE YOU?
HUH?! M-ME?!
I'M ZENNOSUKE KURUMADANI!!
FWIP
I'M THE ELITE SOUL REAPER ASSIGNED TO THIS DISTRICT IN PLACE OF RUKIA KUCHIKI, WHO GOT THROWN IN JAIL FOR SOME CRIME!!
SHAK-ING YET?!
ICHIGO KUROSAKI...
...DEPUTY SOUL REAPER!
DOOM
HERE'S MY BADGE!
WH...
WHAT?!
A DEPUTY BADGE?! I'VE NEVER EVEN HEARD OF SUCH A THING!!
WHAT?
THIS THING'S USE-LESS.
TUMP

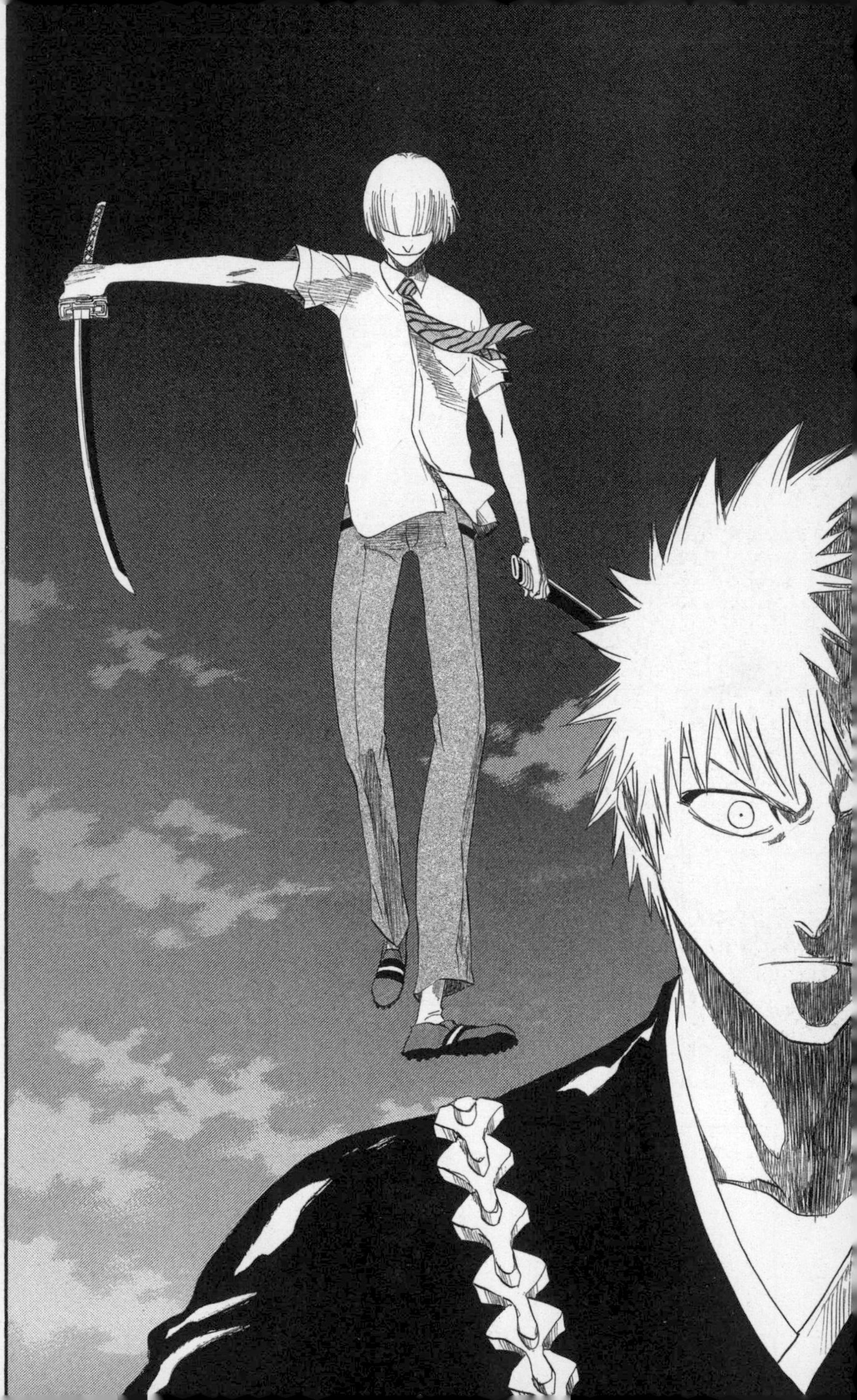

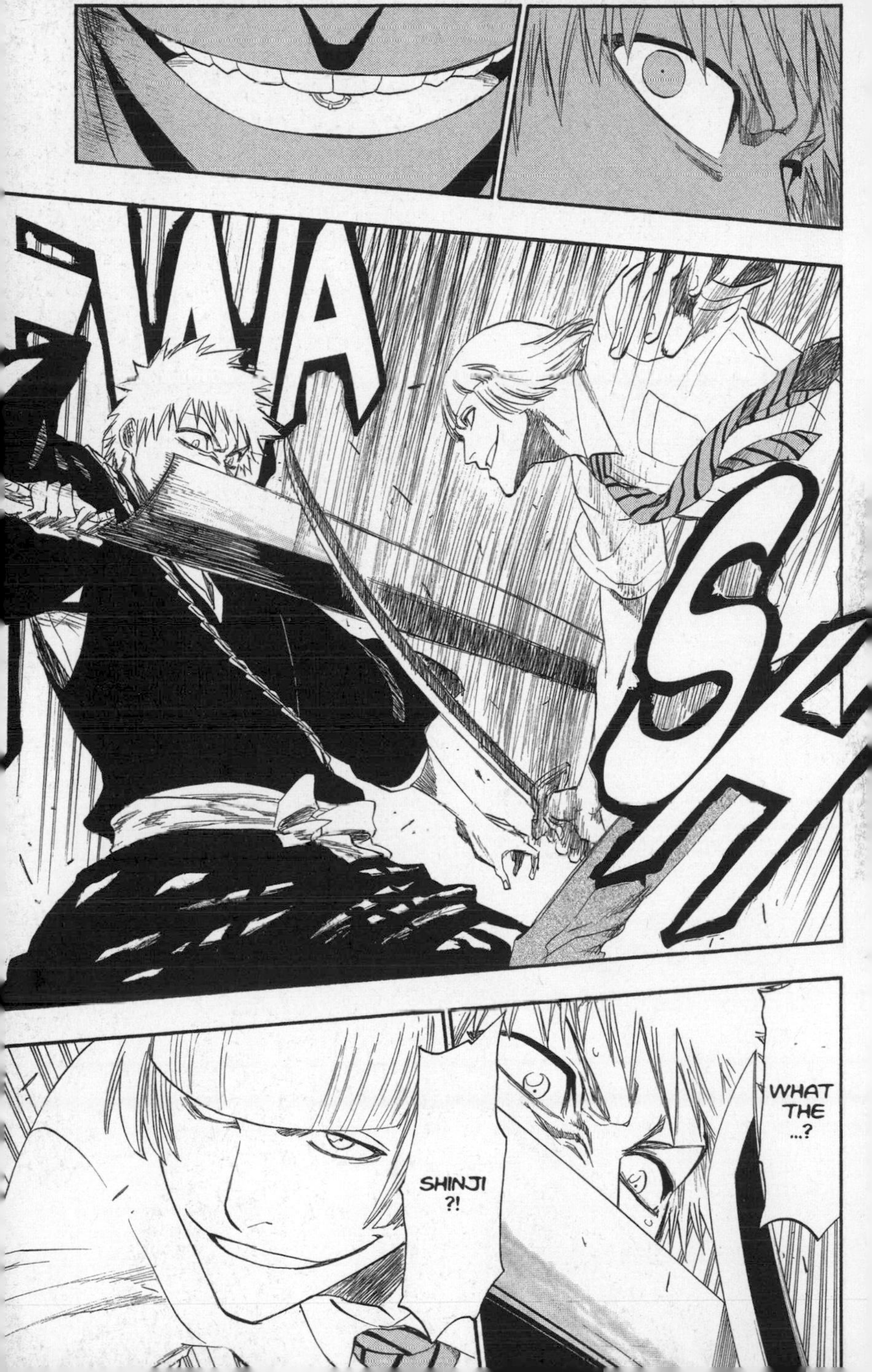
WA
SH
WHAT THE ...?
SHINJI ?!

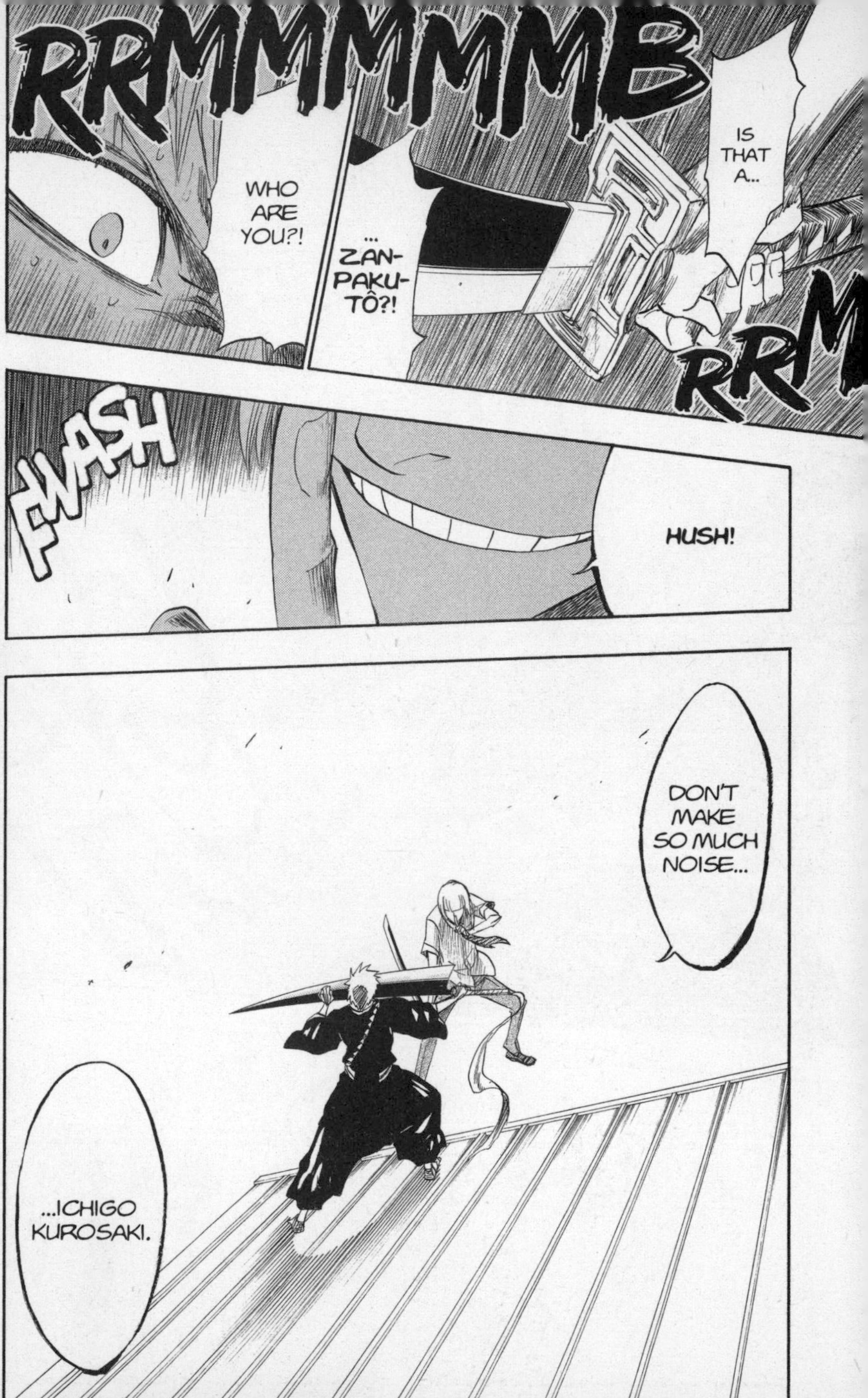
RRMMMMMB
IS THAT A...
...ZANPAKUTÔ?!
RRM
WHO ARE YOU?!
FWASH
HUSH!
DON'T MAKE SO MUCH NOISE...
...ICHIGO KUROSAKI.

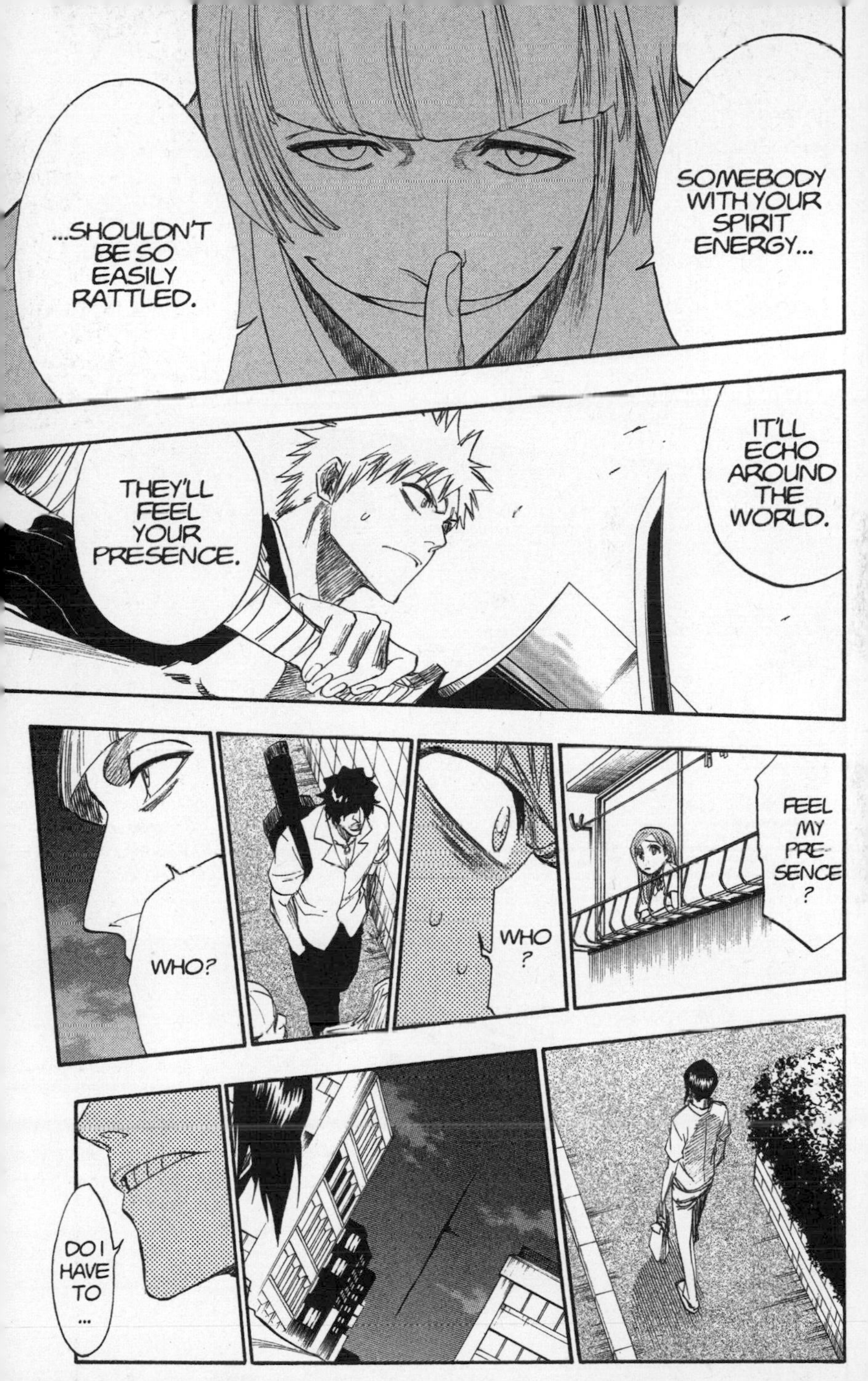
SOMEBODY WITH YOUR SPIRIT ENERGY...
...SHOULDN'T BE SO EASILY RATTLED.
IT'LL ECHO AROUND THE WORLD.
THEY'LL FEEL YOUR PRESENCE.
FEEL MY PRE-SENCE?
WHO?
WHO?
DO I HAVE TO ...

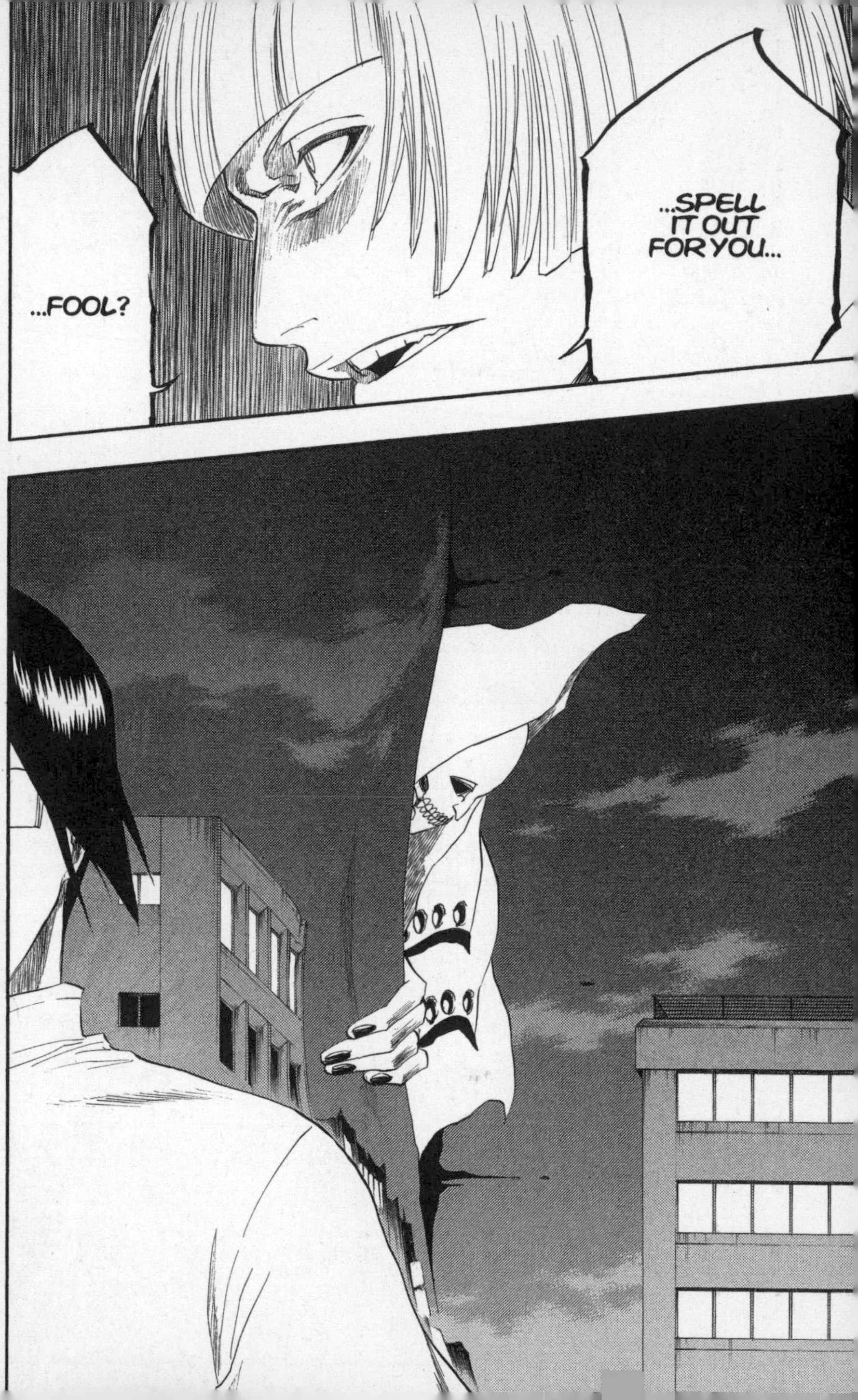
...SPELL IT OUT FOR YOU...
...FOOL?

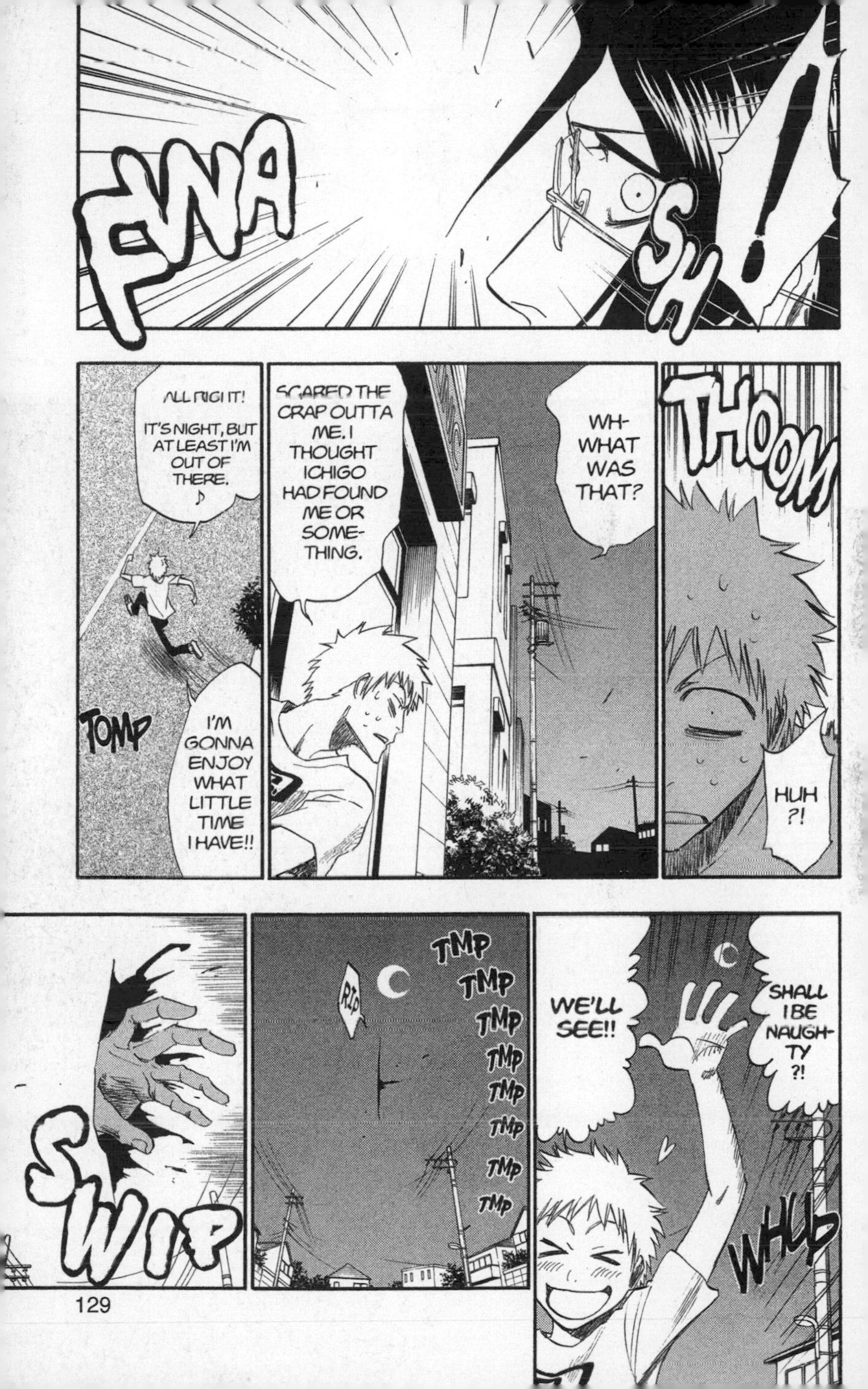
FWA
SH!
THOOM
HUH ?!
WH-WHAT WAS THAT?
SCARED THE CRAP OUTTA ME. I THOUGHT ICHIGO HAD FOUND ME OR SOMETHING.
ALL RIGHT!
IT'S NIGHT, BUT AT LEAST I'M OUT OF THERE. ♪
TOMP
I'M GONNA ENJOY WHAT LITTLE TIME I HAVE!!
SHALL I BE NAUGHTY ?!
WE'LL SEE!!
WHUD
TMP TMP TMP TMP TMP TMP TMP TMP
RIP
SWIP

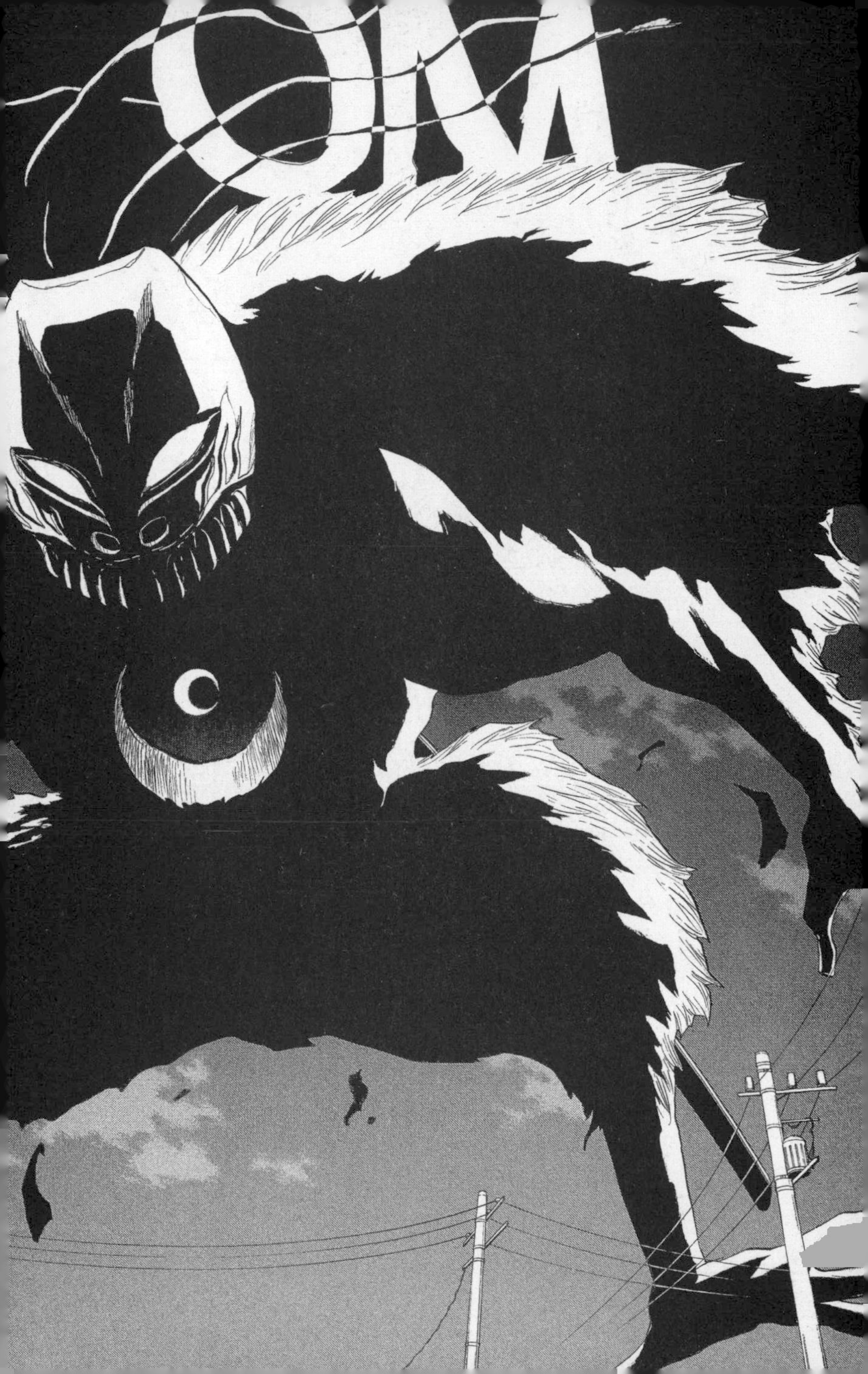
OM

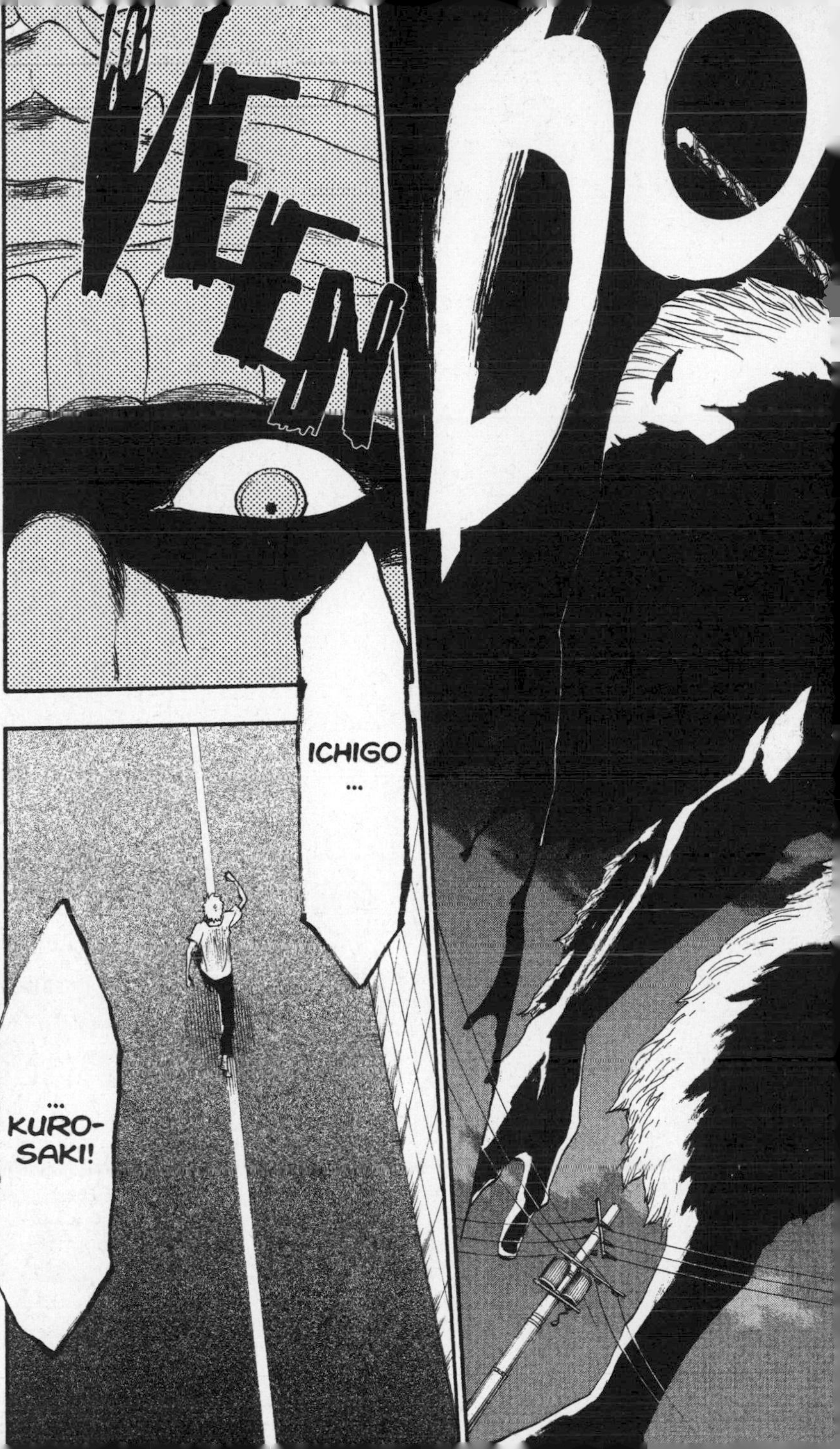
DO
ICHIGO ...
... KURO-SAKI!

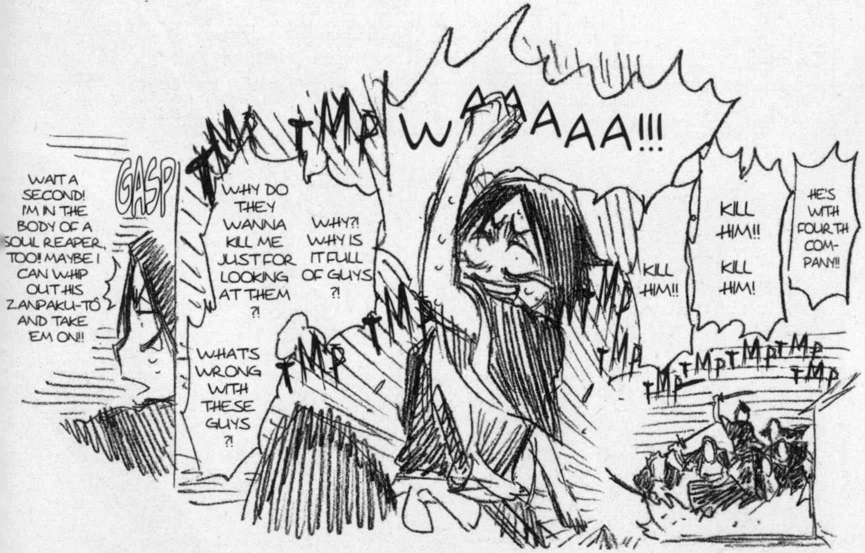
HE'S WITH FOURTH COMPANY!!
KILL HIM!! KILL HIM!
KILL HIM!!
TMP TMP TMP TMP TMP TMP
WAAAAAA!!!
WHY?! WHY IS IT FULL OF GUYS ?!
WHY DO THEY WANNA KILL ME JUST FOR LOOKING AT THEM ?!
TMP TMP TMP TMP
WHATS WRONG WITH THESE GUYS ?!
GASP
WAIT A SECOND! I'M IN THE BODY OF A SOUL REAPER, TOO! MAYBE I CAN WHIP OUT HIS ZANPAKU-TÔ AND TAKE EM ON!!

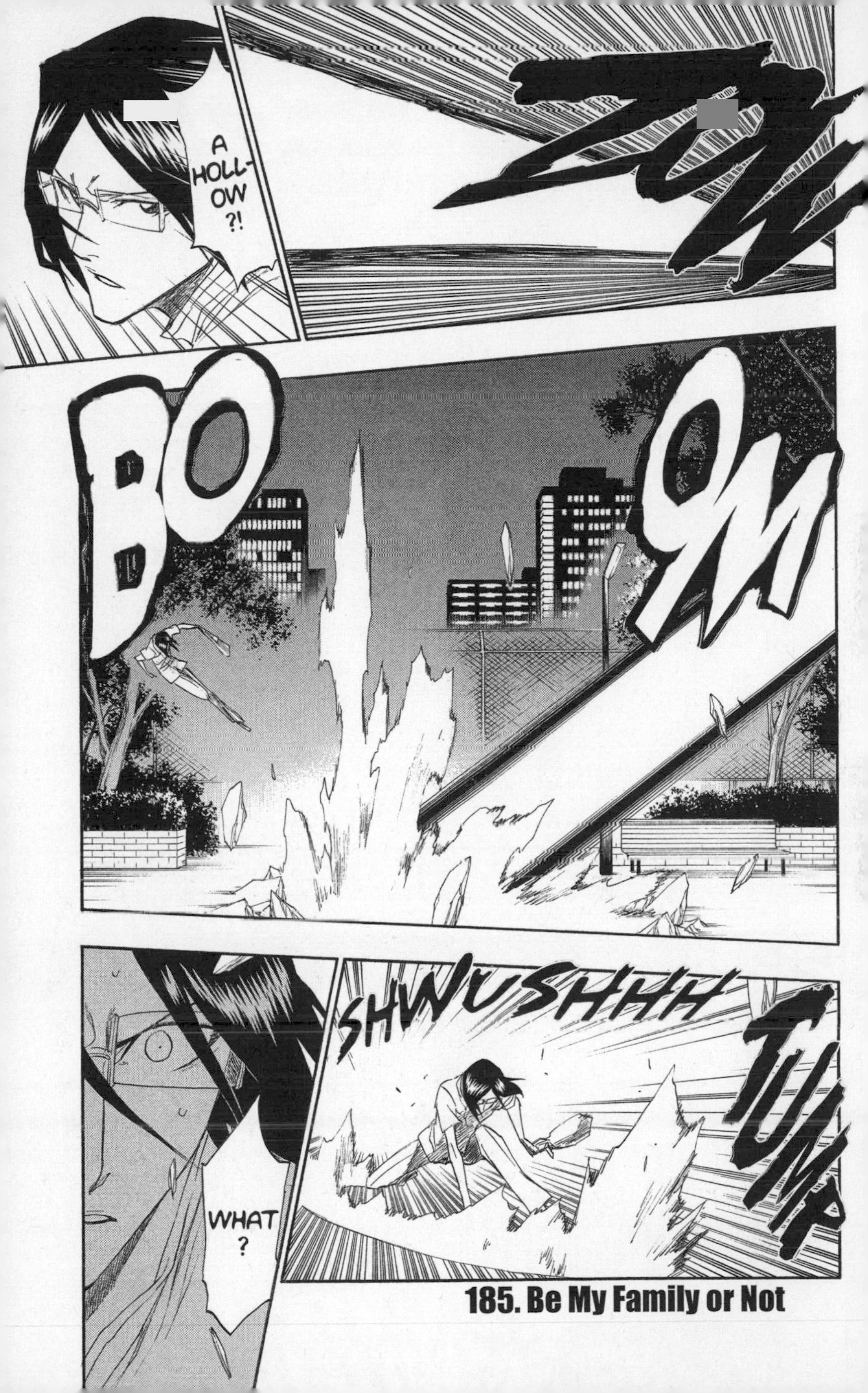
ZOW
A HOLLOW?!
BOOM
SHWUSHHH
TUMP
WHAT?

185. Be My Family or Not

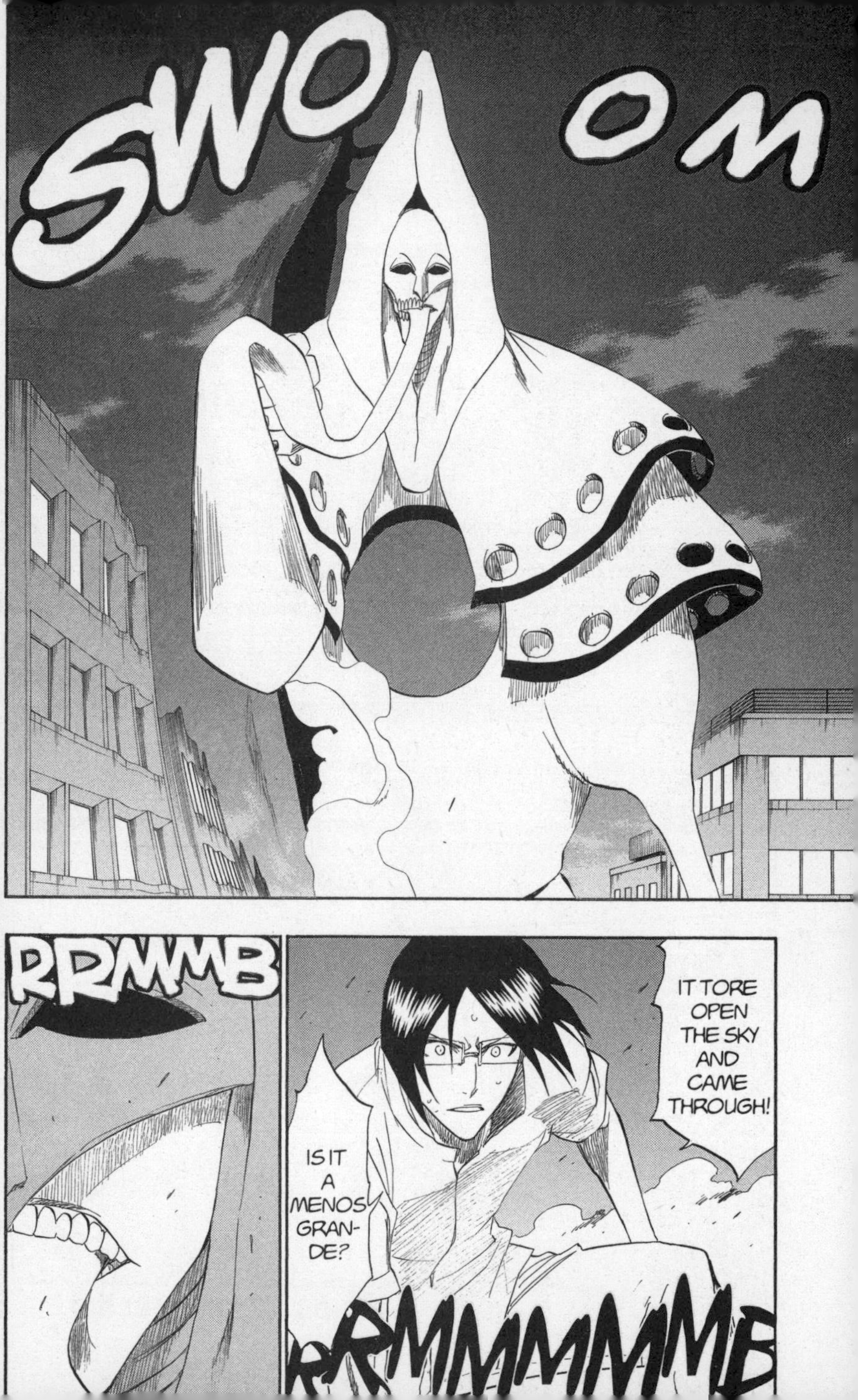
SWOOM
IT TORE OPEN THE SKY AND CAME THROUGH!
IS IT A MENOS GRANDE?
RRMMMMMM
RRMMB

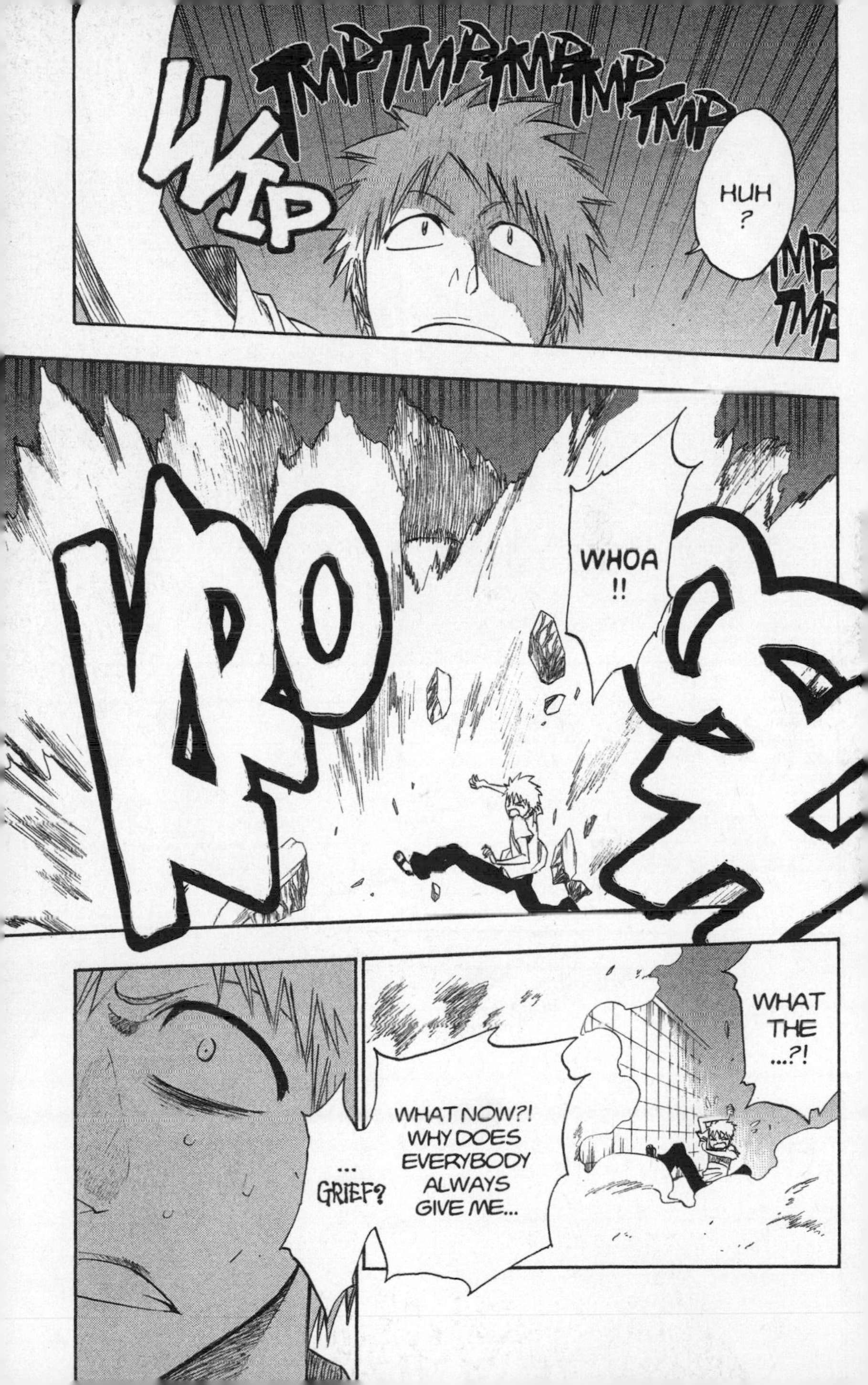
HUH ?
TMPTMPTMPTMPTMP TMP
WIP
WHOA !!
WHAT THE ...?!
WHAT NOW?! WHY DOES EVERYBODY ALWAYS GIVE ME...
... GRIEF?

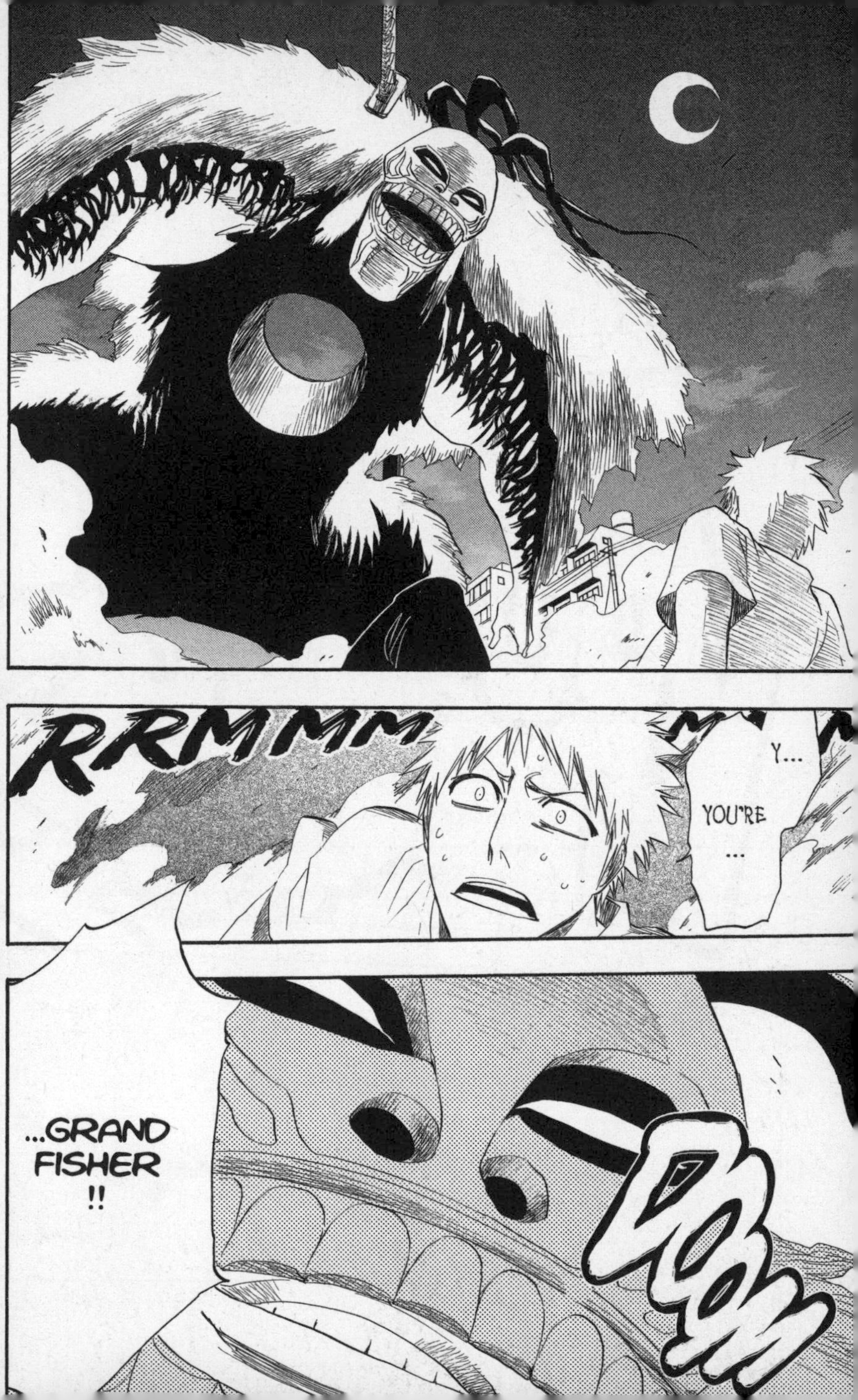
RRMMMM
Y...
YOU'RE
...
...GRAND FISHER !!
DOOM

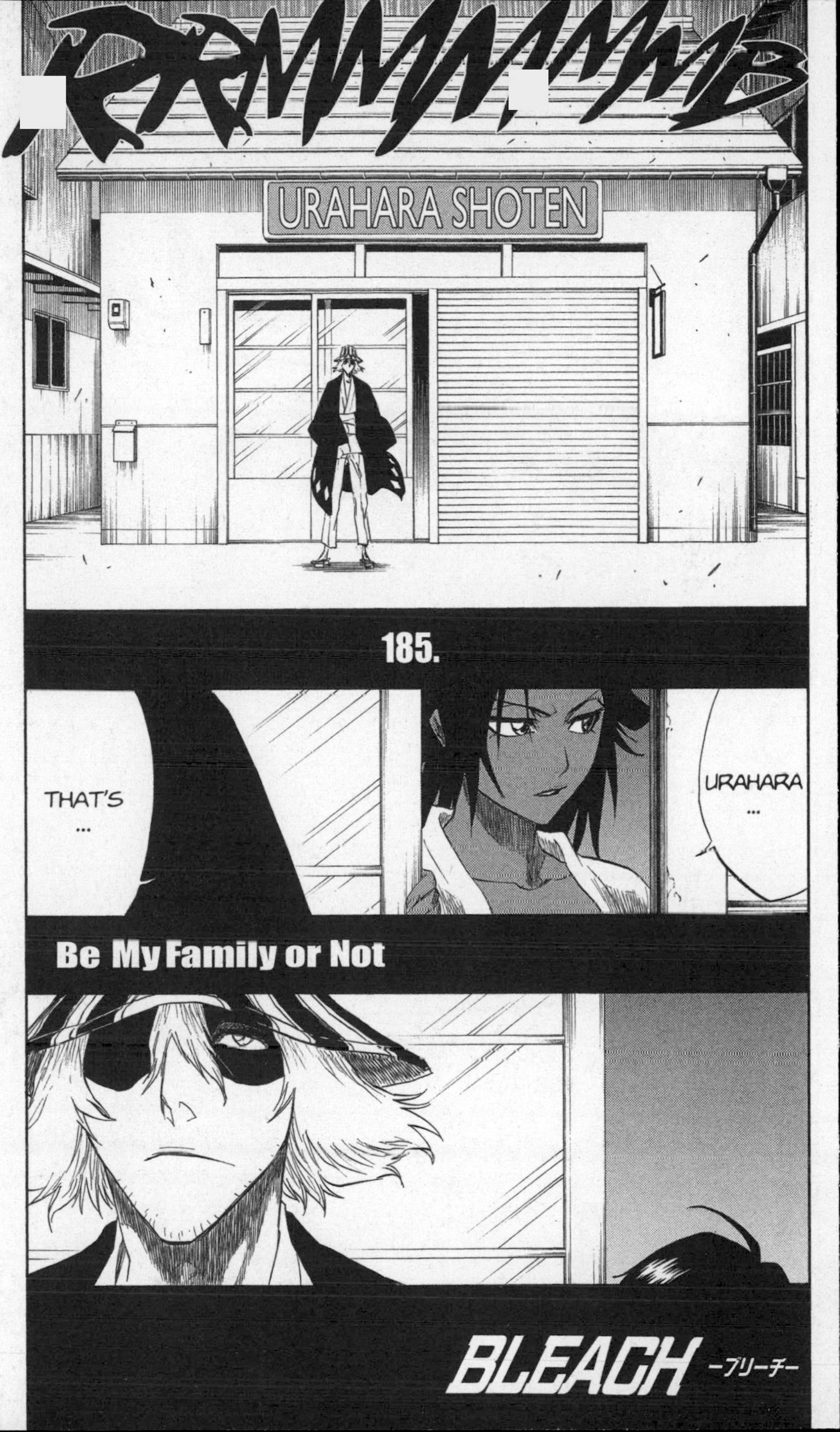
URAHARA SHOTEN
185.
URAHARA ...
THAT'S ...
Be My Family or Not
BLEACH
-ブリーチ-

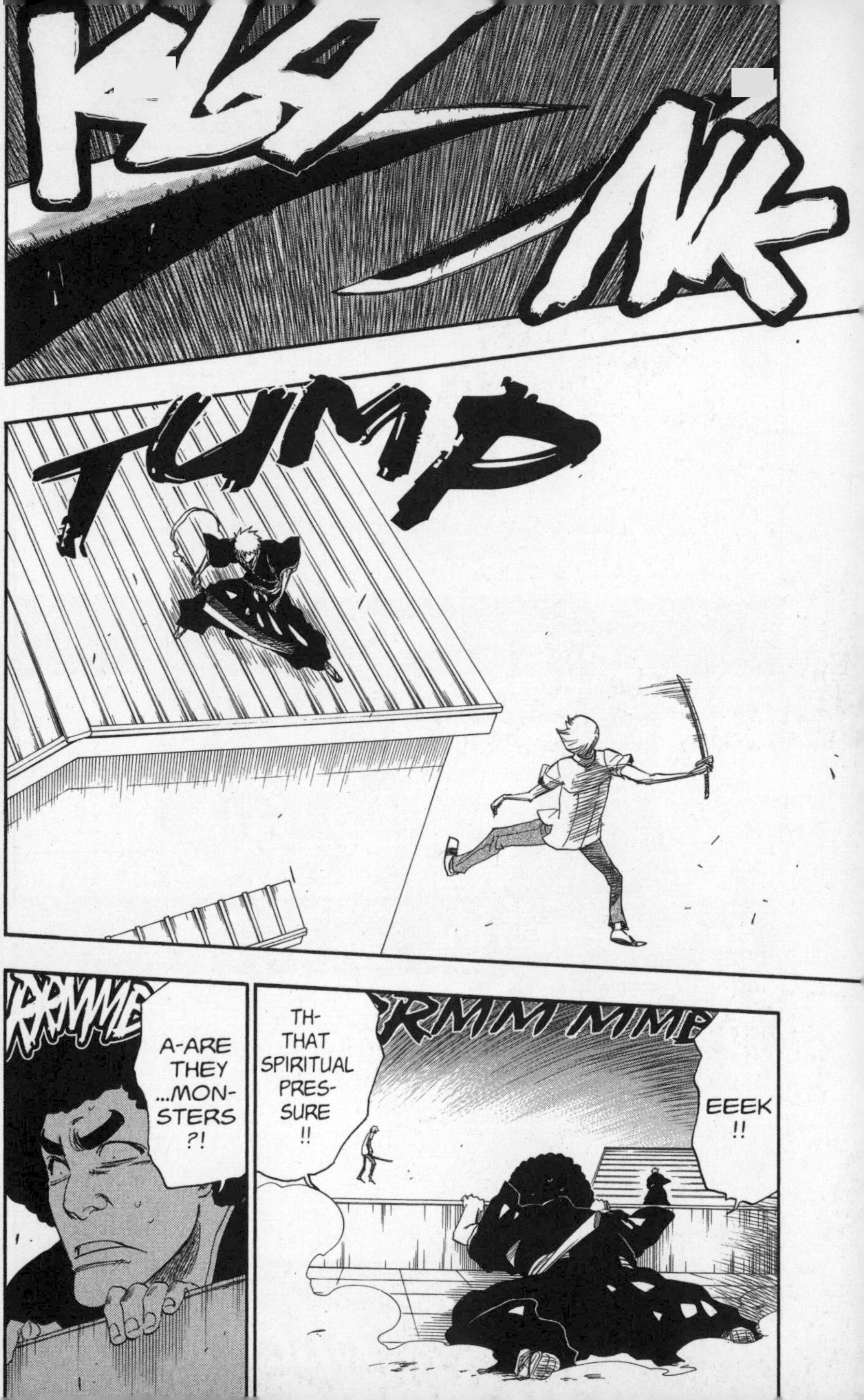
TUMP
EEEK !!
TH- THAT SPIRITUAL PRES-SURE !!
A-ARE THEY ...MON-STERS ?!

READ THIS WAY

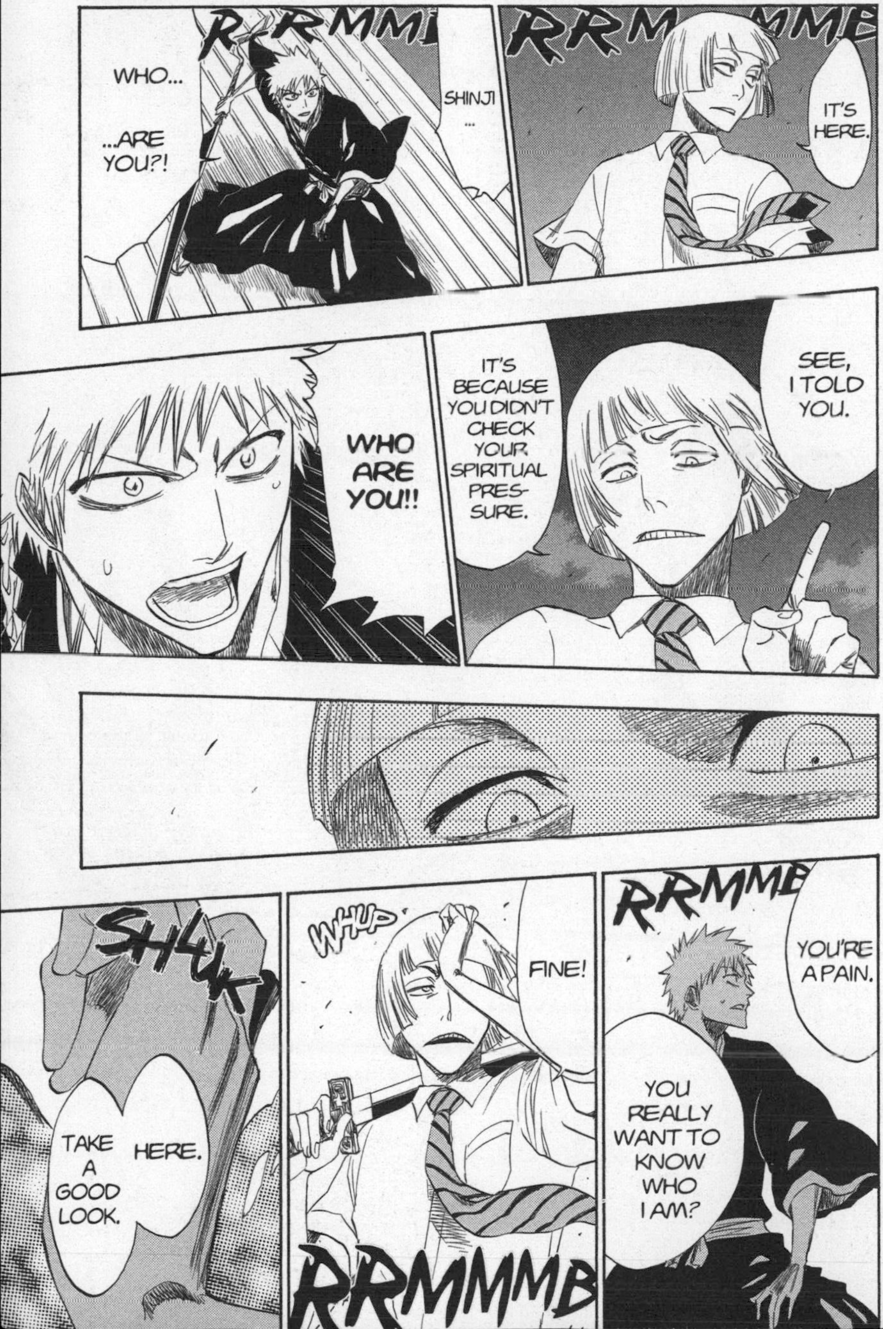
RRM MMB
IT'S HERE.
R-RMMM
SHINJI ...
WHO...
...ARE YOU?!
SEE, I TOLD YOU.
IT'S BECAUSE YOU DIDN'T CHECK YOUR SPIRITUAL PRES-SURE.
WHO ARE YOU!!
RRMMB
YOU'RE A PAIN.
YOU REALLY WANT TO KNOW WHO I AM?
WHUP
FINE!
RRMMMB
SHLUK
HERE.
TAKE A GOOD LOOK.

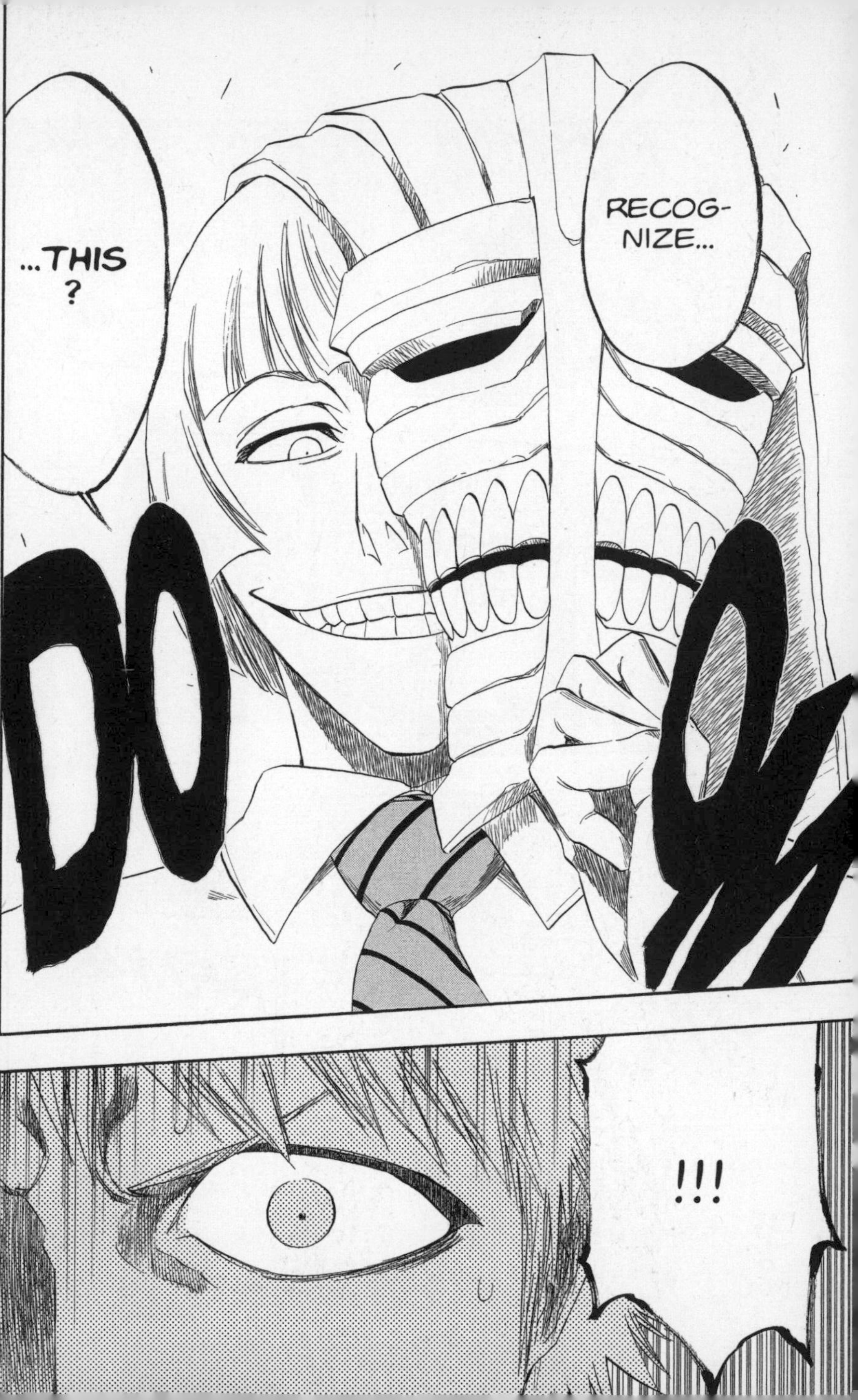
RECOG-
NIZE...
...THIS
?
DOOM
!!!

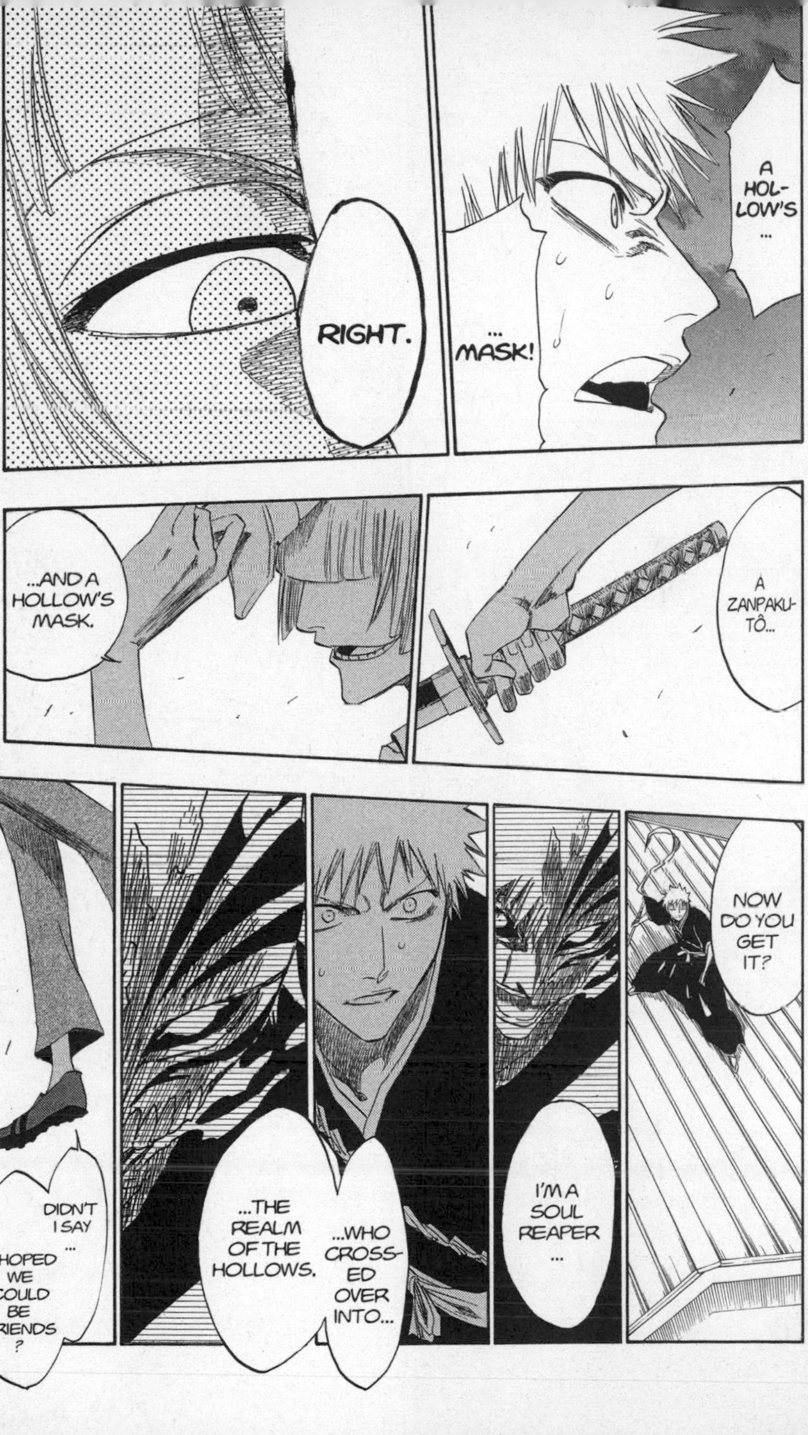
A HOL-LOW'S ...
... MASK!
RIGHT.
A ZANPAKU-TÔ...
...AND A HOLLOW'S MASK.
NOW DO YOU GET IT?
I'M A SOUL REAPER ...
...WHO CROSS-ED OVER INTO...
...THE REALM OF THE HOLLOWS.
DIDN'T I SAY ...
...I HOPED WE COULD BE FRIENDS?

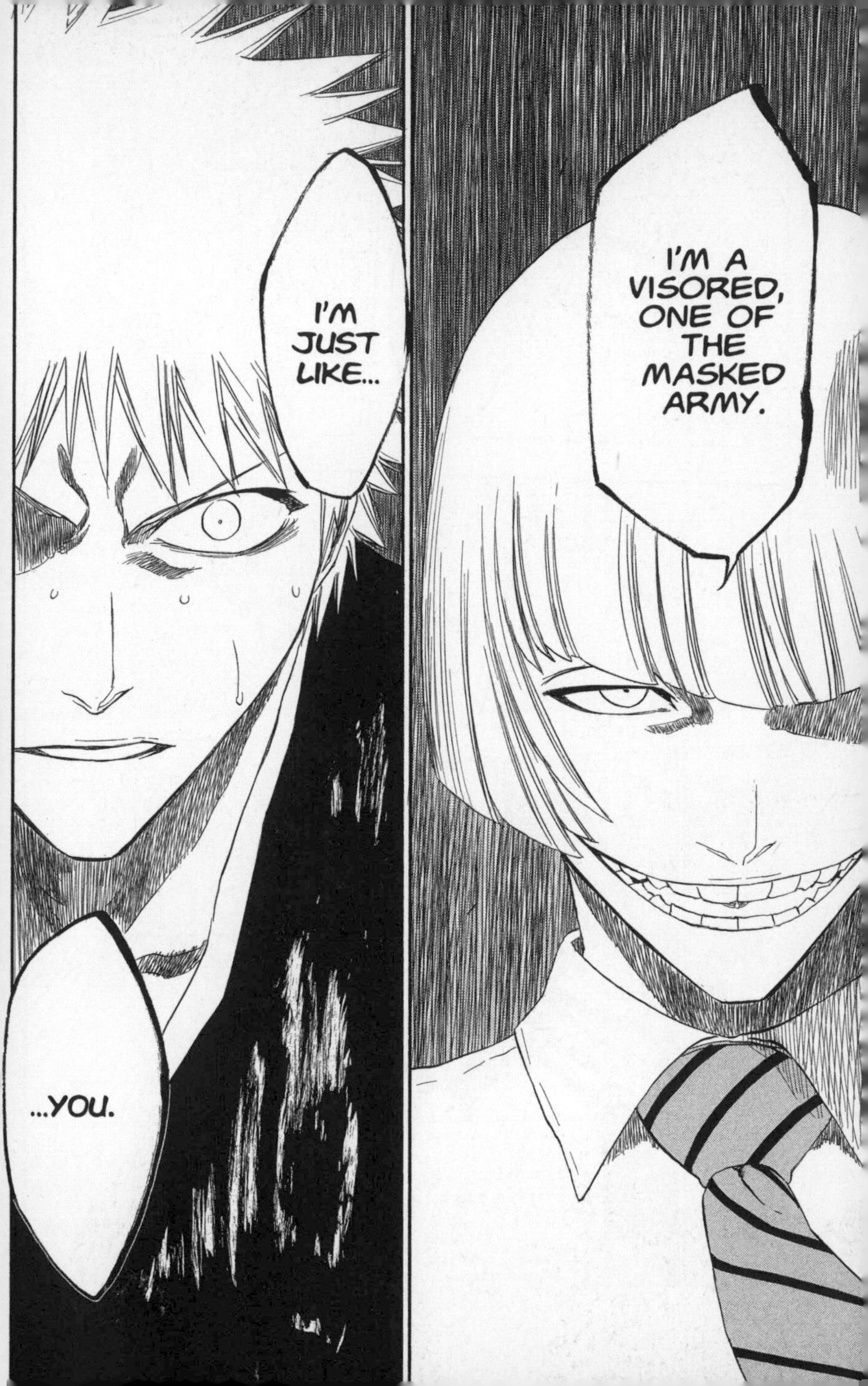
I'M A VISORED, ONE OF THE MASKED ARMY.
I'M JUST LIKE...
...YOU.

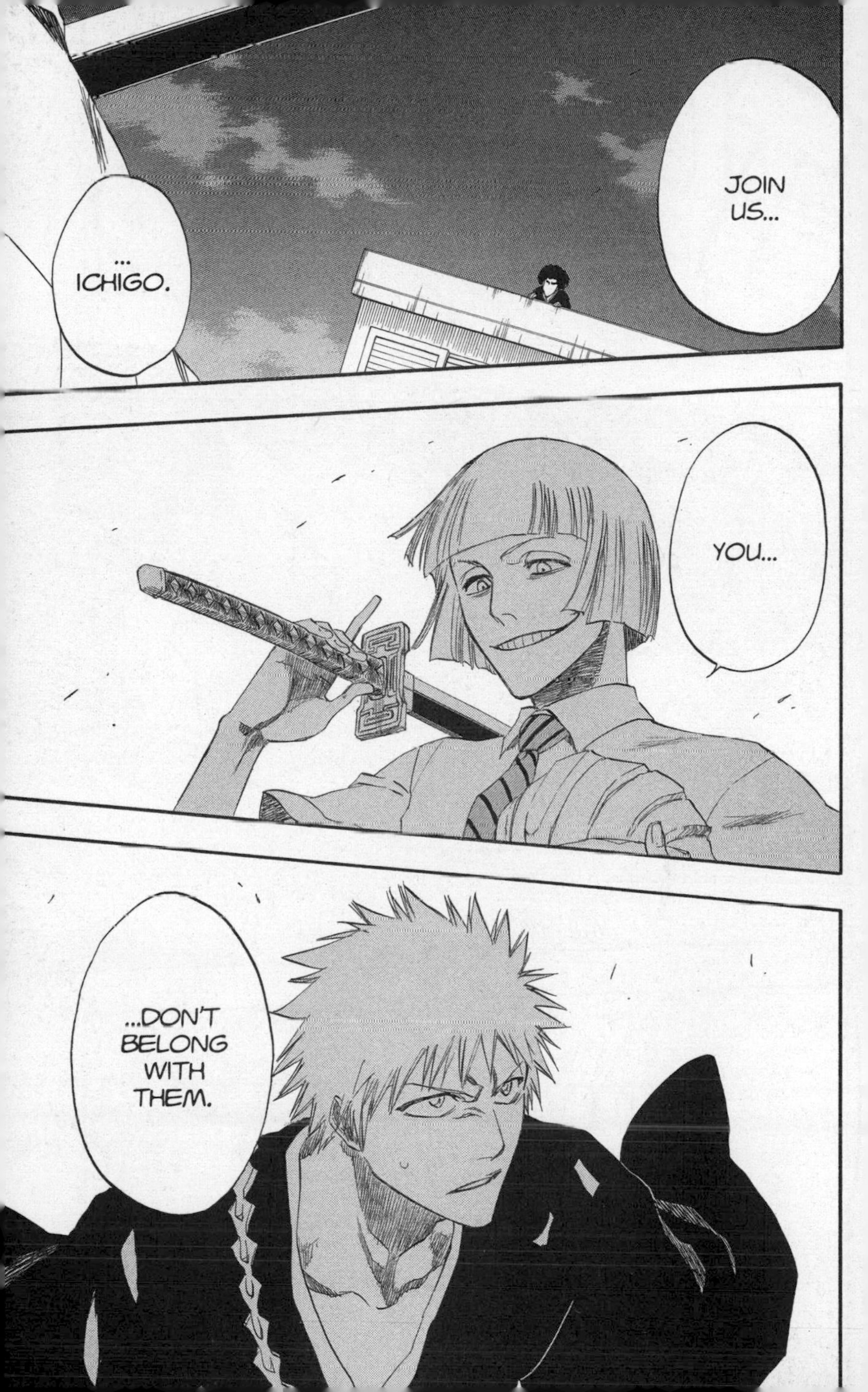
JOIN US...
... ICHIGO.
YOU...
...DON'T BELONG WITH THEM.

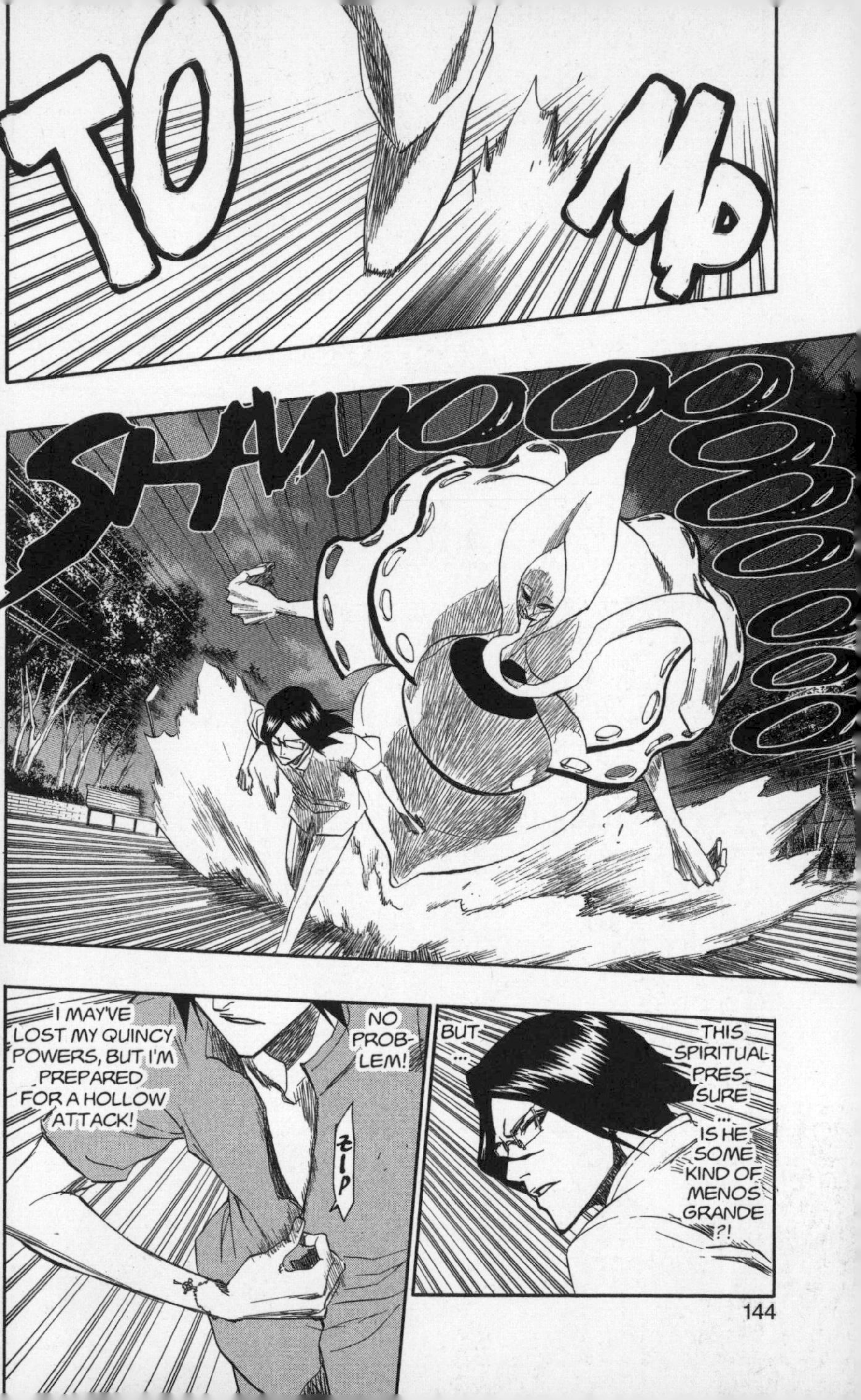
TOMP
SHWOOOOOOOOOOOOOOOO
THIS SPIRITUAL PRESSURE...
BUT...
IS HE SOME KIND OF MENOS GRANDE?!
NO PROBLEM!
I MAY'VE LOST MY QUINCY POWERS, BUT I'M PREPARED FOR A HOLLOW ATTACK!
ZIP

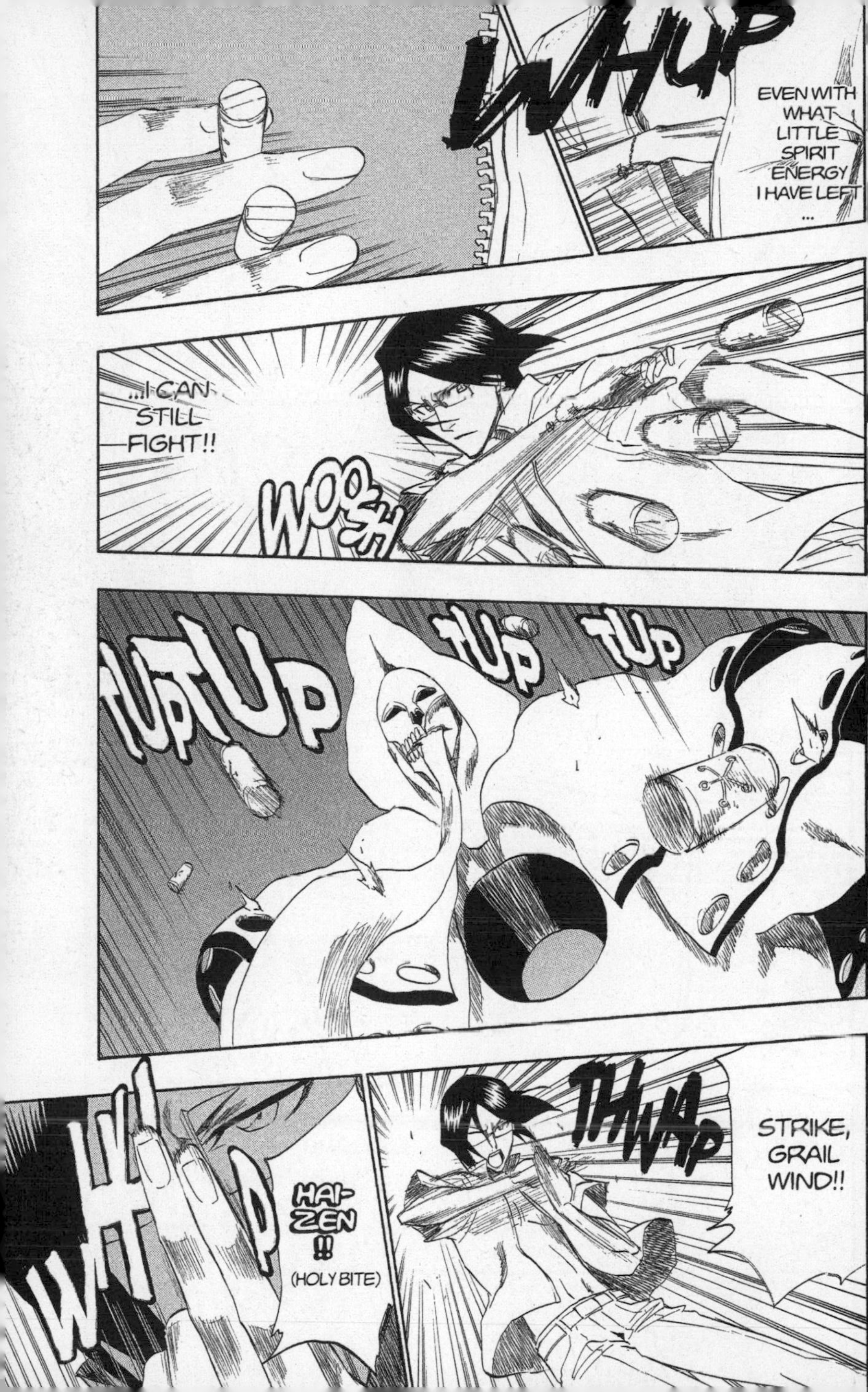
WHUP
EVEN WITH WHAT LITTLE SPIRIT ENERGY I HAVE LEFT ...
...I CAN STILL FIGHT!!
WOOSH
TUP
TUP
TUPTUP
STRIKE, GRAIL WIND!!
THWAP
HAI-ZEN!!
(HOLY BITE)

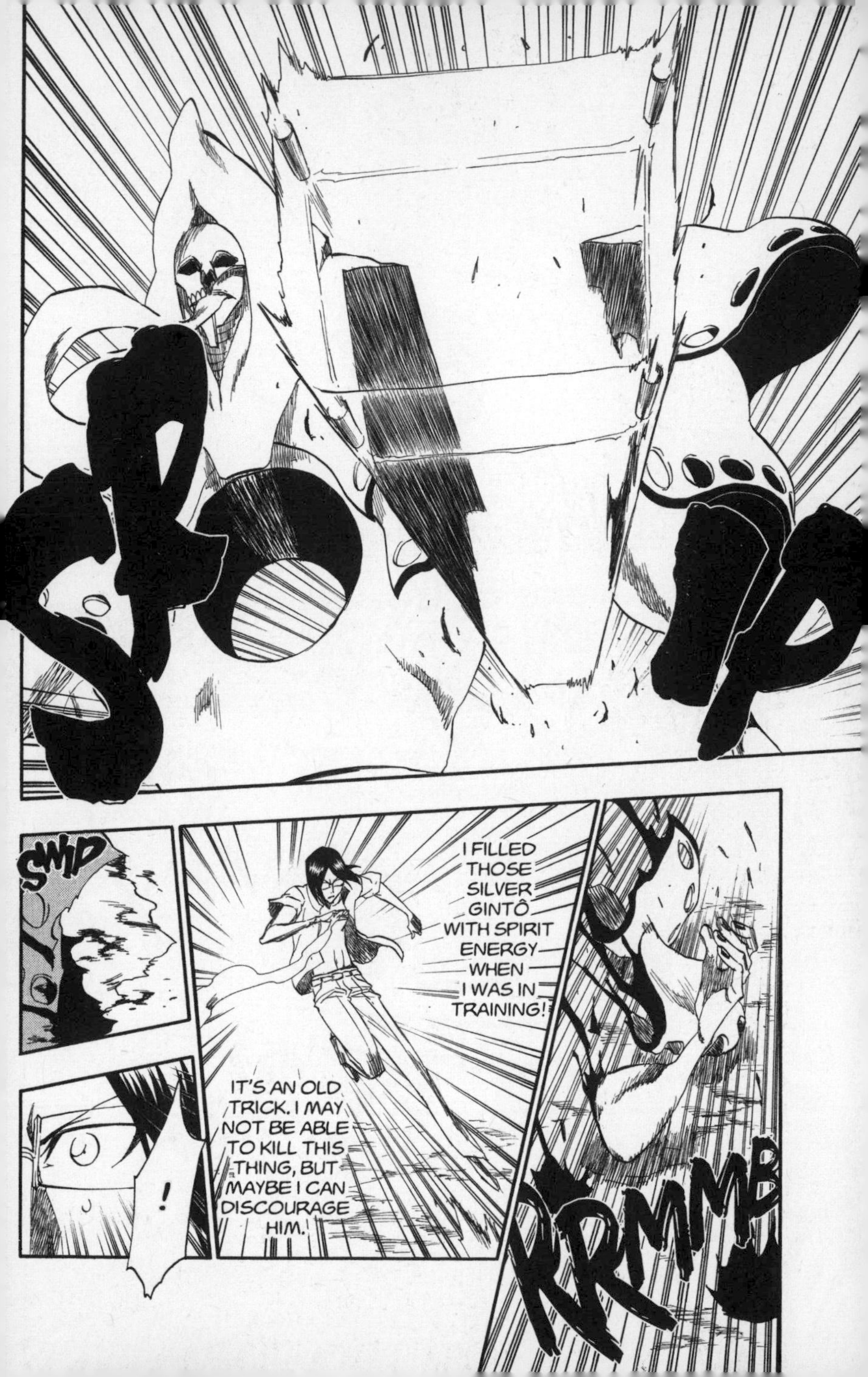
KRMMB
I FILLED THOSE SILVER GINTÔ WITH SPIRIT ENERGY WHEN I WAS IN TRAINING!
IT'S AN OLD TRICK. I MAY NOT BE ABLE TO KILL THIS THING, BUT MAYBE I CAN DISCOURAGE HIM.
SWIP
!

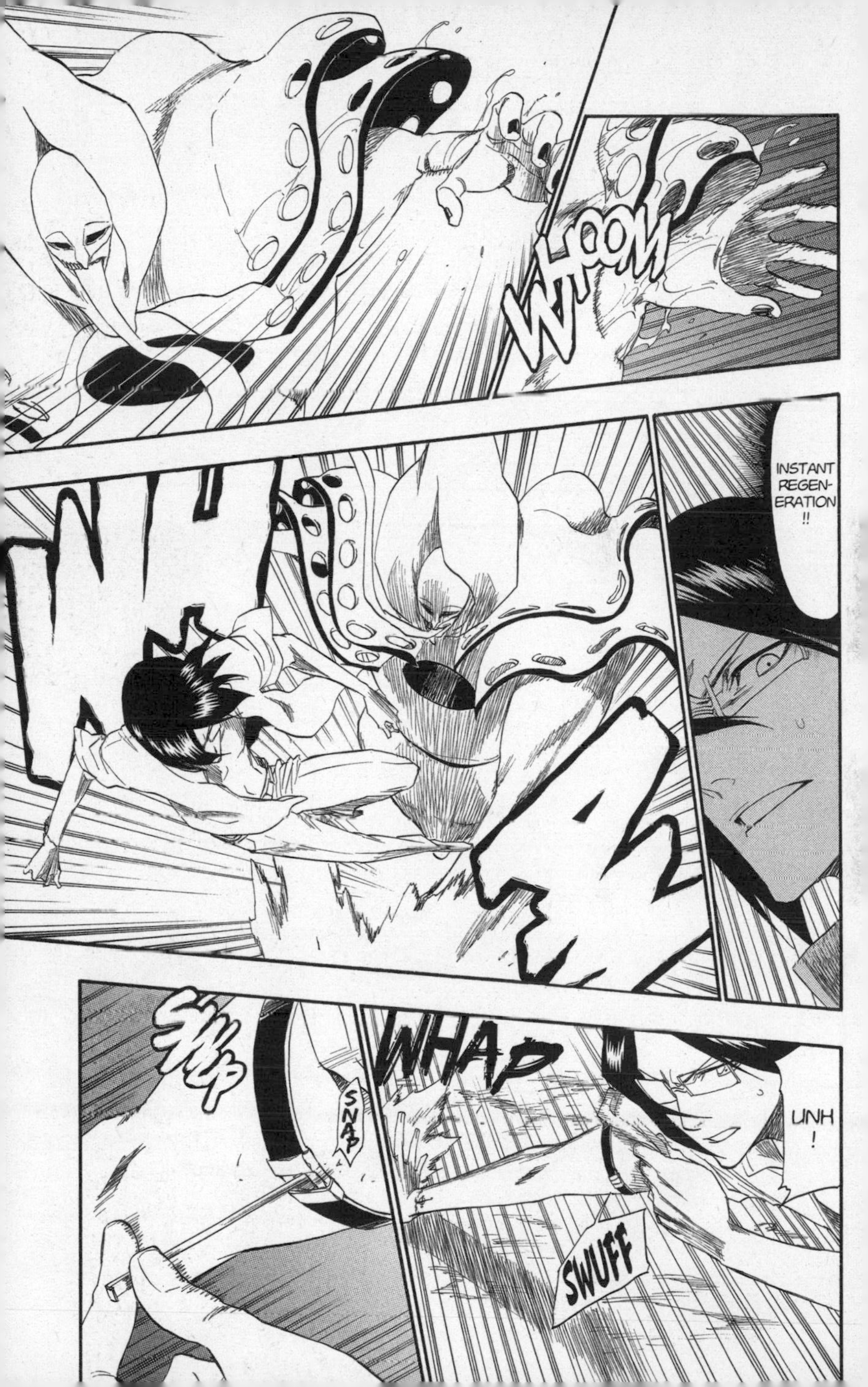
WHOOM
INSTANT REGEN-ERATION !!
WHAP
SNAP
UNH !
SWUFF

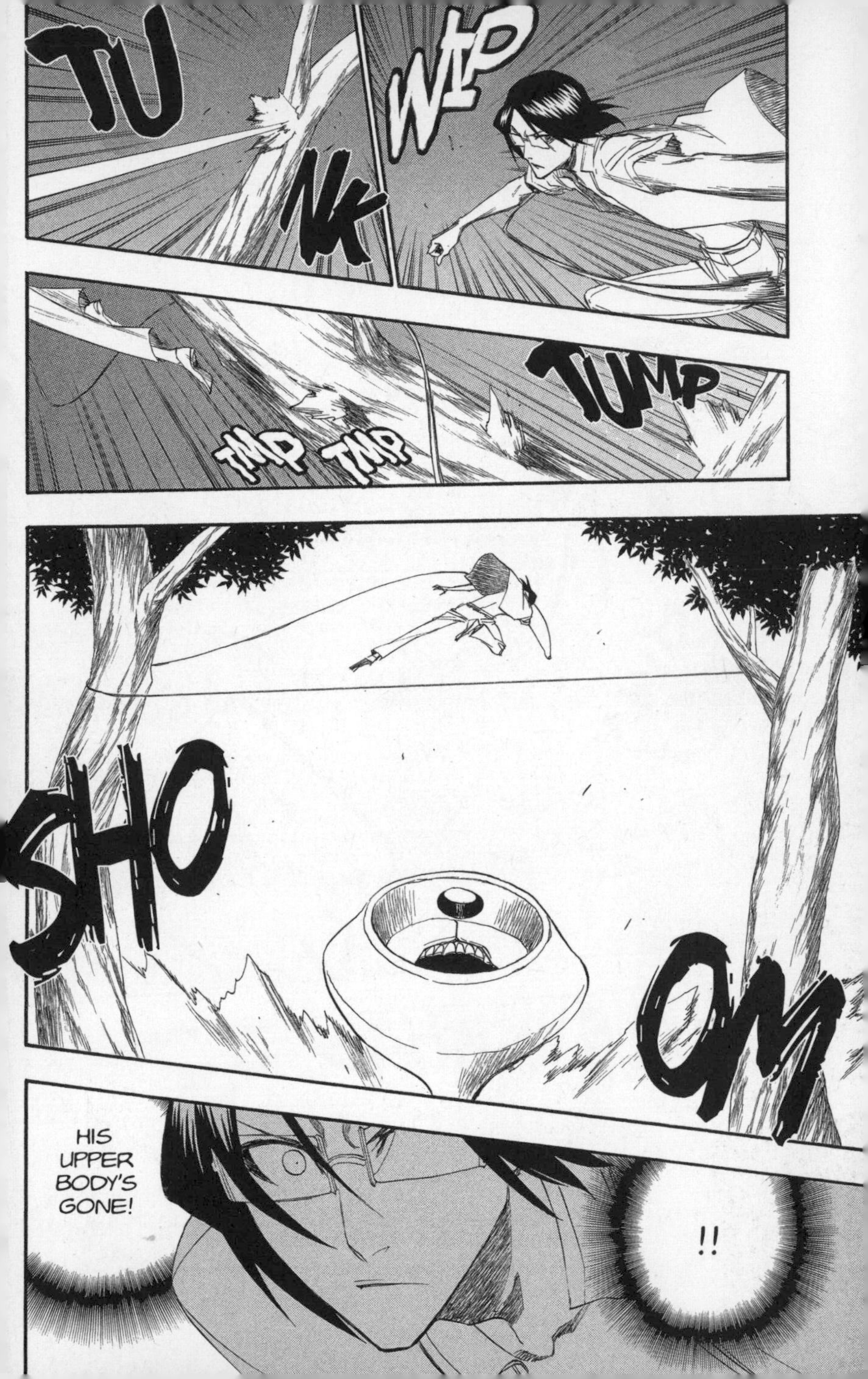
WIP
TUNK
TUMP
TMP TMP
SHOOM
!!
HIS UPPER BODY'S GONE!

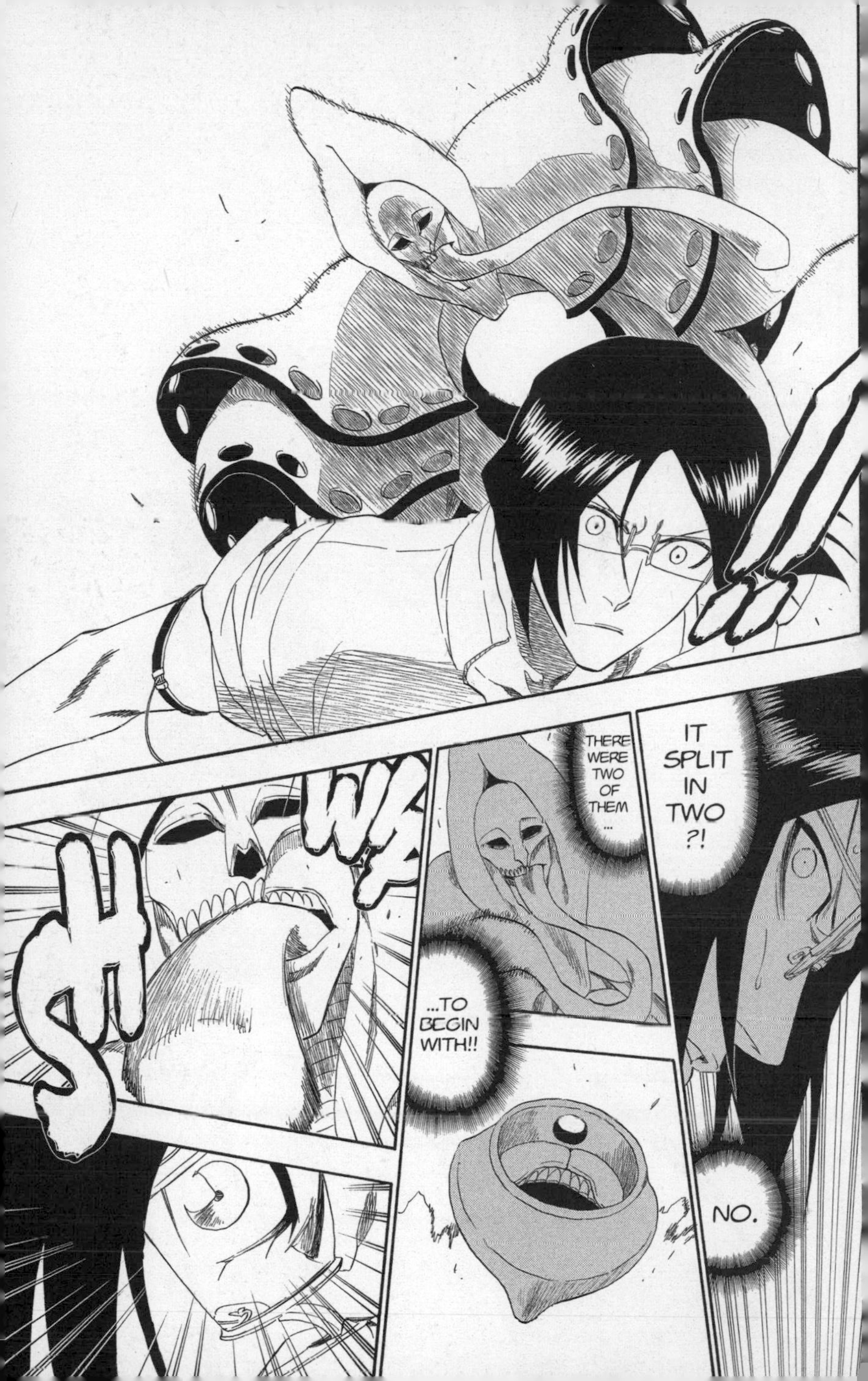
IT SPLIT IN TWO?!
NO.
THERE WERE TWO OF THEM...
...TO BEGIN WITH!!

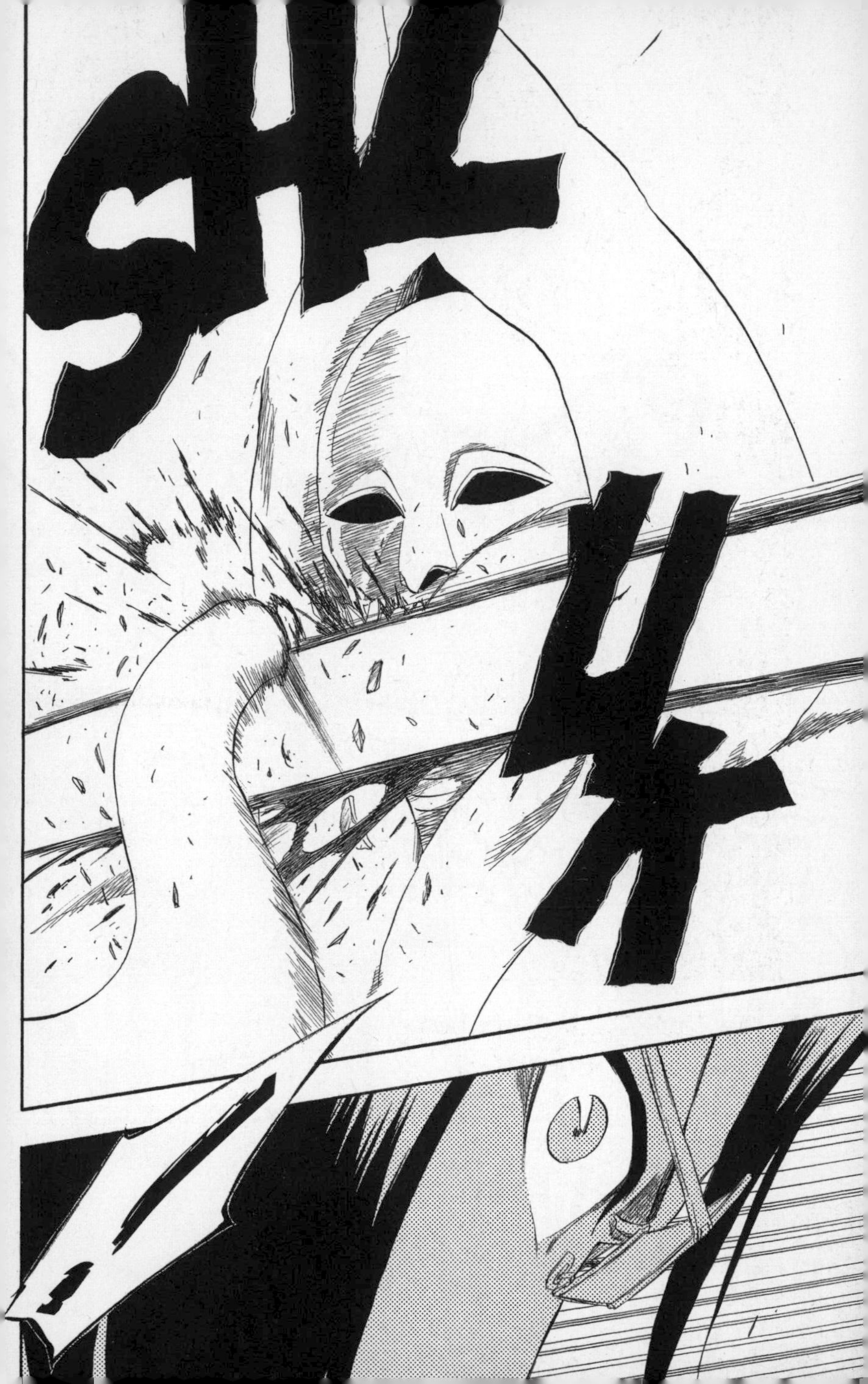
SHL
K

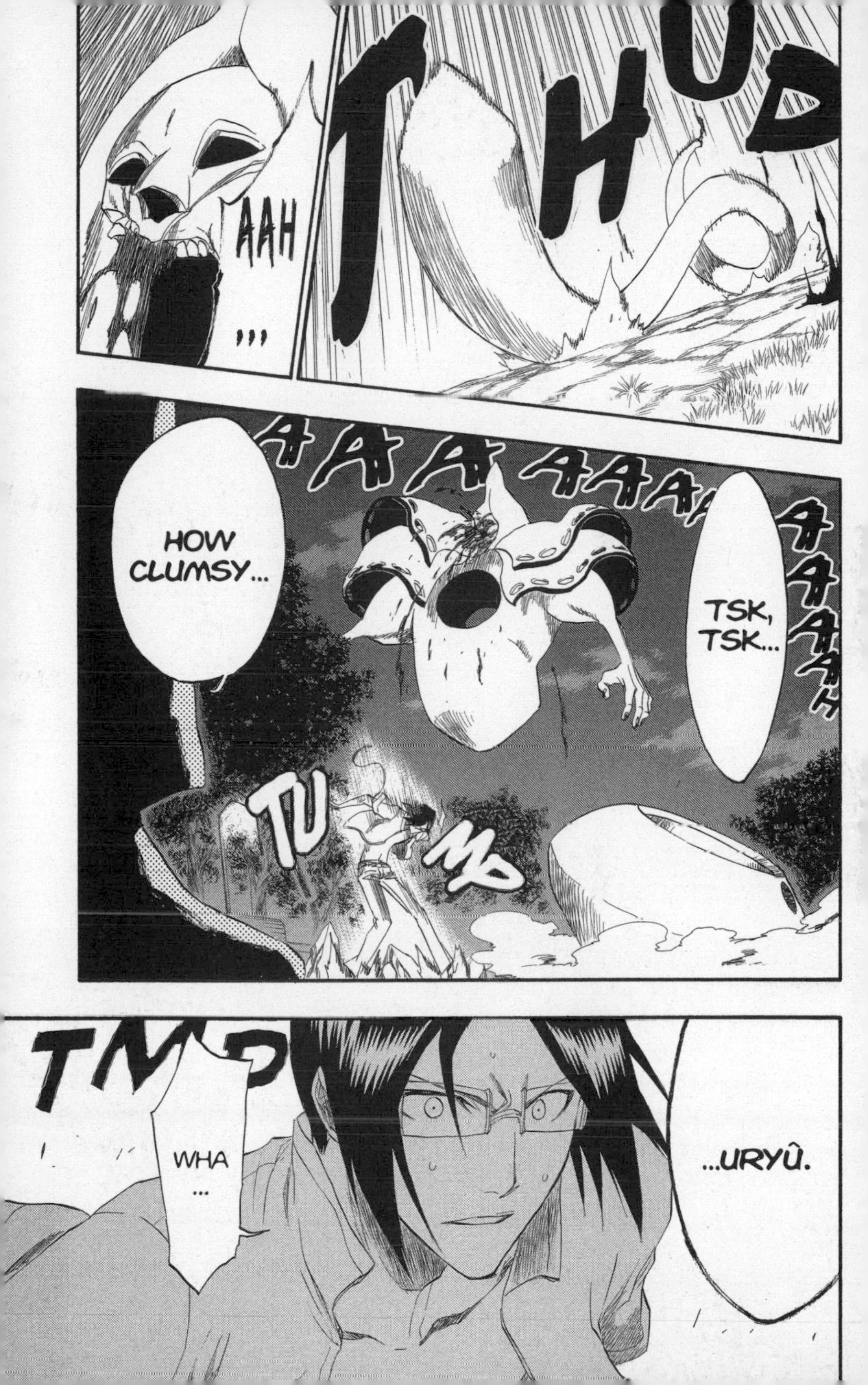
THUD
AAH
,,,
TSK, TSK...
AAAAAAAAAAAAAAAAAH
HOW CLUMSY...
TUMP
...URYÛ.
WHA
...
TMP

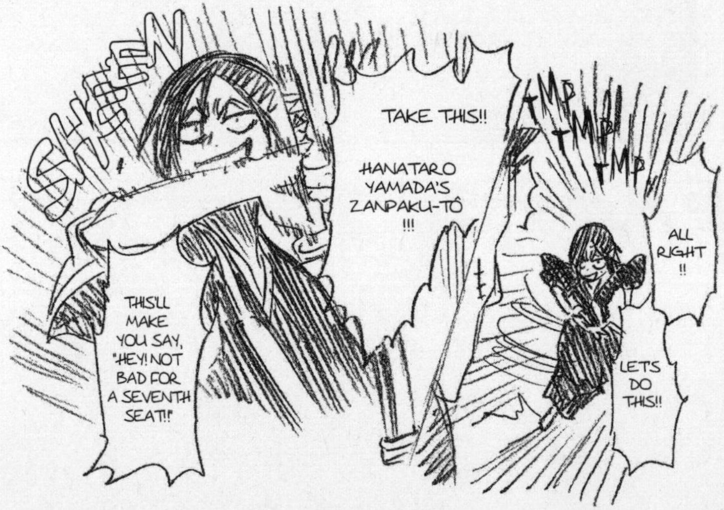
TMP TMP TMP
ALL RIGHT!!
TAKE THIS!!
HANATARO YAMADA'S ZANPAKU-TÔ!!!
LET'S DO THIS!!
SHEEN
THIS'LL MAKE YOU SAY, "HEY! NOT BAD FOR A SEVENTH SEAT!!"

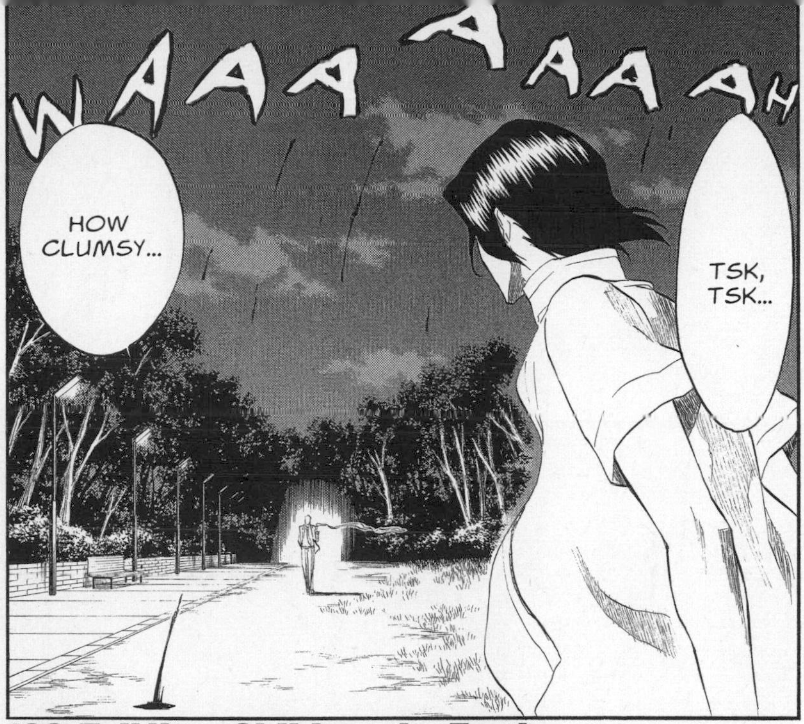
WAAAAAAAH
TSK, TSK...
HOW CLUMSY...

186. Tell Your Children the Truth

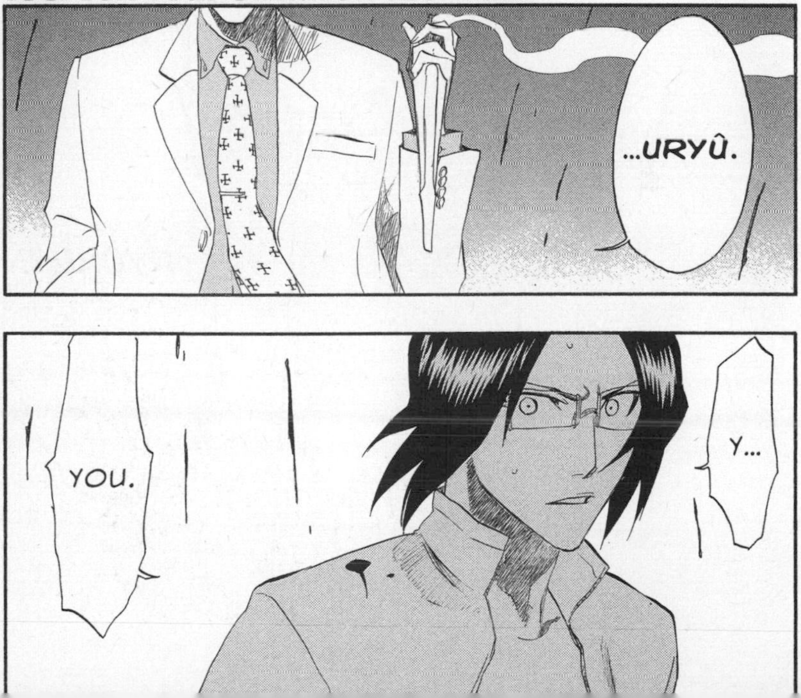
...URYÛ.
Y...
YOU.

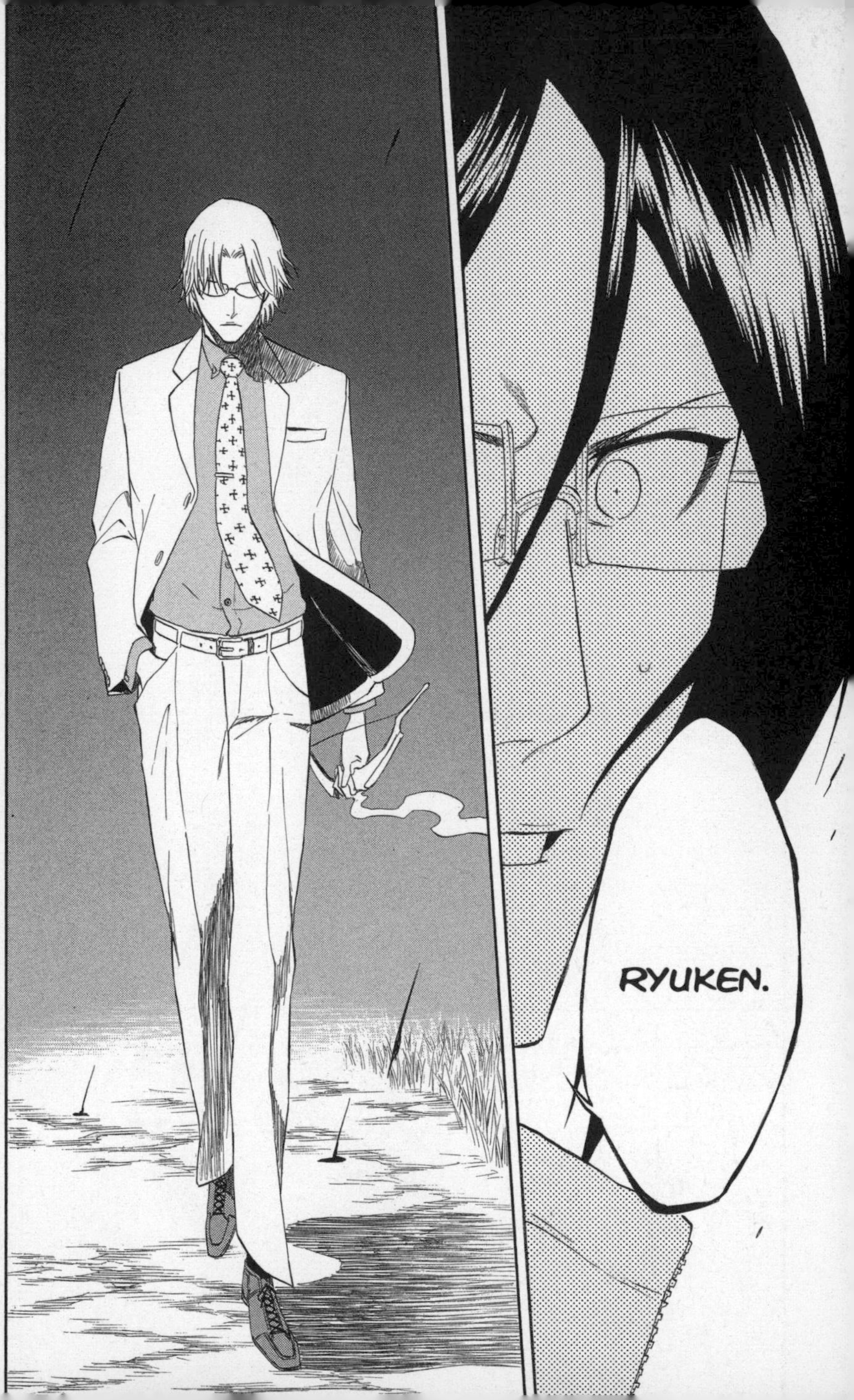
RYUKEN.

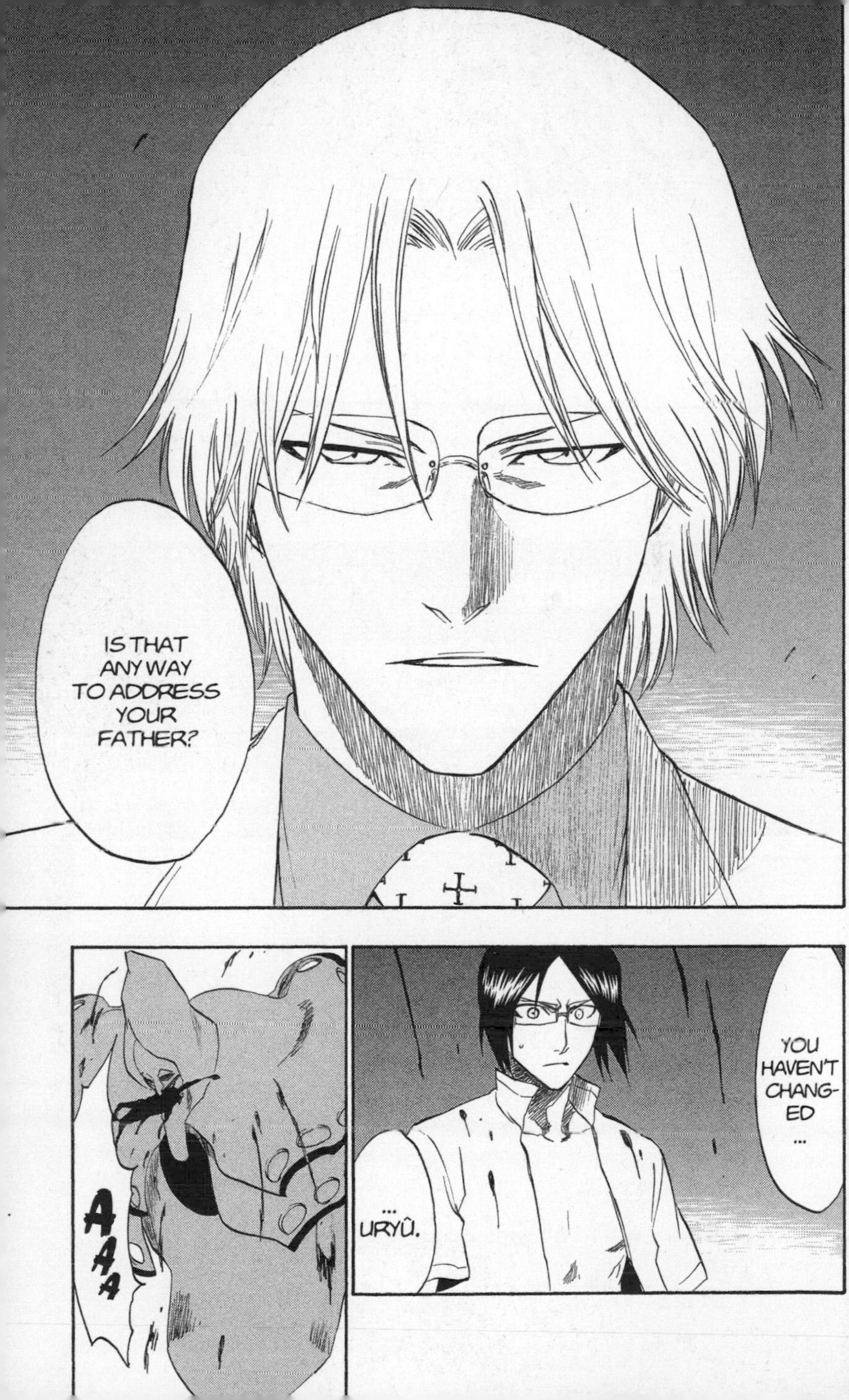
IS THAT ANY WAY TO ADDRESS YOUR FATHER?
YOU HAVEN'T CHANG-ED ...
... URYÛ.
AAAA

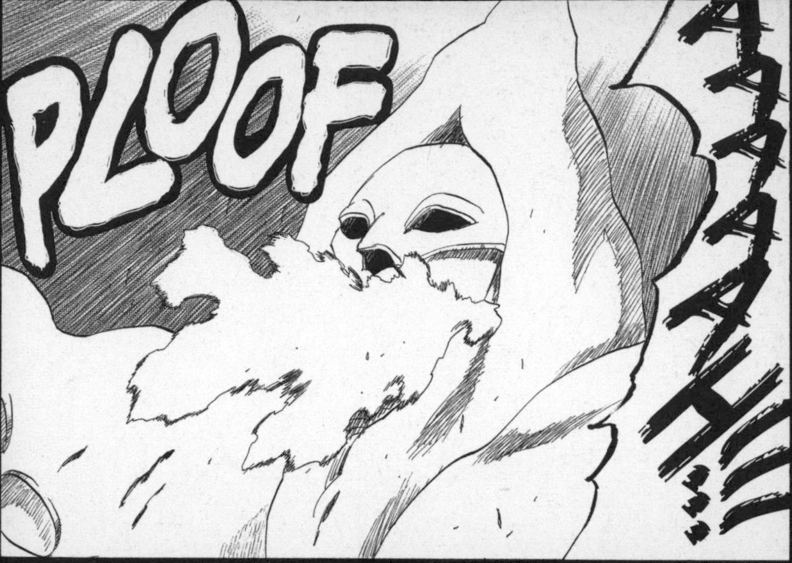
AAAAAH...!!!
PLOOF

Tell Your Children

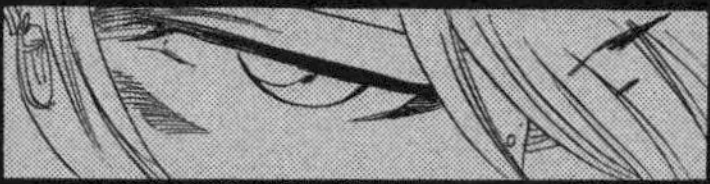

the Truth

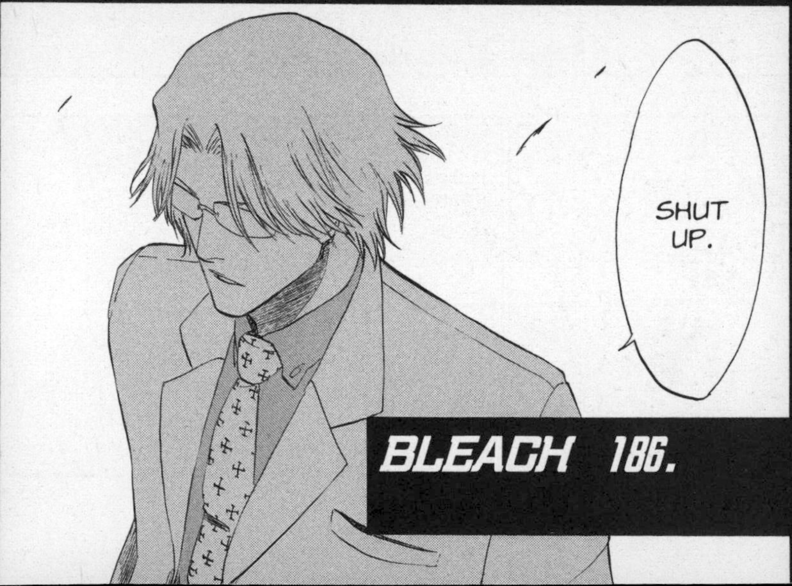
SHUT UP.
BLEACH 186.

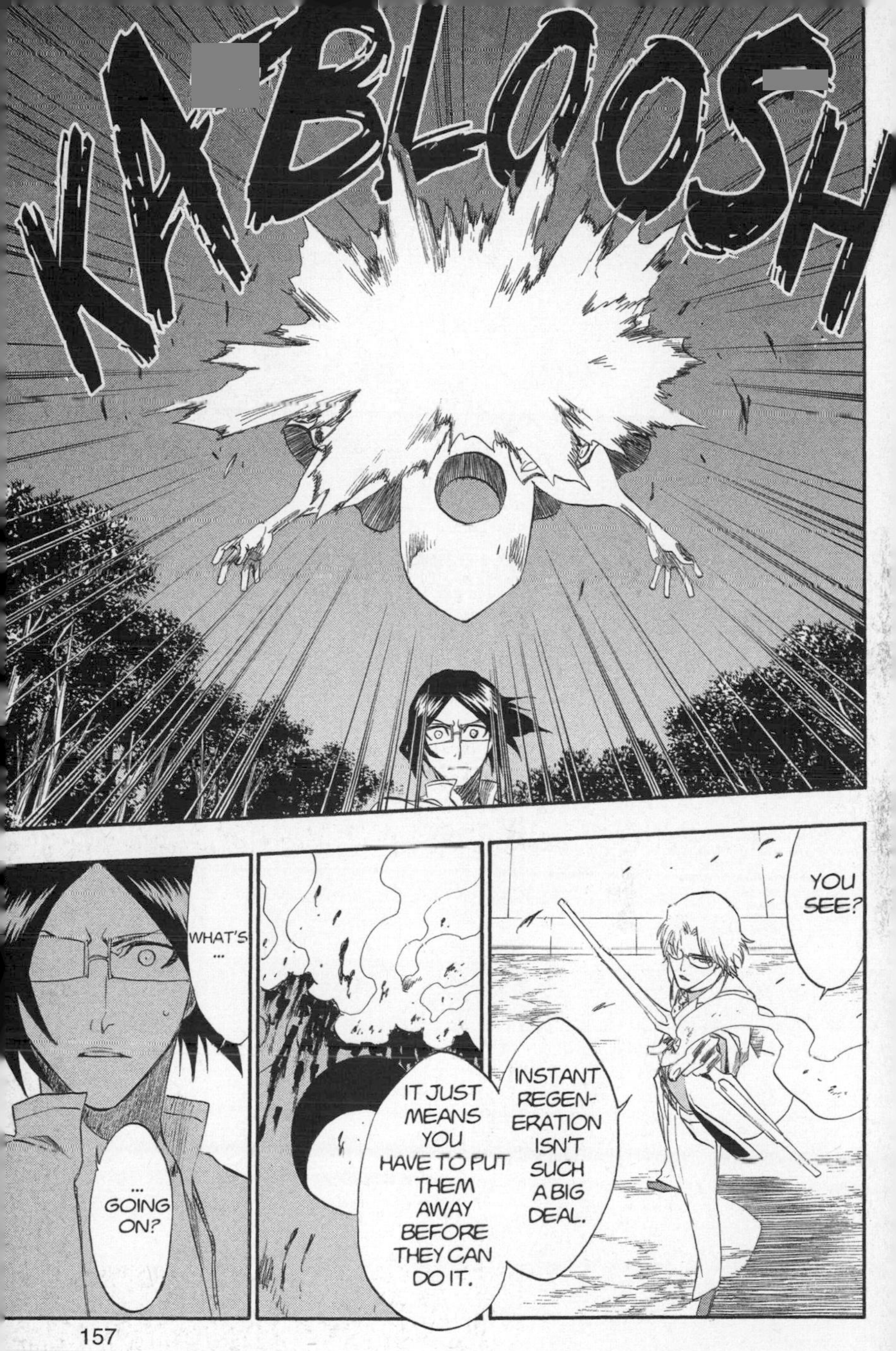
KABLOOSH
YOU SEE?
INSTANT REGEN-ERATION ISN'T SUCH A BIG DEAL.
IT JUST MEANS YOU HAVE TO PUT THEM AWAY BEFORE THEY CAN DO IT.
WHAT'S ...
... GOING ON?

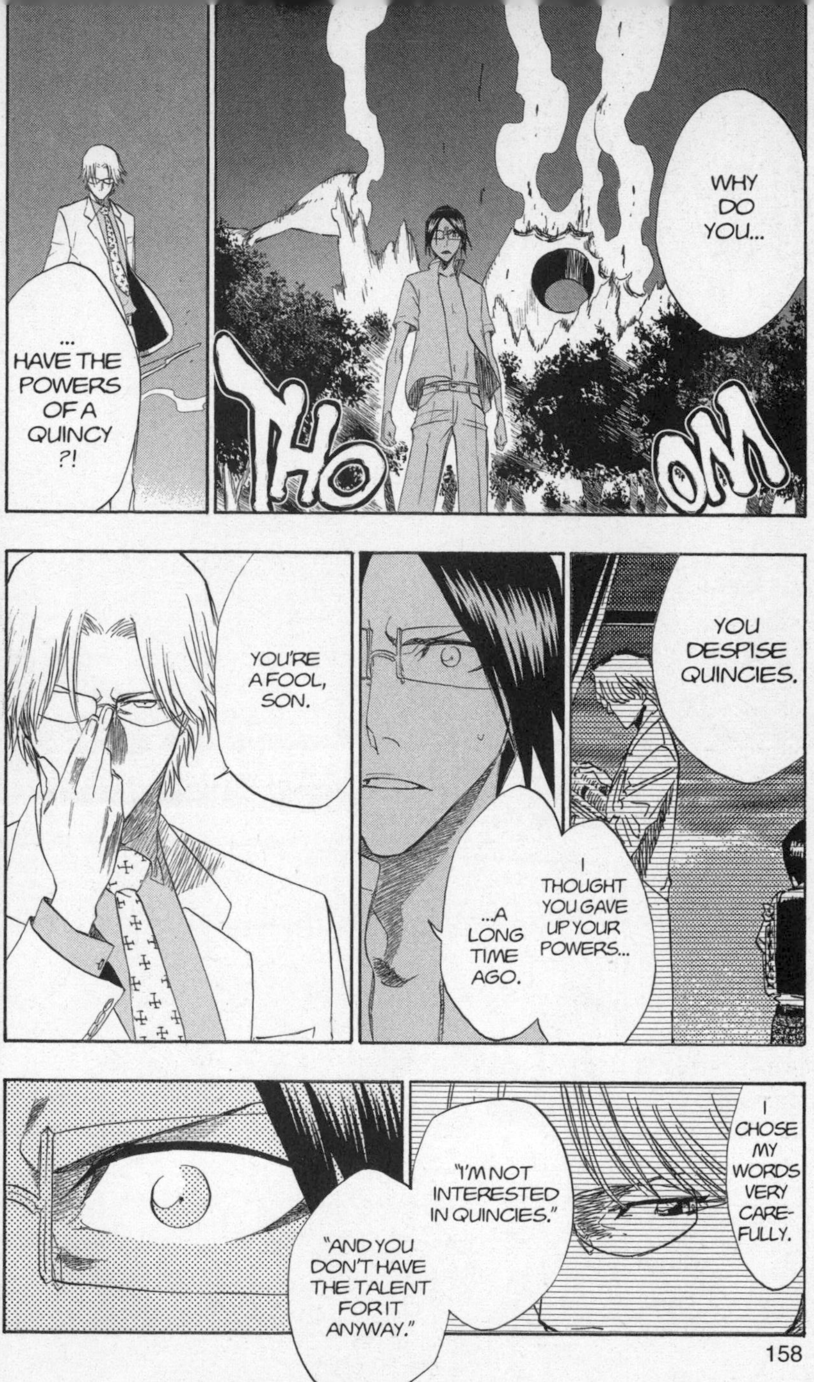
WHY DO YOU...
THO OM
...HAVE THE POWERS OF A QUINCY?!
YOU DESPISE QUINCIES.
I THOUGHT YOU GAVE UP YOUR POWERS...
...A LONG TIME AGO.
YOU'RE A FOOL, SON.
I CHOSE MY WORDS VERY CARE-FULLY.
"I'M NOT INTERESTED IN QUINCIES."
"AND YOU DON'T HAVE THE TALENT FOR IT ANYWAY."

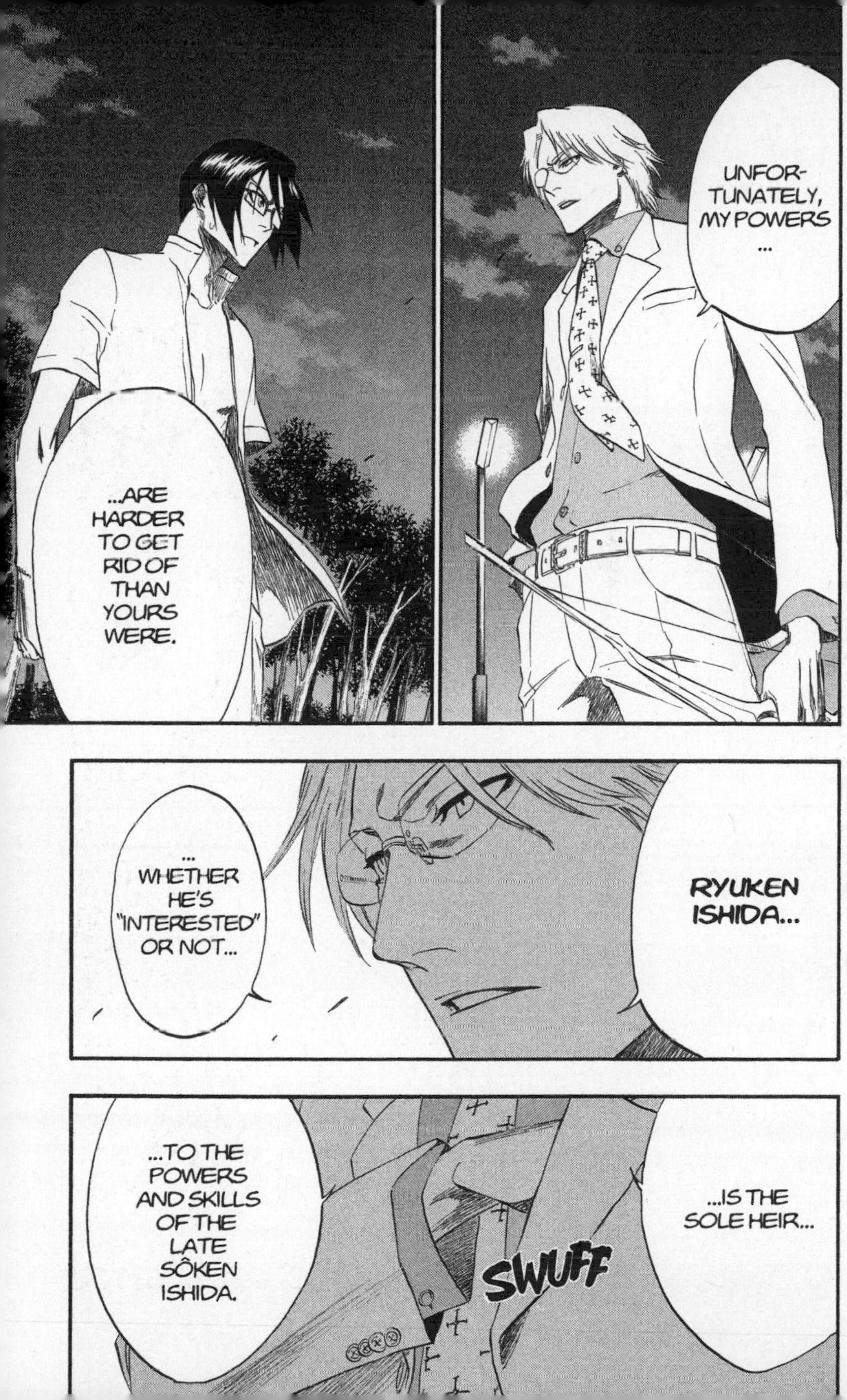
UNFOR-TUNATELY, MY POWERS ...
...ARE HARDER TO GET RID OF THAN YOURS WERE.
RYUKEN ISHIDA...
... WHETHER HE'S "INTERESTED" OR NOT...
...IS THE SOLE HEIR...
SWUFF
...TO THE POWERS AND SKILLS OF THE LATE SÔKEN ISHIDA.

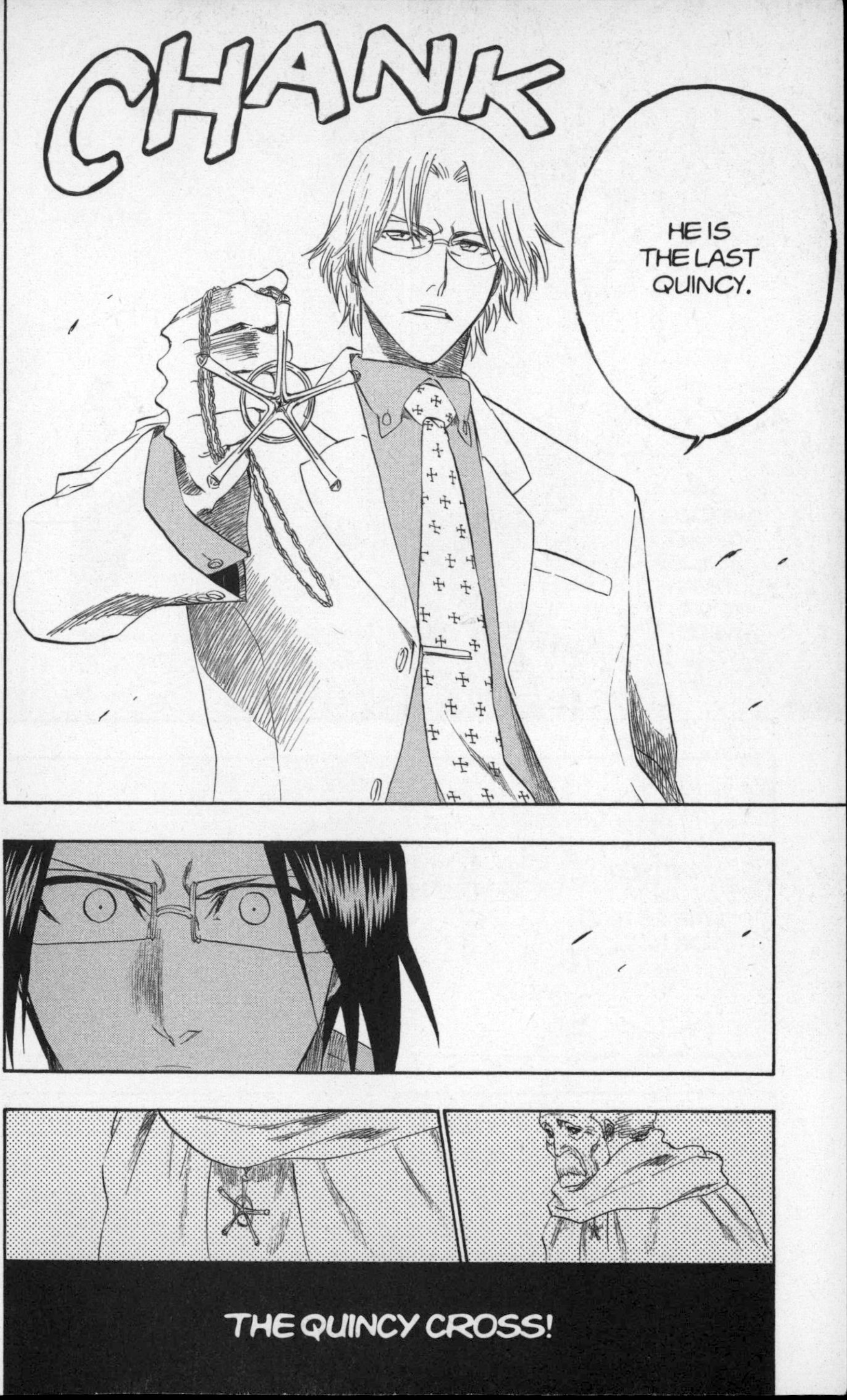
CHANK
HE IS THE LAST QUINCY.
THE QUINCY CROSS!

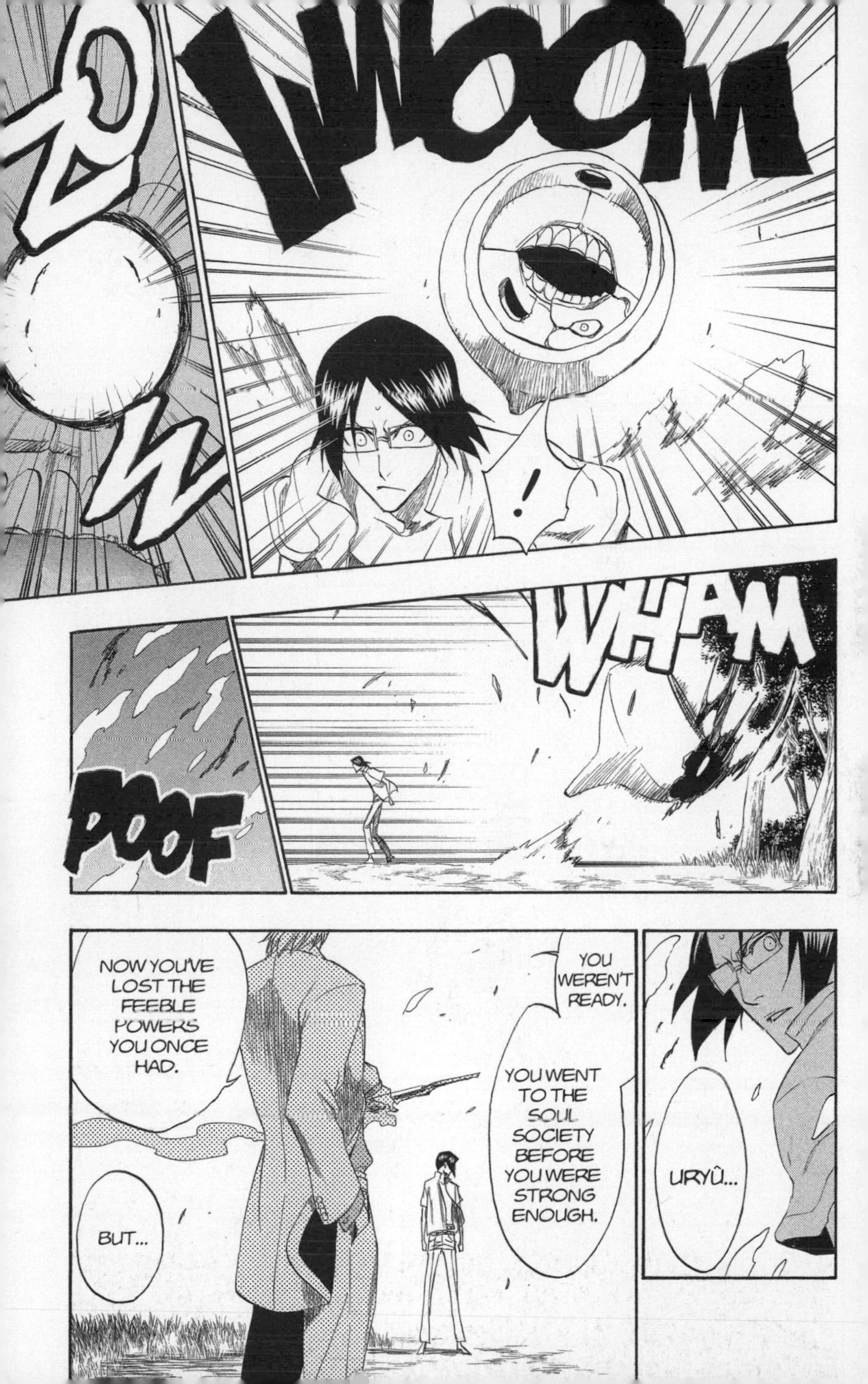
WOOM
!
WHAM
POOF
URYÛ...
YOU WEREN'T READY.
YOU WENT TO THE SOUL SOCIETY BEFORE YOU WERE STRONG ENOUGH.
NOW YOU'VE LOST THE FEEBLE POWERS YOU ONCE HAD.
BUT...

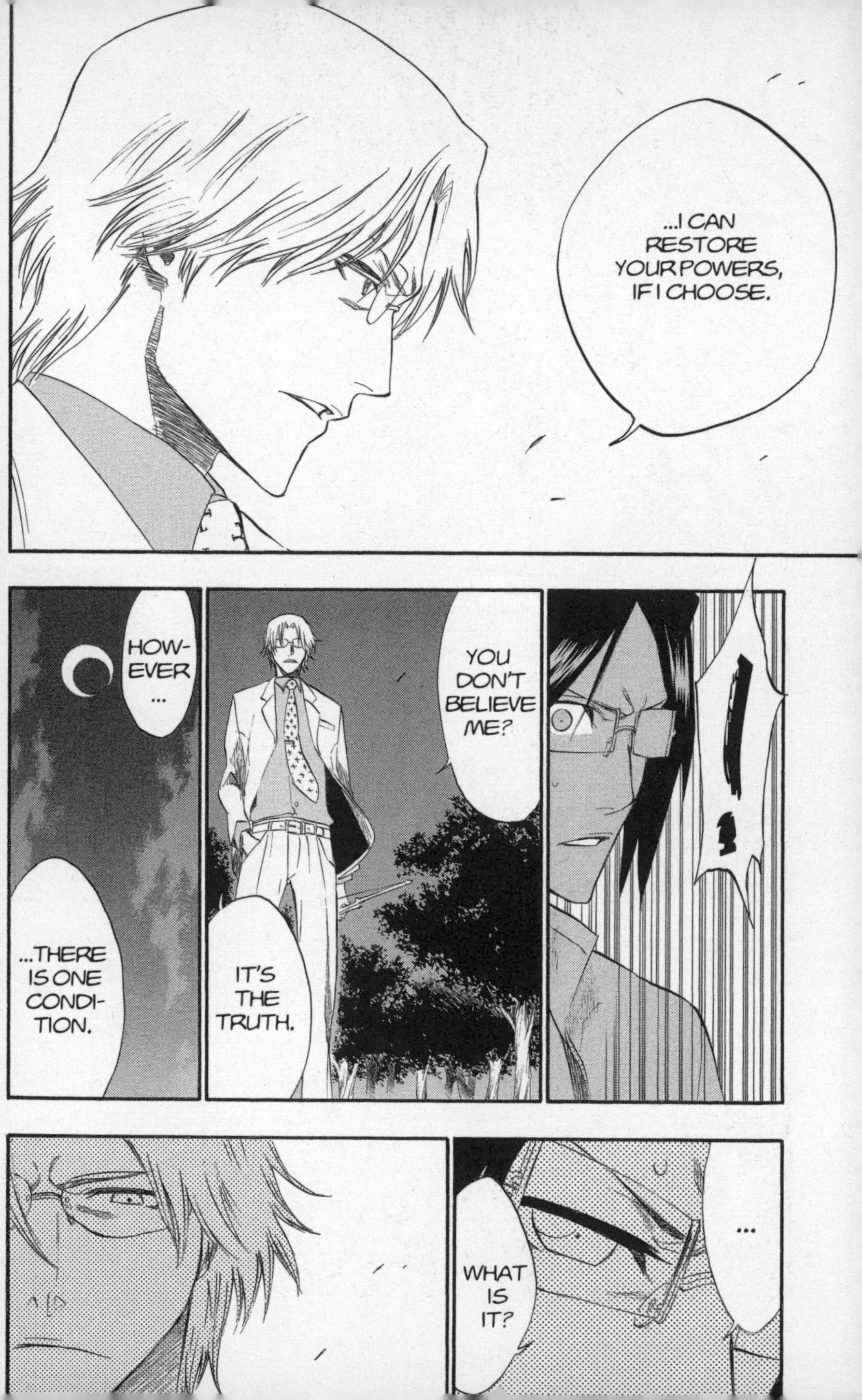
...I CAN RESTORE YOUR POWERS, IF I CHOOSE.
!
YOU DON'T BELIEVE ME?
IT'S THE TRUTH.
HOW-EVER ...
...THERE IS ONE CONDI-TION.
...
WHAT IS IT?

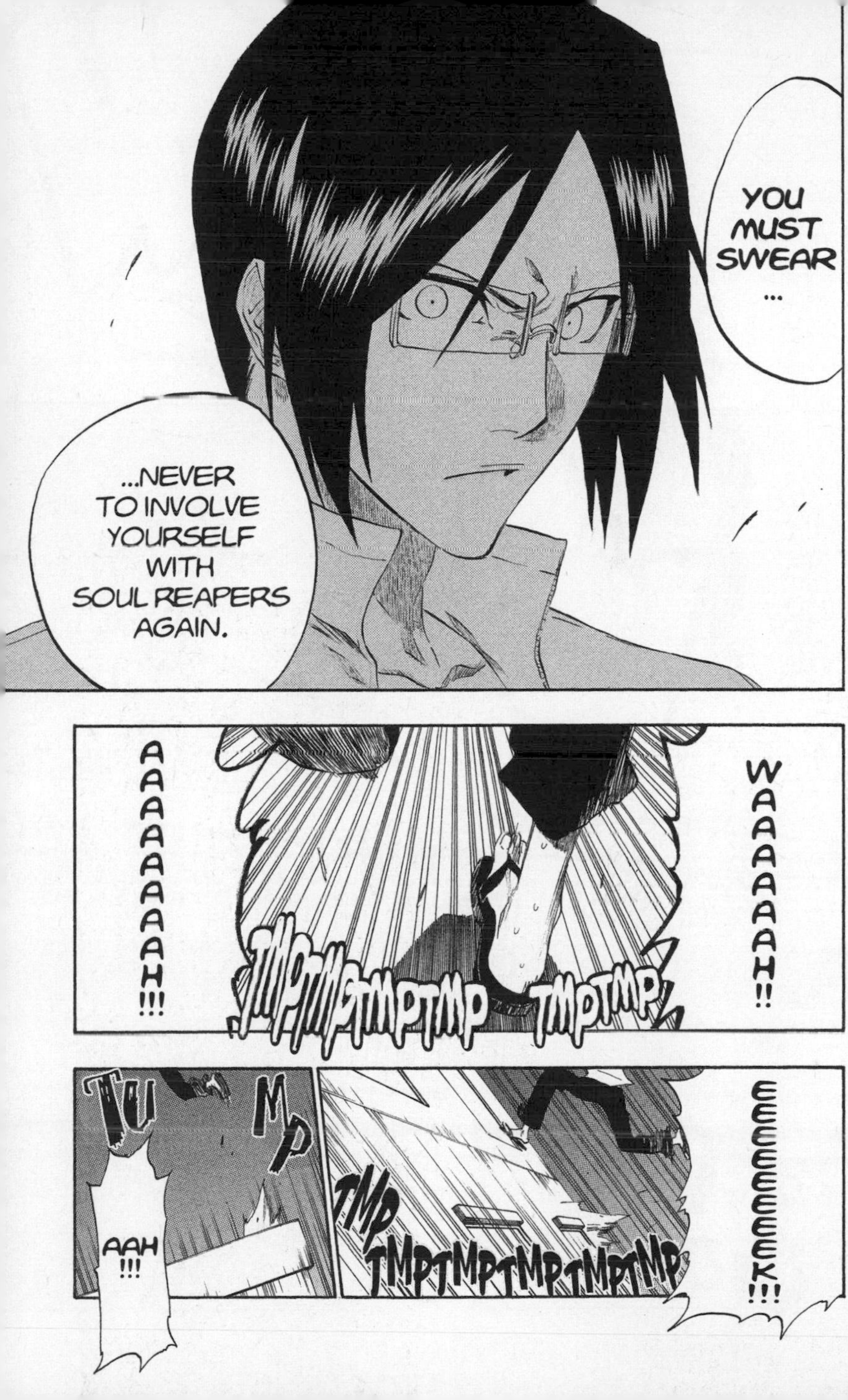
YOU MUST SWEAR ...
...NEVER TO INVOLVE YOURSELF WITH SOUL REAPERS AGAIN.
WAAAAAAAH!!
TMPTMPTMPTMP TMPTMP
AAAAAAAAAH!!!
EEEEEEEEK!!!
TMP TMPTMPTMPTMPTMP
AAH!!!

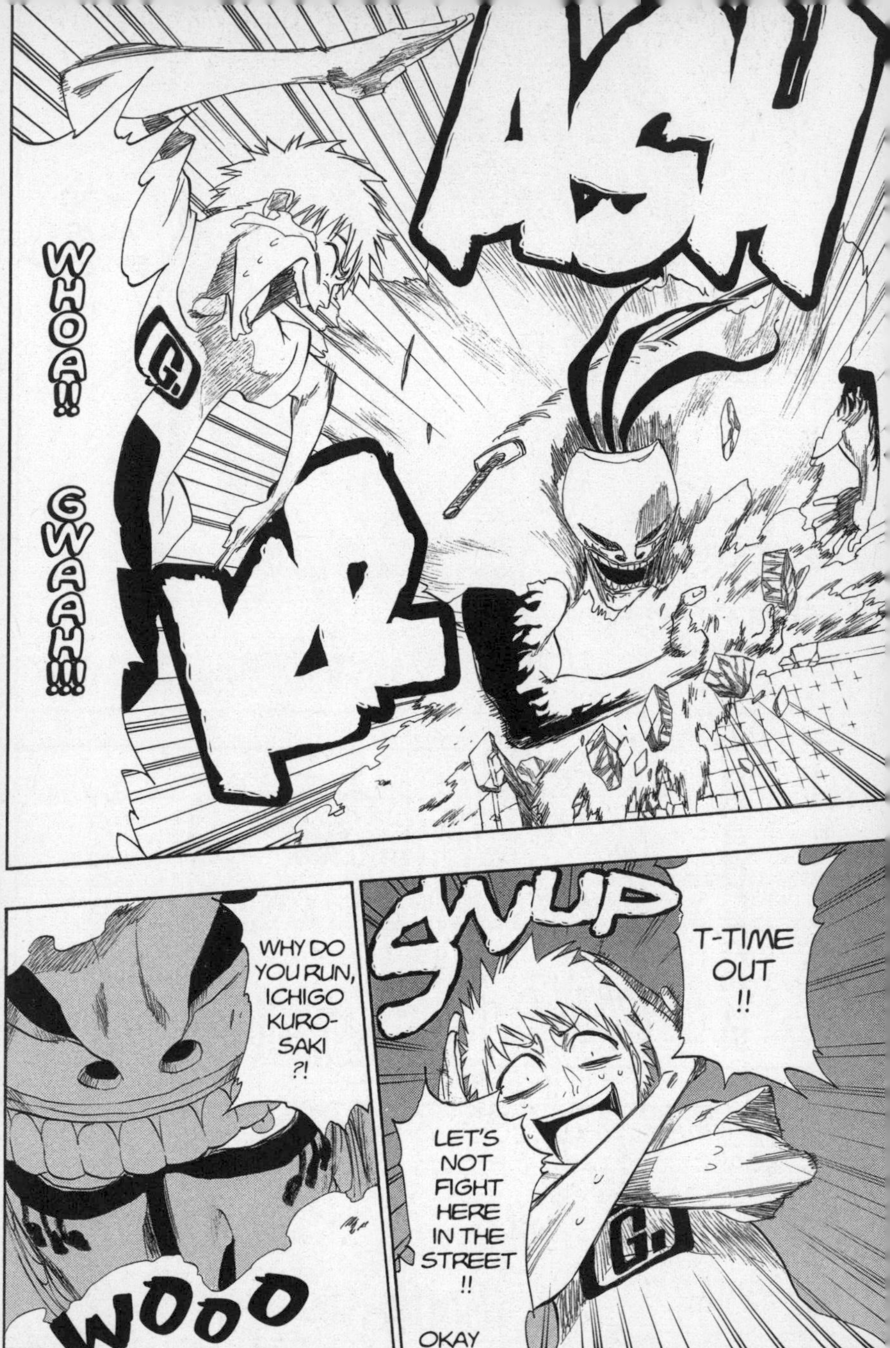
WHOA!! GWAAAH!!!
SWUP
T-TIME OUT !!
LET'S NOT FIGHT HERE IN THE STREET !!
OKAY ?!
WHY DO YOU RUN, ICHIGO KURO-SAKI ?!
WOOO

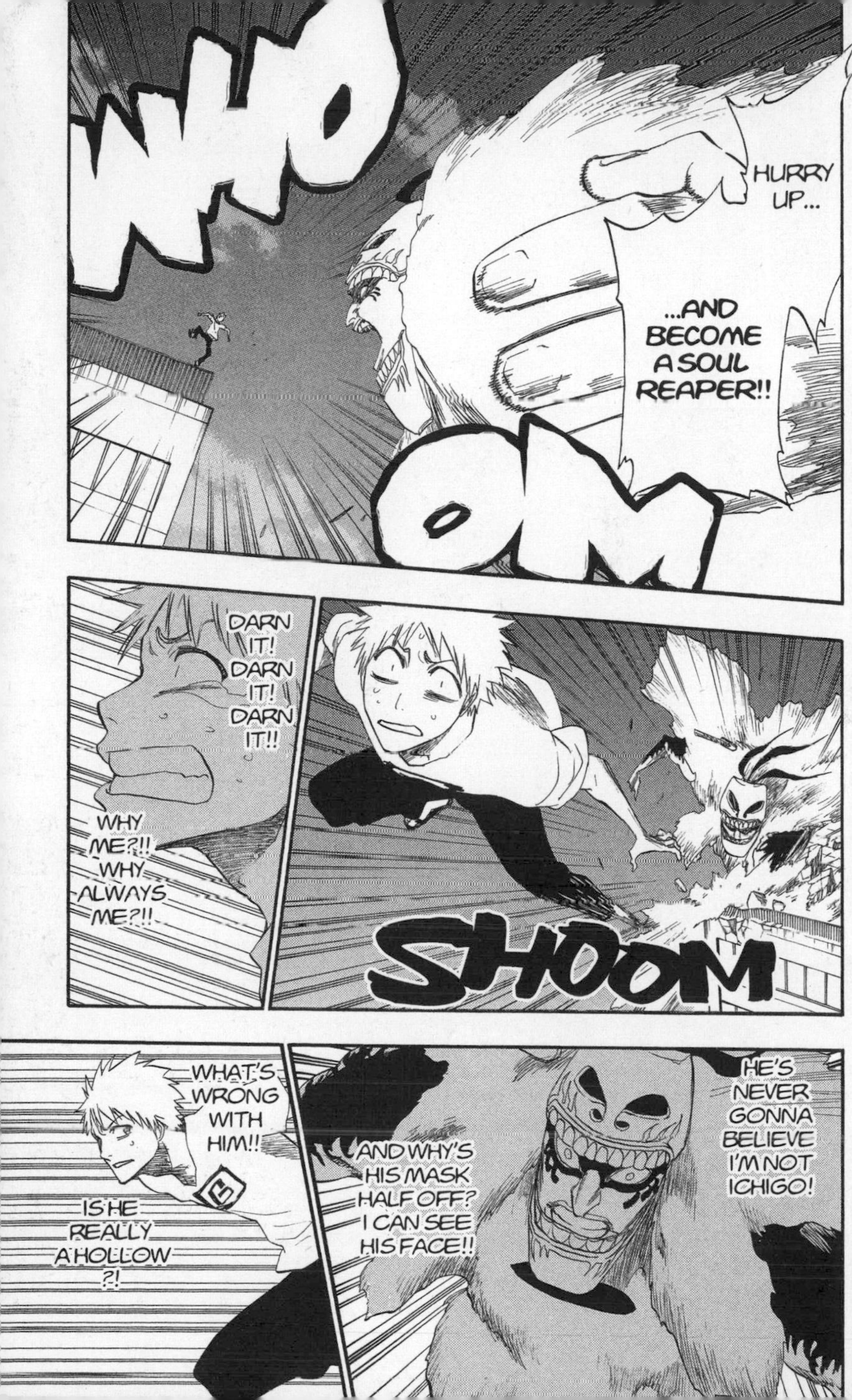
HURRY UP...
...AND BECOME A SOUL REAPER!!
WHOOM
SHOOM
DARN IT! DARN IT! DARN IT!!
WHY ME?!! WHY ALWAYS ME?!!
HE'S NEVER GONNA BELIEVE I'M NOT ICHIGO!
AND WHY'S HIS MASK HALF OFF? I CAN SEE HIS FACE!!
WHAT'S WRONG WITH HIM!!
IS HE REALLY A HOLLOW ?!

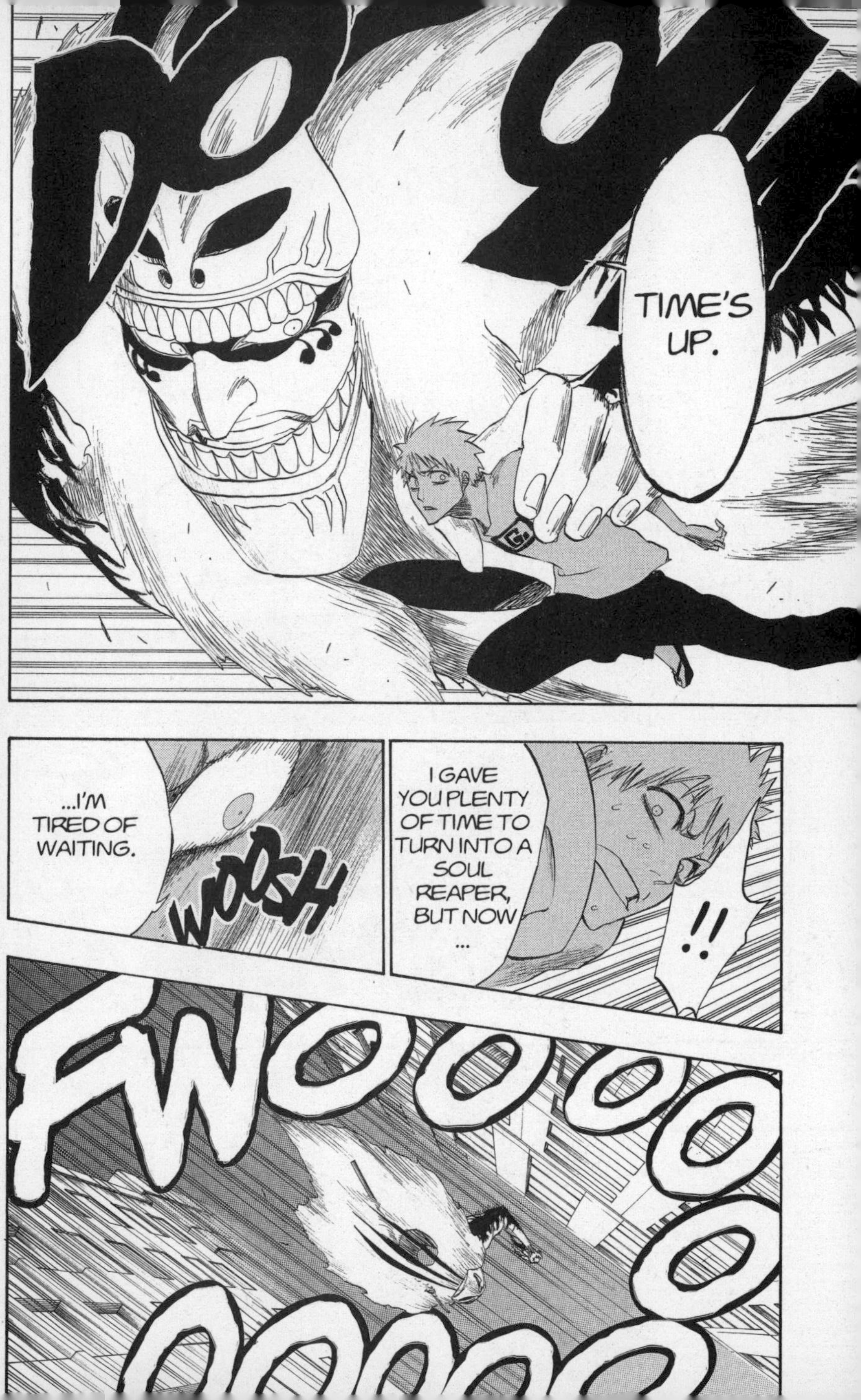
TIME'S UP.
I GAVE YOU PLENTY OF TIME TO TURN INTO A SOUL REAPER, BUT NOW ...
!!
...I'M TIRED OF WAITING.
WOOSH
FWOOOOOOOOOO

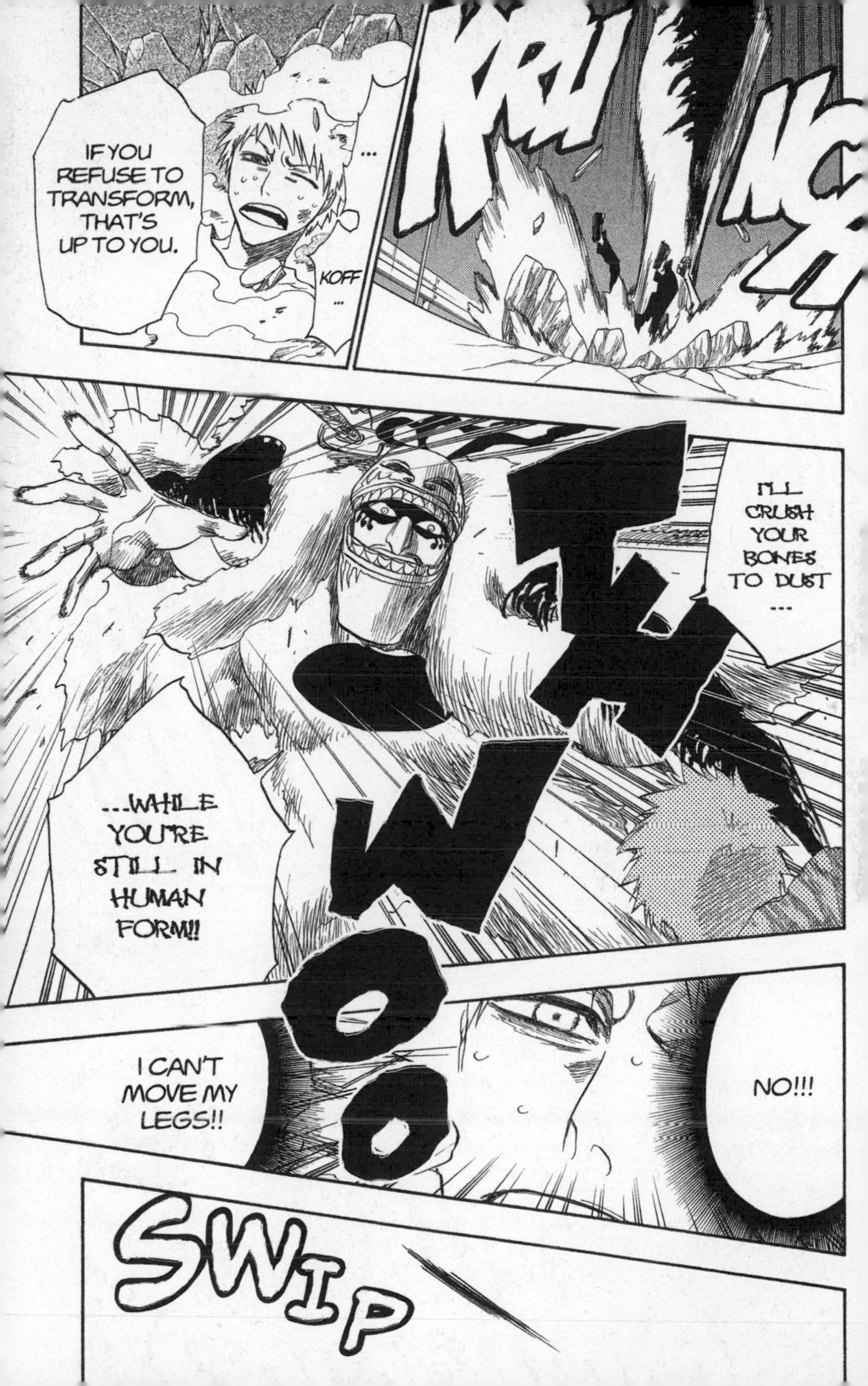
...
IF YOU REFUSE TO TRANSFORM, THAT'S UP TO YOU.
KOFF ...
I'LL CRUSH YOUR BONES TO DUST ...
...WHILE YOU'RE STILL IN HUMAN FORM!!
NO!!!
I CAN'T MOVE MY LEGS!!
SWIP

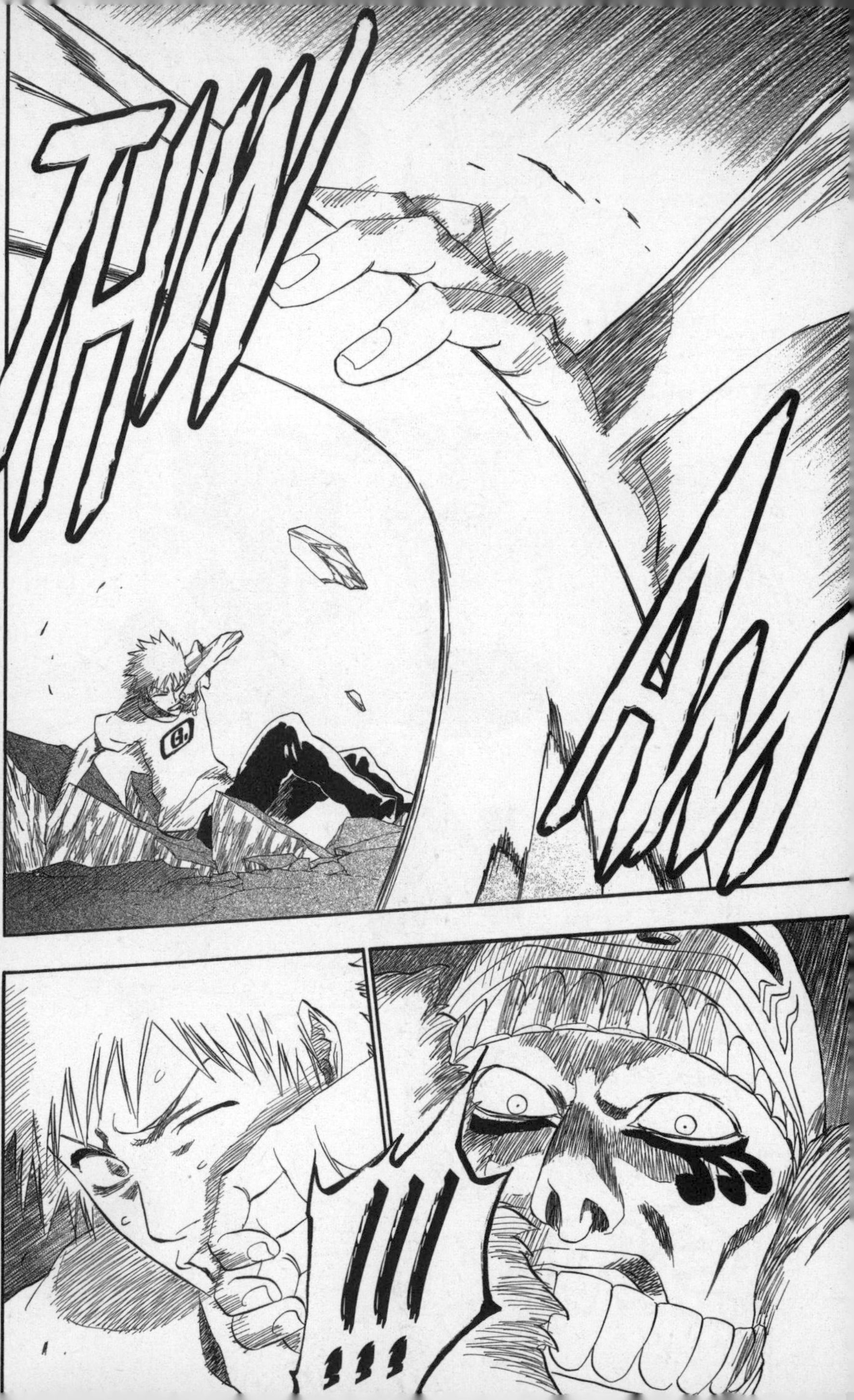
THWAM
!!!

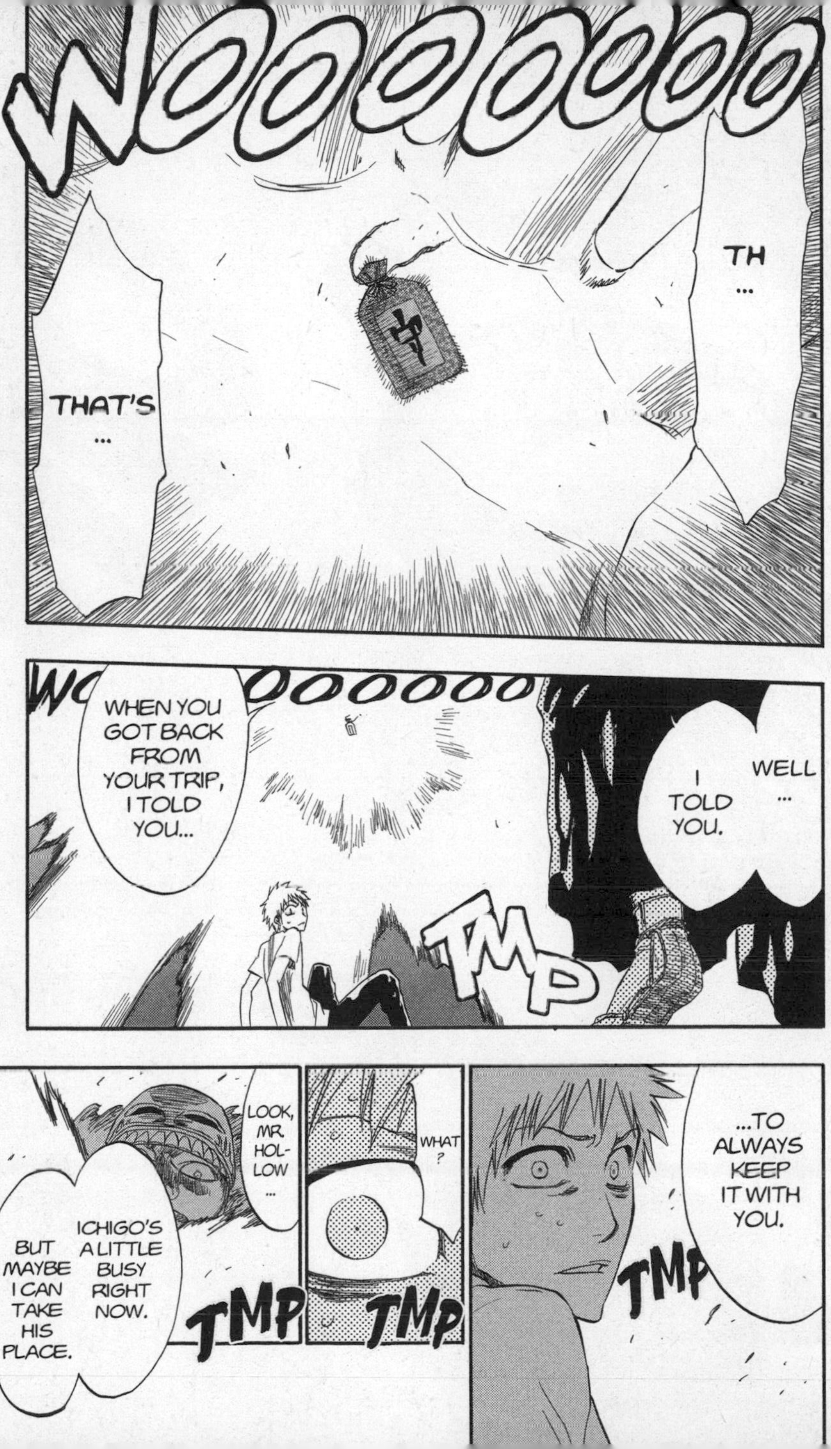
WOOOOOOO
TH...
THAT'S...
WELL...
I TOLD YOU.
WHEN YOU GOT BACK FROM YOUR TRIP, I TOLD YOU...
TMP
...TO ALWAYS KEEP IT WITH YOU.
TMP
WHAT?
TMP
LOOK, MR. HOL-LOW...
ICHIGO'S A LITTLE BUSY RIGHT NOW.
BUT MAYBE I CAN TAKE HIS PLACE.
TMP

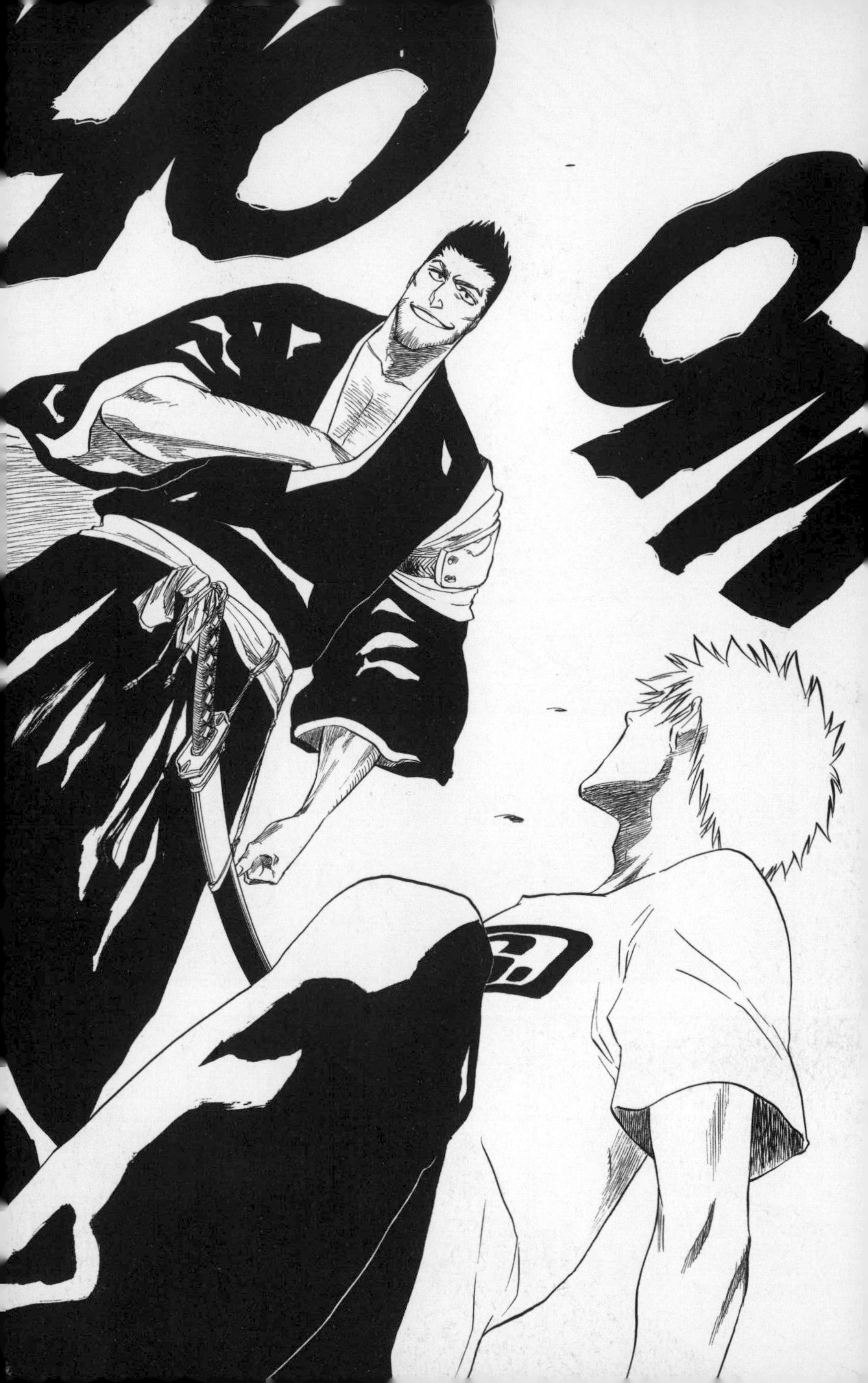

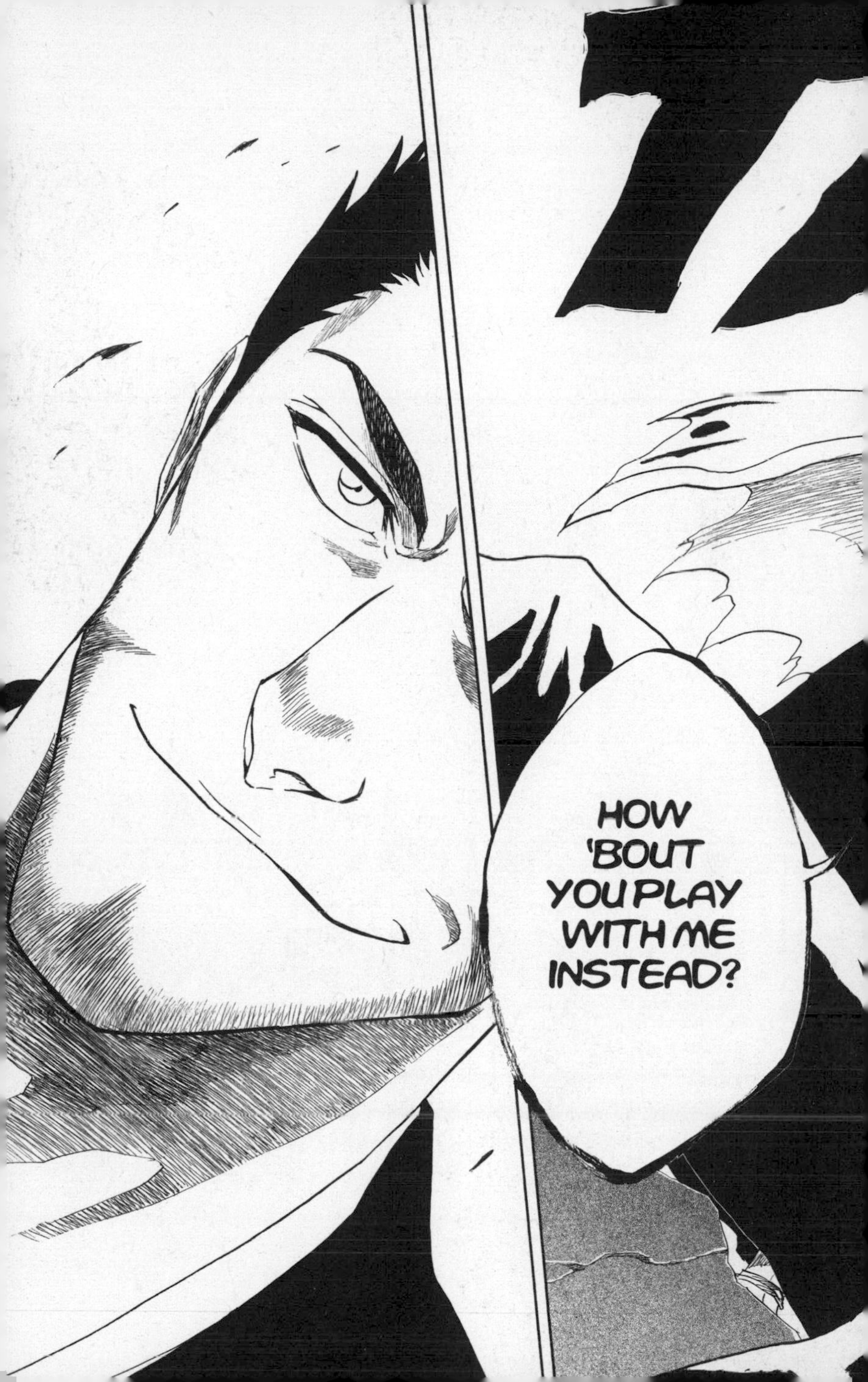
HOW 'BOUT YOU PLAY WITH ME INSTEAD?

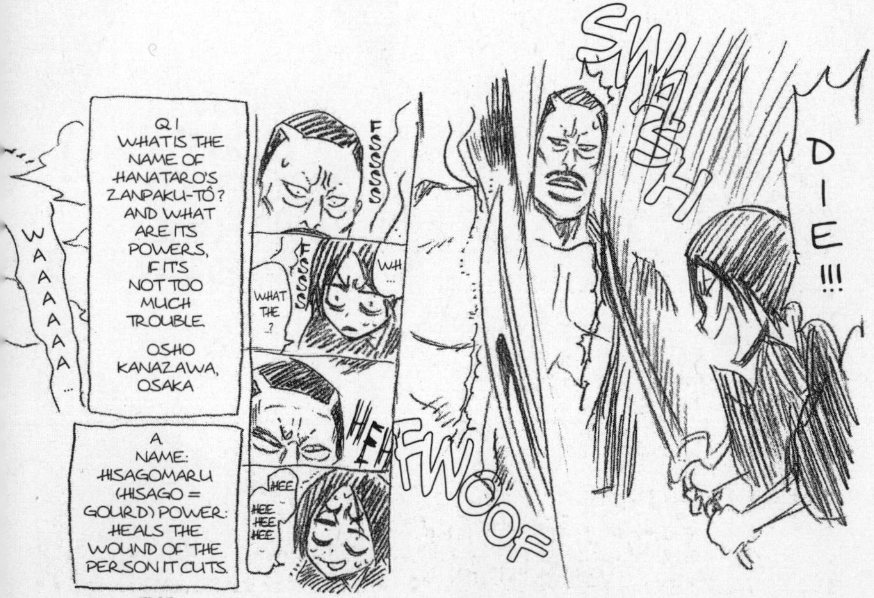
DIE!!!
SWASH
FWOOF
FSSSSS
WH...
FSSSS
WHAT THE ?
HEH
HEE HEE HEE HEE
Q1 WHAT IS THE NAME OF HANATARO'S ZANPAKU-TÔ? AND WHAT ARE ITS POWERS, IF ITS NOT TOO MUCH TROUBLE.
OSHO KANAZAWA, OSAKA
A NAME: HISAGOMARU (HISAGO = GOURD) POWER: HEALS THE WOUND OF THE PERSON IT CUTS.
WAAAAAA...
TO BE CONTINUED

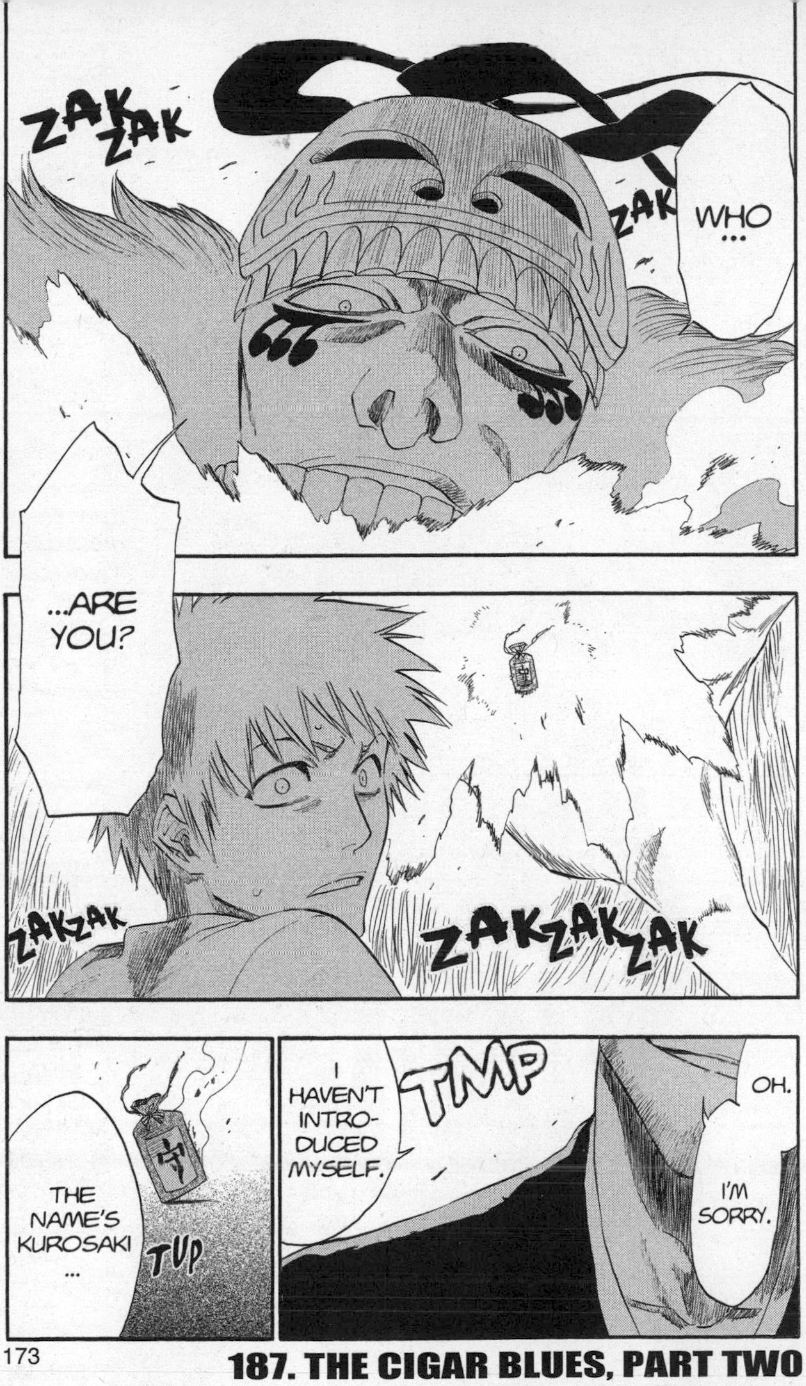
WHO ...
ZAK
ZAK ZAK
...ARE YOU?
ZAKZAKZAK
ZAKZAK
OH.
TMP
I HAVEN'T INTRO-DUCED MYSELF.
I'M SORRY.
THE NAME'S KUROSAKI ...
TUP

187. THE CIGAR BLUES, PART TWO

BLEACH 187. THE CIGAR BLUES, PART TWO

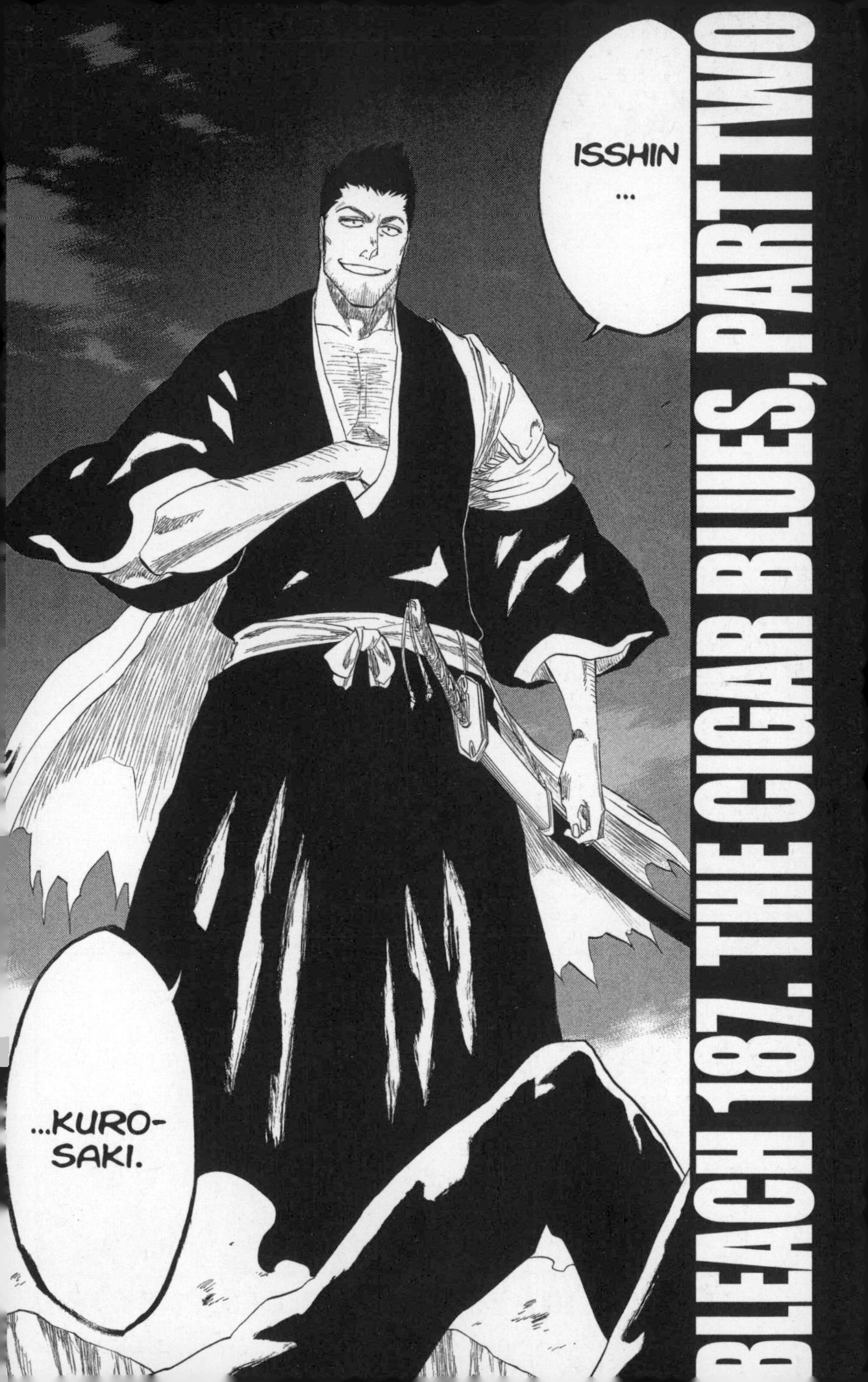
ISSHIN
...
...KURO-
SAKI.

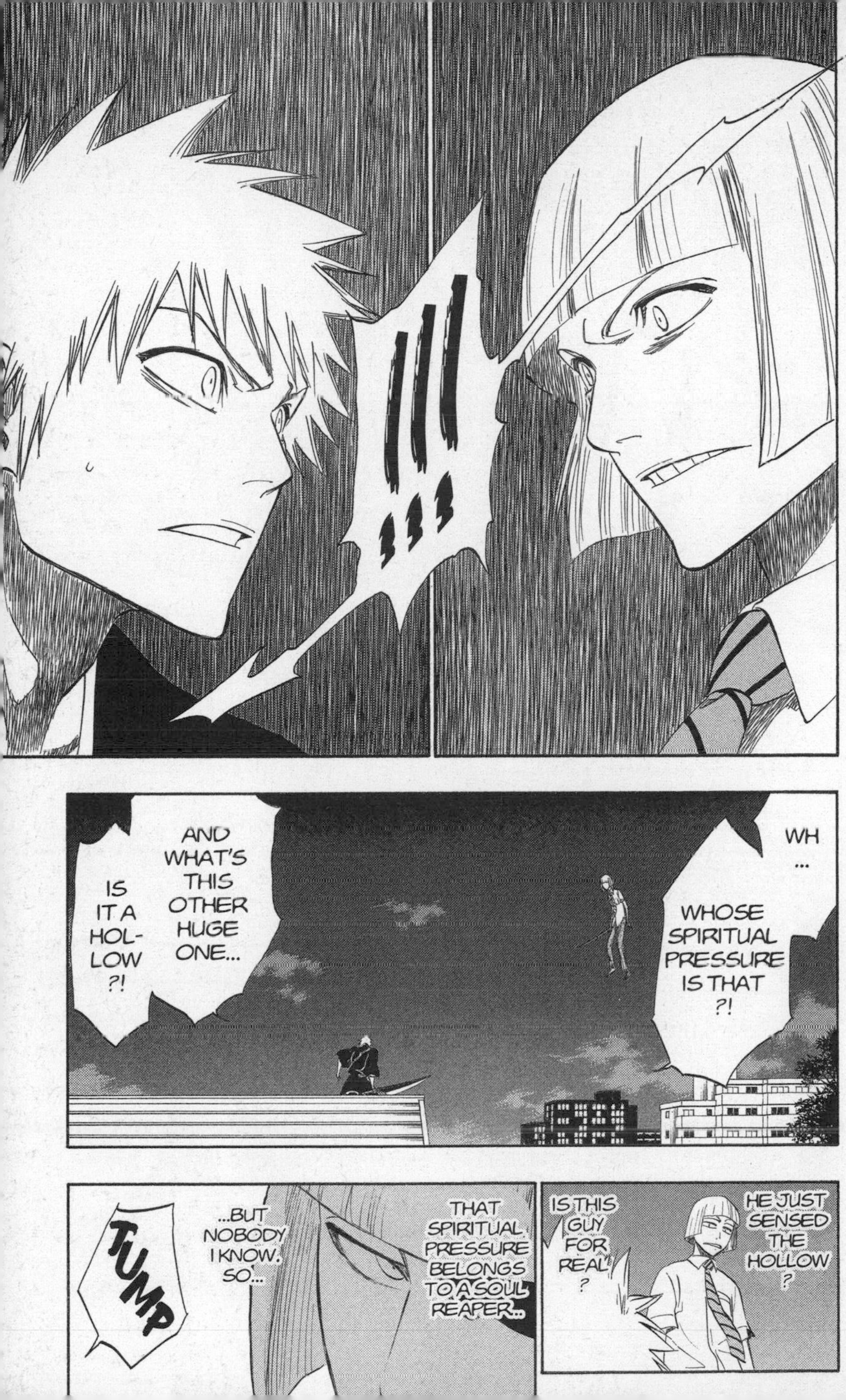
!!!
WH... WHOSE SPIRITUAL PRESSURE IS THAT?!
AND WHAT'S THIS OTHER HUGE ONE...
IS IT A HOL-LOW?!
HE JUST SENSED THE HOLLOW?
IS THIS GUY FOR REAL?
THAT SPIRITUAL PRESSURE BELONGS TO A SOUL REAPER...
...BUT NOBODY I KNOW. SO...
TUMP

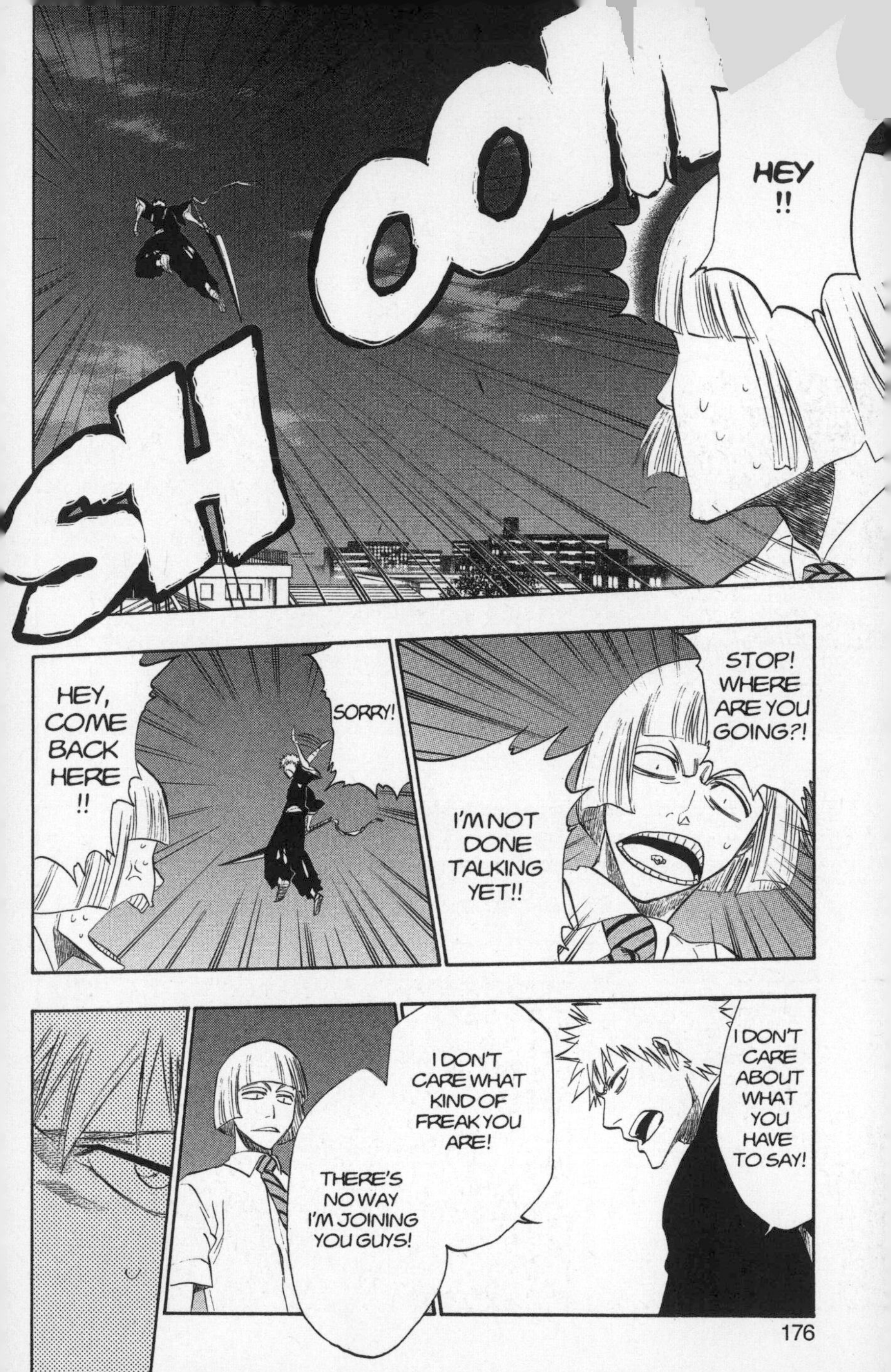
HEY!!
SHOOM
STOP! WHERE ARE YOU GOING?!
I'M NOT DONE TALKING YET!!
SORRY!
HEY, COME BACK HERE!!
I DON'T CARE ABOUT WHAT YOU HAVE TO SAY!
I DON'T CARE WHAT KIND OF FREAK YOU ARE!
THERE'S NO WAY I'M JOINING YOU GUYS!

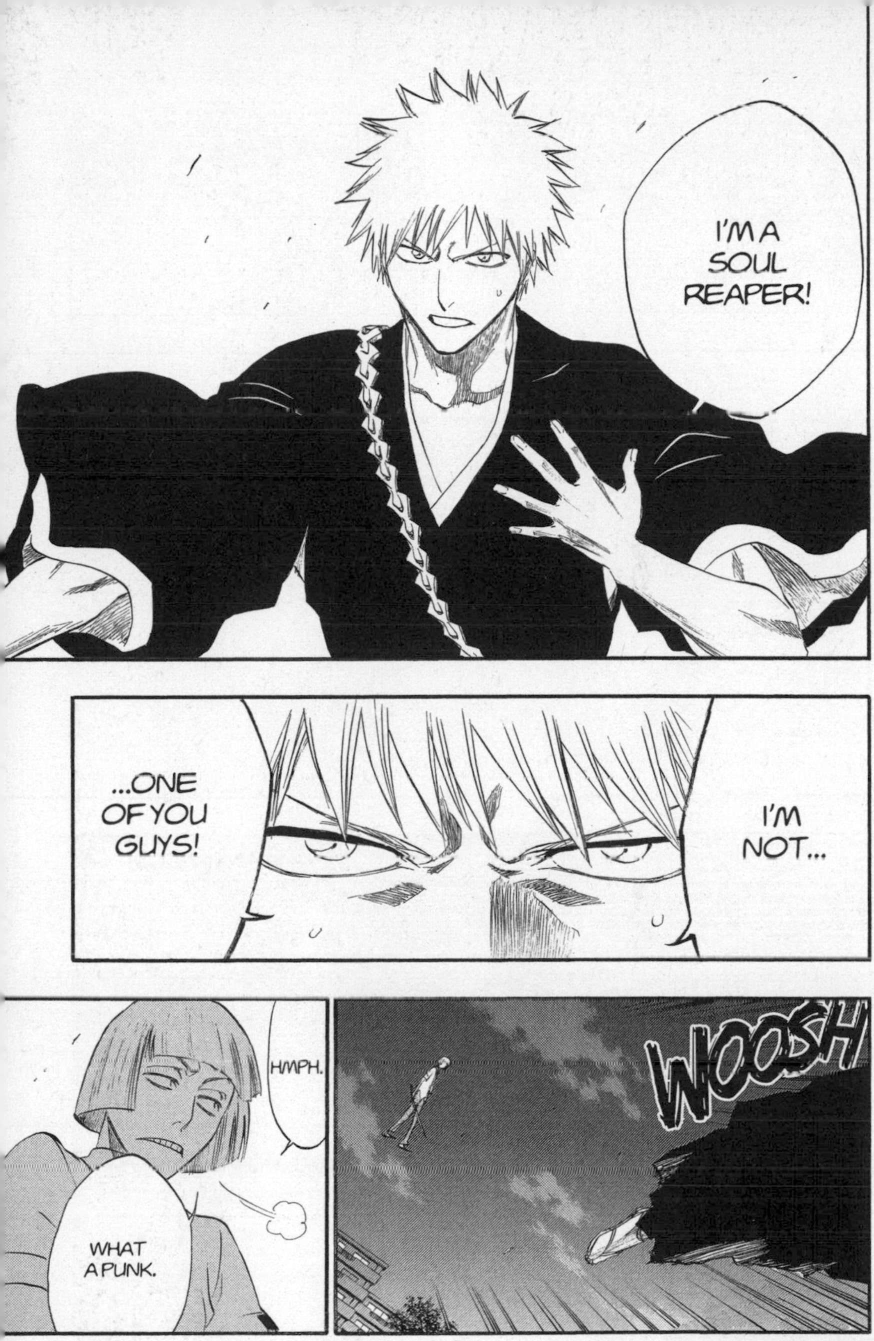
I'M A SOUL REAPER!
I'M NOT...
...ONE OF YOU GUYS!
WOOSH
HMPH.
WHAT A PUNK.

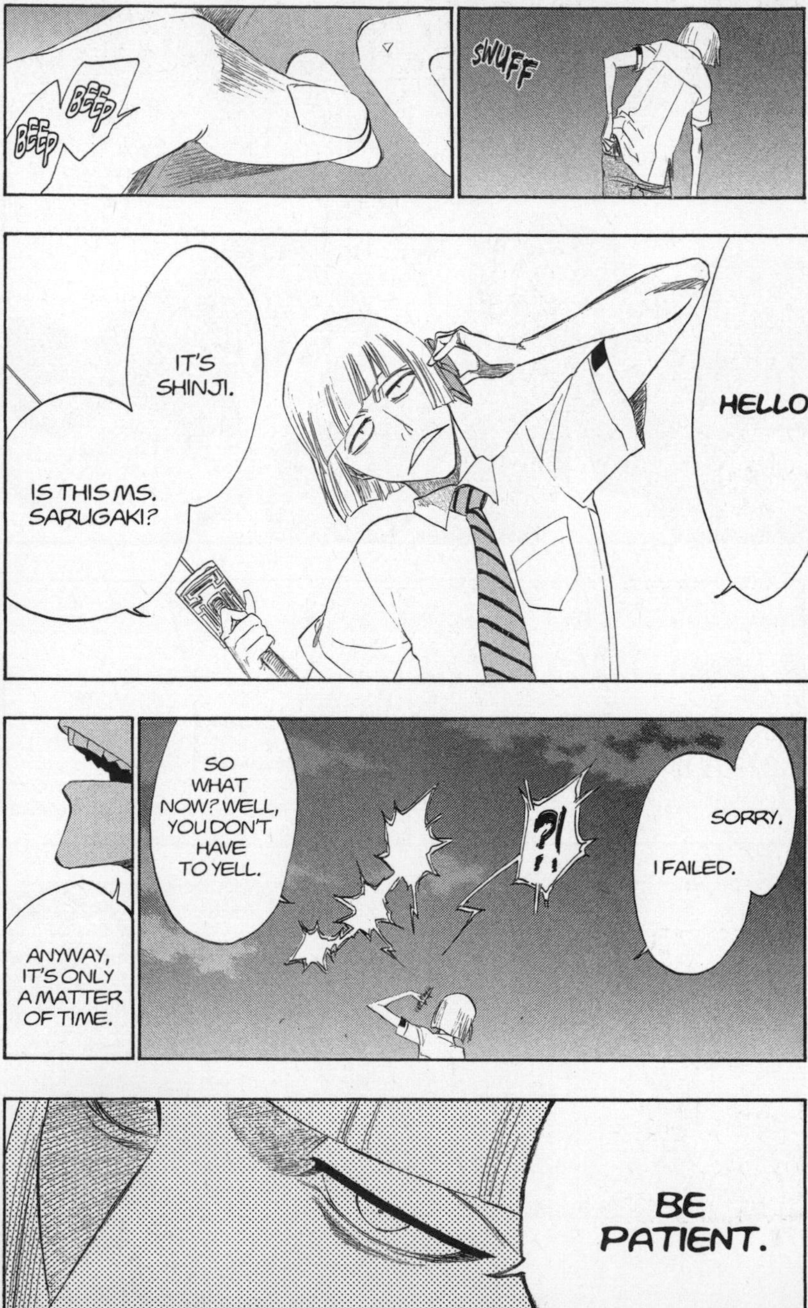
SWUFF
BEEP
BEEP
HELLO?
IT'S SHINJI.
IS THIS MS. SARUGAKI?
SORRY.
I FAILED.
?!
SO WHAT NOW? WELL, YOU DON'T HAVE TO YELL.
ANYWAY, IT'S ONLY A MATTER OF TIME.
BE PATIENT.

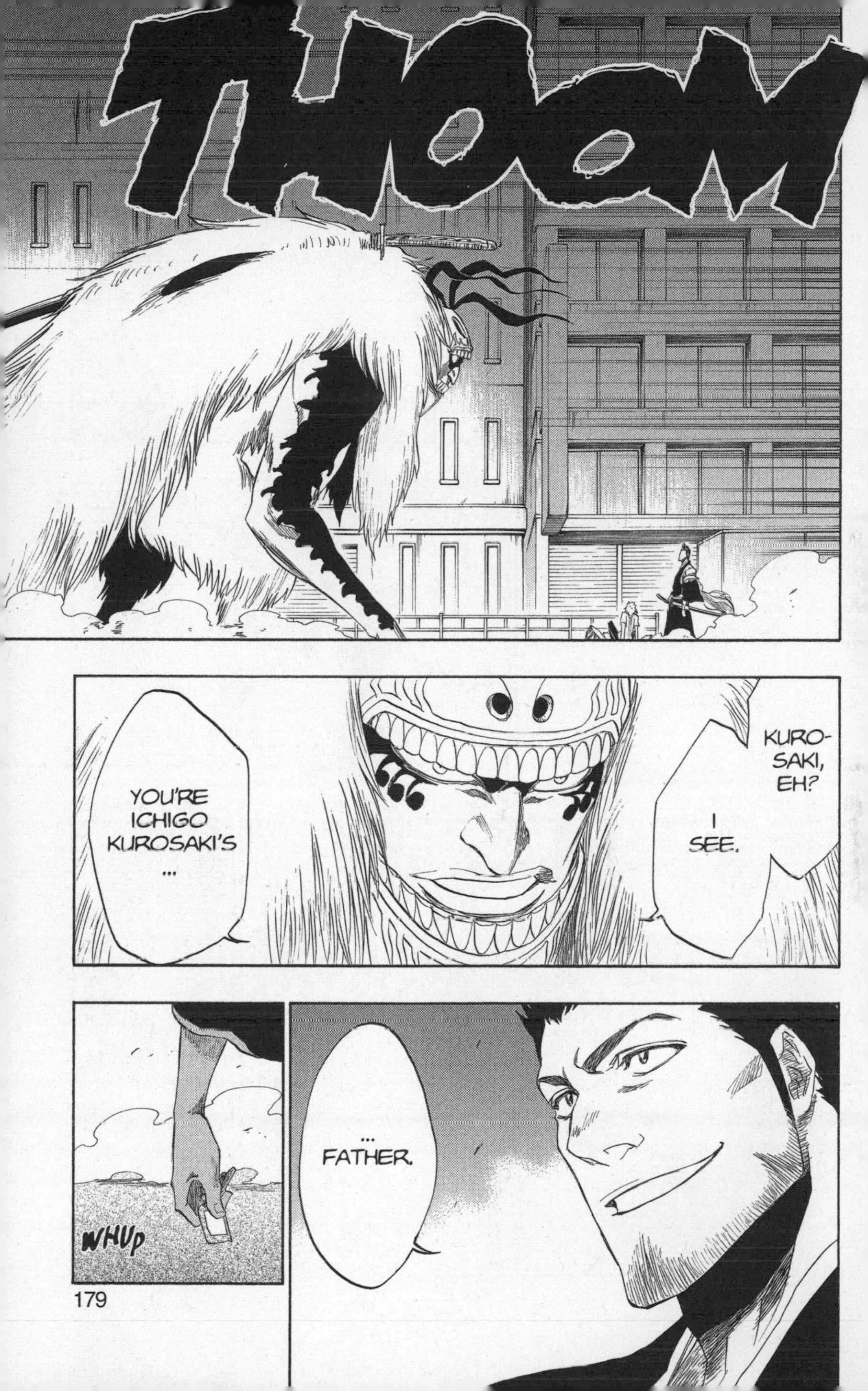
THOOM
KURO-SAKI, EH?
I SEE.
YOU'RE ICHIGO KUROSAKI'S ...
... FATHER.
WHUP

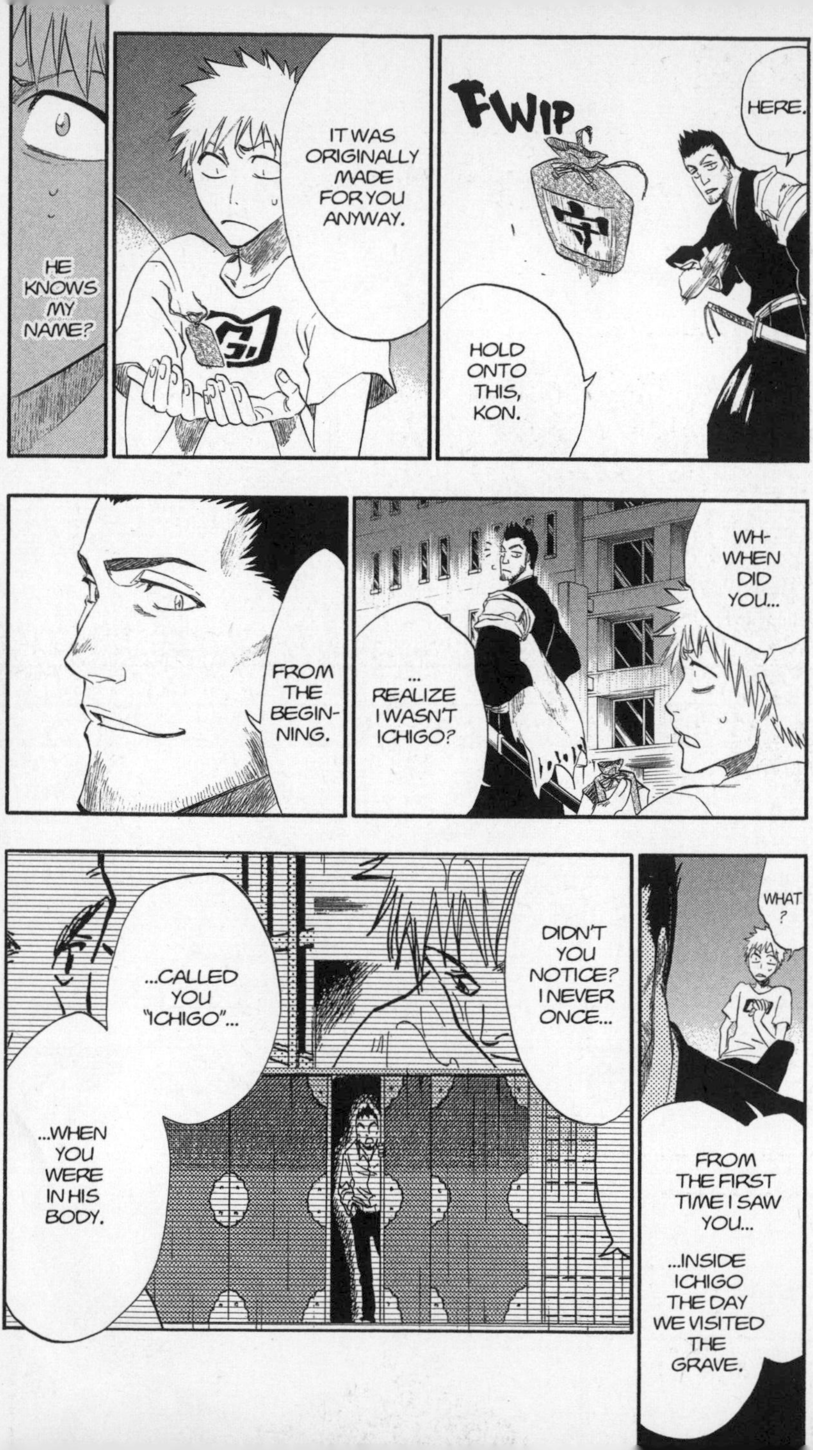
HERE.
FWIP
HOLD ONTO THIS, KON.
IT WAS ORIGINALLY MADE FOR YOU ANYWAY.
HE KNOWS MY NAME?
WH- WHEN DID YOU...
...REALIZE I WASN'T ICHIGO?
FROM THE BEGIN-NING.
WHAT?
FROM THE FIRST TIME I SAW YOU...
...INSIDE ICHIGO THE DAY WE VISITED THE GRAVE.
DIDN'T YOU NOTICE? I NEVER ONCE...
...CALLED YOU "ICHIGO"...
...WHEN YOU WERE IN HIS BODY.

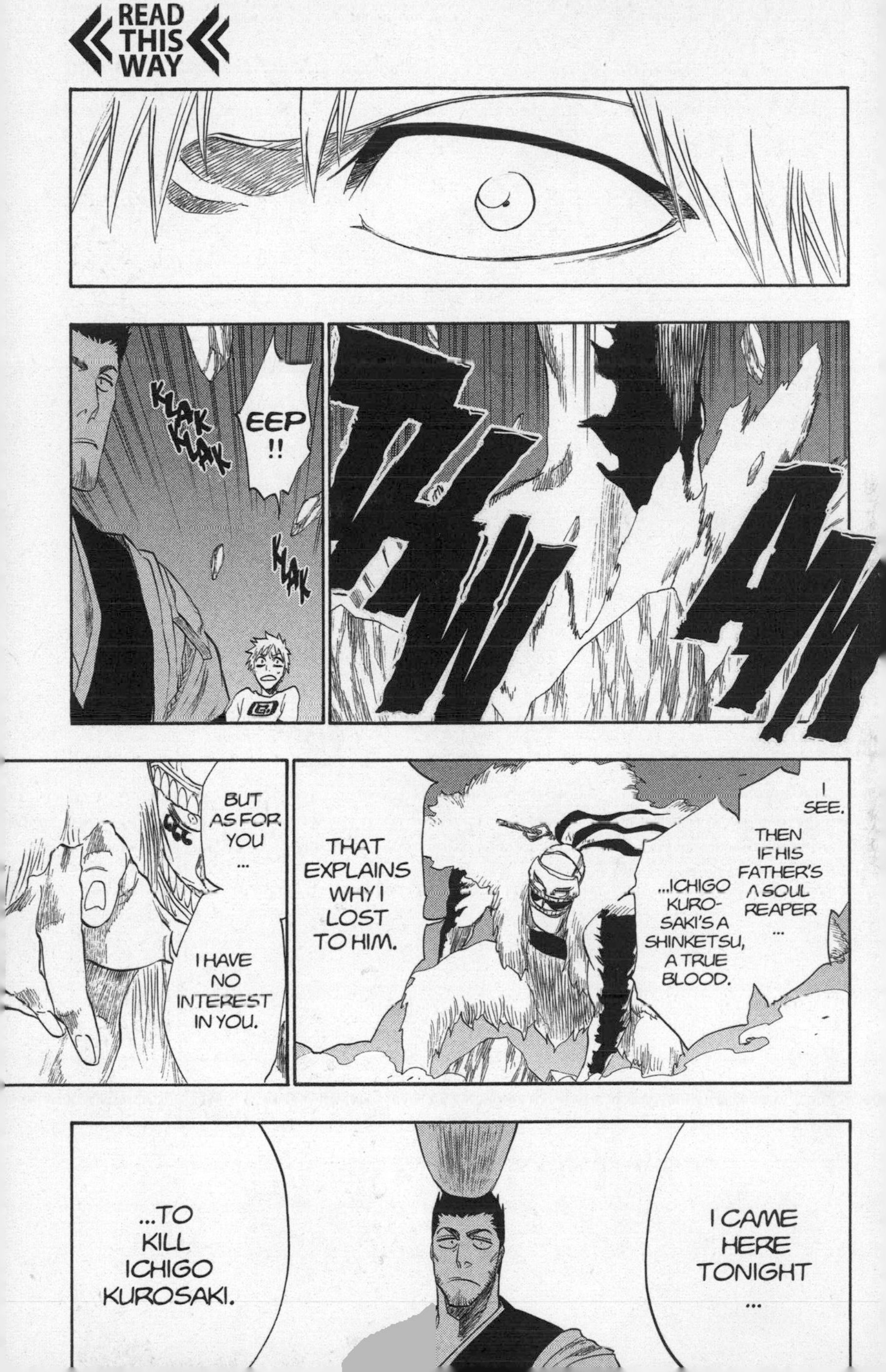
READ THIS WAY
WHAM
EEP !!
KLAK KLAK
KLAK
I SEE.
THEN IF HIS FATHER'S A SOUL REAPER ...
...ICHIGO KUROSAKI'S A SHINKETSU, A TRUE BLOOD.
THAT EXPLAINS WHY I LOST TO HIM.
BUT AS FOR YOU ...
I HAVE NO INTEREST IN YOU.
I CAME HERE TONIGHT ...
...TO KILL ICHIGO KUROSAKI.

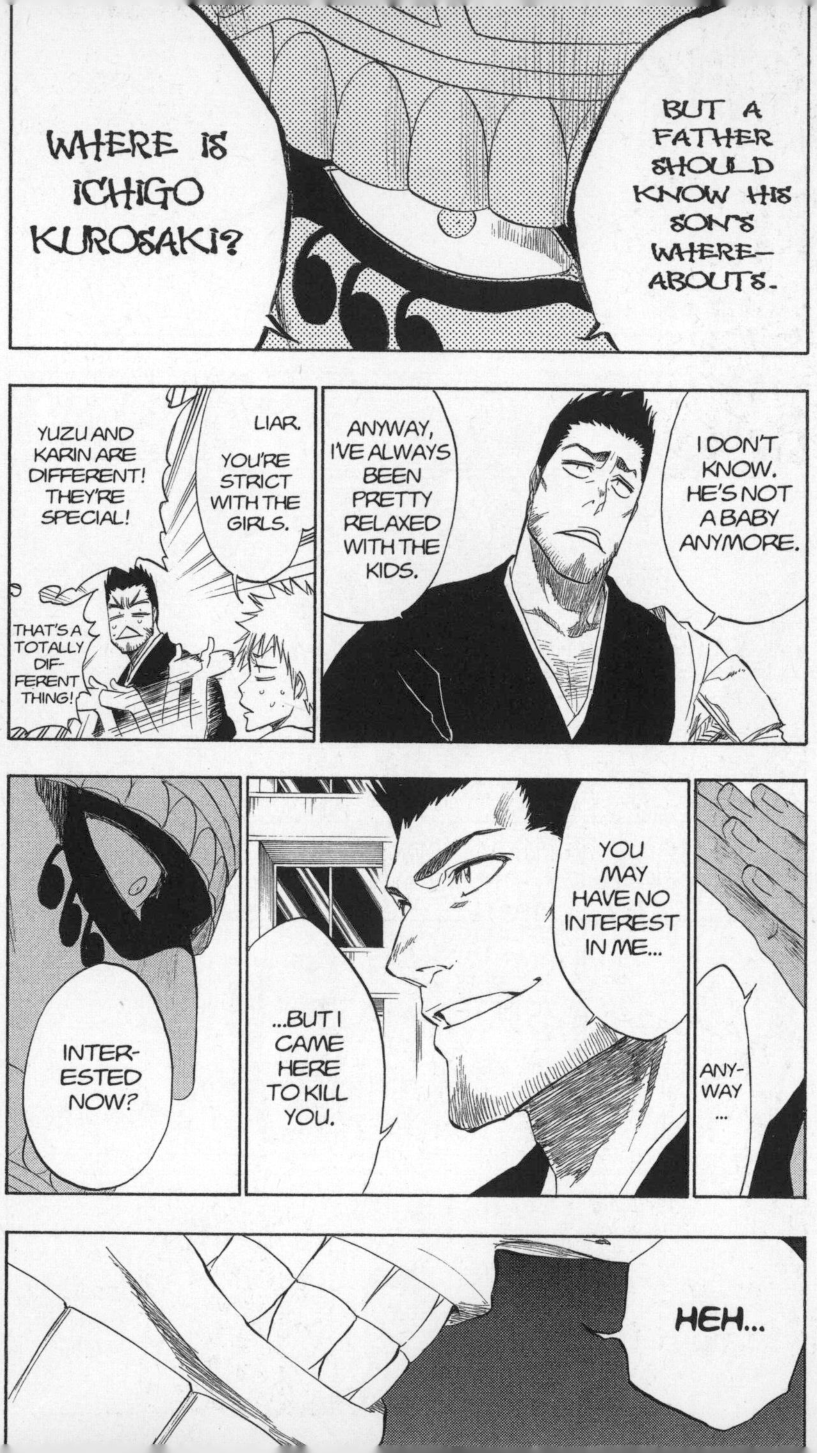
BUT A FATHER SHOULD KNOW HIS SON'S WHEREABOUTS.
WHERE IS ICHIGO KUROSAKI?
I DON'T KNOW. HE'S NOT A BABY ANYMORE.
ANYWAY, I'VE ALWAYS BEEN PRETTY RELAXED WITH THE KIDS.
LIAR.
YOU'RE STRICT WITH THE GIRLS.
YUZU AND KARIN ARE DIFFERENT! THEY'RE SPECIAL!
THAT'S A TOTALLY DIF-FERENT THING!
ANY-WAY ...
YOU MAY HAVE NO INTEREST IN ME...
...BUT I CAME HERE TO KILL YOU.
INTER-ESTED NOW?
HEH...

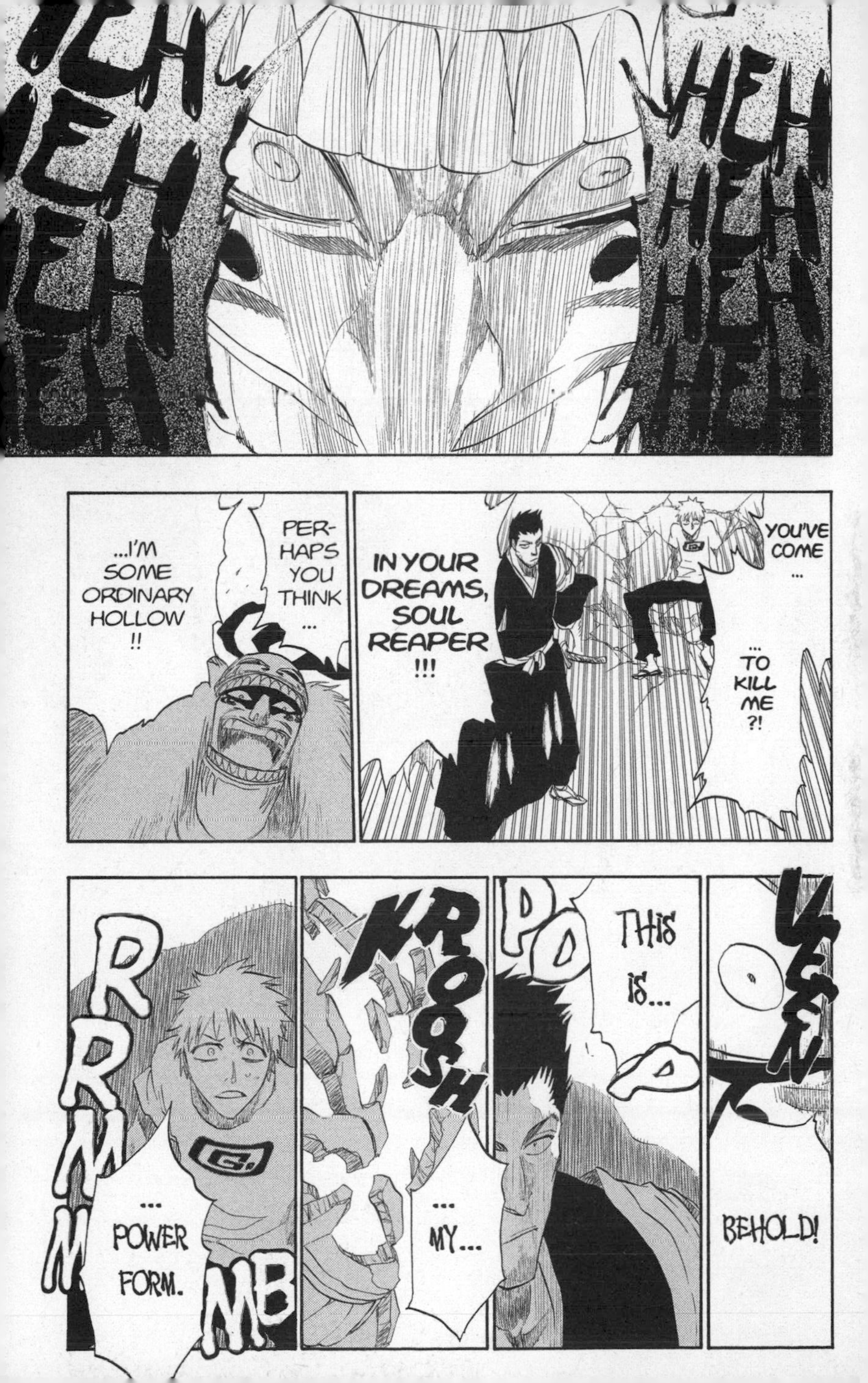
HEH HEH HEH HEH
HEH HEH HEH HEH
YOU'VE COME ...
... TO KILL ME ?!
IN YOUR DREAMS, SOUL REAPER !!!
PER-HAPS YOU THINK ...
...I'M SOME ORDINARY HOLLOW !!
BEHOLD!
THIS IS...
... MY...
VROOSH
... POWER FORM.

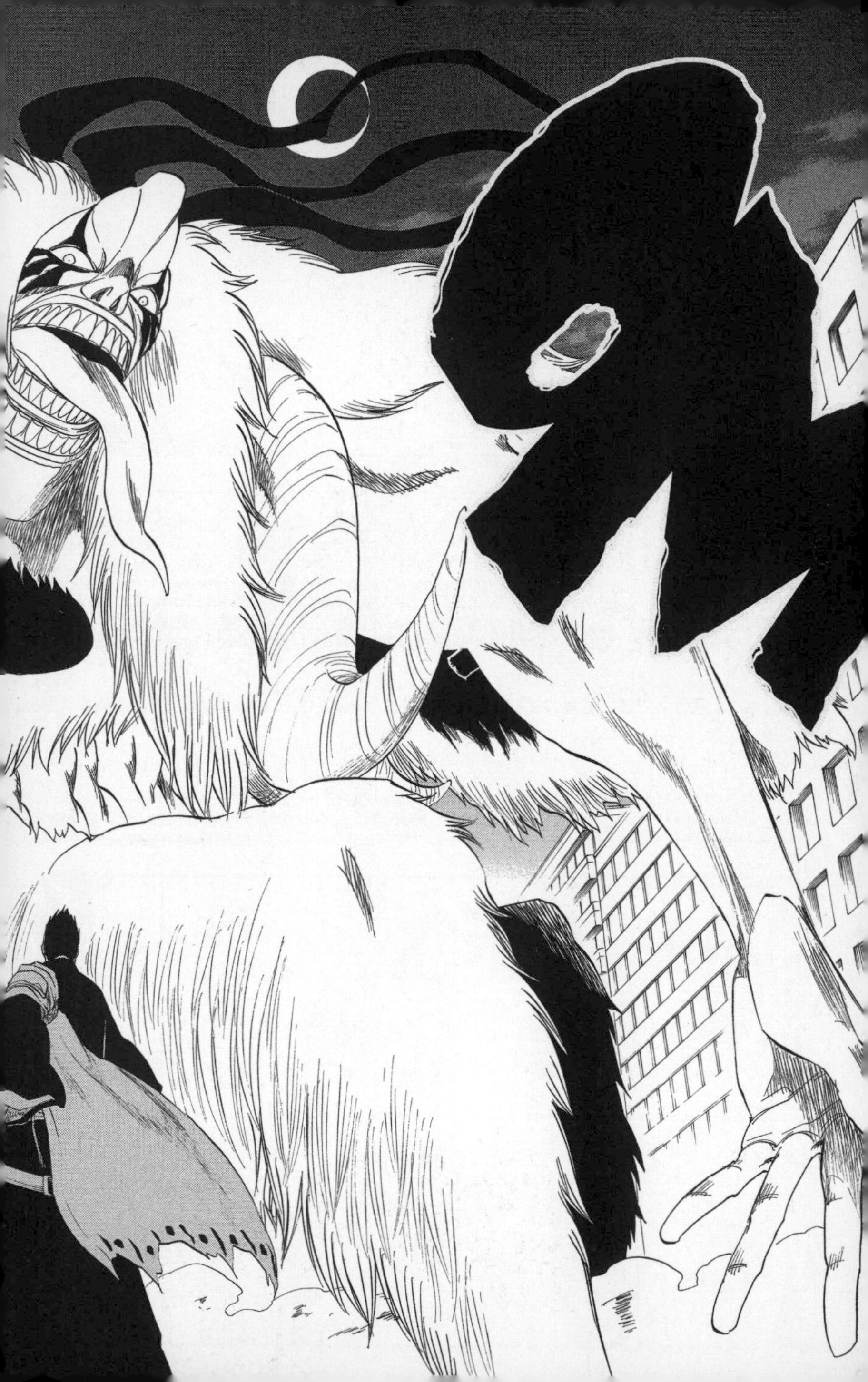

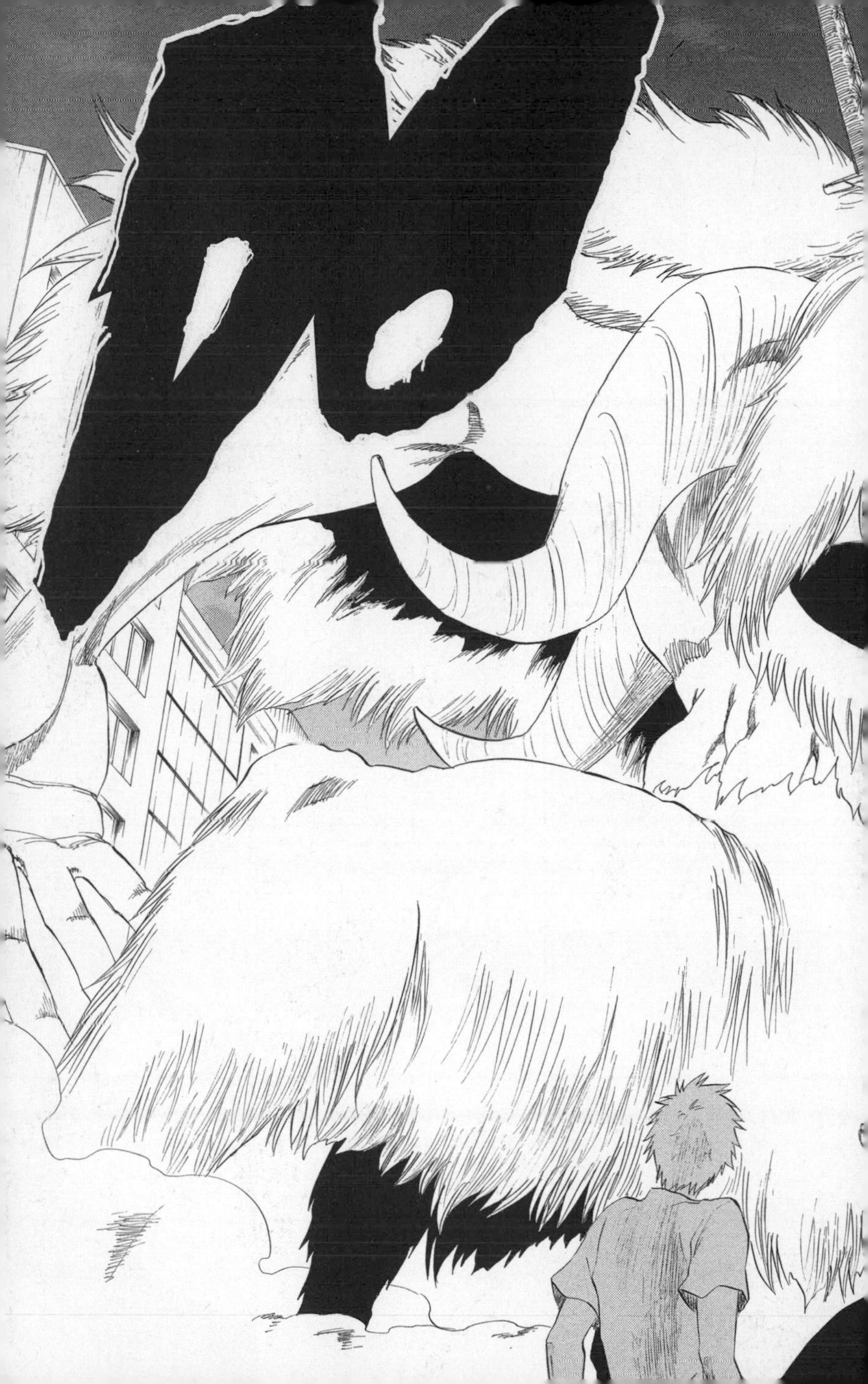

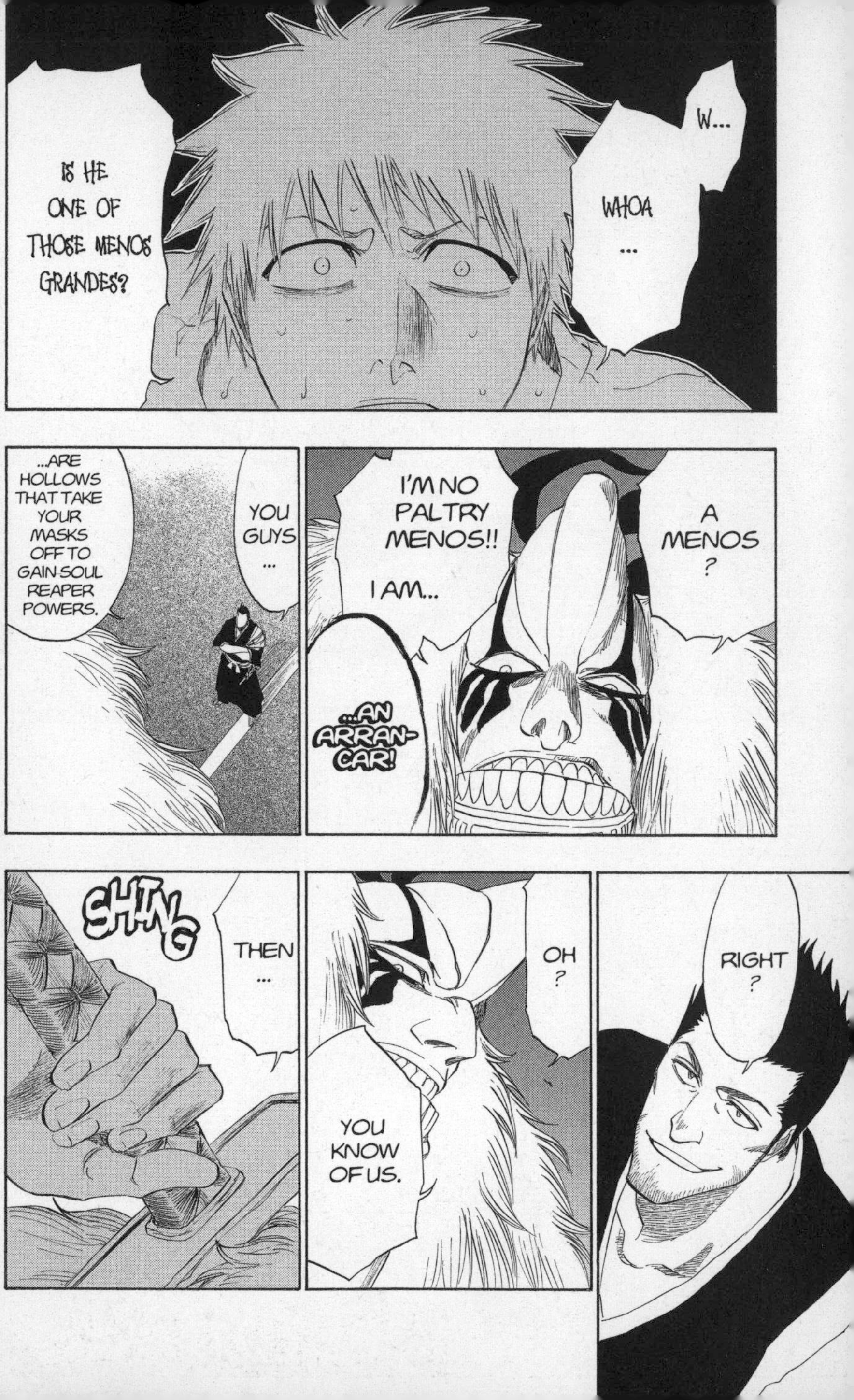
W...
WHOA ...
IS HE ONE OF THOSE MENOS GRANDES?
A MENOS ?
I'M NO PALTRY MENOS!!
I AM...
...AN ARRAN-CAR!
YOU GUYS ...
...ARE HOLLOWS THAT TAKE YOUR MASKS OFF TO GAIN-SOUL REAPER POWERS.
RIGHT ?
OH ?
YOU KNOW OF US.
THEN ...
SHING

READ THIS WAY

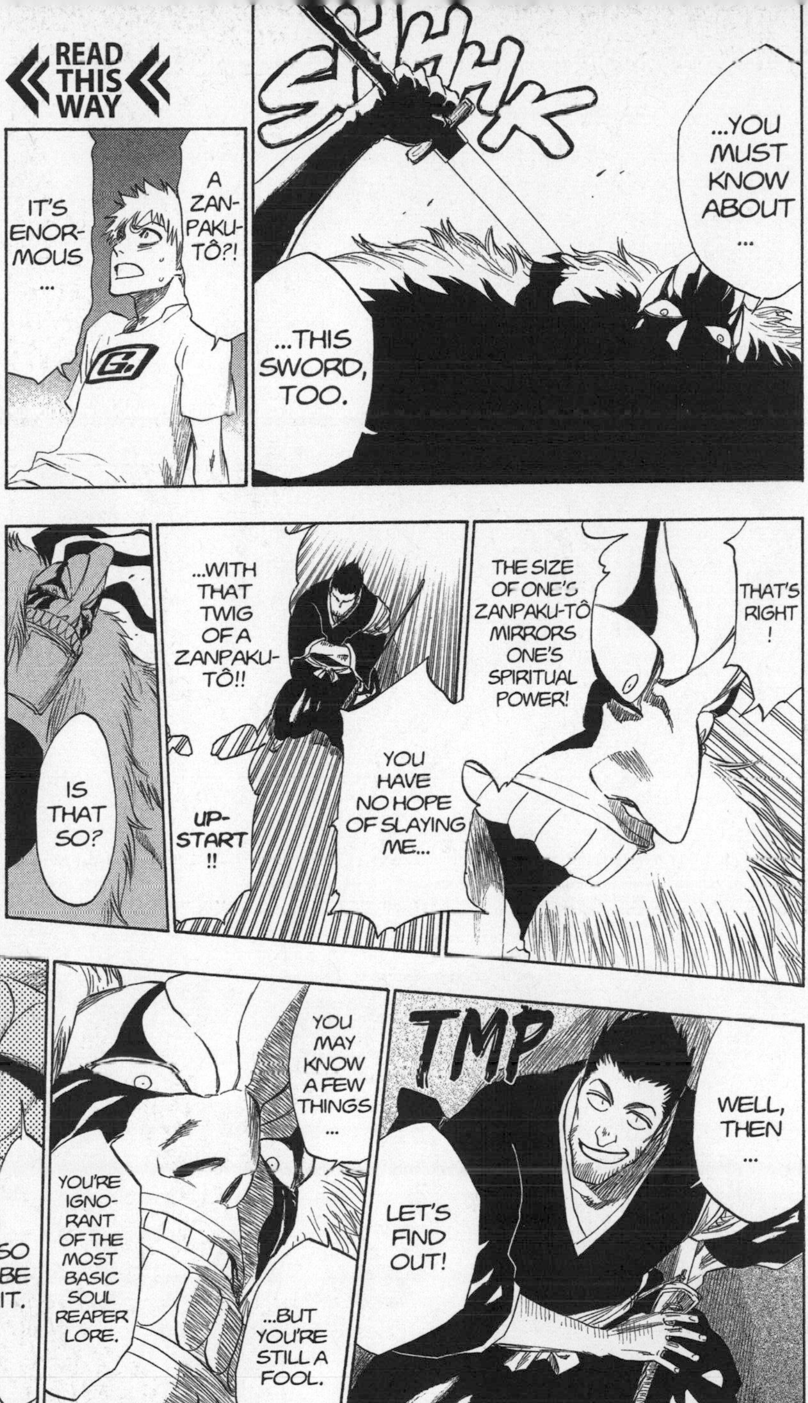
SHHHK
...YOU MUST KNOW ABOUT ...
...THIS SWORD, TOO.
A ZANPAKU-TÔ?!
IT'S ENORMOUS ...
THAT'S RIGHT!
THE SIZE OF ONE'S ZANPAKU-TÔ MIRRORS ONE'S SPIRITUAL POWER!
YOU HAVE NO HOPE OF SLAYING ME...
...WITH THAT TWIG OF A ZANPAKU-TÔ!!
UP-START!!
IS THAT SO?
TMP
WELL, THEN ...
LET'S FIND OUT!
YOU MAY KNOW A FEW THINGS ...
...BUT YOU'RE STILL A FOOL.
YOU'RE IGNORANT OF THE MOST BASIC SOUL REAPER LORE.
SO BE IT.

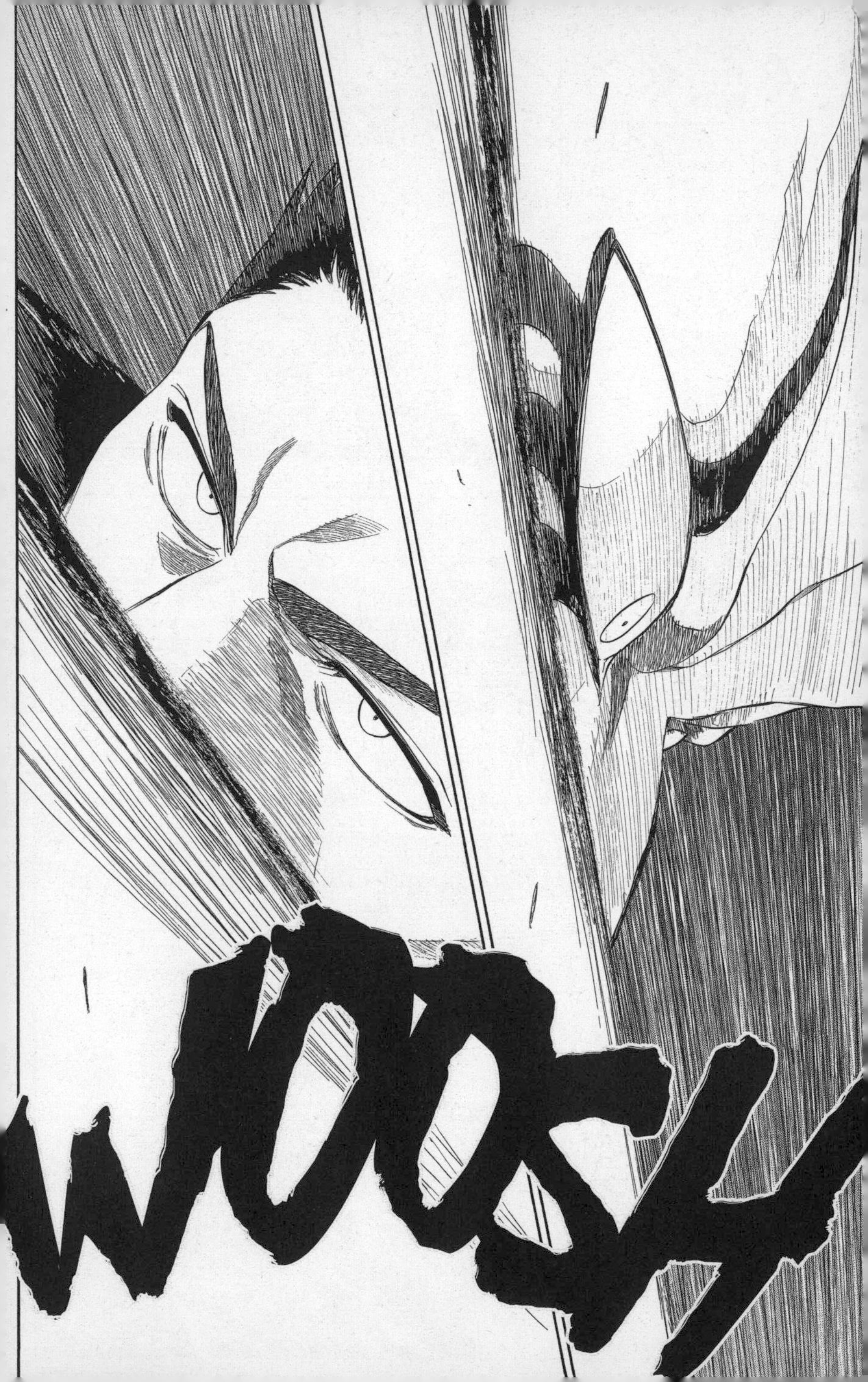
WOOSH

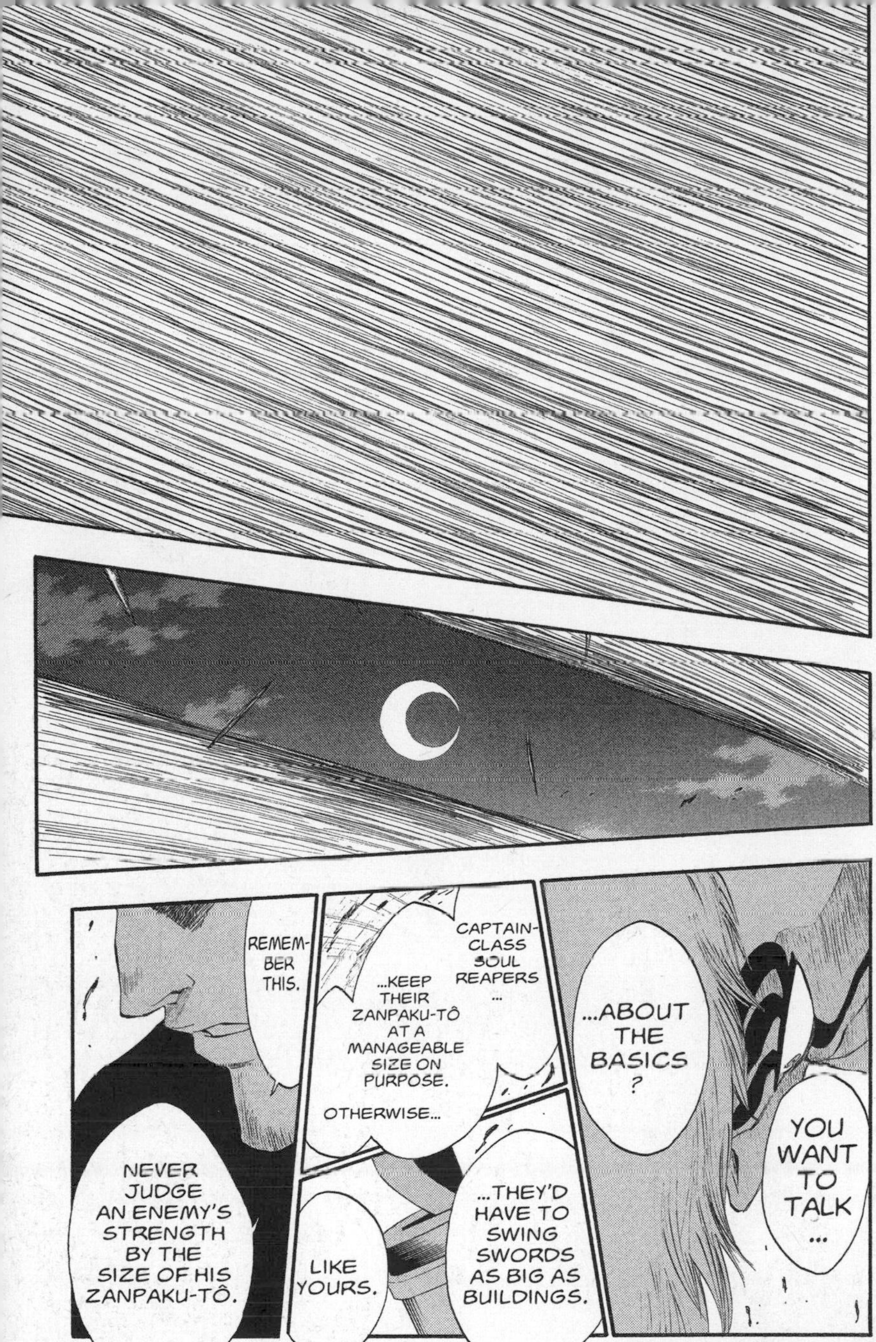
YOU WANT TO TALK...
...ABOUT THE BASICS?
CAPTAIN-CLASS SOUL REAPERS...
...KEEP THEIR ZANPAKU-TÔ AT A MANAGEABLE SIZE ON PURPOSE.
OTHERWISE...
...THEY'D HAVE TO SWING SWORDS AS BIG AS BUILDINGS.
LIKE YOURS.
REMEMBER THIS.
NEVER JUDGE AN ENEMY'S STRENGTH BY THE SIZE OF HIS ZANPAKU-TÔ.

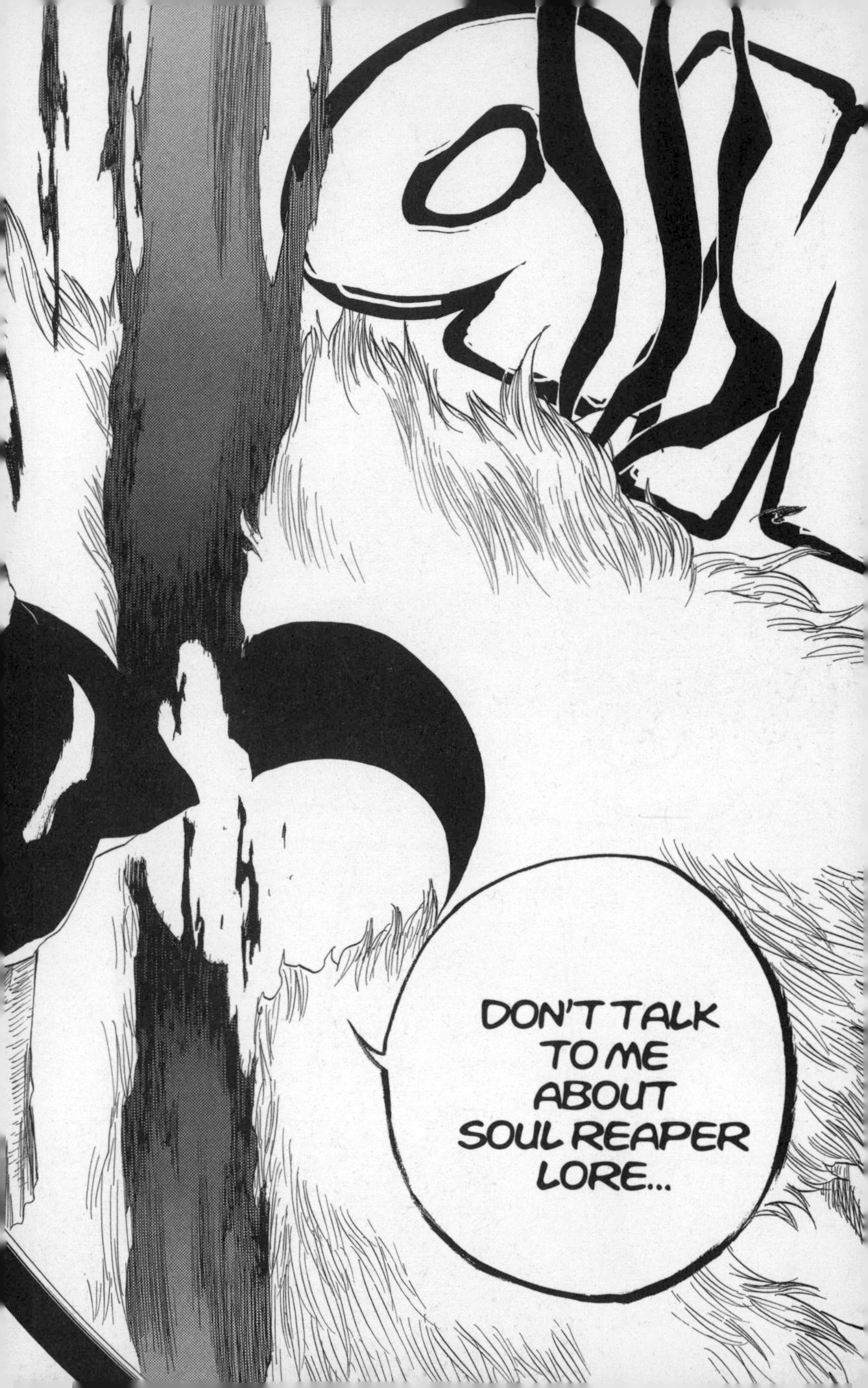
DON'T TALK TO ME ABOUT SOUL REAPER LORE...

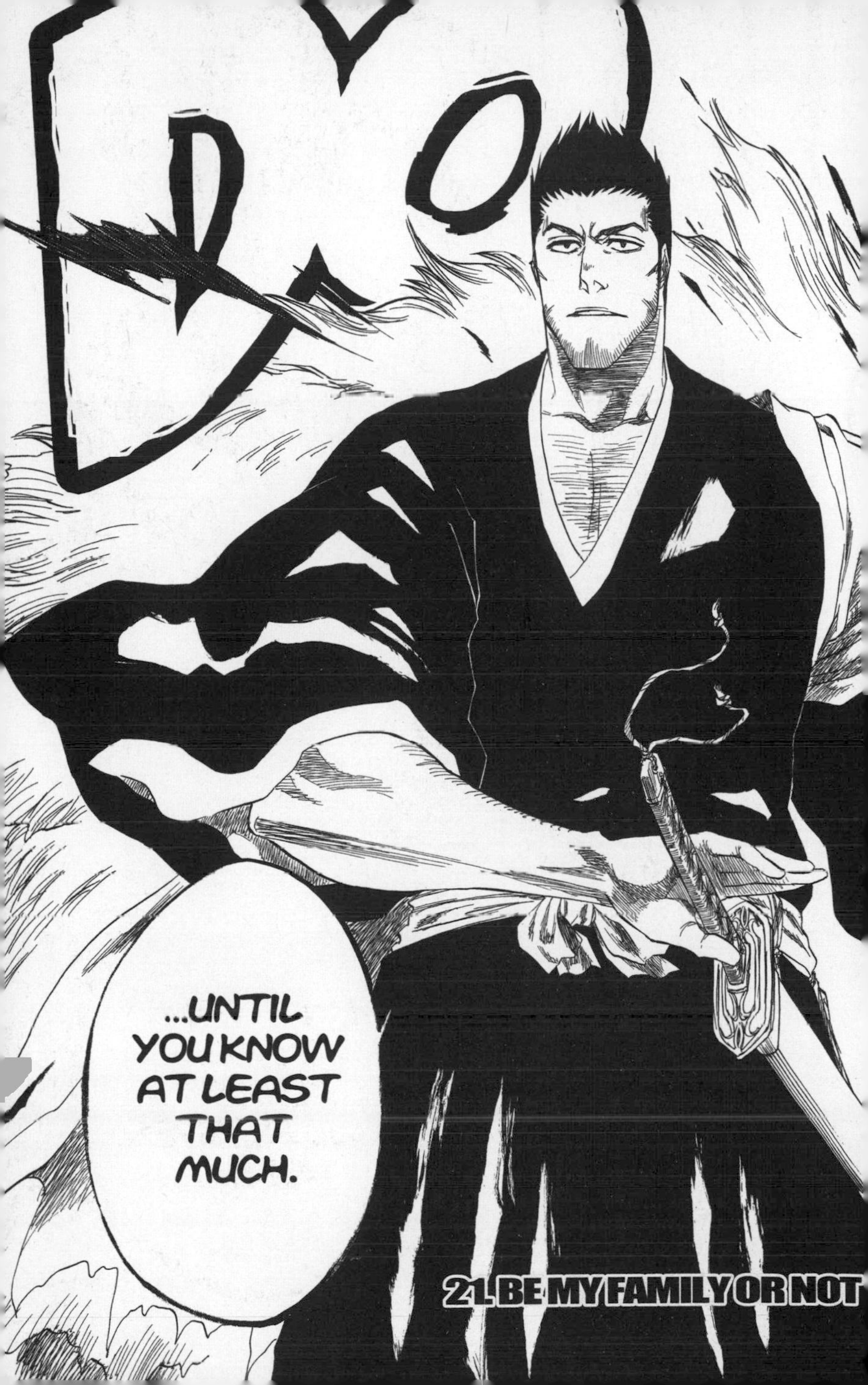
...UNTIL YOU KNOW AT LEAST THAT MUCH.
21. BE MY FAMILY OR NOT

Next Volume Preview

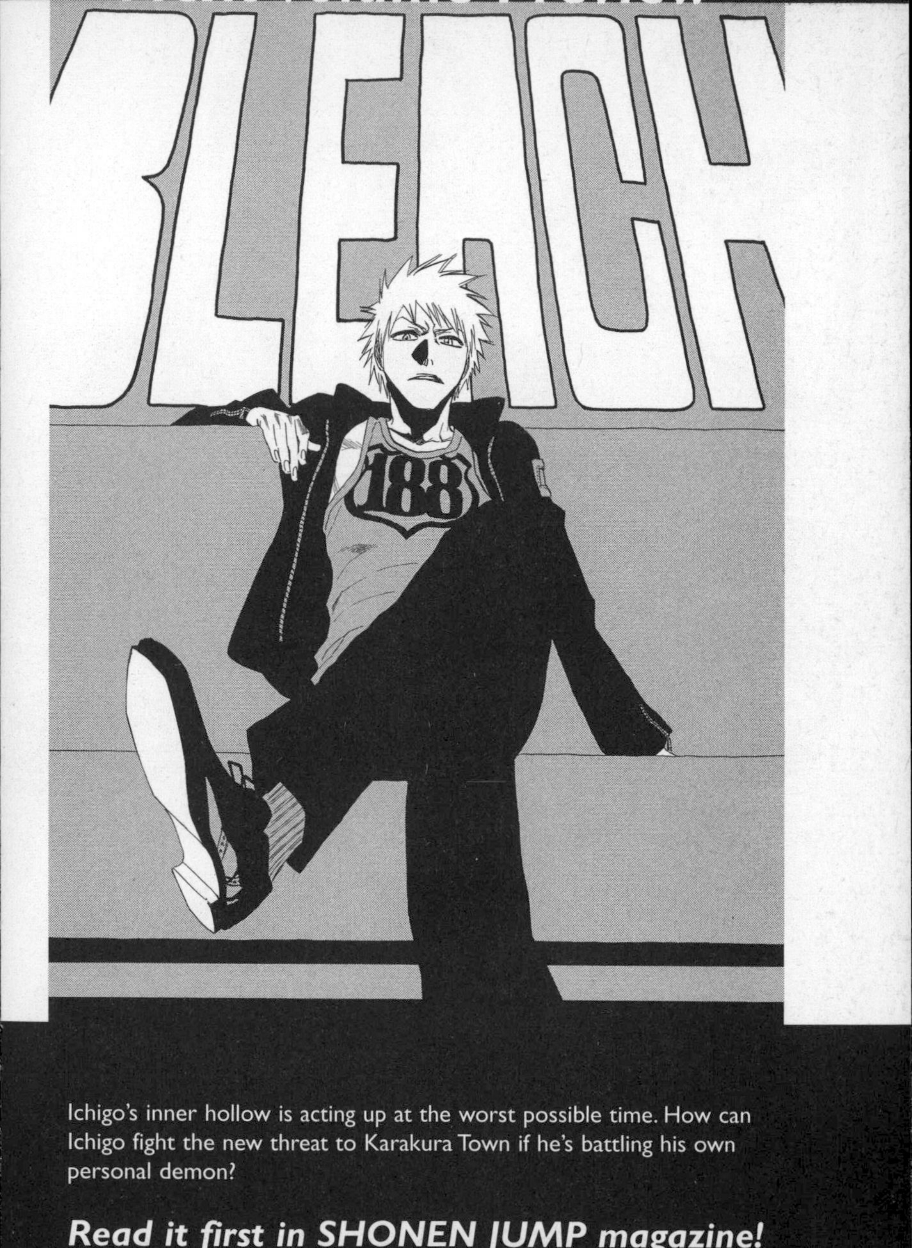
BLEACH
188

Ichigo's inner hollow is acting up at the worst possible time. How can Ichigo fight the new threat to Karakura Town if he's battling his own personal demon?

Read it first in SHONEN JUMP magazine!

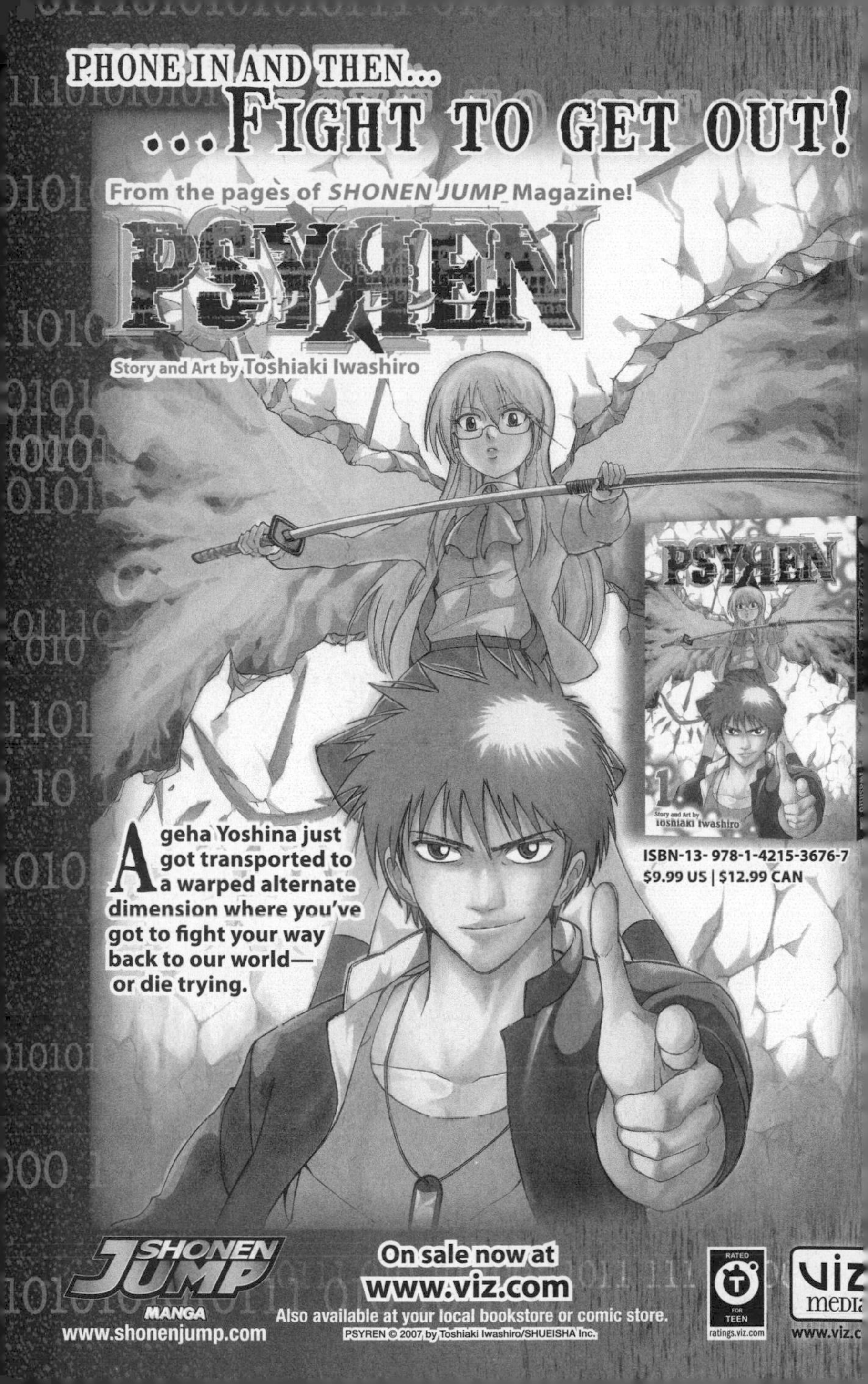
PHONE IN AND THEN...
...FIGHT TO GET OUT!
From the pages of SHONEN JUMP Magazine!
PSYREN
Story and Art by Toshiaki Iwashiro
Ageha Yoshina just got transported to a warped alternate dimension where you've got to fight your way back to our world—or die trying.
PSYREN
1
Story and Art by Toshiaki Iwashiro
ISBN-13- 978-1-4215-3676-7
$9.99 US | $12.99 CAN
SHONEN JUMP MANGA
www.shonenjump.com
On sale now at
www.viz.com
Also available at your local bookstore or comic store.
PSYREN © 2007 by Toshiaki Iwashiro/SHUEISHA Inc.
RATED T FOR TEEN
ratings.viz.com
viz media
www.viz.c

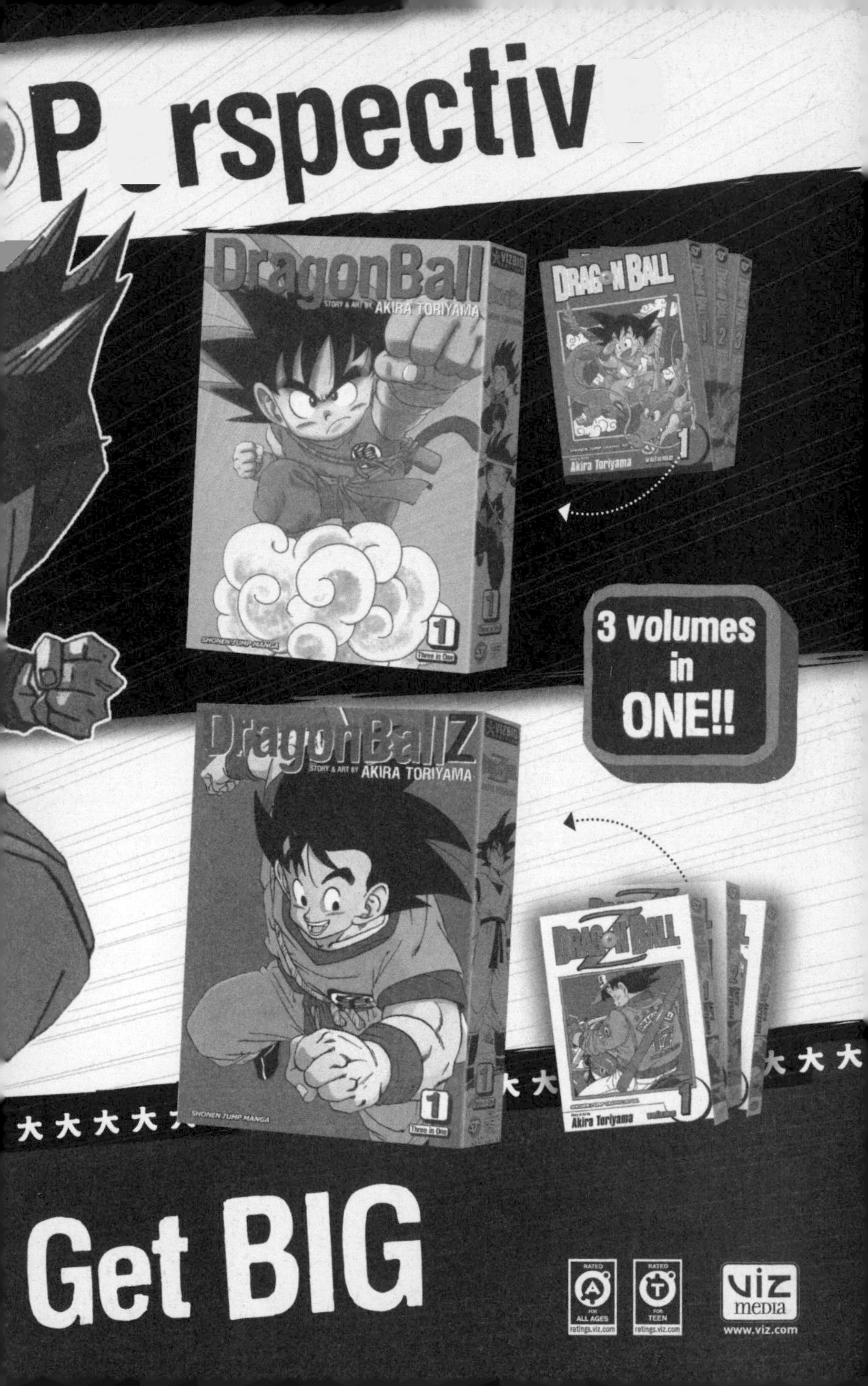
P rspectiv
DragonBall
STORY & ART BY AKIRA TORIYAMA
SHONEN JUMP MANGA
1
Three in One
DRAGON BALL
Akira Toriyama
volume 1
3 volumes in ONE!!
DragonBall Z
STORY & ART BY AKIRA TORIYAMA
SHONEN JUMP MANGA
1
Three in One
DRAGON BALL Z
Akira Toriyama
volume 1
Get BIG
RATED A FOR ALL AGES ratings.viz.com
RATED T FOR TEEN ratings.viz.com
VIZ media
www.viz.com

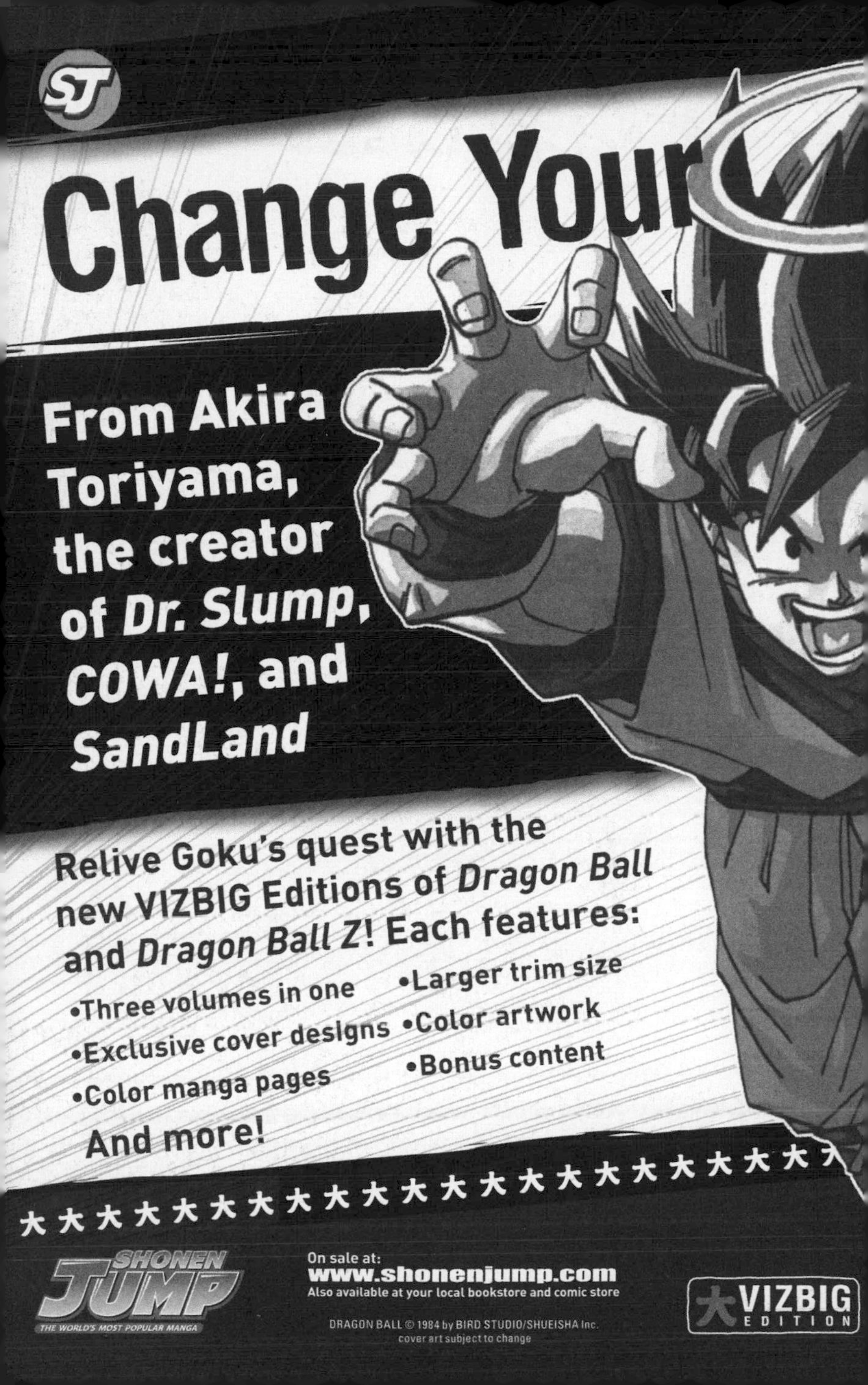
SJ
Change Your
From Akira Toriyama, the creator of Dr. Slump, COWA!, and SandLand
Relive Goku's quest with the new VIZBIG Editions of Dragon Ball and Dragon Ball Z! Each features:
•Three volumes in one
•Exclusive cover designs
•Color manga pages
•Larger trim size
•Color artwork
•Bonus content
And more!
SHONEN JUMP
THE WORLD'S MOST POPULAR MANGA
On sale at:
www.shonenjump.com
Also available at your local bookstore and comic store
DRAGON BALL © 1984 by BIRD STUDIO/SHUEISHA Inc.
cover art subject to change
大 VIZBIG EDITION

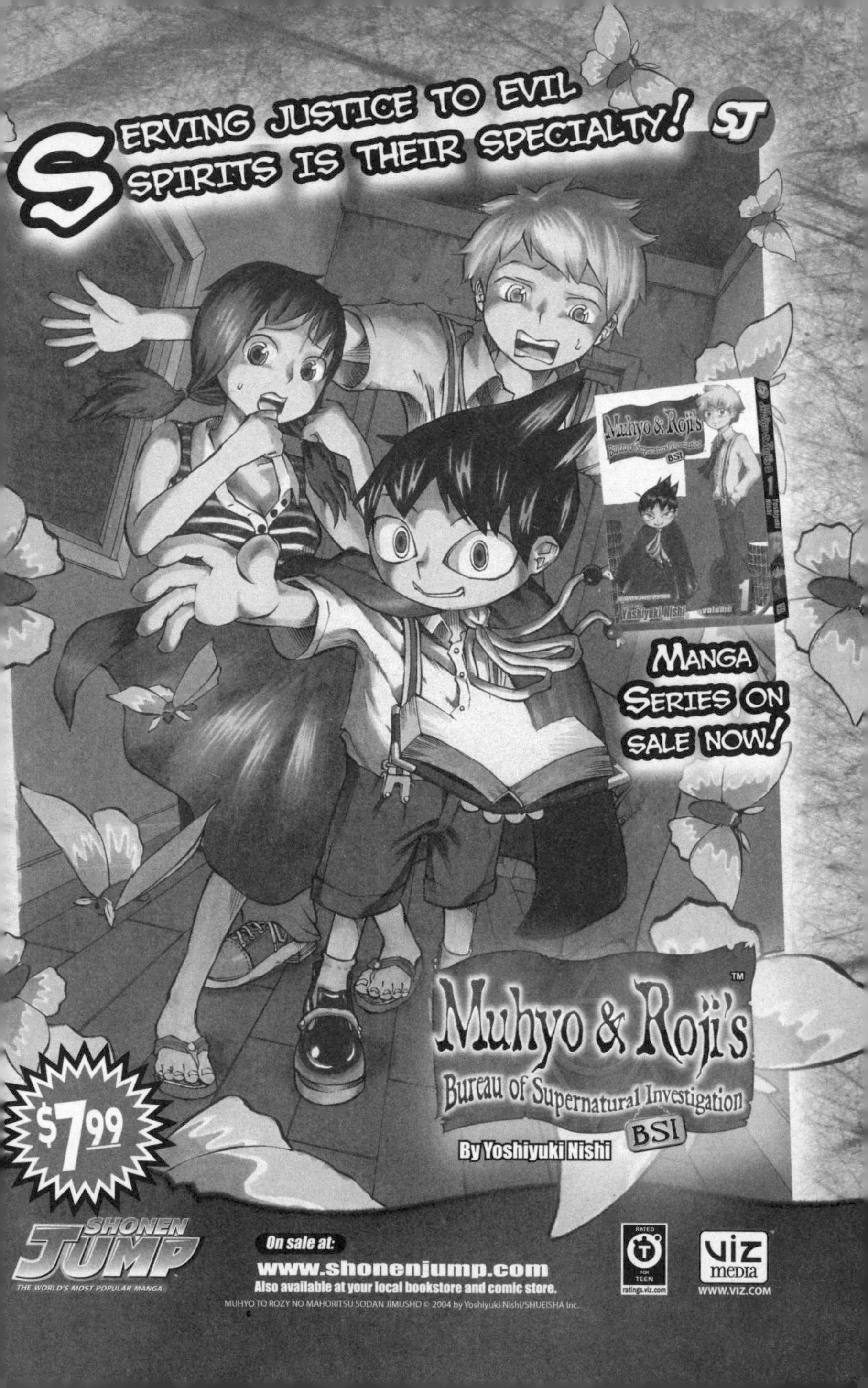
SERVING JUSTICE TO EVIL SPIRITS IS THEIR SPECIALTY!
SJ
MANGA SERIES ON SALE NOW!
Muhyo & Roji's
Bureau of Supernatural Investigation
BSI
By Yoshiyuki Nishi
$7.99
SHONEN JUMP
THE WORLD'S MOST POPULAR MANGA
On sale at:
www.shonenjump.com
Also available at your local bookstore and comic store.
MUHYO TO ROZY NO MAHORITSU SODAN JIMUSHO © 2004 by Yoshiyuki Nishi/SHUEISHA Inc.
RATED T FOR TEEN
ratings.viz.com
VIZ media
WWW.VIZ.COM

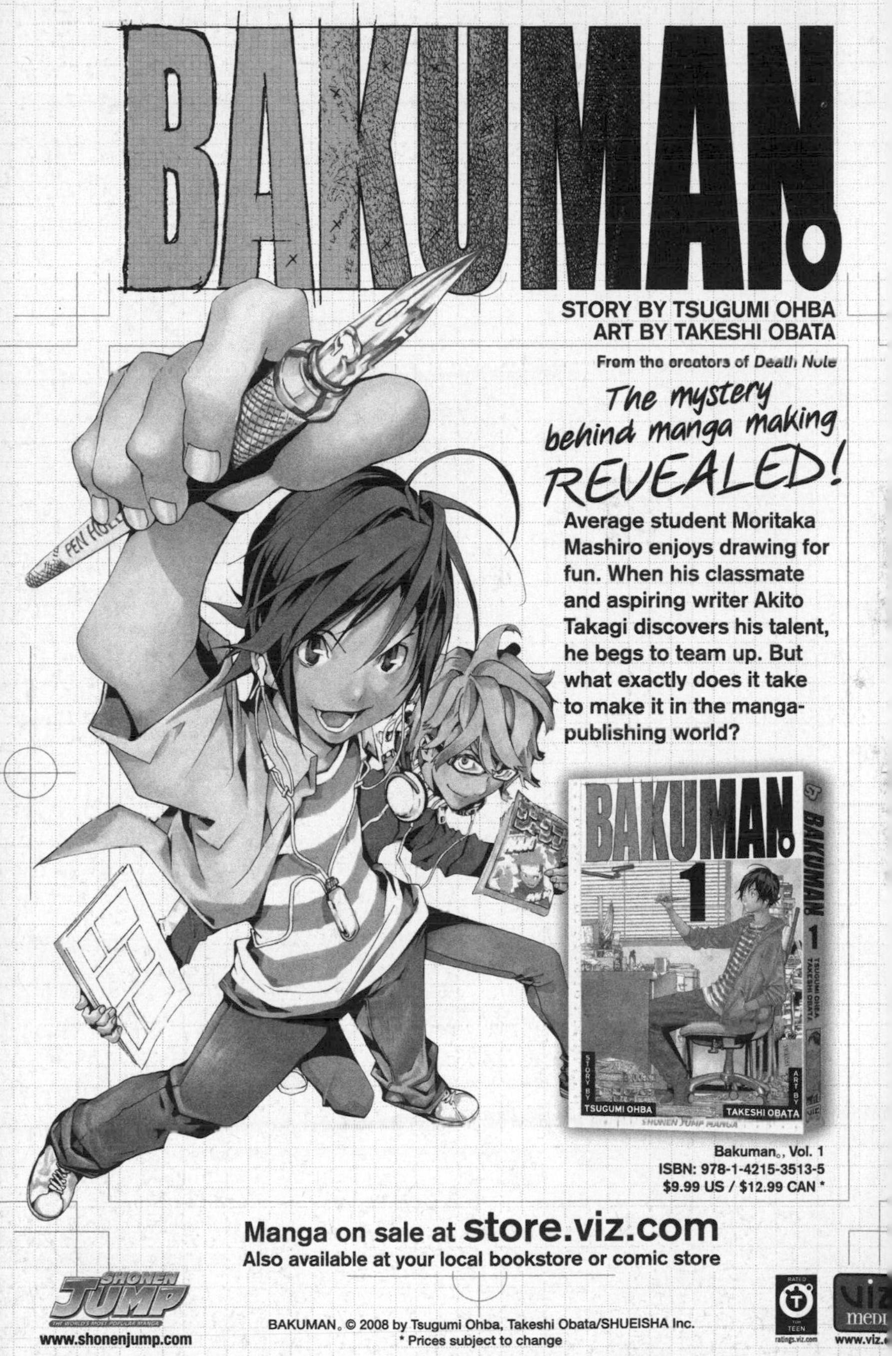
BAKUMAN。
STORY BY TSUGUMI OHBA
ART BY TAKESHI OBATA
From the creators of Death Note
The mystery behind manga making REVEALED!
Average student Moritaka Mashiro enjoys drawing for fun. When his classmate and aspiring writer Akito Takagi discovers his talent, he begs to team up. But what exactly does it take to make it in the manga-publishing world?
BAKUMAN。
1
TSUGUMI OHBA
TAKESHI OBATA
SHONEN JUMP MANGA
Bakuman。, Vol. 1
ISBN: 978-1-4215-3513-5
$9.99 US / $12.99 CAN *
Manga on sale at store.viz.com
Also available at your local bookstore or comic store
SHONEN JUMP
THE WORLD'S MOST POPULAR MANGA
www.shonenjump.com
BAKUMAN。 © 2008 by Tsugumi Ohba, Takeshi Obata/SHUEISHA Inc.
* Prices subject to change
RATED T TEEN
ratings.viz.com
VIZ MEDI
www.viz.

VIZMANGA

Read manga anytime, anywhere!

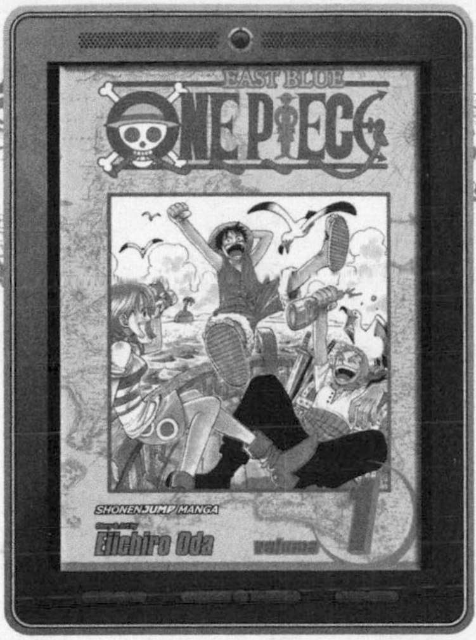

EAST BLUE
ONE PIECE
SHONEN JUMP MANGA
Eiichiro Oda
volume 1

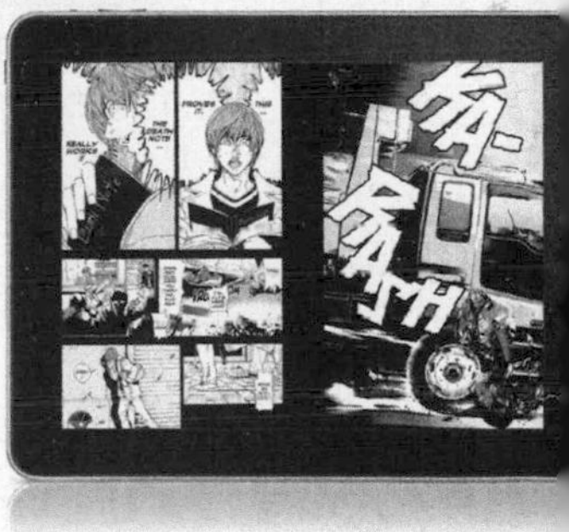

KA-BASH

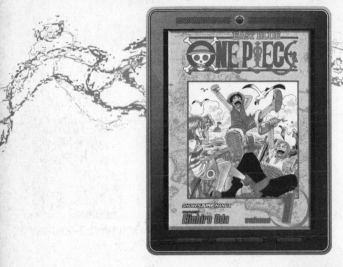

From our newest hit series to the classics you know and love, the best manga in the world is now available digitally. Buy a volume* of digital manga for your:

- iOS device (**iPad®, iPhone®, iPod® touch**) through the **VIZ Manga app**
- Android-powered device (**phone or tablet**) with a browser by visiting **VIZManga.com**
- **Mac or PC computer** by visiting **VIZManga.com**

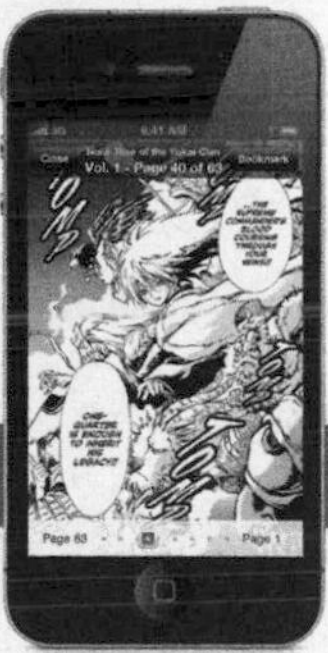

Close
Vol. 1 - Page 40 of 63
Bookmark
Page 63
Page 1

VIZ Digital has loads to offer:

- 500+ ready-to-read volumes
- New volumes each week
- FREE previews
- Access on multiple devices! Create a log-in through the app so you buy a book once, and read it on your device of choice!*

To learn more, visit www.viz.com/apps

*** Some series may not be available for multiple devices. Check the app on your device to find out what's available.**

RATED T+ FOR OLDER TEEN
ratings.viz.com

VIZ MEDIA
viz.com/a

You're Reading in the Wrong Direction!!

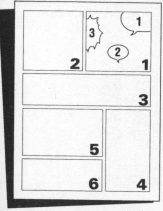

Whoops! Guess what? You're starting at the wrong end of the comic!

...It's true! In keeping with the original Japanese format, **Bleach** is meant to be read from right to left, starting in the upper-right corner.

Unlike English, which is read from left to right, Japanese is read from right to left, meaning that action, sound effects and word-balloon order are completely reversed... something which can make readers unfamiliar with Japanese feel pretty backwards themselves. For this reason, manga or Japanese comics published in the U.S. in English have sometimes been published "flopped"—that is, printed in exact reverse order, as though seen from the other side of a mirror.

By flopping pages, U.S. publishers can avoid confusing readers, but the compromise is not without its downside. For one thing, a character in a flopped manga series who once wore in the original Japanese version a T-shirt emblazoned with "M A Y" (as in "the merry month of") now wears one which reads "Y A M"! Additionally, many manga creators in Japan are themselves unhappy with the process, as some feel the mirror-imaging of their art skews their original intentions.

We are proud to bring you Tite Kubo's **Bleach** in the original unflopped format. For now, though, turn to the other side of the book and let the adventure begin...!

—Editor